LEGENDARY
Lake Pend Oreille
Idaho's Wilderness of Water

Jane Fritz

With contributions by Kevin Davis,
Gary Hassler, Cate Huisman, Marianne Love, Heather McElwain,
Patrick McManus, Jim Mellen and Dennis Nicholls

Foreword by Hazel Hall
Introduction by Francis Cullooyah

KEOKEE
BOOKS
▲▲▲▲▲▲▲▲▲▲▲▲▲▲

SANDPOINT, IDAHO

Keokee Books, Sandpoint, Idaho 83864
© 2010 by Jane Fritz

Second printing, June 2010

Cover painting "Reflections on Lake Pend Oreille" and illustrations
© Karen Robinson

Ross Hall images © Hallans Gallery/The Ross Hall Collection

Printed in the United States of America

Published by Keokee Books, an imprint of Keokee Co. Publishing, Inc.
P.O. Box 722
Sandpoint, ID 83864
208-263-3573

www.KeokeeBooks.com

Publisher's Cataloging-in-Publication Data
Fritz, Jane
Legendary Lake Pend Oreille: Idaho's wilderness of water
        Includes index.
        1. Lake Pend Oreille (Idaho)–History 2. Idaho-history, local 3.Lake Pend Oreille
(Idaho)–Environmental Aspects 4. Lake Pend Oreille (Idaho)-Description and Travel
5. Lake Pend Oreille (Idaho)–Water Supply-Protection. I. Title. II. Fritz, Jane
        979.696.
ISBN 978-1-879628-33-5

For my late mother, Marcia Fritz — for always believing in me. Her remarkable watercolor painting of Lake Pend Oreille that hangs on my wall proves I come from artistic stock.
And for my late father, Frank Fritz — for instilling in me at a young age a love of nature, the wilder the better. His stories of steelhead fishing in Idaho lured me here.
And for my late grandpa, Chester Idczak — for teaching me to embrace beauty. He smiles at me in every rainbow I see.

Acknowledgements

This book would not have been possible without the unwavering support of five women who were truly invaluable to me, midwives to my creative process of birthing it — Jonnie Bradley, Robin Campbell, Becky Kemery, Marie Marek and Shawna Parry. Thank you for being my creative sisters.

I also want to acknowledge the First Peoples here — the Kalispel Tribe of Indians — whose spiritual ties to this remarkable Pend Oreille watershed are forever. I particularly thank my good friend, Francis Cullooyah, cultural director for the tribe, for his review of the manuscript and for his provocative introduction. I also want to honor the memory of the late tribal matriarch, Alice Ignace. She taught many, many people about her culture, the gifts of nature, and how important it is to respect all of life. She was both a mentor and friend to me.

I sincerely thank all the contributing writers, poets, storytellers and photographers whose words, verses, voices and images grace the pages of this book. I am especially indebted to the late Dennis Nicholls for all of his research and beginning work on the manuscript. I am also grateful to Sandpoint artist Karen Robinson for the use of her beautiful watercolor painting on the cover and pen-and-ink illustrations throughout the book; to photographer Dann Hall for the amazing black-and-white photographs from the Ross Hall Collection; and to artists Ward Tollbom and Eileen Klatt for their wonderful fish art. Very special thanks are extended to Jean Maryborn, Linda Hackbarth, Jolanda Van Ooyen, Ivar Nelson and Ron Raiha for their editorial assistance and creative suggestions. Thanks also to Kim Marshall for the gift of her computer when mine gave up mid-manuscript. I also want to thank three women who made sure I was well-fed when the writing of this manuscript threatened to consume me: Ruth Kuster, Susan Green and Darian Fadeley.

I have learned a great deal from working with Keokee Books: Billie Jean Plaster, my editor; designer Laura White; and publisher Chris Bessler. Thank you for enduring my creative process.

I am also extremely grateful to the Grandmothers for their graces and constant guidance. It is a very humbling experience to write about Lake Pend Oreille. It is so very, very precious and sacred, and truly grand and glorious.

—Jane Fritz, author/editor

Contents

Hazel Hall above Talache, circa 1936

Foreword

Author's note: Hazel Hall moved to Sandpoint in 1932 as a new bride. For more than 30 years her husband, Ross, photographed memorable images of the lake, mountains and people of northern Idaho. Together they captured, printed and hand-tinted remarkable works of art. Their Himes Studio was sold in 1963 to the late Duane "Cap" Davis; Ross Hall then focused his keen eye on creating scenic postcards until that business, too, was sold to the late photographer, Will Hawkins. Ross died in 1990. Active to the end, Hazel died August 14, 2009, at age 96 while this book was in production. Son Dann continues to manage the Ross Hall Collection through the Hallans Gallery in downtown Sandpoint. This book contains a special section of Ross Hall's timeless black-and-white images, courtesy of Hallans Gallery.

Never had I seen a lake so vast. I longed to explore it in every direction.

In time, some friends took my husband, Ross, and me far down Lake Pend Oreille from Sandpoint in their speedboat. It was an all-day affair. The return trip offered a full moon shining so brightly on the water that boating through its shimmering path scattered moonbeams on either side of us — a breathtaking experience.

It was at that very moment that I fell deeply in love with the lake of the poetic name, *Pend d'Oreille.*

Ross was the photographer for the Himes Studio and the lake "called" him to take portraits of her. Every chance he had, he would pursue her with his camera. Soon he was taking

Legendary Lake Pend Oreille

photographs of the lake at the request of other people.

These were the days before colored film, and Ross taught me to color some of the photographs with transparent oils. This kind of painting does not take the skill of a real painter, but it does require knowing how to mix and apply the pigments. It is a joy to stir the many shades of blues, greens, yellows and reds to capture nature's myriad moods. Sometimes the lake would be caught in a storm. Other times her passive calm and stillness would make me wonder about her mood. The happiest images made me happy, too.

Sometimes I hiked with Ross for pictures, but mostly he went alone or with male friends who loved strenuous, mountain hiking. Besides, there was always work for me to do back in the studio in order for our business to make a living for our young family. Sadly, the tinted images and the ones taken later on with color film have faded in their vibrancy. But our son Dann cares for Ross' collection of black-and-white photographs, so other people can enjoy vicariously the vantage points Ross sought out of Lake Pend Oreille from those mountaintop trails.

Today, so many decades after my first moonlit encounter, I live at the shore of Pend Oreille. I can still feel her every mood. On the hottest days, there is a soft, cool breeze as if fanned by fairy wings. Other times it is as wild and boisterous as the ocean. I observe daily how this great gem of a lake teems with life: An abundance of waterfowl keeps me ever amused, from the time a hen teaches her little ones to duck and feed, then to file in a straight line to follow the wake of the sibling ahead, and finally, when mature enough, to fly into the yonder. I feel the promise of their return; coming back to raise and teach their own young the next spring.

The great Clark Fork River, large and small streams, and waterfalls supply the lake with fresh, clean water. Most species of western trees grow from the shoreline up the hills into the rocky mountaintops. The islands, the peninsulas, the bays, the cliffs, the white, sandy beaches, its mystic depths — all become one. It is as though the Great Landscaper and Painter closed the book and said, "This is my best Creation. It belongs to all of you — enjoy and take care of it." And so we must.

—Hazel Hall

Preface

Hank Birnbaum and his family live in Talache in what was originally a trapper's cabin and then this mining town's one-room schoolhouse. Like so many people who have made their home at the shores of Lake Pend Oreille, Hank has a special connection to this amazing lake, but he may be reticent to say so. His elderly mother attended school and grew up in his log cabin home, and he's owned property here for more than 30 years, although he's only actually lived here for the last several years. But he says it takes much longer than that — many generations of living — to create a true sense of belonging to such country. Just as it was for the indigenous peoples he has studied, a sense of belonging to a particular place requires a respect for, and a long-term dependency on, its natural environment for survival. Only then can one fully appreciate and understand its generous gifts. Lake Pend Oreille has much to teach.

Hank, his Russian wife, and their children moved here from the shores of our planet's oldest and deepest lake, Lake Baikal. At 400 miles long and 25 miles to 50 miles wide, Siberia's Lake Baikal is also the world's largest (in volume) freshwater lake, holding more water than all North America's Great Lakes combined. To those peoples who have relied on Baikal for subsistence for numerous generations, it is called the "Sacred Sea," in recognition of its immense creative power. The more its mysteries are understood, the more humble and grateful a person becomes.

Lake Pend Oreille is also like that, for my friend Hank and those of us whose stories grace the pages of this book. If you acquired this book because you are new to the area, a tourist or visitor, or because you have lived here a long time and want to learn more than you presently know, either way I invite you to look deeply into why Pend d'Oreille is the great gem of this world. As a creative source of life, it is so much more than the sum of its parts. You are about to encounter magic, where no lives are easy or uncomplicated, but are rich in beauty and spirit.

—*Jane Fritz, author/editor*

Legendary Lake Pend Oreille

Introduction

Since little has been written about the Kalispel, or Pend d'Oreille, Indians, most people don't realize the vastness of our aboriginal territory. As a hunter-gatherer society, my people once lived in the abundant, watery region that stretches from western Montana's Mission Mountains, across the panhandle of Idaho and eastern Washington, and north into Canada's British Columbia — comprising more than 4 million acres. Our traditional villages and seasonal encampments were along the Clark Fork and Pend Oreille rivers, Pend Oreille and Priest lakes, and the many tributaries and stream-fed forested mountains and valleys that empty into the great Columbia River.

Lake Pend Oreille holds many tribal legends. Some of them tell of the origin of our life in this beautiful land when the Earth was very young and evolving and all of its creatures were submerged and lived underwater. It was then that Creator told all the animals that were chosen — from the smallest to the largest being — to emerge from the lake onto its shores. Some of these left their footprints in the soft, still evolving rocks. Closely following was the creation of the Kalispel, or Pend d'Oreille, people placed here to be the caretakers of all creation.

My life as a traditional Kalispel, and the reflections about my people as written by the author, only serve to reawaken for me a way of life that once was and still can be. The simplicity, closeness to nature, and nurturing that our surroundings can give us is still possible, only if and when we can learn to respect what we have.

—Francis Cullooyah, Cultural Program Director
Kalispel Tribe of Indians

CHAPTER ONE

PART I: RECREATION GUIDE TO LAKE PEND OREILLE

Meet Lake Pend Oreille

"The wilderness of water has a spiritual vastness that's almost greater than any wilderness of land."

— *Russell Keene*

ack in 1993, Russell Keene and I went for a ride in his Old Town "Katahdin" canoe from Talache Landing. At age 84, Russell had outfitted his canoe with a rowing machine to get him around on the lake faster, and to keep him in strapping good shape. I quickly got a lesson on proper rowing technique. I recall doing all the rowing that day, hugging the shore as we headed south to Maiden Rock and back again. Russ chided me for my lack of courage to take to open water and cross over to Kilroy Bay, one of his favorite canoe routes. Surely I could accomplish this; after all, he had seen elk swim across in a mere hour and a half. But then it was not unusual for Russ to row all the way to Hope or Clark Fork either. In fact, in the previous five years that he had taken to rowing his canoe on Lake Pend Oreille, he had amassed nearly 4,000 miles in the process. Quoted in a story I subsequently wrote for *Sandpoint Magazine* that summer (reprinted in Part II, chapter 18), Russ exclaimed: "I have great respect for this lake. I know it can kill me. But you got to roll with it. You got to live with the wilderness of water, not just be there. You have to be part of it. This lake gets in your blood, I guess. You're living on your own strength. ... And there's a certain thrill in pitting yourself against a wild thing like this lake, and believe me, when it gets rough, it's wild — terrifying!"

The wildness of Lake Pend Oreille, the largest lake in Idaho, is derived, at least in part, from its sheer size. At 43 miles long and more than 1,100 feet deep, it dwarfs every other lake in the state. It is 20 miles from Sandpoint City Beach east to the Clark Fork Delta and from there it is almost 25 miles south to Buttonhook Bay. The lake is seldom less than three miles wide and at its widest spans nearly six and a half miles from Picard Point to the angular slopes of the Green Monarchs. Being hemmed in by mountains on all sides likely contributes to the lake's tempestuousness as well.

Shimmering beneath the northern Idaho summer sun; churning in the fury of a winter storm; brimming with the icy waters of spring runoff; tranquil in the light of an autumn full moon — Lake Pend Oreille has been the lifeblood of civilizations old and new. It remains the most remarkable geographic feature of northern Idaho.

Geology and Geography

Lake Pend Oreille lies within the Purcell Trench, a chasm in the Rocky Mountain chain that stretches a couple hundred miles from the Idaho Panhandle well into Canada. This steep-sided valley was created by forces deep in Earth's crust hundreds of millions of years ago. Sediments in a vast seabed from the obscure past buckled and rose, forming the ancient mountain range of the Cabinets. Then igneous intrusions pushed their way to the surface and in a cataclysm of mountain building, the Selkirk Mountains were born around 135 million years ago.

The narrow but long valley embraced by these two mountain ranges became the perfect home for big rivers and deep lakes. At its south end, the stage was set for events of gargantuan proportions.

Thousands of years ago the Idaho Panhandle was covered with thousands of feet of ice. The Purcell Lobe of the continental ice sheet blocked the mouth of the Clark Fork River. An immense lake that filled the valleys of western Montana was created. When that ice dam failed, supposedly over and over again, 10 times more water than what flows in all the rivers of the world today rushed into the vacated abyss that now cradles Idaho's most precious gem. Lake Pend Oreille is a remnant of the former glacial valley that preceded it, but Pend Oreille is no less spectacular, no less beautiful than its ancestor, Glacial Lake Missoula.

Perhaps more impressive than its 111 miles of shoreline is its depth. Lake Pend Oreille is the fifth deepest lake in the United States. The deepest part of the lake has been plumbed at 1,158 feet, although there is still question about its exact depth. In the southern lobe of the lake past Indian Point, there's a stretch of water 10 miles long by more than a mile wide where the bottom is consistently more than 1,000 feet below the surface.

Two rivers and nearly two dozen creeks feed the lake. Pack River flows from the north draining the Selkirk Mountains. Trestle Creek comes out of the Cabinets from the northeast. Gold and Granite creeks are the largest streams collecting runoff from the Coeur d'Alene Mountains to the southeast. But flowing from the wide, deep valley creasing the Montana landscape to the east is Clark's Fork of the Columbia, today simply known as Clark Fork River. It supplies 90 percent of the lake's water from a watershed of hundreds of square miles, including Glacier National Park, the Bob Marshall Wilderness and the moon-like landscape of Homestake Pass above Butte, Montana, 280 miles to the south.

Lake Pend Oreille is surrounded by four mountain ranges: the Selkirks to the north and west, the Cabinets to the east, and to the south the Coeur

Taken July 24, 2005, from the International Space Station by NASA astronaut John Phillips (Image courtesy of the Image Science & Analysis Laboratory, NASA Johnson Space Center, http://eol.jsc.nasa.gov)

d'Alenes and the Bitterroots. South and west lie the Rathdrum Prairie and the ponderosa pine forests of eastern Washington. The highest point immediately around the lake is Packsaddle Mountain crowning its east side at 6,405 feet. Looming over the Clark Fork River Delta is the highest summit in Bonner County, Idaho — Scotchman Peak at 7,009 feet, which soars more than 6,000 vertical feet above the lake bottom.

Shown circa 1923, Baptiste Big Smoke stands on the Hope Peninsula near Sheepherder Point. The son of Chief John Big Smoke, he later became the last known Kalispel chief (Compton L. White photo courtesy of Kalispel Tribe)

Human History

There is a long history of human activity around Lake Pend Oreille. Not long after the continental ice sheet receded, native peoples hunted, fished and traded along its shores. For more than 10,000 years indigenous tribes prospered here. Then, in September 1809, David Thompson, a Canadian fur trader and explorer, arrived and set his eyes on this beautiful body of water immediately recognizing its intrinsic value. Written in his later years, his memoir states, "The impression of my mind is, from the formation of the country and its climate, its extensive Meadows and fine forests, watered by countless brooks and Rills of pure water, that it will become the abode of civilized Man, whether Natives or other people."

Thompson initially named the lake "Kullyspel Lake" after the Kalispel Indians who lived here. Perhaps one of his voyageurs gave the lake its French name – *Pend d'Oreille*. Translated, it means "ear pendant," possibly referring to jewelry worn by a Kalispel they encountered, even though it wasn't tribal custom to wear earrings. Or maybe the name described the lake's shape as an ear. This is the name that endured, but sadly with the spelling altered: the d' *(apostrophe)* was dropped in use over the years.

First Avenue, circa 1955, Sandpoint slowly grew into a mining and timber center after first being settled in 1881 (Ross Hall)

After Thompson's initial exploration of Lake Pend Oreille, the remote and wild character of this place changed dramatically over the next 200 years. Steamboats began plying the waters of Lake Pend Oreille in the 1860s; the railroads came in the 1880s; and mining and timbering dominated the landscape at the turn of the 20th century.

Part of the lake's colorful history includes the gold rush era beginning in 1864, when the lake was used as a thoroughfare for prospectors traveling from the Columbia River to the gold fields of Helena. Steamships like the *Mary Moody* took miners from Buttonhook Bay north up the lake and then east up the Clark Fork River as far as the impassable Cabinet Gorge rapids until 1869 when the gold rush died down.

The lake's largest community, Sandpoint, was first settled in 1881 when Emma Lavinia and Burt Weeks opened E.L. Weeks & Co., General Merchandise, and the Northern Pacific (NP) surveyed the area and established the station of Pend d'Oreille. The town grew slowly from then on as a mining and timber center. Hope was once a booming railroad community with the construction of the NP line in 1882. The Chinese who worked on the railroad lived in the community until the 1920s.

A big chapter in the lake's history was written during World War II, when Bayview was the site of the Farragut Naval Training Station through which some 300,000 enlisted men passed. There is still a naval research detachment in Bayview. The community was also busy early this century when mines and lime quarries flourished.

Roads were pushed through the dark forests onto all sides of the lake by the 1950s. However, it remained difficult, if not impossible, to get to every part of the lakeshore. To this day, much of the lakeshore is only approachable by watercraft. Much of Lake Pend Oreille's shoreline is simply too steep and rugged for a road. Highway 200 parallels the northeast side of the lake connecting Sandpoint to Hope and Clark Fork. A few roads have been punched into premium locations like Talache Landing, Garfield Bay and along the lakeshore to Bottle Bay on the west side. At the south end are the communities of Bayview and Lakeview, while the most remote outposts are on the lake's east shore at Granite Creek, Cedar Creek, Whiskey Rock and Kilroy Bay.

Climate

With climate change, the weather patterns are changing. Normally the weather around Lake Pend Oreille is moderate despite the fact that the northernmost tip of the lake is only 30 miles from the 49th parallel and the Canadian border. The primary reason for this is the influence of maritime weather systems that come inland off the Pacific Ocean. Those that arrive from deep in the South Pacific are often called a "Pineapple Express." They bring warm, moist storms during the winter months that can create rain-on-snow events and cause floods throughout the region. On the other hand, systems that move in from the Gulf of Alaska can bring heavy snow and bitter subzero temperatures. Summers are warm.

At Sandpoint, the most populous community in the lake region, weather data has been tracked for more than a century. The record high temperature is 104 degrees. The record low is 37 below zero. But in between that 141-degree extreme is a pattern that is typically characterized by anything but extremes. Taking the entire year's temperatures into consideration, the high temperature at Sandpoint averages 56 degrees, the low 35 degrees. July is the warmest month, averaging a high of 81 degrees. January is the coldest, with the thermometer dropping to an overnight average low of 21 degrees. Frost-free days number around 99 for most years, but there is a probability that one out of 10 years could experience more than 140 frost-free days. The last freeze generally comes in early June while the first freeze arrives in early to mid-September.

Typically a little more than 33 inches of precipitation falls at Sandpoint, with an average of 88 inches of snowfall. Two-thirds of the snow usually comes in December and January and those two months, along with November, are far and away the wettest. They account for 14 inches of rainfall on average. July is the only month that averages less than an inch of rainfall. But there can

Legendary Lake Pend Oreille

be periods during the summer when no precipitation falls at all for weeks at a time.

These averages fluctuate wildly with changes in elevation and location. Schweitzer Mountain Resort a few miles north of Sandpoint typically receives 300 inches of snow each winter and there are places in the high Cabinets to the east that exceed 100 inches of precipitation in a year.

With that in mind, having lived here for 30 years, I would say that global warming is definitely changing every aspect of the local climate. Summer temperatures are hot, rising faster and persisting in the 90-degree range. Winters are milder with less snow, although the winter of 2007-08 approached one of the snowiest on record. It's not just my observation, though. Climate experts say that northern Idaho will continue to experience earlier springs, warmer and drier summers, and less snowpack in the mountains. The summer of 2006 was the driest season in more than a hundred years with very little rain between mid-June and mid-September. The trend may result in longer, more dangerous forest fire seasons.

Regardless of whether or not the area around Lake Pend Oreille is modulated by global climate change, it's likely that we'll continue to have many gray, cloudy days in winter and generous amounts of sunshine during summer. It will remain an excellent climate for a variety of outdoor recreational pursuits.

Bing Crosby, left, and a large Kamloops rainbow trout along with Pike Moon, circa 1948 (Ross Hall)

Fish and Wildlife

Lake Pend Oreille is a big lake and it harbors big fish. The largest taken from its depths was in 1994 by the late Jim Eversole. It was a mackinaw (also called lake trout) that weighed more than 43 pounds. The world-record Kamloops, or Gerrard rainbow trout, was hauled in by Wes Hamlet in 1947 and pushed the scales to 37 pounds. Both of these species are recent transplants. Lake trout were planted here in the 1920s and the Kamloops were brought in from Kootenay Lake in British Columbia in the 1940s. One reason these sport fish reached such enormous proportions was their plentiful prey – kokanee. The kokanee population crashed in the 1990s. Subsequently, the kokanee fishery was closed in 2000.

Lake Pend Oreille is also an important stronghold for a char that is native to the watershed, but on the brink of extinction in much of its historic range – the beleaguered bull trout. Sometimes it is mistakenly called a Dolly Varden, the name of a related species. Though fishing for these giants is heavily controlled, they were once pulled from these waters by the multitudes. The largest bull trout on record to come from the lake weighed 32 pounds.

The lake is still home to native whitefish, northern pikeminnow, char and western slope cutthroat trout along with introduced species such as lake whitefish, and rainbow, brown and brook trout. Warmwater fishes also have been introduced and include species like largemouth and smallmouth bass, northern pike, black crappie and yellow perch.

Waterbirds – resident and migratory – are abundant. From exceedingly rare loons and western grebes to tundra swans, Canada and snow geese, countless ducks of more than a dozen species, heron, and thousands of coots, this lake plays host to a menagerie of waterbirds. In addition, throughout the spring and summer, the cacophony of shoreline birds adds to the din of life around the lake. From the eagles and osprey that soar overhead to the deer that drink quietly at its shores; from the moose wading its shallows to the beaver plying its placid backwaters; from the mountain goats on Bernard Peak's tattered cliffs to the fish swimming its shimmering depths, Lake Pend Oreille is vibrant with wildlife.

A Wilderness of Water

Today, 12,000 years after the ice melted and ancient floodwaters receded, two centuries after the fur traders encountered the indigenous peoples, and at the dawn of a new millennia with perhaps the greatest influx of human residents the region has ever known, Lake Pend Oreille is still Russell Keene's wild and sometimes terrifying "wilderness of water." It still beckons to the adventurer. Yet, for all its wildness, the lake can be a place of serenity as well. Russ said he was never lonely on the lake, even those times when nobody was out there but him. "It is peaceful and a lot like praying," he said. "It's a feeling that you are alone with the Creator, and you listen to the deep calm of it."

In the following pages you are invited to discover Lake Pend Oreille for yourself in a myriad of ways. Experience its wildness and its deep calm. Explore its mountain heights and watery

Legendary Lake Pend Oreille

depths, quiet coves and broad expanses. Enjoy the thrill of fishing and capture majestic wildlife on film. This book will help you get to know this most precious of the Gem State's watery gems — Lake Pend Oreille. As Russell Keene alluded to, its spiritual vastness awaits you.

Lake Pend Oreille is tucked into the northern panhandle of Idaho that, for all its beauty and natural attractions, remains relatively little known and out of the way. This is despite the fact that the area has been receiving a lot of national press in recent years as a great place to visit and live. As part of the rural Inland Northwest, it's still not a place many find accidentally.

The view from Trail 120 above Hope shows the vastness and wildness of Lake Pend Oreille (Jim Mellen)

Lake Pend Oreille lies almost entirely within Bonner County. Only the southwestern tip including Bayview and Farragut State Park falls within Kootenai County. At Sandpoint is where the Pend Oreille River officially is delineated from the lake, west of the Long Bridge, although previously it was at Dover. Thirty miles downstream is Albeni Falls, just beyond the city of Priest River. Built in 1955 by the federal government, Albeni Falls Dam is managed by the U.S. Army Corps of Engineers. It controls the level of Lake Pend Oreille for the purposes of electricity generation, flood control and recreation, raising the lake level each spring and lowering it every fall. At full summertime pool, Lake Pend Oreille is at an elevation of 2,062 feet. Its maximum wintertime drawdown is 2,051 feet. A second dam exists on the east end of the lake, seven miles upstream on the Clark Fork River. The Cabinet Gorge Dam was completed in 1952 and is privately owned and operated by Avista Utilities of Spokane, Washington.

This book describes the many communities, recreation sites and access points to the lake, along with its human and natural history. Part I, in chapters 4 through 10, divides the lake and its major rivers into seven geographical areas. Each area describes in detail all the recreational facilities available at these sites and the variety of ways to enjoy your stay on, in and around Lake Pend Oreille. Each area begins with an overview and a detailed map and then an "Anecdota" — a personal story from someone who has lived here awhile. There are also brief notes or longer stories of American Indian history, pioneer history, wildflower identification, wildlife-viewing opportunities, fishing tales, sailing information, paddle routes, special events and activities, driving and biking tours, and even poetry. Following chapters by area are two more chapters devoted to hiking, mountain biking and horseback riding trails, and fish and fishing.

Part II details the area's human history from prehistory to present day. It includes a 200-year chronology of important social milestones. This book is designed to help you maximize the enjoyment of the lake but also to learn why this is such a remarkable body of water. The information is fairly comprehensive although hardly all-encompassing. You will have the most fun in making discoveries for yourself and creating your own stories to share. And hopefully, like so many of us who are lucky enough to call this area home, you also will develop a deep love and respect for Lake Pend Oreille. Its future depends on it.

Pend Oreille

Encircled by the mountains high,
O'er-arched by an unequaled sky,
Fringed by thy forests, evergreen,
No fairer lake has ever been –
    O Pend Oreille, the Beautiful!

The stars gaze on thy placid breast
In filmy mists so lightly dressed.
The queenly moon the livelong night
Flings in thy deeps her silvery light,
While from the woods, the owlet's calls
Echo along thy massive walls –
    O Pend Oreille, the Beautiful!

I hear the laughter of the loon.
I hear thy wavelets whisper, croon.
I hear the mallard whistling by.
I see the osprey poised on high.
I see the ever-widening rings
Where out thy breast the salmon springs –
    O Pend Oreille, the Beautiful!

And when from out the rigorous North,
The roistering winds come rushing forth,
Lashing thy breast with might and main,
Making thy billows leap again –
I joy in all thy wild uproar,
And linger on thy stormy shore,
Or sail my boat in triumph o'er –
    O Pend Oreille, the Beautiful!

Here with thee would I ever stay,
Forgetting all the sordid way,
Which doth engross the Sons of men,
Bringing them sorrow, sin and pain.
For Heaven hath kissed thee, Pend Oreille,
And lingers near Thee, day by day –
    O Pend Oreille, the Beautiful!

–Sullivan S. Healey
Tacoma, Washington, December 8, 1917

CHAPTER TWO

Activities at a Glance

"If there is magic on this planet, it is contained in water."
−Loren Eiseley

ake Pend Oreille is for people who like big water. Maybe you're the active type who wants to lustily embrace any number of recreational pursuits in, on, under or high above the water. Or perhaps you prefer more passive engagements like gazing out over the lake to catch a spectacular sunset from the deck of a local restaurant. Some activities can even be enjoyed from the comfort of your automobile, like photographing a moose feeding in the shallows of one of the lake's many sloughs. Share in the best of what nature can offer here and you will create lifelong memories. Remember, a body of water this remarkable is a source of life for many and that caring for it ensures their future.

This chapter will give you a broad overview of the various activities that are available here and detailed throughout Part I, as well as provide other information such as etiquette, safety and boating regulations. Think of it as a "things to do" list while in the region and a way to get you planning your unique adventure here.

Powerboats and Waterskiing

On any given day from early spring until late fall, the lake teems with powerboat enthusiasts. Whether you are out for a leisurely tour of the lakeshore in a pontoon boat or are

towing your kids on a wakeboard down the river, there are numerous boat launches and docks to give you adequate access (see insert, Lake Pend Oreille Idaho Recreation Map). Keep in mind that by law no one under the age of 10 is allowed to operate a motor-driven watercraft except under direct adult supervision. This rule includes personal watercraft. Between ages 10 and 14, it is unlawful to operate a motorboat without adult supervision unless it is a motor rated at 10 horsepower or less. To prevent collisions with other watercraft, keep a sharp lookout and maintain a safe speed and distance. Speeding boats and their wakes can pose a hazard to non-motorized vessels.

There are a few boating rules that every operator should follow when encountering other boats. They include:

- If a powered craft encounters a vessel with limited ability to maneuver, like a sailboat under sail, give way to it unless it is overtaking. Slow down when approaching people in canoes and kayaks.
- If towing a water-skier, there must be a third person on board continuously observing the skier and using a skier-down flag.
- When a powerboat is speeding head-on toward your boat, both boats should veer to starboard (right) and pass by one another on port (left).
- If crossing paths with another powerboat, the boat on starboard has the right of way.
- When overtaking another boat, the faster craft should veer from its course sufficiently to safely pass the slower boat.
- Traveling at night can be tricky, but common sense can help avoid trouble. If you see a red light crossing right to left (starboard to port) in front of you, the boat displaying the light

Legendary Lake Pend Oreille

has the right-of-way. Change course to avoid it. On the other hand, if you see a green light crossing in front of you from left to right (port to starboard), you have the right-of-way and should maintain course and speed, but do anything necessary to avoid collision.

• The simplest rule on the lake is to always show courtesy and respect to other boaters.

Especially for Jet Skiers

Although the same rules and regulations govern personal watercraft, there are a few extra things to keep in mind if you're operating a personal watercraft:

• If you allow your engine to idle or shut off during operation, you lose all steering control and will continue in the direction you were headed.

• Allow plenty of room for stopping. Jet Skis don't stop immediately.

• It is illegal to ride personal watercraft without a lanyard attached between yourself and the ignition safety switch. That way if you are thrown from the proper operating position, the engine will shut off immediately.

• Avoid riding where there are strong currents or winds; it could make it difficult to get back on the machine if you fall off and it overturns. Always wear your life preserver and remember that it is legal to ride only between sunrise and sunset.

• Do not jump wakes or ride more than 15 mph within 100 feet of another vessel. A "no wake" zone exists within 200 feet of the entire shoreline.

• Avoid congregating with other personal watercraft users near shore as this can cause excessive noise, and avoid campsites and residential areas, especially early in the morning or just before sunset.

• Do not operate a personal watercraft in shallow water, 24 inches deep or less. Bottom sediments and aquatic plants will be sucked into the machine's water pump doing damage to it and the environment. Stay away from reeds and grasses.

• It is illegal to chase, harass or disturb wildlife or waterfowl with your personal watercraft.

Weather Emergencies

Weather on Lake Pend Oreille can change rapidly and create unexpected situations for vessel operators. Even the weatherman has trouble predicting rapid weather changes. It's a good idea to monitor weather developments by VHF radio broadcasting frequencies (162.4 MHz to 162.55 MHz). If caught in foul weather:

- Put on life jackets and make sure they are properly secured.
- Head for the nearest shore that is safe to approach.
- Head the bow into the waves at a 45-degree angle. Personal watercraft should head into the waves at a 90-degree angle.
- Reduce speed and seat passengers on the bottom of the vessel, as close to the centerline as possible.
- If caught on open water during a thunderstorm, stay low in the middle of the vessel.
- Secure loose items, keep bilge free of water and drop anchor from the bow if your engine stops. If you have no anchor, drop anything heavy on a line that will create drag, and hold the bow into the wind.
- Visually signal for help in the event of an emergency. If you don't have a red flare, use arm signals (arms straight out from body and flap them up and down) or an orange flag during the day, and a flashlight at night with this distress flashing progression: ● ● ● — — — ● ● ● (dot, dot, dot, dash, dash, dash, dot, dot, dot).

The next chapter addresses other topics concerning powerboats, such as boat maintenance, fueling and the spread of noxious weeds.

A Word about Wakes, Boat Speed and Noise

Speeding boats can create large waves that can cause erosion damage to the shoreline, harm nesting waterfowl and their young, and be potentially dangerous to other boaters on the lake, especially to those in small watercraft like canoes and kayaks. Subsequently, deputies from the Bonner County Sheriff's Marine Division enforce a local ordinance designating 200 feet of the entire shoreline perimeter of Lake Pend Oreille as a "No Wake Zone." (For the Clark Fork and Pend Oreille rivers it is 100 feet.) Additionally, the bays at the southern end of the lake around Bayview (Area 1) and the area known as the Pack River Flats (Area 4) are no-wake zones.

Vessels also should slow down to no-wake speed (less than 5 mph) within 200 feet of a dock, swimmer or other person in the water except when safely pulling a water-skier from a dock or near shore, and then the boat must pull outward, perpendicular to the shoreline. Returning to shore, the boat cannot go within the 200-foot zone to release a skier. No wake also extends to the area surrounding bridge structures and within 50 feet of any other vessel. Scuba divers and snorkelers should display a red with white diagonal stripe "diver down" flag when in the water and boats with water-skiers in the water must display an orange "skier down" flag. Boaters must reduce to no-wake speed within 200 feet of the flags (100 feet on the rivers). It's also a good idea to know the hand signals for skiers and to remember that it's illegal to water-ski between one hour after sunset and one hour before sunrise, just in case you're a die-hard water-skier. At night, boaters shouldn't exceed 25 mph on the water.

In addition to 14 navigational lights out on the lake and 16 navigational lights on the Pend Oreille River, the county's Marine Division also occasionally places buoys in sensitive wildlife habitat areas or where there are safety concerns, such as shallow water between islands and shore. Watch for these floating markers and follow their directions. In some parts of the lake there are also mooring buoys, which are painted white with a blue horizontal band, indicating a safe place offshore for vessels to anchor. There are also places on the lake and rivers that are not officially restricted, but are considered generally inappropriate for recreational powerboats and waterskiing. These include Denton Slough, Morton Slough, Perch Bay and the Clark Fork Delta. These areas are designated Important Bird Areas (IBAs) by the Idaho Department of Fish and Game and the National Audubon Society because of nesting or migratory waterfowl. Some birds, like western grebes, actually build floating nests out of aquatic plants and have their nursery area close by. The breeding success or failure of this species is directly tied to powerboats. Wildlife have fewer choices than we do, so please give them ample room. Protect these habitat areas by enjoying wildlife from afar with binoculars in hand.

As the area grows in popularity so does the number of powerboats on Lake Pend Oreille. The county's Marine Division is seeing a significant increase in the number of personal watercraft and larger jet boats on the water and receiving more complaints from other lake users and lakeshore residents about the noise these machines make, especially close to shore. So that everyone can enjoy the lake, remember to be considerate. It's a big lake with plenty of space to enjoy a variety of motorized watercraft.

There are a few other rules regarding navigation that every vessel operator should know. (Did you know that it's illegal to fish or sunbathe on docks where boats are being launched?) For more information on responsible boating, visit www.boatidaho.org, pick up a copy of *The Handbook! Of Idaho Boating Laws and Responsibilities* at any local marina, or check out the Bonner County Sheriff's Office Web site at www.bonnerso.org under the Marine Division tab. One more thing: Idaho law prohibits anyone from operating or being in actual physical control of any vessel while "under the influence" of alcohol (a blood alcohol level of .08 percent for a person 21 years of age and older; .02 percent for under age 21). Penalties are hefty. It is better to follow this simple rule: Don't drink and boat!

Sailing

Lake Pend Oreille doesn't have the protected anchorages and coves that saltwater sailors from the Northwest are accustomed to finding among coastal islands, but adequate shelter and anchorage can be found with a little advance planning and an eye to the weather. And even though it remains at "full pool" during the summer, between late September and early May the lake is drawn down as much as 11 feet for power generation and fishery management. The Bonner County Marine Division deputies of the Sheriff's Department can advise by radio or in person of safe anchorages, docks and ramps for sailors to use.

Sailing with Schweitzer in view

The lake gives cruising sailors a choice of vacation environments. Between Independence Day and Labor Day, it is buzzing with activity. After Labor Day the lake is nearly deserted, although the weather is often clear and frequently windy, and the surrounding mountainsides are at their most beautiful with reddening huckleberry bushes, golden birches and snow on the far peaks. Anchoring and docking options wither, however, as the lake level drops and cruising sailors must plan ahead to make sure there is still water at their destinations. In the spring and up until Independence Day, the lake is relatively quiet, and docking options slowly increase as the water rises. Most ramps and docks have enough water to be used by the middle of May. The public launches at the Hope Boat Basin (if your mast can make it under the highway bridge) and at Bayview are accessible year round.

With its many ramps and easy access, Lake Pend Oreille is a great destination for the trailer sailor. Other sailors can rent Ranger 20s at marinas in Sandpoint and Bayview. These are great camping boats for couples or small families. Those not so rustically inclined can enjoy sailing them from one overnight land stop to another on the lake.

From Bayview, at the south end of the lake, a sailboat with good winds could in a single day race up to Sandpoint at the north end, or spend a week exploring the shoreline and the many small communities, sailing when the wind obliges. One thing is for certain, though: Lake Pend Oreille is a great sailing lake.

The general information on sailing here and elsewhere in the book was written by Cate Huisman, a local sailor. Cate has also written a knowledgeable and helpful column on sailing for each of the seven areas of the lake entitled, "Points of Sail." Specific to that locale, she addresses wind patterns, weather, anchorages, marina access, rentals and other important details for both the casual and serious sailor.

Kayak and Canoe Paddle Routes

As big as Lake Pend Oreille is, it might surprise you to discover that it's also a fine lake to venture out in a canoe or kayak. There are several ideal places for launching non-motorized craft that give you an opportunity to explore some of the quieter areas of the lake, alone or with family and friends. Paddling is a great way to spend a few hours or a few days on the water. And you'll be experiencing the lake in the same spirit as the Kalispel Indians who were the region's first inhabitants. Their primary form of transportation was their unique, sturgeon-nose canoe.

Paddling is also the best way to observe wildlife on the lake, and the quieter you are the more you'll observe. Maybe it's an osprey carrying a trout in its talons back to the nest, a beaver startling you with a sudden slap of his tail on the water, or a great blue heron taking flight with a squawk sounding prehistoric enough to be a pterodactyl. As a canoeist, especially paddling in the Clark Fork River and Pack River

Kayaking past the Cottage Island in Hope (Chris Bessler)

deltas, I've encountered bear in crab apple trees, deer quietly drinking at the water's edge, ravens following me closely going from tree to tree, and river otter and mink swimming alongside the riverbank. I've experienced uncommon events, as well: A mountain goat climbing down a rocky slope to water, or loons that dive underwater not far from my craft only to resurface hundreds of yards away.

You can have similar amazing experiences. Try any of the paddle routes in Areas 1 through 7 including: Sand Creek toward Boyer Slough, Talache Landing to Maiden Rock, Hawkins Point to Fisherman Island, Pack River Flats, Clark Fork Delta, Idlewilde Bay to Buttonhook Bay, Garfield Bay to Green Bay, and Springy Point to Dover Bay. Interested in paddling under the full moons of summer? Read the story in Area 3 on page 153, "Full Moon Paddle" by Gary Hassler. In addition to these paddle routes, floating the Pack River in a canoe, kayak or inflatable boat is also fun.

There are also great places to canoe camp, especially on U.S. Forest Service lands. There are many small stony beaches to explore. I once spent five days alone at a beautiful stony beach I call Loon Beach that was the best meditative retreat and rejuvenating vacation I've ever had. I had never quieted myself for so long in one place to just observe the life around me. I was truly amazed at the abundance and complexity that surrounds us, and the lessons in living life well, if we only take the time to notice.

Leave No Trace (see www.lnt.org)

Plan ahead and prepare.

Travel and camp on durable surfaces.

Dispose of waste properly: Pack it in, pack it out.

Leave what you find, but pack out the trash left by others.

Minimize campfire impacts. Use designated fire rings only.

Respect wildlife.

Be considerate of other visitors.

Camping

The shores of Lake Pend Oreille offer the most diverse opportunities for outdoor camping in the Inland Northwest. Whether you are looking to unroll your sleeping bag on a remote strip of beachfront, or wheel your RV into a designated campground, Lake Pend Oreille covers a range of camping experiences to fit any lifestyle.

Camping areas range from the rarely visited to highly used. There are rustic and modern sites, but not all the campgrounds are designated as such. Some are not even accessible by car.

In fact, many are primitive, which means that no one is directly responsible for their day-to-day maintenance. Wilderness ethics should be applied when visiting these areas.

A good portion of the lakeshore is private property, and some camping areas border these lands. Always obtain direct permission from the property owner if access is required to reach certain parts of the lake. When in doubt, check with the U.S. Forest Service or the maps found in this book. Respecting private property can assure access to public lands in the future.

There are also sensitive cultural sites on the lake with pictographs and petroglyphs that are thousands of years old. Etched into stone by the area's First Peoples, these places are protected by federal law. But vandalism still has occurred. It's important to treat these cultural sites with the utmost respect, whether they are artifacts found in the mud during low water periods or from images on rocks seen along the shoreline. To the descendents of these people, the Kalispel Indians, these items not only represent their history and heritage, they are considered sacred. If you uncover a hidden treasure of the past, leave it there or bury it.

Human impact plays a major role in the overuse of some camping areas. Such impacts range from unsightly trash left behind (including human waste) to landscape alterations (such as cutting live trees or removing native plants), which can be catastrophic to the fragile habitats that support fish and wildlife. The general rule when camping in any area is "Leave No Trace." In all camping areas, from the most primitive to most developed, daily upkeep and maintenance should primarily fall on you — the camper. Such principles will help ensure that this region is preserved for future generations to enjoy.

Swimming, Beaches and Picnics

A brisk plunge into Lake Pend Oreille can be a definitive moment in one's life. In high summer the water temperature reaches into the 70-degree range for a month or so out of the year, but it can be much colder at either end of the season. Swimming in Lake Pend Oreille ranges from a full-day activity under the hot northern Idaho sun to a quick dip taken in between other outdoor pursuits. Though the window of opportunity for swimming can be brief — generally early June through early September — the reward is well worth the long winter wait.

Some swimming areas have roped off areas for safety, designed to protect small children; and some have lifeguards on duty during the busiest summer months. When swimming in the lake, remember that some areas are deep right offshore. Ten feet out and the water can be over your head. Other areas can be fairly shallow a ways out and less of a headache for parents trying to keep an eye on the kids. It's a good idea for parents to check the water depth wherever family members take a dip, just to be safe, as drowning can occur. Swimming in the Clark Fork, Pack or Pend Oreille rivers can be very dangerous in late spring and early to midsummer when the current

Liz Zimmerman takes a refreshing swim at Trestle Creek. The Monarch Mountains are in the distance (Woods Wheatcroft)

flows are swift from runoff of melting mountaintop snows.

Beaches here are either sandy, stony or rocky. Some beaches have colorful, flat stones perfect for a stone-skipping competition. Hand in hand with beaches and swimming are having picnics. A visit to the lake's edge hardly seems complete without a basket of food and a cooler of beverages. You don't need a picnic table, of course, but many public access areas have them. Be aware that some of these sites require a day-use fee. Also, it's illegal to picnic, or sunbathe, on docks that are launch sites or otherwise used by boats.

- - - - - - - - - - - - - - - - - -

Scuba Diving

There is also a way to experience life *underwater*. A relatively new sport here, Lake Pend Oreille is virtually unexplored by divers, partly because there were no dive shops here filling air tanks.

Although the water can be cloudy at times, there are a few popular dive areas with some of the best sites being the southern part of the lake (Area 1, Chapter 4). Steep rock formations, or "walls," go down hundreds of feet just offshore. Another interesting dive area is in shallower water near the Pack River Flats (Area 4, Chapter 7) where in 1904 a train trestle gave way plunging several cars into the water. An undisturbed part of history, three railroad cars are still down there, and you can actually dive into one of them from the lake surface. Scuba diving can also afford a peek into the past. From rocky terrain to smooth gravel beds, lucky divers can often spot bits of history – hatchets, old bottles from Prohibition days and fishing tackle. There are also sunken boats to explore, some of them very old. Divers, however, should be aware they have a duty to leave these artifacts in place and undisturbed; in fact, it's illegal to collect artifacts underwater as well as on land. Please leave them for others to witness, and to preserve the living history for posterity.

Tiffany Windju explores the old Humbird Mill site known as "The Ruins" (Patrick Orton)

Fishing

Fishing was one of the major facets of traditional Kalispel life. Native peoples fished for cutthroat trout, char, chub and whitefish using hook and line, dip nets, spears, at night using torches, and by placing stick or brush weirs at the mouths of tributaries. Fishing was essential to their survival as a tribe. Then with the arrival of settlers, fish became both food and sport with thousands of fish caught. Record-setting fisheries have peaked and crashed here in Lake Pend Oreille. But fishing is still one of the main reasons people come to northern Idaho and Lake Pend Oreille.

Chapter 12 – Fish and Fishing – gives a list of the species of fish that can be caught in the rivers and various areas of the lake, including brief information about the species and their identification. There is also information on the history of fishing in Lake Pend Oreille, the future of the fishery and the K&K Derby, fishing contests held every spring and fall.

Charter Boats and Lake Tours

Locally owned Lake Pend Oreille Cruises can take up to 30 passengers out on the lake to explore its vast shoreline and secluded bays. From Sandpoint City Beach Dock in the summer and Kramer Marina in Hope in spring and fall, the *Shawnodese* captures the romance of an old riverboat and the modern efficiency of a private yacht. In addition to private charters, it offers a variety of public cruises – lunch, dinner, sunset dessert, wine tasting, mountain goat viewing and eagle watching. The cruises are a great way to see the lake, especially for newcomers to the area, and a great deal of history is shared along the way.

Lake Pend Oreille Cruises

Another kind of sightseeing adventure is by flat-water kayak. In addition to the magical Full Moon Paddles, Full Spectrum Tours of Sandpoint has guided half-day, full-day and multi-day tours, including sunset paddles, as well as classes. Equipment, guide, instruction and kayak are provided for the rental fee. It's an opportunity to try a sport with you at the helm.

Besides sightseeing tours, it's also possible to rent a fancy houseboat at Hope Marine Services for a unique, personalized vacation rental. It's a chance to experience living *on* Lake Pend Oreille. These houseboats come fully equipped; some even have Jacuzzi hot tubs on board!

Another kind of charter – and a very popular one – is the charter fishing boat that along with your guide is outfitted with state-of-the-art fishing equipment and fish finders. One charter service even boasts of more than a thousand lures to choose from to catch that big lunker. Some of the fishing charters also offer half- or full-day excursions on modern, comfortable yachts. Some offer overnight tours with spacious sleeping cabins. Fishing charters are moored at Hope Marine Services, Kramer Marina or Holiday Shores Marina – located at Ellisport Bay in Hope. Additional charters are available in Bayview and at Garfield Bay.

Wildlife Viewing, Bird Watching and Photography

Experiencing Lake Pend Oreille and its surrounding landscape with binoculars at the ready is one of the best ways to be prepared for exceptional wildlife viewing, which can include moose, elk, black bear, cougar, bobcat, mountain goats, white-tailed and mule deer, wolves, coyote, beaver, otter, mink, heron, bald eagles, ospreys, hawks, dozens of species of waterfowl including Canada geese and tundra swans, and other species of waterbirds like loons and grebes. We also have, in some people's minds, less glamorous wildlife such as raccoons, skunks, squirrels, packrats, turtles, salamanders and frogs. Please respect these creatures and their habitats.

Moose at Pack River Flats (Chris Bessler)

This place is also a bird-watcher's paradise, with numerous species of songbirds and woodpeckers. A birder from the big city can become ecstatic catching sight of a large pileated woodpecker in a cedar tree along one of the hiking trails. You often hear its prehistoric-sounding cry in flight or its loud hammering on a tree before you actually see it.

Have your camera handy, too. But take caution in approaching wildlife. Remember that these creatures are *wild*, which means that their behavior is unpredictable and can sometimes be dangerous if you get too close. You especially want to avoid getting between a mother moose or bear and their young. It's best to keep your distance. Always keep in mind that animals are free to roam and move as they please. Natural migrations and moving patterns are just that – natural. Animals are always on the move and yet also rely on places that historically have served as habitat for foraging, nesting or shelter. The best areas for viewing a variety of wildlife include the Clark Fork Delta, Denton Slough, Hope Peninsula (David Thompson State Wildlife Preserve), Pack River Flats, Fisherman Island, Oden Bay and Pend d'Oreille Bay.

Endangered Species

There are a few species that are only occasionally seen here because of their diminished numbers and because of their shyness around humans. It's a good idea to know that they are out there, in and around the lake, just in case you come upon them. They are officially listed as threatened or endangered species in Bonner County and protected by federal law. They include the grizzly bear, Selkirk Mountains woodland caribou, Canada lynx, bald eagle and bull trout. Wolverines are being considered for listing. None of these creatures can be harassed or harmed in any way without serious consequences. It's important to know that even a found bald eagle feather is illegal to possess.

Grizzly bear

Snakes and Bats

There are a few other species of wildlife that, at first, you might *not* want to meet up with based on what you've heard but are important to nature's interconnected web of life and are both valuable and interesting to learn about – snakes and bats. We only have three species of snakes in northern Idaho, all nonpoisonous: the nocturnal and burrowing rubber boa (plain brown, black or gray with a yellow belly); the common garter snake; and its relative, the western terrestrial garter snake (both are dark in color, but one has red blotches and the other a yellow or brown stripe along its sides). Garter snakes travel by day and are found on land or in water. All three snakes give birth to living young, eat small prey, shed their skins and hibernate in the winter.

There are several species of bats, a flying mammal found here in northern Idaho. Bats erroneously are considered to be aggressive, blind, dirty and often rabid. They are actually shy and can consume up to one-half their body weight in insects a day. In other words, they'll eat up to 600 mosquitoes an hour! So, try to thank them rather than fear them.

Etiquette Around the Lake's Wild

Traversing the mountain trails that surround Lake Pend Oreille can reveal secrets of nature that can be thrilling for you but create stress for wild creatures merely trying to survive. Smaller animals will usually skedaddle out of sight of a human, but a doe deer startled along the trail could result in the abandonment of its newborn fawn nestled in the grass nearby. On the other hand, coming upon a bull moose or elk during the rut could arouse his territorial ire and result in a challenging charge. Minimize your impacts and avoid disturbing wildlife. Move away from, not towards wildlife; and never shout or scream at a wild animal.

Kootenai Indian elders recall how during huckleberry season in the not-too-distant past, they would pick the berries on one side of the bush and a black bear would feast on the delectable fruits on the other side. Today, typically both species run away from each other.

Other than maybe sharing huckleberries, please don't feed wildlife. The saying goes: "A fed animal is a dead animal." The preservatives and additives found in human food can be poisonous to wildlife, even if they appear to be enjoying the free meal. Animals can become habituated to handouts and more of them will come begging. Some animals, such as bears, will either be relocated or killed by Idaho Fish and Game agents if they become too opportunistic. Pack out all of your trash and food scraps; don't leave anything behind for wildlife to scavenge.

Near water, encounters with wildlife require a more concerted effort to respect their space, breeding and nursery habitats. The creek banks, riverbanks and lakeshore are home to nesting species such as mink, muskrat and otter, and boats that create a wake can cause irreparable harm.

The most vulnerable wildlife are those species that live on water. Many waterfowl and waterbirds use the lake only during spring and fall migrations to and from their breeding territories. Thousands of migrating ducks, swans, grebes and occasional loons can be seen feeding and flocking in some of the lake's shallow bays. Some species – mallards, wood ducks, mergansers and Canada geese – breed here and often become wary of humans during nesting season, so watching with binoculars or spotting scopes from shore is best for them.

Some of these waterbirds, such as the common loon, will live on the lake during the summer without breeding. It's truly a magical event to hear the wail of a loon at dusk while camping along the rocky shore of the Green Monarchs.

One final word about respecting wildlife in their habitat: Avoid bringing dogs to wildlife viewing areas. Dogs have a natural instinct to chase animals that are moving. This can lead to ruined nests, frightened animals and possibly result in injured or dead animals, including your dog.

A little respect can go a long way in preserving wildlife for generations to come while still enjoying this recreationist's paradise. Be an unobtrusive visitor.

- - - - - - - - - - - - - - - - - -

Wildflowers, Native Plants and Photography

What goes hand in hand with the abundance of *fauna* is the abundance of *flora* here in northern Idaho. Many of the native plants, aquatics, shrubs, mushrooms and berries that grow here ultimately become food for wildlife. Since wild herbivores rely on growing things to survive, it is recommended that as much as possible you leave plants, including wildflowers, where they are growing. Enjoy their beauty, their smell (wild roses are incredible!), and preserve these gifts of nature with a photograph, drawing or painting instead of picking them.

Jill Trick viewing native flowers, Indian paintbrush and beargrass (Jane Fritz)

Maybe you'll even want to write a poem about what you see. In early May 1980, my first spring living around Lake Pend Oreille, I wrote in my journal a simple but memorable entry: "Some of the wildflowers I've seen today up at Sam Owen's grave ... Nuttall's larkspur (poisonous), common camas (edible bulb), maiden blue-eyed Mary (tiny!) and shooting stars." Getting to know the vast array of native plants and wildflowers in northern Idaho has been my passion ever since, from the blooming of the first western spring beauty at the edge of melting snows, to the glorious yellow glacier lily and huckleberries in summer, to autumn's clusters of ripened red-orange berries of the mountain ash that hang on the tree until waxwings eat them during the harsh months of winter. Getting to know the ways of native plants all year long is highly recommended.

There are a variety of native plant habitats around Lake Pend Oreille from riparian areas to wetlands to meadows to subalpine forests. The Kinnikinnick Chapter of the Idaho Native Plant Society has created a North Idaho Native Plant Arboretum in Sandpoint's Lakeview Park, adjacent to the Bonner County Historical Museum. It's well worth your time to get to know the plants at the arboretum first, using your field guide, and then go seek them out in the wild.

Hiking, Mountain Biking and Horseback Riding

Lake Pend Oreille is a draw for recreationists of all sorts, including hikers, horse people and single-track mountain bikers. A system of trails practically encircles the lake providing almost 100 miles of dirt and rock paths, some accessing the lake itself while many of them lead to majestic mountaintop vistas. Some trails are designated "Family Fun Hikes." These are trails generally suitable for all ages. They offer a good place to take young children or elderly relatives, as long as everyone is in reasonably good health. Chapter 11 of this book details *all* the trails around Lake Pend Oreille with views of the lake.

The Backcountry Horsemen, a local group of riders, are the people to

Trail running on Scotchman Peak Trail (Doug Marshall)

thank for doing trail maintenance in collaboration with U.S. Forest Service volunteers. They work to keep trailheads accessible to horse and riders and clear fallen timber along the trails after snowmelt. But not all trails are accessible to people on horseback, because access sometimes begins on private property. It's essential to seek permission from property owners before riding onto their property.

Unlike our neighbor to the east – the state of Montana – northern Idaho has few horse trailer parking areas near trailheads. Nonetheless, there are some amazing trails around the lake to experience on horseback. So if you choose to ride rather than hike or bike, be sure that the place you are going has plenty of water and grass for your animal; otherwise, you'll have to pack in weed-free hay, processed grain and water. Some of the best trails for horseback are the two-day ride between Lunch Peak and Lightning Creek in Clark Fork along Trail 120 (see Area 7) and the day ride to the top of Gold Hill (Area 2). A U.S. Forest Service map or topographic map is an excellent companion item for the serious hiker or backcountry camper.

— — — — — — — — — — — — — — — — — —

Driving and Bicycling Tours

Perhaps you don't have the time or inclination to actually get on or in the lake, but you still want to enjoy its fantastic, natural scenery. A good way to do that is from a bicycle or the comfort of your car.

Road biking in northern Idaho is an adventure in its own right, with asphalt that changes with the seasons (i.e., pot holes and ruts), dirt or gravel roads that can be muddy after rains, highways with narrow shoulders, and lengthy loops that make your legs burn. But the rewards are great: sweeping vistas of the lake, exquisite beaches en route, long stretches of open country road, and few other cyclists in sight. Be sure to pack a flat-tire repair kit, extra food and plenty of drinking water.

Given the vastness of the land around Lake Pend Oreille, exploring it by car is a great way to fit it all in if your days here are limited. Those who enjoy leisurely drives through exquisite landscapes and scenery will find the driving tours to be exceptional. It's advisable to plan road trips as half- or full-day outings. Stopping along the way will allow you to take in as much as possible. In addition to the wonderful landscapes and watery scenery, these driving tours pass through historic areas, which also deserve exploration.

Lake Events

Special events take place every spring, summer and fall that have Lake Pend Oreille as

the centerpiece of activities. These events
draw people to the area from throughout
the Northwest. Some of these annual,
community-centered happenings include:
Independence Day fireworks over the water at
Bayview, Sandpoint and Hope; a wooden boat
festival; two fishing derbies; the Long Bridge
Swim; Sunday Concerts on the Lawn; the
dynamic, two-week-long Festival at Sandpoint
at Memorial Field; and the Arts & Crafts Fair
sponsored by the Pend Oreille Arts Council at
Sandpoint City Beach.

Independence Day fireworks at Sandpoint City Beach
(Cory Murdock)

Gianna Heaviland and her dog, Otto, swim at Green Bay after hiking the Mineral Point Trail (Joanne Heaviland)

CHAPTER THREE 3

Caring for the Lake's Future

"Just 20 parts phosphorus to a billion parts water – the equivalent of a single drop of water in a full bathtub – can provoke an algae bloom."

—*National Wildlife Federation Magazine*

Regardless of whether this is your first encounter with Lake Pend Oreille or your hundredth, there are some things you should know about its vulnerabilities and the impacts humans have on its well-being – basically that people are the primary cause of water pollution. This chapter is one that I hope every reader will take seriously.

Historically, the lake has undergone dramatic changes. Seventy years after fur trader David Thompson first came upon Lake Pend Oreille in 1809, pioneer settlers, loggers, miners and railroad men arrived in droves and immediately exploited the area's natural resources. The area's pristine waters were used as the lifeblood of commerce. Over time, however, a different resource ethic began to emerge consistent with the national environmental movement of the 1970s; passage of the Clean Water Act and other protective legislation set a new course of action for how Lake Pend Oreille and its tributary rivers and streams would be treated in the future.

Gradually the natural beauty of the area moved to center stage, and tourism and service industries developed. Lake Pend Oreille's aesthetic and recreational values have contributed to a new, booming tourist economy for surrounding towns and communities.

Many artists, back-to-the-landers and corporate America escapees looking for a simpler life, one more in harmony with the natural world, arrived in the 1970s, including me. There are many of us still living here, and we know how lucky we've been. It's more than the area's incomparable beauty and year-round recreational opportunities; we've enjoyed clean air, clean water and a fruitful earth. We learned from those who had been here for generations to nurture a deep, abiding love and respect for the place. My friend, the late American Indian elder Henry SiJohn, with tears in his eyes once described the tribal life around Lake Pend Oreille as "utopian." I have come to believe that the past 40 years has been the most favorable time to live around Idaho's Lake Pend Oreille since the days of Henry's ancestors.

Now, 200 years after the arrival of that first outsider, dramatic changes are again occurring. The forested mountain lands, grassy meadows and spectacular waters are a magnet for people coming here from all over the country. The area is clearly in the national spotlight, and Lake Pend Oreille is typically the centerpiece of all that attention.

Watershed Awareness

After a region is "discovered," it suffers numerous impacts. Both the people who live and work here and the agencies that regulate and control recreational and development impacts are concerned about the future of the Lake Pend Oreille watershed, particularly the integrity of near-shore waters, shorelines, riverbanks and streams. Development of shoreline properties, herbicide treatment to control invasive aquatic weeds and increasing recreational demands all can have a deleterious effect on the lake. While out enjoying the lake, rivers and surrounding mountains, it's important to minimize our impacts on the lake in order that future generations can enjoy its remarkable qualities.

According to authorities, there's been an increase in illegal waterway activities: careless oil and gas spills from boaters; digging, rip-rapping or building boat docks along the shoreline without a permit; and dumping hazardous wastes into the water. Pollutants, sedimentation and too many nutrients will upset the ecological balance of a lake resulting in a slimy shore, excessive weed growth in shallow bays and mucky, instead of sandy, lake bottoms. There's also the possibility of deadly, blue-green algae blooms. Ultimately it will require personal responsibility to protect Lake Pend Oreille. State water quality officials especially appreciate vigilant citizens who become active land stewards.

Additionally, in recent years, miles of shorelines once given over to meadow or forested land have been converted to numerous individual homesites with manicured grass lawns right down to the water. The chemical fertilizers and herbicides that it takes to maintain such a carpet of green inevitably wind up in the water. According to regulatory authorities, it's not good for the lake or wildlife habitat. The cumulative effect of a developed lakeshore without native vegetation is too many nutrients in the water and pollution near the shoreline.

For more than a decade the nonprofit Tri-State Water Quality Council has worked to improve and protect the water quality of the Clark Fork-Pend Oreille watershed, which encompasses 16 million acres spanning Montana, Idaho and Washington and including Lake Pend Oreille. Made up of everyday citizens and representatives from business, industry, government, local tribes and environmental groups, the council oversees the implementation of a management plan to reduce nutrient pollution in the entire watershed. An increasing level of nutrients, particularly nitrogen and phosphorus, are threatening the lake's water quality and contributing to algal blooms, growth of algae scum on rocks and the spread of invasive aquatics like Eurasian watermilfoil, so much so that it's been designated a "threatened" resource by the state of Idaho. The lake's nearshore waters will likely continue to degrade over the long term unless certain local actions and protective measures are implemented.

Leave No Trace

Perhaps you don't live in Sandpoint or Bayview or spend your summer in a vacation home on Lake Pend Oreille, but come from outside the area to enjoy the lake on the weekend. What impact is your recreational experience having on the lake's water quality?

Recreational use is steadily increasing in step with growth of the area. More and more people from other places are visiting Lake Pend Oreille: as weekend tourists with Jet Skis in tow; RV travelers who park along the water's edge; anglers who cook their catch over campfires on the shore; and bicyclists, canoeists and kayakers who camp overnight. Getting people to voluntarily follow the guidelines of a water quality plan may seem like a pipe dream, but there is a lot a person can do to keep the waterways clean. (See "Leave No Trace," page 20)

Oftentimes, the simplest way to help is by being mindful of your impact and picking up after yourself: Don't build fires near the water's edge (I regularly dismantle fire rings that are too close); haul out your garbage; and never dispose of harmful, toxic or foreign substances on or near the shore.

According to the U.S. Forest Service, that's what every lake user ought to do. It's also why the agency promotes Leave No Trace principles and other low-impact camping ethics in educational brochures and over its Web sites. Camping in undeveloped areas is OK, but Forest Service rangers encourage visitors to stay in developed campgrounds that provide toilets and appropriate fire rings placed back from the water. They also encourage people to stay on the trails, because it protects native vegetation in addition to keeping sediments out of the lake. Sediments build up and when the lake gets muddy, aquatic plants have trouble growing, oxygen for fish and other aquatic species is then diminished, and aquatic organisms and insects get buried alive. Not a healthy picture!

Unfortunately, agency upkeep of the many USFS recreational sites around Lake Pend Oreille is limited. Without the public's self-policing help, the Forest Service will continue to fall behind on what needs to be done, and that can only spell trouble for protecting the waters of Lake Pend Oreille.

Attention Boaters! Spread the Word, not the Weed

With the increase of recreational boating in the watershed, the public also bears responsibility for one other major pollution problem – the growth of invasive weeds. Native aquatic plants are essential to a healthy lake environment for fish, insects, invertebrates and wildlife; but Eurasian watermilfoil, a recent arrival in the shallow bays of Lake Pend Oreille and its tributaries, are choking out native vegetation. The plant also can choke docks and make swimming dangerous, especially for small children. The plant can set seed, but more commonly it propagates by fragmentation. The smallest weed fragment of Eurasian watermilfoil can attach to trailers, boat props, fishing gear, oars and paddles, and boat hulls. When carried from one place to another, the undesired plant part can establish roots and develop new growth. It infests waterways like a cancer, spreading easily and growing quickly. A single plant can multiply into 250 million new plants in one year in nutrient-rich waters. Since Eurasian watermilfoil is readily spread between lakes and rivers, typically by boats, personal responsibility and proactive deeds are key.

Educational signage asking boaters to clean their crafts on shore after lake and river use has not been a significant deterrent in the spread of the unwanted species. Nor has asking boaters to stay out of invasive milfoil growth areas, especially around docks in front of lakeshore homes. The result is that Eurasian watermilfoil growth has become so bad that since the summer of 2006, and every year since, Bonner County has used massive amounts of a variety of toxic herbicides to kill the invasive aquatic plants in several heavily infested areas, including popular public swimming areas in both the lake and Pend Oreille River. But chemical controls have been only marginally successful and the herbicides also kill native milfoils and other aquatic plants, which are important food and shelter for many species of fish and wildlife. Scuba divers are successful at removing whole milfoil plants, but there are few divers trained to do the work. Unfortunately, chemical herbicides are easier and cheaper to use and part of the mindset of a generation accustomed to using toxic chemicals to solve its problems. Current research shows that a small native insect – the Eurasian milfoil weevil – may be an effective long-term control. Its use is being tested.

It's a complex issue: lakeshore property owners want the invasive milfoil eradicated, but many residents, myself among them, want to see more sustainable controls applied that are safer for water users and for fish and wildlife. Doing nothing is unacceptable and unsavory trade-offs are being made; but with more public awareness and stewardship, perhaps Eurasian watermilfoil will be contained enough to keep chemicals out of the lake in the future. Keep your marine vessels clean of this plant. Prevention is the cheapest and most effective way to manage this problem plant.

In 2009, a new invasive species threat emerged, with the potential to wreak as much or more damage as milfoil. *Quagga* and zebra mussels, two closely related freshwater mollusks, were introduced to the Great Lakes in 1988, most likely in the ballast water of a cargo ship from Europe. They have since spread to some Western waters. The mussels attach themselves to various surfaces – rocks, docks, boats – and form massive colonies that obstruct access for humans and gobble up the phytoplanktons that are the primary food supply for fish and other species in a healthy lake ecosystem. The mussels reproduce with tiny eggs and larva that can't be seen with the unaided eye, which means they can be spread unknowingly in contaminated bilge or even mud on the hull of a boat. The threat of mussels requires all boaters to carefully clean their boats before launching in the lake.

The mussels have not yet been identified in Lake Pend Oreille, but the severe threat they pose – to Pend Oreille and all Idaho waters – prompted the Idaho Legislature in May 1990 to launch a mandatory invasive species prevention program. The program requires all boaters, even kayakers and canoeists, to clean their boats to prevent the spread of milfoil, mussels and other invasives. Virtually all watercraft, even canoes and kayaks, are also now required to carry an Invasive Species Fund sticker; boaters are subject to fines for failing to obtain the stickers. Stickers are available at all Idaho state parks, including Farragut and Round Lake. More information at: www.invasivespecies. idaho.gov, phone 1-877-336-8676.

A promising organization that formed in early 2009 that will be directly monitoring and responding to water quality threats in the watershed is the Lake Pend Oreille Waterkeeper. Affiliated with the international organization Waterkeeper Alliance, this group's activist thrust will focus around education, partnership and advocacy. Lake Pend Oreille Waterkeeper will not only work to protect water quality, but also to improve the health and viability of the ecosystems and people that rely upon it, while ensuring that laws and rules are adequate and enforced.

Protecting Lake Pend Oreille's water quality is not simple. It will take diligent and sustained efforts – possibly even sacrifices – to ensure that this remarkable lake, a paradise for many, is healthy another 30 or 40 years from now.

HELPFUL TIPS ON HOW TO KEEP YOUR LAKE CLEAN AND HEALTHY

Don't Feed the Lake

To slow storm-water runoff and minimize nutrient overloading at the shoreline:

- Maintain natural vegetation on banks or terrace steep slopes.

- Leave a buffer zone (riparian area) of native vegetation near the lakeshore to act as a natural filter system.
- Minimize applications of fertilizers, herbicides and pesticides on shore. Instead, use compost. Cut or hand pull weeds. It is illegal to apply any chemicals to the lake without a permit.
- Don't burn yard wastes; compost them well away from the water.
- Minimize soil disturbance during construction and revegetate bare areas as soon as possible.
- Don't burn campfires on the shoreline below the high water mark. The ashes contain nutrients and wash into the lake with rainfall.

Don't Flush Your Lake's Future

What happens on shore can ultimately wind up in the lake:
- Don't dump household cleaners, solvents or pesticides into storm sewers. Discard hazardous contaminants properly.
- Recycle motor oil and other automotive wastes (ask at automotive shops).
- Pick up animal waste and bag for trash pickup.
- Don't bathe, wash pets or wash dishes with soap in the lake.
- Maintain septic systems and make sure gray water drains to the septic system or at least 50 feet from the lake when camping. Never dump gray water directly into the lake.
- Conserve water, so less wastewater reaches the lake.

Where Have All the Wetlands Gone?

Wetlands filter out pollutants and sediments, act as a natural barrier against shore erosion, and provide food, shelter and nursery areas for fish and wildlife.
- Eliminate the need to fill, dredge, drain or alter wetlands and weed beds.
- Protect fish and wildlife habitat.
- Control erosion in wetland areas; sediments suffocate plants and fish eggs.
- Avoid using motorboats and personal watercraft in shallow areas to prevent stirring sediments, spreading invasive weeds or leaking oil and gas in an already stressed environment.
- Many aquatic plants and algae are crucial to the health of a lake. Learn which ones are most beneficial to fish and wildlife.
- Keep livestock out of wetlands.
- Work to control nonnative aquatic plants like Eurasian watermilfoil. Do NOT use chemicals in the lake, but hand harvest and compost the plants.
- Shoreline development can obscure the natural beauty of the lakeshore. Design structures

Legendary Lake Pend Oreille

that are in harmony with the natural features. Keep piers and docks to a minimum, and build your cabin or home back from the water.

Adapted from "Get in Tune To Your Lake," Lake Management Program, Wisconsin Department of Natural Resources, Madison, Wisconsin. Used with permission.

Eurasian Watermilfoil Identification

Eurasian watermilfoil can be difficult to identify and can be confused with several species of native watermilfoil. To distinguish the native plant from the invader:

- Each milfoil leaf is made of pairs of small leaflets. Leaves are arranged in whorls of four around the stem. A segment of Eurasian milfoil leaf shows 12 to 24 pairs of leaflets; a native milfoil leaf has only six to 10 pairs.
- Eurasian milfoil has a finer, more feathery appearance.
- Eurasian watermilfoil leaves tend to collapse around the stem when removed from the water. Native milfoil species have thicker stems and are usually more robust and keep their shape.
- Eurasian watermilfoil's flower spikes form above the water's surface and stems branch several times near the surface forming a dense mat. The upper stems often develop a reddish color.

Clockwise from above: Idaho Invasive Species Fund sticker, required for all boats in Lake Pend Oreille; Eurasian watermilfoil tangled up with a boat (Tom Wolf); close-ups of milfoil and zebra mussels

How You Can Help Control the Spread of Invasive Species

One plant segment of milfoil can root and propagate a dense colony of new plants and infest shallow areas of the lake. Mussels can spread by virtually invisible eggs or larva in bilge water or mud.

- Always remove plant fragments from your boat hull, trailer, motor, paddles and oars, and anchor before launching and after leaving the water.
- When swimming, remove plant fragments floating on water.
- Dispose of plant fragments in the trash or on high, dry ground.
- Clean fishing tackle and any other equipment that has made contact with weed beds. Inspect all exposed surfaces (vehicle, trailer, anchor, dock lines, live wells, bilge, motor, hull, trailer axle and rollers). Small mussels feel like sandpaper and are invisible to the eye.
- Wash the hull of each watercraft thoroughly (steam clean if possible).
- Drain all water and dry all areas.
- Drain and dry the lower outboard unit.
- Clean and dry all live-wells.
- Empty and dry any buckets.
- Dispose of all bait in the trash.
- Wait five days and keep watercraft dry between launches into different fresh waters.
- Spread the word to neighbors and friends who also use northern Idaho lakes and rivers.

Boat Maintenance and Sanitation

The biggest pollution threats to water quality in Lake Pend Oreille while boating come from the materials needed to keep a powerboat's engine running smoothly. Oil is especially dangerous because only a single cup of oil spilled into the water can contaminate an area the size of a football field. By following some simple steps, we can all contribute to a cleaner lake.

- Keep engines well tuned: routinely check for engine fuel leaks and use a drip pan under the engine.
- Maintain a clean engine: Watch for and correct small leaks before they become bigger problems. Use absorbent pads to clean engine spaces, but minimize the use of engine cleaners.
- Use a spill-proof pump or vacuum tank when changing oil and transmission fluid. When removing an oil filter, slip a plastic bag over it to contain oil that normally drips from the filter and use an absorbent pad to wipe up oil drops.
- Do not change antifreeze while on the lake: orange and pink-colored antifreeze is less toxic than the blue- and green-colored ethylene glycol. When winterizing your inboard engine block, be sure not to dump the antifreeze on the ground or in water. Dispose of it properly. Antifreeze is also deadly to pets. Used oil, antifreeze, cleaners and gas/oil absorbent pads from private, noncommercial boats can be taken to the Bonner County Recycling/Transfer stations for disposal.

- Cleaning your boat: A lot of things can make a boat dirty, but when cleaning it, keep in mind what happens to the dirt, paint chips, solvents and other grime that might wash off your boat into the water. Clean all parts of the boat ashore over hard surfaces where potential contaminants can be contained. Use cleaning products that are non-toxic and free of phosphates. If the label says "do not get in eyes" or "always wear gloves," the chances are the product you are using can harm you and the environment. Consider using alternative cleaners like baking soda, lemon juice, vinegar and employ a little elbow grease. And clean frequently. A boat that looks clean is easy to keep clean.

- Fueling: Oil, diesel fuel and gasoline can quickly cause serious pollution. Follow some basic steps to ensure these substances do not enter the water. Never overfill or "top off" your fuel tank. Know that capacity and stop at 90 percent. Avoid backsplash at the nozzle, and use absorbent pads around the fuel nozzle in case of backsplash. If filling the boat tank from a gas can, make sure the nozzle collar has a washer and the collar is tight, don't pop the air vent plug until the nozzle is in the tank filler tube, and don't try this method of filling the tank if the boat or dock is bobbing. Never leave a fuel nozzle unattended during fueling. If you have a spill, immediately contact the National Response Center at 1-800-424-8802 and call local authorities using 911. Do not use emulsifiers or soaps on fuel spills. These products simply break up the petroleum into small droplets that sink to the lake bottom or remain in the water column. It is illegal to use them. Instead use absorbent pads, pillows or brooms to soak up as much petroleum as possible before the slick drifts away. Absorbent pads and spill containment kits are available at marinas or boating supply stores.

- Bilge care: Prior to pumping, inspect the bilge for petroleum sheens, oil droplets, hydraulic fluid and grease. If bilge water is oily or has a sheen, do not discharge into the lake. Use absorbent materials (see above) and remove the petroleum. Routinely check and fix oil or fuel leaks.

- Sanitation: It is illegal to discharge or dump sewage from marine toilets, boat holding tanks or portable toilets into Lake Pend Oreille and other waters. Whenever possible, use onshore restrooms rather than onboard ones. If your boat has a toilet/holding tank, use the pump-out stations located around Lake Pend Oreille. State law requires that the tank must be sealed to prevent spills. If your boat doesn't have a toilet, take a portable toilet on board your vessel and only empty it at a dump station or home. Keep fats, solvents, oils, emulsifiers, paints, poisons, disposable diapers and sanitary napkins out of toilets.

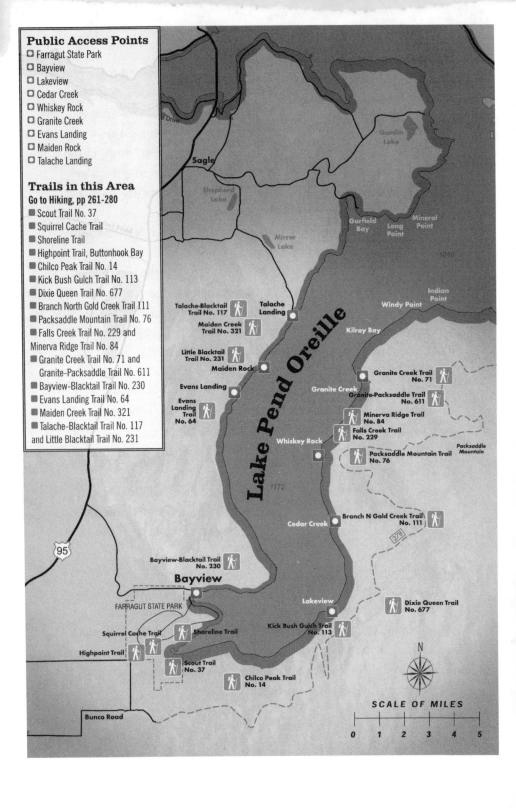

Public Access Points
☐ Farragut State Park
☐ Bayview
☐ Lakeview
☐ Cedar Creek
☐ Whiskey Rock
☐ Granite Creek
☐ Evans Landing
☐ Maiden Rock
☐ Talache Landing

Trails in this Area
Go to Hiking, pp 261–280
■ Scout Trail No. 37
■ Squirrel Cache Trail
■ Shoreline Trail
■ Highpoint Trail, Buttonhook Bay
■ Chilco Peak Trail No. 14
■ Kick Bush Gulch Trail No. 113
■ Dixie Queen Trail No. 677
■ Branch North Gold Creek Trail 111
■ Packsaddle Mountain Trail No. 76
■ Falls Creek Trail No. 229 and
Minerva Ridge Trail No. 84
■ Granite Creek Trail No. 71 and
   Granite-Packsaddle Trail No. 611
■ Bayview-Blacktail Trail No. 230
■ Evans Landing Trail No. 64
■ Maiden Creek Trail No. 321
■ Talache-Blacktail Trail No. 117
and Little Blacktail Trail No. 231

Lake Pend Oreille

Sagle

Gamlin Lake

Shepherd Lake

Mirror Lake

Garfield Bay   Long Point   Mineral Point

Indian Point

Windy Point

Talache-Blacktail Trail No. 117

Talache Landing

Maiden Creek Trail No. 321

Kilray Bay

Little Blacktail Trail No. 231

Maiden Rock

Granite Creek Trail No. 71

Granite Creek

Granite-Packsaddle Trail No. 611

Evans Landing

Evans Landing Trail No. 64

Minerva Ridge Trail No. 84

Falls Creek Trail No. 229

Whiskey Rock

Packsaddle Mountain Trail No. 76

Packsaddle Mountain

1172

Cedar Creek

Branch N Gold Creek Trail No. 111

278

95

Bayview-Blacktail Trail No. 230

Bayview

FARRAGUT STATE PARK

Lakeview

Dixie Queen Trail No. 677

Squirrel Cache Trail   Shoreline Trail

Kick Bush Gulch Trail No. 113

Highpoint Trail

Scout Trail No. 37

Chilco Peak Trail No. 14

Bunco Road

N

SCALE OF MILES
0   1   2   3   4   5

CHAPTER FOUR

AREA 1, BAYVIEW

Eastern Shore to Kilroy Bay
Western Shore to Talache Landing

OVERVIEW:

*I*n the hearts of many people, myself included, the spirit of Lake Pend Oreille is likened to that of a woman – the Lady of the Lake. Perhaps then, the southern tip of the lake near the present-day town of Bayview is found at the lady's feet, her ankle at Cape Horn. Looking at the lake's shape on a modern map, she appears to be pirouetting between mountain ranges.

Whether you arrive by boat or car, south from Sandpoint, southwest from Clark Fork, or north from Coeur d'Alene (only 26 miles off Interstate 90), getting to and on the lake is easy in and around Bayview with several developed marinas, a city dock and Farragut State Park next door. To reach public sites east of Bayview, rugged mountain roads provide the main access. See "Tour on Wheels" in this chapter. But there are small and relatively few access points by car as you travel much of the surrounding geography, so it's OK to explore by boat and camp on the tiny, pebble beaches that dot the shorelines amidst established recreational sites.

Most of this area is remote, magnificently beautiful and steeped in history. Established

Aerial view of Buttonhook, Idlewilde and Scenic bays, with Bayview on the right (Jay Mock)

boat launches and docks soon give way to primitive beaches, accessible only by water. It's best to discover these remarkable beaches, coves and scenic splendors for yourself.

The southern end of Lake Pend Oreille near Bayview to Kilroy Bay on the eastern shore, then across the lake to Talache Landing on the opposite shore, is where weather and winds typically build, flowing northward up the lake's long, narrow body. This area is a sailor's heaven whether soloing or joining a regatta of boats from the Lake Pend Oreille Yacht Club out of Bayview. There is also a U.S. Naval Acoustic Research Detachment here — one of only two in the country — and unusual for an inland body of water. The federal government conducts deepwater sonar research for Navy ships and submarines, and supports research on fish done by the state and University of Idaho. The Navy also records data from weather buoys on the lake below Three Sisters Peaks, daily information that is available to the public via the Internet. Google "Pend Oreille Lake."

This is also the most mysterious part of the lake. It is where the water is the deepest. There is more than 1,100 feet of water beneath your boat a nautical mile from either the east or west shoreline. This area of the lake clearly falls under the rubric, "wilderness of water." Wild also describes the rocky, steep slopes that rise from the lakeshore. Largely National Forest lands, they are home to more wildlife than people, including white, shaggy mountain goat families on the vertical slopes of Bernard Peak.

If civilized amenities are what you seek, they can be easily found in Bayview, and to a lesser extent across the lake in the small community of Lakeview. Southwest of Bayview at the far southern tip of Lake Pend Oreille is Farragut State Park. During World War II, it was the Farragut Naval Training Station. Today, as a state park, it features more than 40 miles of trails for hikers and bikers to explore, including more than 20 miles also open to equestrian use; numerous campsites; a swimming beach; a museum and historic brig; disc golf course; volleyball area and playground; and ample boating facilities. At the head of this bay and around a small peninsula lies Buttonhook Bay. This protected, southernmost toe point of the lake lies completely within Kootenai County.

Traveling northeast and northwest from Scenic and Idlewilde bays, it is wild again for nearly 20 miles. There is public access at Lakeview, Cedar Creek, Whiskey Rock and Granite Creek on the east shore, and at Evans Landing, Maiden Rock and Talache Landing on the west shore. Of those three on the west shore, two are accessible only via trails or by boat — Evans Landing and Maiden Rock.

Most of the land on the eastern side of Lake Pend Oreille is Forest Service-managed public land. The centerpiece of this side of the lake is the looming hulk of Packsaddle Mountain (6,405 feet), which is the magnet to the many trails weaving through the forests from stream bottoms to ridgetops. Framing the deep waters of the lake on the west shore is a string of low hills that separate Pend Oreille from the main valley of the Purcell Trench from Gold Hill to Cape Horn Peak. These hills are heavily timbered, easily accessible and have well-managed Forest Service trails. For detailed trail information, refer to chapter 11, "Hiking, Mountain Biking and Horseback Riding Trails."

This area of the lake affords recreational experiences you won't soon forget. So go explore!

- -

Anecdota: Life on a Houseboat

It was an exciting life for a girl growing up in Coeur d'Alene in the late 1950s. Come summer, Carrie Nylund's duffel bag was already packed and zipped when her mom, Judy Freeland, said, "It's time to pack up and go to the lake!" Lake Pend Oreille, that is, at Bayview where the family's houseboat was moored. Back then, Lake Coeur d'Alene had hydroplane races and it was too hectic being on the water.

In contrast, those summers on Lake Pend Oreille were idyllic. Carrie and her two older brothers spent extended weekends living on the houseboat that her dad, Gene Soper, and family friend Jim Doyle built in 1958. They called it the *Doylie-Bob*. It was a simple, rectangular deck strapped onto 55-gallon drums to serve as pontoons with a flat-topped, wooden structure

Carrie Nylund and family aboard the *Doylie-Bob* (courtesy photo)

centered on the deck that served as the "house." One of the earliest photographs of the *Doylie-Bob* was of Judy standing on deck very pregnant with Carrie; so her life on a houseboat spanned from being in the womb until adolescence.

Carrie, her mom, brothers and Elvina Doyle spent weekdays on the lake moored at Bayview until the weekends when the men would arrive. All together, they would motor down the lake from Scenic Bay to Buttonhook Bay, and moor for the night. They would count the deer along the way, which sometimes numbered over 50 animals, and Carrie would look for mountain goats on Bernard Peak using binoculars. Or they would motor northeast towards Lakeview trolling for kokanee salmon or rainbow trout, and then fry up the fish for breakfast. They would swim, fish some more, and find a beach to tie up to for the night. This summertime routine of pure enjoyment went from Memorial Day through Labor Day.

Carrie recalls as a small girl falling asleep among the life jackets and deck pillows kept in a storage box located on the fore deck. It was also her special hiding place during storms on the lake. She had to constantly wear a life jacket on board, but only until she was old enough to easily swim encircling the houseboat. The only thing that sometimes frightened her was swimming in that deep, deep water – only because her brothers would tease her about the "Pend Oreille Paddler" or some enormous sturgeon about to nibble at her toes from the depths below.

Being out on the lake today takes Carrie back to those memorable, long-ago summers. Carrie believes that her experiences on the lake as a youth shaped her active, adult life as a kayaker and scuba diver and is what nurtured her love of the outdoors. Today Carrie and her husband, John, live in Sagle and paddle Lake Pend Oreille in every season. They go canoe camping and have favorite spots for scuba diving – Bayview, Maiden Rock and Talache Landing. The steep walls and interesting rock formations fascinate them, and they watch for big bass and look for lost fishing tackle and sunken boats. The couple once tried staying on a modern houseboat with full kitchen and a waterslide on deck. But Carrie says it was too plush, like you never left home at all. The *Doylie-Bob* was more like going camping and she liked that better.

As a lifelong lake enthusiast, Carrie's advice to people new to Lake Pend Oreille is to find something you enjoy doing that will bring you in close contact with the lake and at the same time won't take away from its remarkable splendor. It's a good give-and-take formula for the lake's future.

Scenic Bay Marina in Bayview (Linda Lantzy)

 BAYVIEW

A free, public boat launching facility managed by Kootenai County occupies a narrow slot leading to the water in the center of Bayview, next to Boileau's Resort.

What's it like?

Located on Scenic Bay next door to Farragut State Park, this is the gateway for Lake Pend

Oreille for those approaching from the Spokane-Coeur d'Alene area. In fact it was Spokane entrepreneurs who built it as a resort community, welcoming its first permanent residents in 1910. There are numerous private marinas, restaurants, shops and other amenities available, including marine tours and charters. Private property crowds this launch site and parking is limited.

Bayview also has something familiar to visitors from the Puget Sound area – old limestone kilns. A cement industry flourished in the area in the early decades of the 20th century, and lime was shipped first by barge north to railheads at Hope and Sandpoint, and then directly by rail to Spokane. You can view the ruins of the kilns from Scenic Bay Marina.

This lakeside community is home to hundreds of sailboats, and you'll see a lot of float homes and houseboats moored in the marinas, too. They have been a part of the Bayview experience for generations. This is one of the most popular boating and sailing areas on the lake.

The residents of Bayview host a major annual event that draws crowds of tourists from around the region – Bayview Daze. It's a community celebration that happens around July Fourth and culminates in a spectacular fireworks display over the water.

The U.S. Navy has maintained an acoustic research facility in Bayview since the 1950s, including work on the *Seawolf* class attack submarine. One-fifth scale models of the Navy's equipment are tested on Lake Pend Oreille, but the newest facet of the Navy's research is surface water warfare testing with a 133-foot, quarter-scale model of a destroyer that launched in 2005. The *Sea Jet* operates on the lake between Bayview and Garfield Bay.

FACILITIES: concrete boat ramp; public dock; gas, rope crane, marine supplies and repair at private marinas; sailboat, fishing boat, houseboat and canoe rentals and moorage; boat cruises, tours and charters; restaurants, groceries, retail shops and lodging

ACTIVITIES: sailing, boating, paddling, fishing, houseboat camping, picnicking, wildlife viewing, scuba diving

How to get here:

Take Idaho State Highway 54 east from U.S. Highway 95 at Athol and travel six miles, passing through Farragut State Park to reach Bayview at the northeast corner of the park.

Points of Sail
By Cate Huisman

Wind and Sailors:

The Lake Pend Oreille Yacht Club (http://web.lpoyc.org) is based in Bayview, home to hundreds of sailboats, thanks to water depths that enable owners to keep their boats in the lake year-round. The club has both cruising and racing calendars, with races on Wednesday evenings in summer, a spring and fall series, and even a frozen New Year's Day race for those who haven't drifted off to the ski slopes. The Bitter End Marina is home to the majority of the masts, and races begin from there or MacDonald's Hudson Bay Resort.

The wind here follows a fairly reliable pattern in summer, due to the thermal effects of Packsaddle Mountain across the lake. In the morning, cold air flows down the mountain and generates a northeast wind, which usually

Sailing from Bayview (Chris Bessler)

dies at midday. In the afternoon, as the sun heats the mountain, warm air begins to flow back up, creating a west or southwest wind.

Anchorages:

The south end of the lake includes several secure anchorages, several docks and marinas, and several exposed mooring buoys off lovely shorelines. Buttonhook Bay in Farragut State Park at the very south end of the lake is popular on summer weekends but not crowded at other times. If the docks are full, you can drop the hook in the bay, which is fully enclosed and completely protected from winds coming from any direction, but beware of logs on the bottom.

The public docks along the east side at Lakeview, Cedar Creek, Whiskey Rock and Granite Creek provide secure places to tie up. However, these docks are in relatively shallow bays that can be exposed to winds from both the north and south, so they won't necessarily make for a calm night. Because of this lack of protection, none provides good options for overnight anchorage. Shoal-draft boats that can get far back into the bays have the most options. Whiskey Rock provides the best protection from the south. There are also two mooring buoys at Whiskey Rock that, according to the Bonner County Sheriff's Marine Division, will secure any size vessel.

On the west side, there are five additional secure county mooring buoys – three at Maiden Rock and two at Evans Landing – but they are fully exposed.

Launching and Hauling:

There is an excellent launch site at Eagle Boat Landing in Farragut State Park with more than ample parking, but there's a nominal fee to get into the park. When launching from the Bayview ramp, check whether you will hit the overhead power lines before stepping your mast. MacDonald's Hudson Bay Resort has a crane that provides access when water has fallen too low to use the launch ramps.

Float homes at Bayview (Chris Bessler)

- - - - - - - - - - - - - - - - - - - -

Lore Along the Shore: Scenic Bay

The first white settlers arrived in the 1880s and 1890s as a result of the mining boom for lime and named the sheltered cove Squaw Bay. By 1910, the town of Bayview was platted and the bay's name was changed to a more respectful Scenic Bay. Bayview became a lumber, fishing, mining and railroad

Legendary Lake Pend Oreille

center. It has often been called "the town that floats" because of more than a hundred float homes moored there.

Near Bayview the lakeshore extends east and then bends north around a forested elbow of land called Cape Horn Point. (You are now in Bonner County.) This was the route for the hauling of lime to Sandpoint and Hope by barge. In 1904, a barge capsized, dumping 40 tons of the mineral into the lake where it is over 800 feet deep.

Idlewilde Bay

Clasped between Blackwell Point and Steamboat Rock is one of the largest bays on the lake – Idlewilde Bay. From 1942 to 1946, the U.S. Navy operated Farragut Naval Training Station on its north shore. Farragut is now a popular state park.

Rising almost vertically above the lake across the bay from Blackwell Point is one of the most stunning geologic features on the lake – Steamboat Rock. Just to the east of Steamboat Rock is Echo Bay.

- - - - - - - - - - - - - - - - - -

Lore Along the Shore: Kalispel Culture

Blackwell Point, the fertile peninsula between Scenic and Idlewilde bays, was an aboriginal winter village of the Upper Kalispel Indians. The Kalispel name *Ncame'p* meant "the head, or gateway to the lake." Another Salishan group, the Coeur d'Alenes, whose traditional territory was to the south, came to hunt deer to the south of this village. This area was also a place where native peoples collected gray, black, and striped red and black pipestone for making various objects. There are also petroglyphs in this

Kalispel tribal members Louise Andrew, left, and Lucy Seymour riding on Kalispel ground in 1907, which later became the reservation in 1914 (Northwest Museum of Arts & Culture/Eastern Washington State Historical Society, Spokane, Washington, William Ryan, S.J. Collection. Digitally restored, for authorized publication, per financial support of the Kalispel Tribe of Indians, L87-410.10).

area, prehistoric carvings etched into rock, which for the Kalispel people are extremely important cultural sites with spiritual power. They are deserving of the greatest respect and protection.

In 1900, the Indians started being displaced as the Leibergs, John Bernard and his wife, Carrie, a doctor, arrived and homesteaded 165 acres of the peninsula. It became known as Leiberg Point. Later F.A. Blackwell purchased the property and the landform assumed his name.

On some maps Blackwell Point is identified as Jokulhlaup Point. *Jokulhlaup* is an Icelandic term for a glacial-outburst flood, reminding visitors that Lake Pend Oreille was a product of glacial activity and catastrophic flooding more than 10,000 years ago.

- - - - - - - - - - - - - - - - - - - -

Paddle Route: Idlewilde and Buttonhook Bays

Eagle Boat Launch is a large, modern facility at Farragut State Park located just south of Blackwell Point on the west side of Idlewilde Bay. Canoeists and kayakers can find easy access to the lake launching from Eagle Boat Launch. Another launch site for paddle craft, at the very end of the lake, is Buttonhook Bay. This small, sheltered bay offers a serene, placid sojourn for paddlers who can carry their watercraft down the short trail to the docks. It's a two- to three-mile paddle one-way (two to four hours round-trip) to Steamboat Rock from either launch site.

- - - - - - - - - - - - - - - - - - - -

Scuba Diving: An Underwater Heaven

Several years ago, Joe Foelsch started thinking about how much water actually covered the earth. It led him to ask: "Why not go beyond land for outdoor adventures?" So he and his wife, Jill, took up scuba diving as a family activity.

"There's a lot of life under the lake," says Joe, full of stories about his underwater adventures. He's come face to face with a 6-pound largemouth bass and seen some pretty large trout. He's also gathered a lot of lost fishing tackle snagged on underwater rocks. But it's the rocky vertical walls that drop from the lake's surface hundreds of feet down into Pend Oreille's depths that really get him excited. He says what they call "wall dives" are the most exciting scuba diving experiences here, and the southern part of Lake Pend Oreille offers some of the best, which Joe calls "truly awesome."

Favorite dive spots are usually guarded secrets, like favorite fishing holes; but Joe did reveal some of the best places for wall dives. On the east side from Bayview, the most spectacular dives are at Whiskey Rock, Graham Point (at Lakeview) and Echo Bay. Evans Landing and Talache Landing on the west side are also premier sites. Joe's personal favorite is Whiskey Rock, where he once dove 130 feet down and the wall continued to plummet beneath him out of sight.

Although summer is usually a scuba diver's favorite season, Joe says diving in Lake Pend Oreille can be a year-round sport if you have the proper gear. To get started in the sport as a beginner, though, all you really need is a dive mask, fins and snorkel.

 ▶ **FARRAGUT STATE PARK**

This is a fee area managed by State of Idaho Parks and Recreation.

What's it like?

It was named for Admiral David Farragut, the first Navy admiral appointed by Congress for leadership during the Civil War, who was known for his famous cry of "Damn the torpedoes! Full steam ahead!" This once-expansive, inland U.S. naval base was the second-largest naval training facility in the world. Farragut was integral to the nation's World War II effort, having trained almost 300,000 sailors (see chapter 16).

Acquired by the state in 1965, today Farragut is one of the premier state parks in Idaho. It encompasses 4,000 acres of pine forests, open meadows and spectacular sandy beaches and lakefront. Besides being one of the largest camping areas in northern Idaho, it offers facilities for a variety of year-round recreational opportunities and is a popular cross-country skiing area in the winter. Year-round attractions include a visitor center, the Brig Museum, which tells its Naval history, and an interpretive

Eagle Boat Launch with Bernard Peak in the distance (Richard Heinzen)

walking tour of the park. Part of the park is co-owned by Idaho Fish and Game and is managed as a wildlife refuge. Farragut Park has hosted National Girl Scout and Boy Scout Jamborees over the years, giving more than 130,000 scouts the experience of a lifetime.

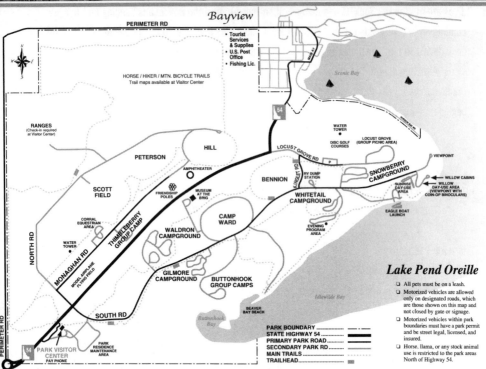

Boaters, sailors and paddlers enjoy Farragut because of its sheltered location on the lake. The high, steep cliffs tumbling off Bernard Peak protect the two bays – Scenic and Idlewilde – that anchor the south end of Lake Pend Oreille. Eagle Boat Landing is a large, modern facility that accommodates most types of marine vessels. It is located just south of Blackwell Point on the west side of Idlewilde Bay.

Hiking, bicycling and mountain biking opportunities in the park are extensive, ranging from easy excursions of less than a mile to all-day adventures of 20 miles or more. Detailed maps are recommended and available for purchase at the park visitor center. The most popular trails include: Squirrel Cache Nature Trail – a self-guided interpretive trail (a portion of the trail was originally a horse and wagon route in the 1860s); Shoreline Trail that winds along the shoreline from the Blackwell Point Viewpoint south to Eagle Boat Landing, past Beaver Bay Swimming Area, around Buttonhook Bay, and then upland through a pleasant forest environment where it joins the Highpoint Trail – a three-mile trail that affords hikers a variety of options and terrain including spectacular vistas of the lake. Beaver Bay is one of the nicest areas for swimming on the lake.

Horseback riders and llama users are also welcome at Farragut but are restricted to the trails north of Highway 54. The newly developed Corral Area provides equestrians and llama users easy access to these trails, which are also accessible to hikers and bikers. The Corral Area, located just north of the Thimbleberry Group Area and east of park headquarters, is made up of two public access areas of temporary holding stalls. Here you'll find ample parking, overnight campsites, hitching posts and a watering trough. But beware if your horse spooks at loud noises: The park's shooting range is also in this area. Future plans for this area include a basic riding arena, shelter, equestrian experience course and improved trail linkage.

Shoreline Trail on Idlewilde Bay (Richard Heinzen)

The Sunrise and Willow day use areas at Farragut offer picnic shelters, tables and lakeview cabins that can be reserved for gatherings and events. The Willow Day Use Area also has coin-operated spotting scopes for viewing mountain goats on the Bernard Peak cliffs across Idlewilde Bay.

Farragut State Park offers lots of camping choices. There are nearly 200 overnight sites at five campgrounds, plus two group camp areas. Overnight fees vary, and trailers and RVs up to 32-feet long can be accommodated. Campgrounds offer boat ramps, docks, dump stations, flush toilets, hot showers and potable water. For reservations, call 208-683-2425 or log onto www. reserveamerica.com.

At the western end of the park, just past the visitor center, is a large, open area for flying model airplanes. One of the newest attractions at Farragut, an 18-hole disc golf course is located at the east end of the park near the Locust Grove Picnic Area and water tower. The course offers hours of challenging fun in a forest of mixed-age trees. Keep a close eye on your flying disc, though, as it is easy to lose in the summer foliage.

Farragut State Park is one of the best places in northern Idaho for family-centered outdoor adventure. Come for an afternoon picnic and swim, or camp for several days and explore the surroundings. For more information about this park, go online to www.idahoparks.org and search for Farragut.

FACILITIES: concrete boat ramp, docks, fish-cleaning station, group picnic areas, group and individual campgrounds, amphitheater, picnic tables, restrooms, hot showers, dump station, RV hookups, sandy beach, horseshoe pits, volleyball courts, drinking water; hiking, horseback and biking trails; photographic viewpoints, coin-operated spotting scopes, shooting range, model aircraft field, disc golf course, visitor center and Brig Museum

ACTIVITIES: camping, boating, sailing, canoeing, kayaking, scuba diving, fishing, swimming, picnicking, hiking, biking, horseback riding, wildlife viewing, horseshoe and volleyball games, model aircraft flying, target shooting, disc golf, museum tour

How to get here:

From Athol on U.S. Highway 95, turn west on Idaho State Highway 54 and travel four miles to the main entrance just past the traffic circle. The visitor center is on your right and has maps, campground information and interactive displays about the wildlife and geology of the park. Farragut State Park is open year-round.

- - - - - - - - - - - - - - - - - - -

Brig Museum

Between 1942 and 1946, when the Farragut Naval Training Station operated, this was the place where an unruly naval recruit would wind up when someone decided: "Throw him in the brig!" The concrete block building is one of the few structures that remain from the 776 buildings that once made up the training center. The Brig still has its barred windows, gates and jail cells, but today it's a museum for the public to learn about World War II and naval history. The Brig houses the memorabilia of boot camp days and is dedicated to the nearly 300,000 seamen who received their basic training at Farragut before it was decommissioned in 1946.

The Brig Museum preserves some of the original jail cells that were used to house sailors who went absent without leave. The remaining cells were remodeled into interpretive displays, an audio-visual theater and a gift shop. Donations to the museum of mementos from "The Greatest Generation" continue to come in, so expansion plans are under way. A veteran's plaza out in front of the building will showcase a bronze sculpture of a naval recruit, initialed by the attendees of the 2006 veterans reunion of the sailors who trained there. The project is a way to commemorate Farragut's history as the second-largest naval training center in the world during World War II.

Lore Along the Shore: Southernmost Bays

At the southernmost tip of Lake Pend Oreille is the small, sheltered cove of Buttonhook Bay. In the late 1800s, Buttonhook Bay was a vital link in the mail route between Walla Walla, Washington and Missoula, Montana. A steamboat, *Mary Moody*, carried the mail brought in by horseback riders up the lake to Cabinet Landing on the Clark Fork River, and east to Montana from there. It's also the site of the second-oldest community in northern Idaho, settled in 1866 and called Pen d'Oreille City. The town name later changed to Steamboat Landing because the steamboat era on the lake had taken hold, offering transportation for miners and mail riders. (See chapter 15, page 358.) The *Mary Moody* was the first steamboat built by Zenas Moody and named for his wife. Steamers hauled passengers, freight, horses and wagons from Buttonhook Bay to Cabinet Landing, and north to Pack River and Boyer's Slough, a boat trip of only a few hours. Eventually other landings along this route were developed including Lakeview, Cedar Creek, Whiskey Rock and Granite Creek.

The *Northern*, owned by Northern Navigation Company, had a dance hall in the upper cabin. After owner Ed Elliott fired the boiler early one morning in the 1920s, she caught fire and burned at City Dock (Bonner County Historical Society)

Boating northwest from there is Echo Point (also known as Bernard Point) and Steamboat Rock. Rising almost vertically above Lake Pend Oreille, Steamboat Rock is one of the most beautiful geologic features on the lake. Just around Echo Point is Echo Bay. The high, steep cliffs of Bernard Peak made a great amphitheater for steamboats when they went chugging by. The captain would sound the horn and the high-pitched bellow would echo across the bay. Echo Bay was sometimes also referred to as Flintstone Beach because of the flint that could be found there for sharpening knives.

In 1962, a significant landslide created a glaring scar on the steep face of Bernard Peak — the Bernard Slide. When the rocks and debris crashed into the lake, it sent waves all the way to

Bayview that damaged docks. This rugged mountainside is also home to mountain goats. Narrow rocky beaches afford a landing at the base of the cliffs, but watch for falling rocks.

- - - - - - - - - - - - - - - - - -

Etiquette in the Park: Making Friends with People and Wildlife

Farragut State Park is a popular Idaho destination and despite its heavy use, it can afford a high-quality outdoor experience. But a few rules apply: Use only designated trails to protect vegetation; keep pets on a leash and clean up after them; whatever you pack in, please be sure to pack out; and lend a hand in maintaining the trails by removing obstacles when you encounter them (trash, rocks and tree branches). Try to avoid trails that are muddy or may be subject to erosion and don't blaze your own trails, especially cutting across switchbacks. Bikers should yield to all other trail users and helmets are encouraged.

Farragut is home to many species of wildlife, and they deserve respect as well as caution from human visitors. Numerous species of birds are found here in varied habitats. Small mammals and white-tailed deer roam the park. And potentially more dangerous animals are also present: elk, moose, black bears, cougars, bobcats and coyotes roam the vast forests stretching in and beyond the park's borders. It's best to keep your distance. Never feed wild animals and don't leave food scraps along the trails as they can attract wildlife and potentially pose problems both for people and animals. If wildlife is encountered on the trail, it is best to quietly leave the area and safely observe them from a distance. Report any problems to park personnel.

- - - - - - - - - - - - - - - - - -

Wildlife Viewing: Bernard Peak Mountain Goats

One might not think of seeing mountain goats when out plying the waters of Pend Oreille, but indeed there is a place that offers just such an opportunity. Bernard Peak rises nearly 3,000 feet above the shores of the lake near its southern terminus. On the steep cliffs towering above the lake surface, it is not unusual to see several brilliantly white spots on the gray rock – these are mountain goats *(Oreamnos americanus)* with thick white coats. Occasionally they may even be seen on a rugged outcrop just above the water. Nanny and billy goats are similar in appearance with black, slender horns and white beards. Both genders also have large shoulders for near-vertical climbing, only

the males are slightly larger in size and are usually solitary animals. The best way to enjoy viewing the goats on Bernard Peak is with binoculars from a boat, although at Farragut State Park's Willow Day Use Area there are coin-operated spotting scopes to see them from land.

The Bernard Peak goats are one of only four herds in Idaho's Panhandle. They inhabit a two-mile vertical radius and are fairly easy to see. Scan the cliffs for billy goats, nannies and kids that are born in May and June. Since this area is both their summer and winter habitat, it's important to watch them from a distance so they don't expend a lot of energy trying to evade humans if they come to the water's edge for a drink.

Mountain goat on Bernard Peak (Chris Bessler)

Wildflower Notes: Oregon Grape

Oregon grape, also known as holly grape, is common along the Scout Trail, flowering in April and May. The clusters of bright yellow flowers

transform into tart, bright purple berries that are an important food source for birds and other wildlife. The evergreen, holly-like leaves are another identifying characteristic. A low-lying shrub, it seldom exceeds a foot or two in height. While the most common species is *Berberis repens,* you might notice a group of plants that look a lot like Oregon grape, but their compound leaves appear different. This is a rarer species of *Berberis* called *B. aquatifolium.* It stands out because of the nine pairs of leaflets along the leaf stem.

Oregon grape (Billie Jean Plaster)

Wildlife Viewing: Cavity Nesters

While passing old tree snags along the Squirrel Cache Trail, you might see round holes of various sizes made by birds called cavity nesters — red-shafted flickers, a variety of woodpeckers and tiny nuthatches that are adept at scaling tree trunks upside down. After these birds have raised their young, they will abandon their homes only to have secondary cavity nesters move in. These new tenants include chickadees and owls, but flying squirrels, pine squirrels and raccoons might also take up residence. The Kalispel Indians consider old snags in the mountains to have *sumesh* (see Lore Along the Shore, page 52).

And keep your eyes open, as well as your ears for a loud hammering sound, to catch the largest woodpecker in the region excavating rotting or dying trees looking for its favorite meal, carpenter ants. Look for rectangular rather than round cavities in fallen timber, dead stumps or at the base of mature trees. The pileated woodpecker is the Northwest relative to the ivory-billed woodpecker of the Southeast, a bird thought to be extinct until recently. A sighting of the crow-sized pileated woodpecker with its large, "Woody Woodpecker" red crest (both male and female) and black-and-white plumage is an exciting experience. Consider yourself lucky if you see this large bird or hear its loud *kak, kak, kak, kak*. In the creation legend of the Kootenai Indians, a people who visited the north shore of Lake Pend Oreille, this bird was the chief of the animal people.

Pileated woodpecker (Jon Shaver)

Tour on Wheels:
The High Drive

The High Drive is perhaps the finest mountain-to-lake motor tour in the Lake Pend Oreille region. This drive essentially follows the eastern arc of the lake south of Farragut State Park northeast to Clark Fork. You can travel the road one-way in either direction, or you can use the High Drive to circumnavigate the entire lake.

The tour begins with Bunco Road No. 332 at U.S. Highway 95 near Silverwood Theme Park, approximately eight miles southwest of Bayview. Once on the saddle between Chilco Mountain and Bernard Peak, Road 332 remains on the high ridges of the Coeur d'Alene Mountains on the backside of Packsaddle Mountain all the way to the Montana line. It is a rugged road, requiring four-wheel drive in many places, so don't follow it for this tour.

Instead, take the road which branches off Road 332 near Chilco Mountain – the Johnson-Lakeview Road No. 278. It's a more traveled, decent dirt road, which begins by dipping down to the lake's shore (think "Low Road" for this section of the drive) to the communities of Lakeview, Cedar Creek, Whiskey Rock and Granite Creek. But from Granite Creek, Road 278 climbs high again to the ridgeline of the Green Monarch Mountains and winds around for many miles until it eventually drops down into the Clark Fork Valley onto Johnson Creek Road. Johnson Creek Road parallels the Clark Fork River and ends where you cross a bridge to the town of Clark Fork. It's approximately 45 miles to Clark Fork from where Road 278 branches off the Bunco Road 332. If you want to continue driving around the lake back to where you started at Bunco Road or Bayview, access Idaho State Highway 200 in Clark Fork and travel west about 27 miles to Sandpoint. Then take U.S. Highway 95 south another 20 to 27 miles depending on your originating point.

Along the route, you can stop at two fantastic overlooks – the Bernard Overlook at the south end near Farragut (from Road 332 turn onto USFS Road No. 2707) and the Johnson Point Vista at the northeastern end of the lake almost to Clark Fork. This is a full-day outing that is unparalleled in terms of unique lakeside position and mountain scenery. Side-trip opportunities range from fishing and swimming to mountain peak hiking.

If you decide to use the High Drive to circumnavigate the lake, you'll cover 110-miles of scenic roadways including paved highways, gravel or dirt logging roads that climb high into the Coeur d'Alene Mountains. The drive is generally suitable for most passenger cars. Seasonal changes to the roads do exist, however, and snow can be an issue until midsummer. Logging activities can result in road closures or the hair-raising experiences of having a Mack Truck bearing down on you. (Note: Logging trucks always have the right-of-way on forest roads). It is advisable to carry a cell phone and ample amounts of food and water on this type of excursion and be sure you have tire-changing tools and a decent, inflated spare tire. The roads are typically impassable in winter.

Length: approximately 110 miles roundtrip from Sandpoint

Road Type: Mixed pavement and dirt/ gravel; be sure to have a Forest Service travel map on hand so you can negotiate the maze of logging roads on the east side of the lake.

Road Conditions: good to fair (depending on seasonal conditions)

Attractions: numerous opportunities for wildlife viewing (moose are often seen bounding along Road 278); sweeping photographic viewpoints overlooking Lake Pend Oreille at Johnson Point Vista and Bernard Overlook; and beach access at Farragut State Park, Lakeview and Whiskey Rock

Facilities En Route: Numerous facilities are located in Hope and Clark Fork on Idaho State Highway 200 east of Sandpoint. However if you're driving southwest towards Bayview, please note that Clark Fork is the last outpost for provisions (including potable water) for 25 miles of dirt road until you reach Whiskey Rock Bay Campground. There is no gas available at Whiskey Rock or anywhere else along the east side, so top off the tank before leaving Clark Fork.

Alternative Loop Drive: Clockwise from Sandpoint

Travel east from Sandpoint on Idaho State Highway 200 to the town of Clark Fork, where you turn south onto Stephen Road near the gas station. Cross the railroad tracks, bear left and then cross the Clark Fork River. Turn right directly after the bridge and follow Johnson Creek Road until it climbs into the Coeur d'Alene Mountains. You are now on Road No. 278. At milepost 4, look for the turnoff to the right and travel a mile to Johnson Point Vista for a breathtaking view across the north end of the lake. Road 278 then drops back down to the lakeshore at Granite Creek and Whiskey Rock and continues through wooded countryside to the junction with the access road to Lakeview. From there it is just over a mile to the lakeshore. From Lakeview, Road 278 climbs into the mountains again and joins the Bunco Road No. 332. This road goes over a saddle and descends into the valley among farms and forests. Once back on pavement, it is about seven miles to U.S. Highway 95.

A variation of this loop, but not as good of a road, is to turn south on Forest Road No. 1066 at Johnson Saddle until it ends at Bunco Road No. 332. Turn southwest and follow Road 332 to Bernard Peak – the section where the High Drive actually gets its name.

⟩LAKEVIEW

PUBLIC ACCESS

This area offers free public facilities managed by Bonner County. Tying boats up overnight on docks is OK if not near the gravel launch, but picnicking on docks is not allowed.

What's it like?

Flanked by private property, the small community of Lakeview is surrounded by abandoned limestone mines. It is a serene and pleasant place, and surprisingly much of the town is situated on a bench well above the lake with the majority of houses lacking a view of the lake. Three miles above Lakeview is the Happy Hermit Resort that operates year-round, catering to snowmobile enthusiasts in the winter. There are numerous small beaches from here to Whiskey Rock.

FACILITIES: gravel boat ramp, docks, sandy beach, vault toilet
ACTIVITIES: boating, fishing, swimming, scuba diving

How to get here:

Follow the Bunco Road No. 332 just over seven miles east to where the pavement ends at a large parking area. From there the road climbs into the mountains south of the lake. Drive another six miles to the junction with Road No. 278, which descends from Road 332. From there, it's approximately 12 miles to Lakeview. The narrow road down to the lakeshore is steep and rutted. There is parking for only three or four vehicles.

Pend d'Oreille
It lends to us the atmosphere
Of all its changing moods;
A sermon there, on patience,
Which we spurn:
Its pensiveness, its surging strength,
Its quality of depth,
Are lessons in philosophy for those
Who pause to learn.

It cools the stars in indigo,
It liquefies the moon,
It captures dawn's first promise
Of the day;
It holds the lavish pageant of
The sunset's cloud parade;
Content am I whose sands of life
Run out on Pend d'Oreille.

—Paul Croy
Pioneer Pencil Dust, 1976

Lore Along the Shore: Ghost Towns

Just past a small promontory called Graham Point are the remains of a defunct cement plant and the town once known as Concrete. A little ways up Gold Creek is another ghost town called Chloride, where a well-publicized gold rush fizzled in the 1880s. The discovery of gold on Gold Creek, which was first called Marble Creek, led to a mining boom around 1890, which established the new communities of Lakeview and Chloride. It is reported that upwards of 5,000 people lived here during the height of the gold fever. The town of Chloride, about four or five miles uphill from the lake, died out with the depletion of ore in the mines. Only Lakeview, once known as Gray's Landing, has survived.

Mining limestone was big business on Lake Pend Oreille as early as 1881, when the first

International Portland Cement Company ruins near Lakeview
(Chris Bessler)

limestone claims were filed near Lakeview. The International Portland Cement Company built its first quarry north of Lakeview in 1912. All that remains now are concrete and timber footings. Southwest of Lakeview, another cement plant called Portrock was built in 1921. Parts of the original buildings are still standing. There's also a tunnel opening where limestone was brought to shore by an electric train.

This part of the shoreline is rocky, rugged and remote, but somewhere in this area among the jumbled rocks is one particular flat rock that local people call Table Rock. Try to find it!

CEDAR CREEK

PUBLIC ACCESS

In 1882 John "Jack" Downing Needham rowed his boat across Lake Pend Oreille and homesteaded here. He's credited as being the first permanent white settler on the east side of the lake. The Jack Needham family homestead cabin can still be seen about a quarter-mile from the beach. This ghost town situated halfway between Lakeview and Whiskey Rock was originally named Clara. Clara Needham was the first postmistress and the wife of Fred Needham. Mail was carried by steamboat to the post office that operated here from 1903 to 1913. The Clara Cemetery is three miles from shore on the north side of the road. A small sign reveals its location. After 1920, the town's name changed to Cedar Creek Landing, as it became a stop on the *Northern* steamboat circuit. Cedar Creek and the other east shore communities are still part of a marine mail route out of Bayview's post office (see page 69). For a small fee, individuals can ride with the mail boat operator (contact the Bayview post office). Recreation facilities available today at Cedar Creek include a county dock and a put-in for cartop boats.

WHISKEY ROCK

PUBLIC ACCESS

Managed by the U.S. Forest Service, this is a no fee area that has 13 campground sites accessible to small motor homes and travel trailers. Campground limit is 14 days.

What's it like?

Shaded by big ponderosa pines and Douglas firs, this remote site is a great destination on the lake's eastern side. The rocky shoreline makes for some interesting exploration along the edge of the lake, while a pleasant grassy area adjoins the beach. It is a picturesque, wooded cove with sweeping views of the lake and its western shores. There is a dock here for boats arriving by water, but there is no public launch ramp. The primitive launch site here is private for use only by Whiskey Rock residents. Car-top boats can access the lake from the gravel beach.

Whiskey Rock (Chris Bessler)

FACILITIES: campground (no electrical hookups or large RVs), drinking water, telephone, dock, picnic tables, vault toilets, gravel beach

ACTIVITIES: camping, picnicking, boating, fishing, swimming, scuba diving

How to get here:

Road access is from Johnson Creek-Lakeview Road No. 278. The access dirt road to the boat ramp is narrow and rough; large RVs are not recommended because there is only a small turnaround. An approach across the lake from Garfield Bay or Bayview is a better idea. It is also accessible by hiking down Packsaddle Mountain Trail No. 76.

--- --- --- --- --- --- --- --- --- --- --- --- --- --- ---

Lore Along the Shore: Whiskey Nomenclature

There are numerous stories as to how Whiskey Rock and its companion features, Whiskey Bay and Whiskey Point, got their names. One tale claims a jug of whiskey was a prize for a swimming match held here. Another interesting yarn tells of two men forced by darkness to wait out a storm. Upon waking the next morning they realized that they had landed on a small rocky island and that their boat had drifted away during the night. Stranded for three days with nothing but their jug of whiskey to keep them going, they were finally rescued.

A more probable explanation suggests that this place was a drop-off point for whiskey runners during Prohibition. "Rum Runners" from Bayview would meet up with Canadians here who were smuggling whiskey and rum bound for Spokane. The headquarters for these illegal activities was a mile south at Cunningham's Castle, a reported bordello. Today all that remains is a crumbling cement structure with twisted metal protrusions.

PUBLIC ACCESS ▶ GRANITE CREEK AND SULLIVAN SPRINGS

The fish weir at Sullivan Springs is maintained by Idaho Fish and Game for kokanee reproduction. The dock is managed by Bonner County as a day-use, no-fee area, but tying up to the dock overnight is allowed.

What's it like?

Mining claims were established here during the 1880s, and a small community sprang up as a result. Today Granite Creek ranks as the most valuable spawning stream on Lake Pend Oreille for several species of fish, especially kokanee. Sullivan Springs is a magnificent, natural spring upstream from the lake about one-half mile. Granite Creek is accessed by water. In late autumn, bald eagles dot the trees along the shoreline and feed on fish that spawn and die.

FACILITIES: dock, porta-potty

ACTIVITIES: boating, swimming, fishing, scuba diving, wildlife viewing

Echo Rock

A short distance north by boat from Granite Creek brings you to Granite Point and Echo Rock. A rugged ridge descends from Schafer Peak to the east and plunges into the lake at Granite Point. An immense vertical cliff rises straight up out of the water here, providing an amphitheater of sorts that gives a great echo to any exclamation. This is one of the most impressive topographic features around the lake. Less than a mile from shore, the lake depth is more than 1,100 feet.

Fish Tales: Granite Creek, Sullivan Springs and Spawning Salmon

The kokanee fishery in Lake Pend Oreille has seen better days.

Forty years ago, sport fishermen caught on the average an annual harvest of 1 million of the fish. Kokanee are a land-locked species of salmon that washed into Lake Pend Oreille carried by floodwaters from Montana's Flathead Lake. Once established here, numerous tributaries of the lake began to teem with the spawning adults. Also called silvers or bluebacks, the kokanee were prey for world-class Gerrard rainbow, bull and lake trout. But today these predator fish outnumber its prey. Other factors contributed to the crash of the kokanee fishery, not the least being the Cabinet Gorge and Albeni Falls hydroelectric dams on the watershed. As a result, the kokanee fishery was closed in 2000 and limits on fishing for rainbow trout and lake trout have been liberalized. Idaho Fish and Game awards cash prizes to fishermen who catch the rainbows and lake trout, a creative attempt to save the beleaguered kokanee. Bull trout, protected as a threatened species in the Columbia River system, also prey on kokanee; hence, a limited season for bull trout on Lake Pend Oreille was instituted in 2008. Elsewhere in the system if these fish are caught, they must be released.

According to sportsman and fish aficionado Ron Raiha, Granite Creek is the only credible and viable spawning stream left on Lake Pend Oreille for ensuring kokanee survival. Twenty-seven miles long and fed by the pristine waters of Sullivan Springs, the creek is also a spawning stream for bull trout and cutthroat trout. From mid-November to Christmas, Raiha works with Idaho Fish

Granite Creek (Chris Bessler)

and Game biologists to spawn adult kokanee caught in the weir at Sullivan Springs. (The rest of the year he's an officer with the Bonner County Sheriff's Marine Division.) While some of the spawning salmon are allowed to fulfill their lives naturally, those that are caught produce millions of fertilized salmon eggs. The fertilized eggs are then taken to the Cabinet Gorge Fish Hatchery on the Clark Fork River where they grow into salmon fry to be released eventually back into the lake. It's a project that dramatizes how man can facilitate the kokanee's reproductive journey.

In their red color phase similar to sockeye salmon, the spawning kokanee that returned to Granite Creek in 2006 were the largest fish seen there since the 1970s; some of the males were up to 16 inches long and weighing up to a pound. The fish managers are not sure why 2006 was such a good year, but such healthy, beautiful fish, seemed liked good news. Filling the hatchery that year for the first time with 18 million eggs from Sullivan Springs, it was hoped that it would give the kokanee fishery the incredible boost it needs to thrive again.

However, in late 2007 the tide turned; an extremely low number of spawners returned to Sullivan Springs, resulting in one of the worst egg harvests on record, says Raiha. Fewer than half a million kokanee eggs were taken to the Clark Fork Hatchery for growing, and Idaho Fish and Game had to make up for the shortfall by obtaining eggs from Washington's Lake Whatcom and southern Idaho lakes.

In good spawning years and in lean, dotting the trees along the shoreline are dozens of bald eagles feeding on the spawned carcasses of the fish. The many pounds of dead fish and fish eggs in the gravel beds of the creek will be the winter food for ravens, mallard ducks, weasels, marten, raccoon, and many other species of wildlife in addition to the eagles. It's nature's way of creating balance, sustaining life from death.

Kilroy Bay

Just past Granite Point and Echo Rock is the small, privately owned settlement of Pine Cove. Beyond Pine Cove is the larger settlement of Kilroy Bay, which is also private. Both hamlets are at the foot of Shafer Peak's steep terrain and are accessible by automobile via USFS Road No. 2711, a spur four and a half miles from Johnson-Lakeview Road No. 278. Kilroy Bay is named for a Butte, Montana newspaperman who built a summer home here back in early pioneer days. A creek by the same name flows from a small basin 2,000 feet above Lake Pend Oreille at two small lakes — the Kilroy Lakes.

The former Kilroy Bay Resort is now a private residence, and a couple dozen other families live here seasonally with some folks living here year-round. One of the largest forest fires in recent years originated at Kilroy Bay in October 1991.

Anecdota: Riding the Mail Boat to Kilroy Bay

John Thaxter used to have a desk job. But along with the lure of more time to fish, when opportunity knocked he found himself a storm-worthy vessel and commenced delivering mail for the Bayview post office — by boat.

Despite scorching sun, thick winter fog and furious winds that pound the hull of his boat with spectacular waves, Thaxter has delivered mail to the remote outposts of civilization on the east side of Lake Pend Oreille since 1993, six days a week, all year long.

In addition to his contract with the U.S. Postal Service, he also delivers packages for UPS and FedEx. Upon request, he's also happy to bring a dozen eggs or a loaf of bread from the Bayview Mercantile or maybe deliver something a little bigger, like a new washer and dryer. He also offers taxi service.

Deliveries to this side of the lake are much easier to make by boat than by car or truck. The roads through the surrounding mountains, maintained by the U.S. Forest Service, are primarily dirt roads. It takes one and a half hours to drive the 19 miles to Lakeview from Bayview, but by boat it takes only 10 minutes. It can take all day to deliver something to Kilroy Bay (just ask the Sears delivery man who swears he'll never do it again). But for Thaxter, Kilroy Bay is merely the last stop on his well-traveled lake route; in less than two hours he's back at the dock at MacDonald's Hudson Bay Resort in Bayview after also visiting Lakeview, Cedar Creek, Whiskey Rock, Granite Creek and Pine Cove. The only way to reach these human enclaves once the snow flies is by water because the roads eventually become impassable. So Thaxter is also a lifeline to the residents on this side of the lake during the winter months.

"There's never a dull moment," says Thaxter, adding that he really enjoys his work. (But for the record, he actually has less time for fishing.) He particularly likes the challenge of making deliveries on wintry or stormy days, although the near-80 mph winds and 10-foot waves in November 2006 were downright frightening – the worst weather he's ever seen on the lake.

At each stop along the east shore, most of the residents come down to the docks to meet

him and exchange mailbags and friendly news. Thaxter always has biscuits for the dogs. Most of the time he doesn't even have to get out of the boat: "It makes it a little nicer, especially when the wind is blowing 30 miles per hour."

One can imagine the swell of residents who arrive to spend their summers on this isolated side of the lake, but what sort of people lives here year-round? This particular July day, I'm hitching a ride on the mail boat all the way to Kilroy Bay and back to find out.

Argyle Mydland is a former Angus rancher from Montana who, along with three other year-round families, is enjoying his retirement living at Whiskey Rock. He was used to remoteness, but because of the lake's effect of moderating temperatures, he finds that Whiskey Rock is warmer in winter and cooler in summer than his former home.

John Thaxter delivers mail by boat to Kilroy Bay residents (Woods Wheatcroft)

Mydland really appreciates the old-fashioned hospitality that Thaxter offers to residents like him on Lake Pend Oreille's east shore, especially during wintertime. "If it wasn't for John," he jokingly says, "people here probably wouldn't get anything to eat!"

"It's more fun if you do more than what you're supposed to do," Thaxter says. Folks like Mydland may be customers, but they're also friends. "I don't mind bringing the groceries," he

Legendary Lake Pend Oreille

says. Sometimes Thaxter will even get a phone call in the middle of night. "I make emergency runs, too, sometimes for medications." Once he helped take a resident to the hospital. After all these years and clocking more than 150,000 miles on the lake, he says he could probably do his route blindfolded. With fuel as expensive as it is (in summer 2007 he was spending around $400 a week) he performs the extra duties because he enjoys doing them, not because there's much money in it.

At Kilroy Bay, there are three year-round residents and 24 families who arrive during summertime. Lou Crisler, a naval retiree from Spokane, has lived here for 22 years. Since Johnson Creek-Lakeview Road No. 278 is several miles away, he usually goes by his own boat across the lake to Garfield Bay when he needs to go to Sandpoint. Lou's neighbor, Velda McTighe still enjoys living at Kilroy Bay even after her husband John's death. Surprisingly, no one admits to getting cabin fever here. Instead they spend their days hiking, doing crafts, socializing, watching the storms pass through and viewing wildlife — eagles that flock to Granite Creek for a feast of spawning kokanee in the winter, and moose, deer, elk, mountain goats and cougar who come to shore year round. McTighe says some of the ungulates, recalling a cow moose and her calf, will swim across the lake to Garfield Bay. "It's a little bit of heaven," says Crisler. "I wouldn't go anywhere else."

On the boat heading back to Bayview on this lovely July morning, John Thaxter reveals that although every day on the lake is special, his favorite season of being a mailman on the water is during the winter months when there isn't a lot of human activity. He says the lake's monochromatic landscape with ice sculpting the shoreline and wildlife peacefully drinking at the water's edge is like a beautiful charcoal drawing. Most days he just can't wait to get out on the water. And as far as jobs go, it's the best one he's ever had.

 **EVANS LANDING**

Managed by the U.S. Forest Service, this is a no-fee area.

What's it like?

Primitive and remote, this site caters to hikers and boaters and is accessible only by foot or boat. It is a popular area for paddlers kayaking or canoeing south from Talache Landing. Hiking in is along Evans Landing Trail No. 64. Sweeping views across the lake toward the Coeur d'Alene Mountains are unmatched from this beach, and the area is often overlooked, especially on busy summer days. The remains of an old cabin are found here.

Evans Landing in winter (Jim Mellen)

Between Evans Landing and Cape Horn is a narrow bench of land below the Three Sisters Peaks called Grasshopper Point. By some accounts, the lake is well over 1,200 feet deep just offshore. The U.S. Navy maintains an offshore barge just north of here, which is off-limits to the public.

FACILITIES: rustic, primitive campsites (spring until late fall), pebble beach, picnic tables, porta-potty
ACTIVITIES: camping, picnicking, boating, fishing, swimming, hiking, scuba diving, kayaking, canoeing

How to get here:
To find the trailhead for Evans Landing Trail No. 64 that leads to Evans Landing, see directions in the hiking chapter on page 276.

Maiden Rock (Chris Bessler)

MAIDEN ROCK

Managed by the U.S. Forest Service, this is a day-use, no-fee area.

What's it like?

A primitive and remote site, it is accessible only by trail or boat. The area is adjacent to a unique geologic feature on the lake – Maiden Rock, a huge outcropping that drops steeply into the lake next to a beautiful pebble beach. A jagged ridge tumbles from the summit of Blacktail Mountain into the cold waters of the lake near the mouth of Maiden Creek. The last drop-off of several hundred feet is along the angular, stair-step cliffs.

FACILITIES: picnic tables, fire pit, stony beach, vault toilet
ACTIVITIES: boating, picnicking, fishing, swimming, scuba diving, hiking, camping

How to get here:

To find the trailhead for Maiden Creek Trail No. 321 that leads to Maiden Rock, see directions in the hiking chapter on page 277.

Fire on the Mountain!

Forest fires always loom as a possibility in northern Idaho and one of the largest in recent years broke out the morning of October 16, 1991. Visual evidence of the conflagration that burned nearly 3,000 acres of National Forest land before it was brought under control can be seen climbing the flanks of Green Monarch and Shafer Peak mountains behind Kilroy Bay.

Kilroy resident Ken Gonser and his son Jim discovered the fire while out hunting that morning. A storm blew in and as the men made their way back to their cabin, they smelled smoke. The howling winds had blown a large tree across a power line and it was already blazing wildly because of intense winds and the extreme dryness. They reported the fire but the lake was too rough for the sheriff's boat to venture out across the lake.

This image taken at Kilroy Bay at 8 p.m. on October 16, 1991, shows the firestorm's progression up the hillsides above the bay (Ken Gonser)

The flames were spreading quickly, so the Gonsers rounded up the few men at Kilroy Bay to fight the fire using Lou Crisler's small pumper truck and a long hose down to the water. They were able to save most of the seasonal cabins, losing only two, those belonging to Bob Marksbury and Grant Luden. The residents worked together to fight the blaze and protect each other's homes until the Forest Service's crews and water trucks arrived. Shaken, but safe, the Kilroy Bay residents fought hard. Because of steep terrain and lack of air support due to high winds and smoke, the fire spread around Windy Point up the Monarchs Ridge and burned nearly 3,000 acres before it was contained a week later. Even a helicopter went down into the lake, but the crew was safely rescued.

Lore Along the Shore: Maiden Rock

Pioneer legend has it that an Indian maiden was distraught, scorned by her lover. In a fit of despair, she stepped to the edge of a cliff and threw herself into the tumultuous waves, crashing on the rocks far below. Surprisingly, from certain vantage points out on the water, the cliff's rugged outline does resemble a woman's form. So the name Maiden Rock was given to one of Lake Pend Oreille's most prominent geologic features by the early boatmen who traveled the waters from Bayview to the Clark Fork Delta.

At the shore north of Maiden Rock is the site of the failed mining community of Blacktail, founded by James Ferguson in the early 1900s. Early prospectors dug all over Blacktail Mountain that looms behind, looking for evidence of precious metals. In 1912, Spokane lawyer Winn Gilbert and his brother-in-law bought the property, and, since that time, generations of nine families have shared this 700 feet of lakefront and have made it their mostly summertime home.

North of Blacktail was the small mining town of Talache, active in the 1920s. Talache was named for the small, one-handed pick that originated with the Aztec Indians and was used to extract silver ore from rock. The area is cradled between Butler Mountain and Blacktail Mountain to the west and south respectively, and Grouse Mountain to the north. The broad point of land just north of Talache Landing is Grouse Mountain Point, once called Umbrella Point. Around this point is Garfield Bay (see Area Two, chapter 5).

PUBLIC ACCESS ▶ TALACHE LANDING (TALACHE BEACH)

Accessed from U.S. Highway 95 via the Bonner County-maintained Talache Road in Sagle, south of Sandpoint, Talache Landing is a popular put-in area for kayakers and canoeists coming from Sandpoint and Sagle, as well as a popular swimming area for local residents and scuba divers. Talache Landing is covered in Area 2, chapter 5, along with Garfield Bay.

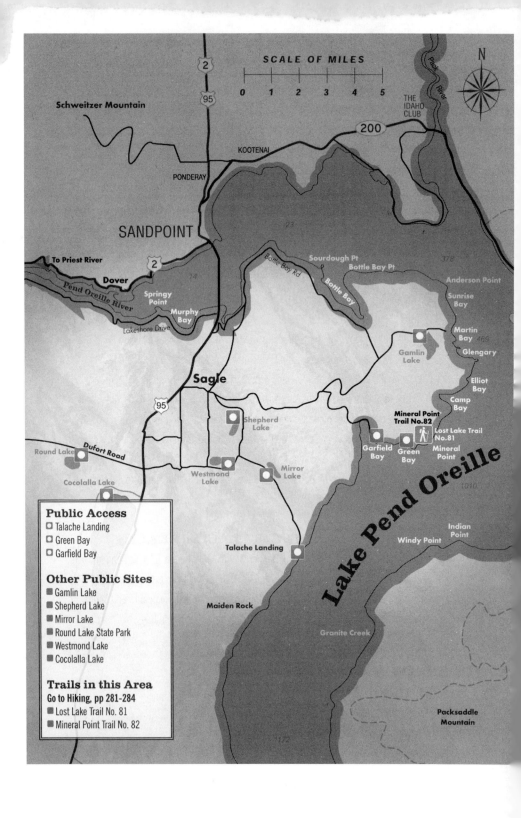

CHAPTER FIVE 5

AREA 2, GARFIELD BAY

Garfield Bay Southwest to Talache Landing
Garfield Bay Northeast to Anderson Point

OVERVIEW:

*W*hen you come driving into Garfield Bay on a sunny summer day, it feels like you are descending into a small fishing village on a seacoast that time has forgotten. The open cove with its marina, boats and rustic homes is idyllic.

Garfield Bay is 15 miles from Sandpoint and found inland from U.S. Highway 95 along winding, county roads. With its large campground uphill from the day-use park and beach, restaurants, convenience stores and marine services, Garfield Bay is an ideal family destination. Garfield Shores Resort and Marina Club offers overnight boat slips to rent as well as long-term moorage. It also has courtesy tie-ups and is the only source of boat gas. Continuing along gravel roads, you'll reach Green Bay and the popular Mineral Point area – Forest Service lands.

By boat, Garfield Bay is an 18-mile boat ride to either Sandpoint or Bayview – making it the halfway point on the lake's western shore. Many boaters come to Garfield Bay from communities on the eastern shore, such as Kilroy Bay, or from Sunnyside, Hope or even Clark Fork. Other

Garfield Bay at sunrise (Ryan McGinty)

adventurous boaters explore the distance around the Sagle Peninsula from Sandpoint or Bottle Bay. Coming by boat from either direction takes you past a number of lovely bays and points that are entirely private property – Camp Bay, Elliot Bay, Picard Point, Glengary Bay, Martin Bay, Sunrise Bay and Anderson Point. You'll see a few houses along this shoreline and a medieval-like wall constructed across a high bluff. Because of the steep, western slope, the shoreline is heavily timbered and dark. The Kalispel Indians traditionally hunted bear and fished with hook and line while camped on this peninsula.

Rounding Picard Point from either direction, views of the Cabinet Mountains remain outstanding. Pearl Island lies due east from here, a mile offshore from Hope. Sunrises are spectacular from anywhere on Lake Pend Oreille, but perhaps some of the best are seen from Sunrise Bay just before Anderson Point, as the sun comes up over the rugged peaks and ridges of the Cabinets.

Heading south of Garfield Bay takes you to Grouse Mountain Point and then Talache Landing with its small but scenic swimming beach, a popular put-in area for kayakers and canoeists. By car, Talache is accessed via Talache Road, another county road that begins just over a mile from U.S. Highway 95 off Sagle Road. About half the shoreline from Garfield Bay south to Talache is public, while all of the shoreline from Green Bay north to Camp Bay is public.

Garfield Bay is a well-protected bay for canoeing or kayaking, although as you round the point toward the beautiful, cobble beaches of Green Bay it can get choppy. Green Bay has primitive

Legendary Lake Pend Oreille

campsites with picnic tables and fire rings.

Inland, the Mineral Point Trail opens to fantastic vista points of Lake Pend Oreille looking across the lake toward the Green Monarchs and south toward Three Sisters Peaks. The trail provides access to the water's edge at Green Bay and connects to an upland trail to Lost Lake, an easy route to experience forest wetlands and possibly see wildlife.

Several picturesque, small lakes dot the Sagle Peninsula landscape: Providence, Gamlin, Livermore, Beaver, Eaton, Mirror and Shepherd. Some of those lakes are private while some allow public access. Some of the most beautiful and popular public recreational attractions in northern Idaho are in this area.

--- --- --- --- --- --- --- --- --- --- --- --- --- --- --- ---

Anecdota: Love and the Lake

Sandpoint is a nice town, but it's Lake Pend Oreille that pulls on people, says Eileen Klatt, an artist who grew up in a large family with nine siblings at the water's edge on Garfield Bay. There were few houses back then – mostly small vacation cabins tucked back into the woods, home to weekend visitors from Spokane. Garfield Bay was in its heyday as a resort community in the late 1950s and early '60s when commercial fishing for kokanee salmon allowed a catch of up to 250 fish a day. Life was full and abundant.

"Summer mornings we were sent out to weed the vegetable garden," says Eileen, "but we didn't get far into it before our mom would let us go swimming." When not on the beach, she and her siblings would either be fishing off the docks, following creeks up into the woods, or picnicking on the shore of one of the many coves between Garfield and Green bays. Their mom didn't drive a car and so trips into Sandpoint were few, but there was always plenty of gas for the motor of their boat. So until they all got drivers licenses to take them to town, she and her siblings hung out together and took turns driving the boat. They went waterskiing or explored other parts of the lake – the Green Monarchs, Talache Landing, Green Bay and Glengary Bay.

"There is more than one side to living on the lake," says Eileen. For all its good times, there were also difficulties and dangers. She remembers their boat coming loose from its mooring and running aground more than once. Tragedy struck when her youngest brother drowned in the lake, slipping from the dock during high water. But despite her brother's death, she and her siblings were allowed the freedom to be out on the lake. Her connection with the lake's magic, its vastness and its special places, and even the life cycle of the kokanee salmon, all contributed to the development of an aesthetic and her strong affinity for water. Lake Pend Oreille has always been her standard for measuring beauty. No other place could ever measure up to the sheer beauty of this place, she says. It casts a spell. It's not so surprising then that her professional life is as a watercolor artist — a painter of fish.

Painter Elieen Klatt, one of 10 children in the Klatt family, grew up on the water at Garfield Bay. Shown above in 1956 as a child with six of her siblings (sitting on middle step, fourth from the left) and below in her studio (courtesy photos)

"Fish have always been a part of my life," Eileen says. She remembers catching them when she was as young as 7 years old. The kokanee were especially interesting to her, how they would change in color from silver or bluebacked in summer to red or rusty during the autumn spawning. When the fishermen stopped bringing boatloads of kokanee to the Garfield Bay dock, she realized that somehow the fish were in danger. Once the Albeni Falls Dam went in and the lake was drawn down in the fall, she would walk along the shore and see so many kokanee left high and dry at the mouths of tributaries. What Eileen didn't fully grasp then was how man was disrupting the life cycle of the fish by

Legendary Lake Pend Oreille

changing its spawning habitat.

Eileen now lives overlooking the lake in the town of Hope. She painted her first fish – a perch that her husband caught – in 1985. A series of paintings and prints of trout soon followed. Today her favorite subjects to paint are salmon, especially those species that are endangered. A collection of her watercolors called, "A Litany of Salmon," has been exhibited in major galleries in the region.

"Their life cycle is a beautiful embodiment of our soul's journey in life," says Eileen. "How we are born into the world, emerge and go out into the world, and we are called to return to our true nature, our inner origin, our source of life. Salmon do that so beautifully with their beauty and persistence. They receive a call to come home with the precious elixir to give to the beings left. It is a heroic journey." For Eileen Klatt, this parallel journey of human and fish life, death and new life was learned from this remarkable body of water – Lake Pend Oreille.

- - - - - - - - - - - - - - - - - -

Lore Along the Shore: From Midas to Garfield

In days past, Green Bay was a logging camp. But Garfield Bay has a mining history. Copper ore was found in this area and a town sprung up here after a mine opened in 1909. James McNicholas, a shyster who bilked Eastern investors into thinking the surrounding mountains were loaded with gold, named the town Midas. By the time folks discovered that he had simply laced the mines with some of the precious minerals, McNicholas had run off to Oregon.

Charles Flaty, a homesteader and conductor for Northern Pacific Railroad, renamed the town in admiration for President James Garfield. It has served as a fishing and resort community since the 1950s. In 1976, several men erected what was known as the "White Cross" just above Garfield Bay that could be seen all the way across the lake to Hope. It eventually fell into disrepair but was rebuilt in 1991.

PUBLIC ACCESS ▶ ## GARFIELD BAY

The recreation site is managed by Bonner County and is a free day-use area, but there are fees for the campground. There are private marinas, campgrounds, lodging, stores and restaurants found here as well.

What's it like?

The day-use facilities and adjacent beaches are tucked back and protected at the head

Sandy Bessler and Crystal at Garfield Bay's beach (Chris Bessler)

of the bay with its pleasant green lawn and plenty of space for relaxing and playing. It is open year-round. The campground winds up the slope across the county road and has pullouts for 25 campers with water at each site and restrooms nearby.

A protected bay, Garfield is well-suited to canoeing or kayaking. From here to Green Bay, the shoreline is rocky, but there are some nice cobble beaches to enjoy swimming and picnicking. Launching from Garfield Bay it is a one- to three-mile one-way paddle to Green Bay, depending on where along the shoreline you land.

FACILITIES: campground for tents and trailers (up to 22 feet with no hookups), concrete boat ramp, docks, sandy beaches, picnic tables and barbecues, children's playground, drinking water, vault toilet
ACTIVITIES: camping, boating, sailing, swimming, picnicking, paddling, fishing

How to get here:

There is paved access from U.S. Highway 95, five miles south of Sandpoint at the community of Sagle. Turn east on Sagle Road and go 7.2 miles to Garfield Bay Road. Veer right and travel 1.25 miles to the paved parking area. The campground is across the road and is RV-accessible.

Looking northeast at Talache Beach in Sagle (Linda Larson)

TALACHE LANDING (TALACHE BEACH)

At the end of Talache Road, a road maintained by Bonner County, is a small area that provides a day-use, sandy-to-rocky beachfront called Talache Landing. There is limited parking for one or two vehicles along the road. Note that this spot is actually on private property. Forest Service land is north and south of this area.

What's it like?

This is a popular put-in area for kayakers and canoeists coming from Sandpoint and Sagle. From the water, it's a short paddle to reach Forest Service public lakefront north of Mirror Creek (the original landing from which iron ore was shipped by barge) or south of Talache Beach, toward Maiden Rock once you pass several homes. It is a convenient put-in for those paddlers who would like to try primitive camping on one of the colorful, pebble public beaches mostly in the southerly direction. On hot summer days, Talache Beach is also a popular swimming area for local residents and scuba divers.

FACILITIES: mixed rocky, gravel and sand beach, convenient put-in from shore for paddle craft

ACTIVITIES: canoeing, kayaking, fishing, swimming, scuba diving

How to get here:

Access is from U.S. Highway 95, five miles south of Sandpoint at the community of Sagle. Turn east on Sagle Road and go just over a mile. A litte ways past South Sagle Road, take the fork to the right on Talache Road and travel about six miles to the end of the road.

Lore Along the Shore: Talache Lodge
By Marianne Love

Harlan and Margaret Walker could be considered resort pioneers and extraordinary promoters of Lake Pend Oreille. Along with Ruth and Wayne Anderson, the Walkers turned 800 acres of the old Talache mining community into a thriving fishing lodge. During its heyday from 1948 to 1962, celebrities like Bing Crosby, Lon Chaney, Phil Harris and Adlai Stevenson (shown below) stayed at the Talache Lodge. Along with the Walker's famous hospitality, steak dinners and sumptuous breakfasts, the main attraction for guests was the opportunity to catch a Kamloops rainbow lunker. When lodge guests caught a big fish, Harlan would cook it for them.

Politician Adlai Stevenson II, at the wheel, prepares to tour Lake Pend Oreille with Fred Kennedy (right), then owner of Kenmore Marina, and Al Coleman, Bonner County chairman of the Democratic Party, in 1952, the first time Stevenson ran for president against Dwight Eisenhower (Ross Hall photo courtesy Bobbie Kennedy)

The Walkers purchased the property in 1947, and along with the land came 63 buildings remaining from silver mining days in Talache. Some of the employees of the lodge lived in the old village site. Harlan, a former Farragut naval recruit, was drawn back to the area after hearing stories about the world-record Kamloops Gerrard rainbow trout. Even though at first his wife, Margaret, took some convincing, she eventually came to love the area.

Harlan took visitors to a spot on the lake beneath the Green Monarchs where they would fish from Granite Creek to Deadman Point and then back across the lake towards Camp Bay and Mineral Point. This area of the lake was soon dubbed the Kamloops Triangle. Unfortunately, the Talache Lodge burned to the ground in the winter of 1962 and was never rebuilt. All that was left were the two native rock chimneys that stood until they were knocked down in the early 1990s. During its final season of operation, guests at Talache Lodge caught 34 trophy fish weighing more than 10 pounds apiece. Harlan and Margaret Walker indeed had found pay dirt at the former mining site, but not from silver ore; it was the simple pleasure of going fishing.

Talache Beach

The pebble,
no bigger than a marble,
is one color underwater,
another when dry and piled
on shore with its kind.
There, it will be lost until, unless,
a wave splashes it.

—Robens Napolitan
Sagle, Idaho

Points of Sail
By Cate Huisman

Wind and Sailors:

The prevailing southerly winds are typically in your face as you head out of Garfield Bay, so sailors tack their way out of the bay or use the convenience of a motor. Once clearing the bay, on a breezy day sailors can often enjoy a fast, broad reach directly across the lake to the foot of the Green Monarchs on the opposing shore, to Windy or Indian points. Other nice sailing out of Garfield Bay is to simply stay along the near shore and head northeast to nearby Green Bay, Mineral Point and Anderson Point; or conversely head south, generally upwind, toward the more distant Talache Landing or Maiden Rock. Note, it's not unusual for those prevailing southerly winds to decline in late afternoon, so don't get stranded. Northerlies coming

Sailing at Green Bay (Mathew Hall)

down the Purcell Trench are less common but can come at any time of year and also can be quite strong.

Anchorages:

Winds in Garfield Bay tend to drop as you approach the head of the bay, and it is often possible to anchor at a mooring buoy off the park at the northern end of the bay, but you are still exposed to winds from the south.

From Garfield Bay to Anderson Point there are few fully protected anchorages and little public access. Beautiful Green Bay has four fully exposed mooring buoys, secure but bumpy. Anchors can drag here in the rock bottom off the shore, so anchoring is not a good idea unless you are able to watch your boat constantly, as winds come and go. Glengary Bay is generally protected from the prevailing southwest winds in summer, and a side-tie may be available in the small marina there; call 208-265-2752. Otherwise, you can anchor in the mud bottom of the bay.

Several more mooring buoys are within reach of Garfield Bay: five scattered below the Green Monarchs; two at Whiskey Rock; three at Maiden Rock; and two at Evans Landing. In general, in this area of the lake, the bottom is rocky, and a Bruce, plow or CQR is necessary.

Launching and Hauling:

The only public ramp is at Garfield Bay. A ramp at Glengary Bay is available with a launch fee. When the water is drawn down for winter pool, they become increasingly difficult to use.

Lake Pend Oreille from above Ellisport Bay, August 29, 2004

Sandpoint from Mickinnick Trail, October 17, 2005

Lake Pend Oreille south from Cape Horn, July 27, 2002

GREEN BAY

Managed by the U.S. Forest Service, this is a no-fee area.

Green Bay (Jon Shaver)

What's it like?

Though it faces due south into strong winds that often blow up the length of the lake, this is one of the more beautiful places on Lake Pend Oreille's shore. The water is exceptionally clear and rock outcroppings punctuate the shoreline. Long Point and Mineral Point are landforms on the eastern edge of Green Bay. The entire region – with its lakeside access, cliffs, picturesque shoreline, superb hiking and biking trails, and a sense of solitude even when it's crowded, make this place a true favorite for locals and visitors alike.

The high bluffs of the Mineral Point Trail overlooking Green Bay offer marvelous views of Lake Pend Oreille. Along the trail is a memorial plaque dedicated to the memory of Brent "Jake" Jacobson, a Forest Service law enforcement officer who gave his life in the line of duty. The upper trailhead has a lovely picnic area with ample parking and a viewing bench to sit a spell. Connecting to this trail is an easy forest trail to Lost Lake, making up part of a loop completed in 2007 by Pend Oreille Pedalers (see box, page 88).

Despite the steep and narrow access road, Green Bay is worth the extra effort. Spending a few nights camping, anytime between snow thaw in spring until late fall, among the pines near the lakeshore, and swimming, hiking or just relaxing during the day is an experience every northern Idaho visitor should have. For sailors there are four mooring buoys just a little ways off shore.

FACILITIES: rustic campsites, picnic tables, viewing benches, barbecue grills, cobble beaches, vault toilets, self-guided interpretive trail, hiking/biking/horseback riding trails, mooring buoys

ACTIVITIES: camping, boating, sailing, swimming, picnicking, hiking, biking, fishing, paddling

How to get here:

The Green Bay campground is 16 miles southeast of Sandpoint. From U.S. Highway 95 about six miles south of Sandpoint, turn east onto Sagle Road and follow it 7.2 miles to Garfield Bay Road. Take it 1.4 miles to Garfield Bay and the Green Bay Cutoff Road, which bears left and uphill, with a road sign that's not easy to see. Go a third of a mile to Mineral Point Road No. 532 and turn right. This is a narrow dirt road. Take it 1.2 miles to its junction with Green Bay Road No. 2672 and follow that narrow road – a rough, steep 0.8 mile – to the parking area and lower trailhead at Green Bay; or continue on Road 532 another 1.9 miles and turn right onto Road 532A, a spur road that leads just over 0.5 mile to the middle trailhead. Each parking area accommodates up to eight vehicles. There are vault toilets at either trailhead. This site is also accessible by boat, but there are no docks – only mooring buoys.

Pend Oreille Pedalers

Formed in 2004, the Pend Oreille Pedalers is a group of local singletrack and road riding addicts who wish to preserve and improve bicycling opportunities in Idaho's panhandle. The bicycle club is an International Mountain Biking Association and League of American Bicyclists affiliate. Shortly after forming, club members got busy clearing and building trails and creating the annual Sandpoint Bike Week, a weeklong spate of activities devoted to bicycling. During the riding season, the club hosts weekly rides and a monthly club ride. This passionate group of cyclists first built two miles of trail on private land off Syringa Heights Road and then secured a grant to build additional trail at Mineral Point, connecting Lost Lake and Mineral Point trails to create a loop. Learn more about the Pend Oreille Pedalers by looking up www.pendoreillepedalers.com, where a fantastic guide to area rides is also posted.

Wildlife Viewing: Nesting Ospreys at Lost Lake

A pair of ospreys has chosen a giant ponderosa pine snag for their nesting site next to Lost Lake. A resident migratory raptor that eats fish, the osprey is common to the Lake Pend Oreille area and lives here between April and September. Because of habitat loss, they will often use bridges (even very noisy ones), manmade platforms and utility poles for places to nest. But in the wild they like big snags close to water or very tall conifers whose tops have died out. The adult birds need perches close to their nest to guard the eggs and nestlings from predators such as ravens and eagles. If they survive their winter in Central America and subsequent long spring migration

north, the adult pair will return to the same nest year after year to breed and raise their young. The osprey offspring, when mature enough for breeding, will also return to their home habitat and build their nests in the forest "neighborhood" relatively close to their parents. One of the most exhilarating wildlife-viewing experiences a person can enjoy is seeing an osprey dive into the water with a violent splash, completely immersed, and then ascend with heavy, wet wings and a fish in its talons to feed itself and its brood.

Osprey (Jay Mock)

Wildflower Notes:
Arrowleaf Balsamroot and Yarrow

Amid the pines along the Mineral Point Trail from late April to early July, the large, golden yellow flower heads of arrowleaf balsamroot color the hillsides. A member of the aster family, *Balsamorhiza sagittata*'s silver-gray leaves, up to a foot long, arise from the base of lengthy flower stems. American Indians would peel and eat the young flower stems and bake the tough woody roots in a fire pit until palatable. The plant also had medicinal value to native peoples. The large leaves were used as a poultice for burns; the roots were boiled and the liquid was used to treat wounds or was drunk as a tea for respiratory ailments.

Another member of the aster family that blooms a little later in this area is yarrow. The leaves of *Achillea millefolium* have a fern-like appearance and a strong scent, and its tiny white flowers are clustered at the top of the

Left: Yarrow
Above: Arrowleaf
balsamroot (Jay Mock)

long, hairy stem. Yarrow is a valuable plant to have in the outdoors: The leaves when crushed and mixed with water can be applied as a poultice to ease sunburn or to stop the bleeding from cuts and wounds. The alkaloid chemical in the plant actually reduces the clotting time of blood. A tea made from the leaves can also reduce a fever and ease suffering from a cold.

GLENGARY BAY

A mix of the old and the new coexists here: huge, expensive homes with a line of Sea-Doos on shore juxtaposed next to small, weathered cabins with old wooden boats in dry dock. Glengary Bay Marina is a private marina that was built by one of Lake Pend Oreille's most famous wooden boat builders and craftsmen – Herrick "Swede" Heitman. Swede has passed on, but the private marina is still owned and operated by his family (see Anecdota: Boatbuilding as a Family Tradition, page 91). They have been working on restoring some of Swede's wooden masterpieces and the old docks and breakwaters have been undergoing much-needed repairs. Boat slips at the marina are available for lease by the week, month or season.

Glengary Bay is also home to the world-renowned inventor of lifesaving medical equipment, – Dr. Forrest Bird. Bird is also a pilot whose unique Bird Air Lodge can be seen from the water, and his Bird Aviation Museum and Invention Center is worth visiting as well (see box below). It opened to the public in 2007 and was featured on television's *60 Minutes* in a segment about Dr. Bird.

 Bird Aviation Museum and Invention Center

Founded by Dr. Forrest Bird, a recipient of the National Medal of Technology and Presidential Citizens Medal and a member of the National Inventors Hall of Fame, this museum is a 16,000-square-foot facility with a gift shop and exhibits on aviation, inventors and their inventions. His vast collection of memorabilia is on display: vintage aircraft and automobiles, limited edition art, and prototypes of numerous inventions, including his own generations of ventilators and respirators. The museum is an incredible tribute to dozens of entrepreneurs and their inventions, from Les Paul and his electric guitar to Bob Smith and his ski goggles. Exhibits also honor local entrepreneurial companies such as Coldwater Creek and Litehouse Foods.

Dr. Bird's wife and museum curator, Pamela Riddle Bird, Ph.D., was instrumental in planning the facility and collecting material to exhibit. A pilot like her husband, Pamela is the author of *Inventing for Dummies* and the founder and CEO of Innovative Product Technologies, a consulting business specializing in market commercialization. Not surprisingly, their common interest in aviation and inventing brought the Birds together.

Bird Aviation Musem and Invention Center is located near Glengary Bay in Sagle, about 17 miles southeast of Sandpoint, off Sagle Road on Bird Ranch Road. Open year-round for groups with reservations and seasonally from May to October, Mondays through Saturdays. Admission is free. Look up www.birdaviationmuseum.com or call 208-255-4321.

Lore Along the Shore: Names Bear Legacies

The bays and landforms along this part of the lake are named for early residents. Martin Bay is named in memory of Johnny Martin, who once lived on this bay but tragically drowned in the lake.

In the early days of settlement around the lake, a popular book was *The Man from Glengary*. Some people speculate that this is how Glengary Bay acquired that name. But other people claim that settlers by the name of O'Donnell named it that because it reminded them of the terrain in Glen Garry, their former home in Scotland. Glengary Bay was also an important steamboat landing.

Picard Point was named for a railroad worker who built a stone house on this point decades ago. Elliott Bay was named for Ed Elliott, the president of the Northern Navigation Company, which operated several steamboats on the lake. Camp Bay was home to early pioneers; a homestead from the 1890s or early 1900s is still visible on the banks.

Anecdota: Boatbuilding as a Family Tradition

There's a photograph on the wall of the late Swede Heitman's workshop at Glengary Bay Marina of him standing next to the last wooden boat he built, a sailing dingy. It was taken sometime in the 1980s, and he's wearing that famously warm smile. His shop is a glimpse into the past: There are old boat props on the wall, even older pinup calendars, the smell of aging lumber and lots of old woodworking tools, some so unusual you wonder how in the world they might be used. Some of these tools he made himself.

Just prior to Swede's death in 1995 at age 84, Marjorie Trulock, his daughter, and her husband, Tom, moved home to northern Idaho from where they had been living in Utah. Marjorie looks very much like her dad – the same welcoming eyes, sincere voice and kind smile. The Trulocks took over the marina, dock restoration tasks and cleaning out the shop. There's a spirited renaissance going on since Marjorie, her husband and their two daughters have also taken on the work of restoring some of Swede's old boats crafted during the 50-plus years that he made Glengary Bay home.

Swede Heitman with the last boat he built (courtesy Marjorie Trulock)

Self-taught, Swede ultimately became a master boatbuilder, crafting amazing wooden boats as well as the commonplace. The *Mary Marge* was built in the 1940s for local dentist Mac McKinnon and named for the doctor's daughter and wife. The 30-foot Husky design is an enormous boat out of the water and has an interior that Swede custom-built, wide and hefty like the physique of Dr. McKinnon.

"Boats were different back then," Marjorie says. "Dad crafted the entire boat, every part of it." It wasn't launched until 1954. "There were letters from Mac wondering when the boat was going to be done. I don't know what my father's response was, but he probably didn't speed up any." That was Swede, too. He did things his own way in his own time. Of course, he also had a lot to deal with, keeping a marina operating and a family provided for, not to mention the many years he served on the Bonner County Planning and Zoning Commission. About 10 years after moving back, the Trulock family reacquired the *Mary Marge*. They have done extensive restoration work, especially on the mahogany and Alaskan cedar hull.

Swede's close friend and Glengary Bay neighbor, Hal Hargreaves, is helping the family with the tedious work. Swede taught Hal how to build and restore wooden boats; his first was a runabout and the second, the *White Raven*, is the boat that Hal and his wife, Ruth, keep at Glengary Bay Marina for use on the lake.

"It's very cool," says Marjorie. "We need to put this boat back in the water and enjoy it as much as Dad would have wanted somebody to enjoy it. It's pretty interesting to be living in this place and to have his things around and be using his tools and shop." She remembers what the *Mary Marge* was like in the water. "It's got a very distinctive sound — it rumbles along. The bow is really high, but it will move right out. Dad thought it was the easiest-moving boat on the lake. We think it will be a nice, big, stable all-weather boat."

Another friend of Swede's, Liam Fitzgerald, also is helping out, but with the labor-intensive marina work. He worked for Swede for 15 summers many years ago, living in a little cabin Swede built on the edge of his property.

"I spent most of my time keeping the marina together so he could concentrate, at least some of the time, on building and repairing boats," Liam says with a look that reminds me of Swede. "They were certainly some of the best years of my life. Not only was he someone you could admire so much; he was a pleasure to be around. He was a great teacher, a great companion, and it was easy to come back here every year."

Another of Swede's boats that is still in use on the lake is a hand-lining kokanee boat he built for Bill Zinter at Bottle Bay Marina in 1956. Ron Raiha now owns the trustworthy vessel and uses it every year for hand-lining lake whitefish in the winter.

The more commonplace boats Swede built were little runabouts. One of these is in the shop, a boat built in 1953 that the Trulock family got at an auction. Marjorie's oldest daughter, Piper, is doing the restoration. They call it the *'53 Swede*. "He made billions of these, lots and lots and lots," says Marjorie. "Inboards and outboards. All the same hull with different cabin configurations made with marine plywood and a fiberglass bottom." Swede loved his grandchildren, although they weren't around him much before his death. Still, Piper won't let anyone else work on her grandpa's boat.

Glengary Bay Marina has 50 boat slips and permits to replace some of the original breakwaters that Swede built. Swede bought the place in 1943. One of the buildings was the old post office and store from when Glengary was one of the steamboat landings. He started operating the marina by the mid-1940s and built sheds and docks, breakwaters — everything with only levers, pulleys and an old Ford tractor that he traded for 100 feet of lake frontage. The marina needs constant attention: Nails pop out, boards rot, logs start to sink and pilings break off. Marjorie and Tom work hard, but both have day jobs. They actually don't want it to be much different anyway. A lot of the people who have slips have old cabins nearby, and a few sailors and local fishermen moor here as well.

"We really don't have many amenities out here," says Marjorie. "We have an outhouse. One yard light. We have a sign at the top that says, 'Private.' People don't come down here." For boaters arriving by water, they typically only have slip moorage available in the winter, since they fill up fast in the summer.

Of all the marinas on the lake, this one is unique, not because very little has changed; but because the spirit of Swede Heitman is still here, alive and well. And just like that photo hanging in his shop, you just know he's proudly grinning about it all.

OTHER PUBLIC ACCESS SITES IN AREA 2 WITH PROXIMITY TO LAKE PEND OREILLE:

Gamlin Lake

Managed by the Bureau of Land Management and the Nature Conservancy, this is a no-fee, day-use area for canoes, kayaks and small fishing boats with electric motors only. This area is also perfect for hiking, mountain biking, wildlife viewing and bird-watching. Besides wetland and waterfowl habitats, the moist coniferous forest around the lake is home to at least 27 nesting bird species including pileated woodpeckers. Roadside parking is off Glengary Bay Road; vault toilet, information kiosk and a two-mile loop trail around this small, quiet and picturesque lake.

Shepherd Lake

Fishing is managed by Bonner County. There are campgrounds and public boat launch docks available on both sides of the lake managed by U.S. Forest Service.

Mirror Lake

Private and public access from adjacent U.S. Forest Service lands. Camp Stidwell, a Boy Scout and Girl Scout summer camp, also is located here.

Round Lake State Park

Managed by the Idaho Department of Parks and Recreation; fees for day use and camping.

What's it like?

Established in 1965, this 58-acre and relatively shallow lake is small but delightful, with exceptional fishing and splendid hiking trails. A glacier-carved pothole lake left behind after the last ice age, Round Lake is home to a wide diversity of plant and animal life, including ospreys. Round Lake makes for a perfect family camping experience; reservations recommended at this thoroughly modern campground. Campfire presentations at the outdoor amphitheater are a summer attraction for visitors. But Round Lake is a year-round park and one of the best ice fishing lakes in northern Idaho. The trails in the park are also very popular for cross-country skiing.

FACILITIES: tree-shaded campsites accessible to RVs up to 24 feet (no hookups), boat launch, docks, dump station, toilets, restrooms with showers, sheltered picnic area, picnic tables and barbecue grills, drinking water, visitors center, and Stewardship and Trappers trails for interpretive nature hiking, biking or horseback riding

Aerial taken by remote control airplane over Gamlin Lake with Lake Pend Oreille in the distance (Jerry Luther)

ACTIVITIES: boating (non-motorized only), camping, fishing, swimming, scuba diving, picnicking, canoeing, wildlife viewing, bird-watching, hiking, biking, and horseback riding trails, campfire programs

How to get here:

Coming from Sandpoint, take U.S. Highway 95 south for 10 miles, turn right (west) on Dufort Road. Follow Dufort Road for two miles to the Round Lake State Park entrance. Dufort Road is 36 miles north of Coeur d'Alene, just north of Westmond.

Westmond Lake

This is a small kettle lake, a deep pothole of water surrounded by seasonal wetlands located at the end of Westmond Creek not far from the intersection of South Sagle Road and East Dufort Road in Sagle (it is not labeled on maps). Most of this property is now owned by Idaho Fish and Game because it has been designated an IBA – Important Bird Area – by the National Audubon Society. It provides significant nesting and migratory habitat for various species of waterfowl and shorebirds and is also valuable nesting habitat for at least 10 pairs of black terns. In fact, this area is likely the largest black tern colony in northern Idaho. A great spot for bird-watchers!

Cocolalla Lake

Located alongside U.S. Highway 95 about 12 miles south of Sandpoint and 34 miles north of Coeur d'Alene is Cocolalla Lake. There are half a dozen primitive campsites available here, some with fire rings, a boat ramp and vault toilet. It is managed by Idaho Fish and Game.

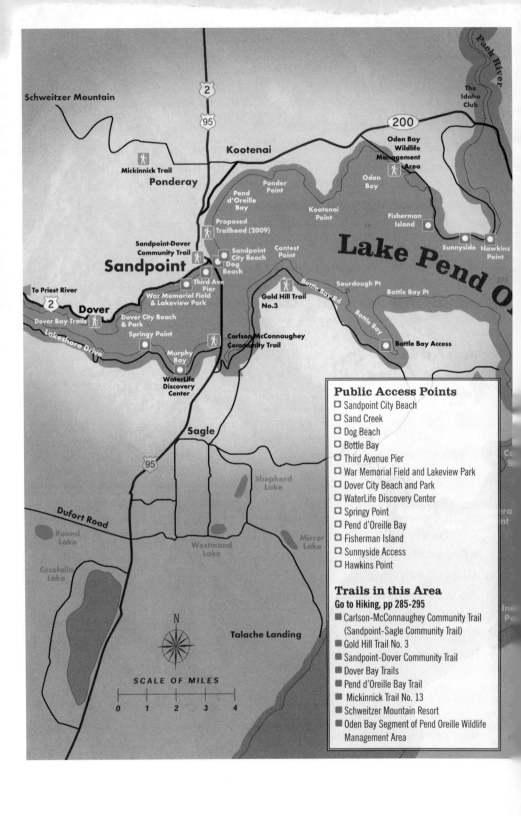

Public Access Points
- ☐ Sandpoint City Beach
- ☐ Sand Creek
- ☐ Dog Beach
- ☐ Bottle Bay
- ☐ Third Avenue Pier
- ☐ War Memorial Field and Lakeview Park
- ☐ Dover City Beach and Park
- ☐ WaterLife Discovery Center
- ☐ Springy Point
- ☐ Pend d'Oreille Bay
- ☐ Fisherman Island
- ☐ Sunnyside Access
- ☐ Hawkins Point

Trails in this Area
Go to Hiking, pp 285-295
- ■ Carlson-McConnaughey Community Trail (Sandpoint-Sagle Community Trail)
- ■ Gold Hill Trail No. 3
- ■ Sandpoint-Dover Community Trail
- ■ Dover Bay Trails
- ■ Pend d'Oreille Bay Trail
- ■ Mickinnick Trail No. 13
- ■ Schweitzer Mountain Resort
- ■ Oden Bay Segment of Pend Oreille Wildlife Management Area

CHAPTER SIX

AREA 3, GREATER SANDPOINT

Downtown Sandpoint
East to Bottle Bay
West of the Long Bridge
North Shoreline to Sunnyside

OVERVIEW

*O*n any August weekend that is warm and sunny, the expanse of water below a cliffside viewpoint northwest towards Sandpoint from Bottle Bay Road becomes what you might call the Boaters Triangle. It's an area buzzing with the sound of jet boats, powerboats with water-skiers in tow and personal watercraft. Bordered by the railroad trestle and Long Bridge to the west, Sandpoint City Beach directly across the way, and around Contest Point to the east towards Sourdough Point and Bottle Bay, this is undoubtedly one of the busiest parts of the lake. It is the most popular recreation area on Lake Pend Oreille that's centered in the town of Sandpoint, where major highways intersect and tourist facilities include resorts, motels, restaurants, shops and marinas.

The open water, as compared to other areas of the lake, is shallow here, only 20 to 40 feet

97

Boating past the third Long Bridge, now a pedestrian bridge, in the area that could be called the "Boaters Triangle," circa 1968 (Ross Hall)

deep. Sailboats brave passage amid the crisscrossing wakes, but because of the boat traffic, canoes and kayaks should use caution during the summer season and keep close to shore.

Driving south from Sandpoint across the Long Bridge, the lakeshore turns east towards Comeback Bay. Bottle Bay Road parallels the lake shoreline at first with rocky, steep cliffs that edge Gold Hill's northern slope, then winds down along the water's edge, followed by more curves and hills, at times as exciting as a roller coaster ride.

This narrow paved road showcases some of the most expensive homes in the area, some cantilevered out over rocky cliffs, with the lake a stone's throw off the deck, and others built on rock outcroppings dotting the hillside on newly built roads to catch the view. This section of shoreline all the way to Anderson Point is private property. However, Bottle Bay Marina and Resort offers public amenities — a restaurant and lounge as well as cabin, canoe, paddle boat and kayak rentals. It's a pleasant drive or boat ride from Sandpoint to Bottle Bay to enjoy dinner or, for a modest fee, to moor your boat for a summer night on the water.

The Long Bridge that crosses Lake Pend Oreille is more than a highway over the water leading to and from Sandpoint. It is also where people tend to notice that the lake starts to narrow to the west, and so over time, the bridge has become the commonly accepted boundary between the lake and the Pend Oreille River. According to Idaho Fish and Game, however, the official nautical demarcation between the two waterways is the railroad bridge over the lake just east of

Legendary Lake Pend Oreille

the Long Bridge. The natural channel of water that existed prior to higher "reservoir" levels caused by Albeni Falls Dam was a meandering river only 30 to 40 feet wide and 33 feet deep.

Since many people still consider the waters west of the Long Bridge to be part of the lake all the way to Dover, this guidebook on Lake Pend Oreille will take you at least that far. From Sandpoint, U.S. Highway 2 travels west, coming first to Dover, then on to Laclede, Priest River and Oldtown. This section of U.S. Highway 2 from Sandpoint to the Washington state line is part of the National Scenic Byway system and is called the "Panhandle Historic Rivers Passage." This byway is also the southern leg of the International Selkirk Loop linking Idaho, Washington and British Columbia, Canada.

From the Long Bridge to Dover, both riverbanks are mostly private property, but there are a couple public access sites worth visiting. While in Sandpoint, you can stroll from downtown to the Third Avenue Pier city park and enjoy watching an osprey fish the waters by day, or spot a falling star on a warm summer night. It's a quiet respite from all the noisy city traffic. A few blocks farther west along Ontario Street leads you to War Memorial Field and Lakeview Park, the location of the Bonner County Historical Museum and the Native Plant Arboretum. Memorial Field is also the site of the annual Festival at Sandpoint outdoor music festival held in August – a magnet for thousands of music lovers.

Heading west, the City of Dover Public Beach and Park is the next public access site on the north riverbank set within the boundaries of the new Dover Bay waterfront community.

Exploring farther downriver to Albeni Falls, 26 more miles, is recommended; there are several public access sites along the way, and despite increasing development of its banks, it is still a beautiful river. Keep in mind that you can't get a sailboat under the Long Bridge, so if you would like to sail the river, you'll have to trailer your boat to Springy Point, Memorial Field or Dover Bay for access.

Traveling south from Sandpoint, when you cross the Long Bridge, you'll find Lakeshore Drive at the south end of the bridge. Resorts and homes dot most of the southern riverbank from the Long Bridge along Lakeshore Drive to Dufort Road. The exceptions are the WaterLife Discovery Center near Murphy Slough – an educational center developed by Idaho Fish and Game – and Springy Point, a large and inviting public campground, boat dock and beach area managed by the U.S. Army Corps of Engineers. Lakeshore Drive also is part of a road tour that loops you to Priest River and back to Sandpoint along U.S. Highway 2.

North of downtown Sandpoint, the highway splits at the stoplight with U.S. Highway 95 going to Schweitzer Mountain Resort and Canada, and Idaho State Highway 200 – the Pend Oreille Scenic Byway – going east to Montana. Nearly all the shoreline from Sandpoint to Sunnyside is privately owned and skirts the small communities of Ponderay and Kootenai.

Public access to the lake isn't available again until you reach the Sunnyside Peninsula on Sunnyside Road, a few miles east of Ponderay and Kootenai off Highway 200. Sunnyside Road is paved for several miles and then becomes dirt along the shoreline to Hawkins Point. The road continues to wind around the peninsula until it meets up with Highway 200 again near The Idaho Club, a golf community, and the Pack River.

There is a small parking area for a couple of vehicles where the road crosses Raymond Slough just before the Perch Bay Road. This area and some of Oden Bay and its shoreline are part of the Lake Pend Oreille Wildlife Management Area managed by the U.S. Army Corps of Engineers. The only other public access sites are along a half-mile section of lakeshore parallel to the gravel portion of Sunnyside Road just before you reach Hawkins Point. This beach area with a gravel launch is called Sunnyside Access and is managed by Idaho Fish and Game. Hawkins Point is the primary public access launch site on Sunnyside, at the far eastern point of the peninsula and just to the west of Pack River Flats.

Going along by boat, the northeast shoreline is some of the lake's shallowest water — less

Sandpoint City Beach (Marie-Dominique Verdier)

than 20 feet deep. From Sandpoint City Beach to Kootenai Bay, you'll cross a bay whose name won't be on any maps. Known as Pend d'Oreille Bay (see page 136) by locals, it's just north of the Seasons at Sandpoint resort marina. The bay curves past historic Black Rock around to Ponder Point where there are private docks, condos and lakeshore homes.

Next you cross Kootenai Bay, the mouth of Boyer Slough, and turn south along a populated peninsula shoreline to Kootenai Point. Around the point is Oden Bay, the largest bay on this side of the lake, wide but very shallow. This area is popular with sailors who triangulate the lake from Sandpoint City Beach to Sunnyside and across the lake to Bottle Bay or Anderson Point.

The often calm, shallow water between Oden Bay and Perch Bay is ideal for kayaking and canoeing. Paddling among the tiny, unnamed islands just offshore of Sunnyside Peninsula is a perfect way to spend a summer afternoon. Look for

Legendary Lake Pend Oreille

longtime resident Terry Anderson's handcrafted wooden sea serpent and the buoy that is a stone version of a sand castle – a generous tie-up for your paddle craft so you can take a quick swim. Fisherman Island is the largest of this cluster of islands and a destination for paddlers to watch for nesting bald eagles. Although camping on the islands is not allowed, a paddle under a full summer moon is spectacular, starting from the public boat ramp at Hawkins Point.

Numerous trails, including miles and miles of paved trails, can be found in Greater Sandpoint. Connecting downtown to the small community of Sagle adjacent the Long Bridge is the Carlson-McConnaughey Community Trail. In Sagle, above Bottle Bay, Trail No. 3 explores Gold Hill and Gold Mountain, with its iconic views overlooking the bridges across Lake Pend Oreille leading to Sandpoint and surrounds. Downtown Sandpoint is also connected to the small community of Dover via part of the Sandpoint-Dover Community Trail. Paved and flat, it's a pleasant three-mile walk to Dover that runs parallel to U.S. Highway 2. That trail leads to more than 9 miles of trails, all open to the public, at Dover Bay, along the water and through natural preserves, and to a beautiful new park with panoramic views.

The Pend d'Oreille Bay Trail is a proposed two-mile-long shoreline trail under development that begins just north of Sandpoint City Beach and will eventually extend to Black Rock in Ponderay and to Kootenai; access is limited via permission from private property owners. A brand-new Forest Service trail that climbs high on a ridge north of Sandpoint, the Mickinnick Trail provides the most extraordinary views of the Pend Oreille River, Lake Pend Oreille, Sandpoint and the Cabinet Mountains. North of there, Schweitzer Mountain Resort holds dozens of trails with sweeping views of Lake Pend Oreille; some are exclusively for hikers and some for mountain bikers. Of course, the mountain has numerous other recreational opportunities in winter and summer. East of town at Sunnyside, a short walking trail takes hikers through the woods to the lakeshore at Oden Bay Wildlife Management Area. For detailed trail information, refer to chapter 11, "Hiking, Mountain Biking and Horseback Riding Trails."

Anecdota: Sailing the Circle

Not all the boating on Lake Pend Oreille is of the motorized variety. On most summer Saturday mornings, members of the Sandpoint Sailing Association will be racing towards Contest Point from the Windbag Marina next to Sandpoint City Beach. Sailboats of various sizes will catch the wind, sails billowing as they quietly tack and traverse towards the Gold Hill shoreline, then lean towards Bottle Bay around Contest Point, and circle back again towards Kootenai Bay for the return to Sandpoint, about two miles due west. Contest Point is the northernmost point of the lake's southern shoreline. A fleet of nine boats sailing past a high cliff viewpoint off Bottle Bay Road creates a serene and natural scene, like a flock of doves soaring through a sky of blue.

A spectator will get a totally different perspective on sailing from the shoreline near City Beach, one that captures the excitement of a race about to begin. On most Thursday evenings in summer, the Sandpoint Sailing Association holds short-course races off the end of the breakwater near the Windbag Marina. Out on the lake are large, orange inflatable buoys that mark the circular course. By 6 p.m., a couple dozen skippers have readied their boats and crews. A northeasterly wind is blowing and few powerboats are on the water.

Terry Jensen and his distinctive black sailboat (John Harcus)

According to Terry Jensen, this August evening portends a pleasant race. As this race's timekeeper, his black 34-foot sailboat is the first one to leave the marina for open water. One by one, the other sailors exit the harbor and capture the wind that will put their boats into racing mode. While not as picturesque as the view from the cliff, it is as exhilarating.

The Spud Cup over Labor Day weekend is the group's biggest race event for the season. It draws sailors from throughout the region and hosts two days' worth of short-course races in various boat classes. It is a wondrous sight to behold 40 to 50 sailboats on the lake from any viewpoint. But the club isn't only about racing, Terry says. There are barbecues and overnight outings and great camaraderie. He says the group was formed to unite those who have a common love for sailing and to introduce other people to the sport, a mission that first began with the Pend Oreille Yacht Club back in the 1970s.

Jensen, an attorney in Sandpoint, began sailing back in the late 1970s when Keith Sheckler, then owner of the Windbag Marina, took him out for his first lesson on Lake Pend Oreille.

Since then he has owned three different boats and spent a good deal of time sailing among the Northwest's coastal San Juan Islands and Canadian Gulf Islands. In 1992, he was part of a three-person crew that sailed across the Atlantic Ocean from Maryland to Portugal. Terry says that sailing Lake Pend Oreille is similar to sailing the Northwest coast, but here the water is warmer and strong currents and tides aren't issues. The forested mountain scenery is just as pretty and crossing long stretches of open water is thrilling.

"Going 5 miles per hour in a sailboat is a whole lot more exciting than going 40 miles per hour in a power boat," he says. But he's also been caught in storms that have blown his sails out, with sudden 50 to 60 mph gale winds that come over a mountaintop catching him unaware. Terry tries to get his boat on the lake at least twice a week during an eight-month sailing calendar from March into November, well past the racing season. So much time on the water has afforded him some wonderful memories: One late spring morning, after an overnight stay on his boat near Hawkins Point, he awoke to "a hundred chickadee-like birds making the boat their home, poking their heads inside, chattering away on the rigging, pattering across the deck." Then there was the clear and cold (10 degrees) early November day with the wind out of the north at 25 mph, sailing from Sandpoint to Glengary Bay, where the spray from the lake instantly froze, encrusting the entire boat in clear ice. Some people actually do sail Lake Pend Oreille in winter, he says, but during those months Terry Jensen would rather be up at Schweitzer skiing.

SANDPOINT CITY BEACH

Managed by the City of Sandpoint, this is a day use area only, with no fee for public access.

What's it like?

This is the quintessential recreational site on Lake Pend Oreille. It covers 6 acres of grassy lawn and sandy beach and boasts all of the amenities associated with playing at the water's edge.

Two marinas – Sandpoint Marina and The Windbag – straddle City Beach public docks and offer additional boat-slip moorings for powerboats and sailboats respectively. Gas is available at Sandpoint Marina, which is located at the mouth of Sand Creek at The Old Power House building. The Windbag Marina caters to sailors and windsurfers. It is accessed by turning north of City Beach on Railroad Avenue, past the

The south end of Sandpoint City Beach (Chris Bessler)

Best Western Edgewater Resort and down the gravel road and rock jetty that leads to a city water building, which is also a great place to fish for bass.

The center of Sandpoint is only two blocks away across the bridge over Sand Creek where there are shops, inns, art galleries, the Panida Theater, Cedar Street Bridge and many fine restaurants.

Sandpoint City Beach historically was a traditional Kalispel Indian village called *Qp Qepe*, then a site for saloons and tar paper shacks in the 1890s, and later a railway center – called the "Railroad Funnel" because of the three main lines established here. Today the shoreline north of City Beach and the Windbag Marina is home to a multimillion-dollar condominium resort called The Seasons at Sandpoint.

City Beach is also the site of the Pend Oreille Arts Council's annual summertime activity, the Arts & Crafts Fair held in mid-August, a two-day event free to the public that showcases more than 100 booths of original, handmade artwork from artisans across the West. There are also kids' arts activities, entertainment, artist demonstrations and food booths.

Also at City Beach is a miniature replica of the Statue of Liberty at the end of a concrete pier; a Peace Pillar with greetings in several languages on the north side of the park; and on the north beach, "Barbara's Bench," dedicated in 2009 to the late Barbara Veraniam, who was a local social activist.

FACILITIES: concrete boat ramp, docks including the city-owned Windbag Marina, public parking, paved walkways (wheelchair accessible), sandy beaches, roped swimming area with lifeguards (summer only), picnic tables, group shelter, barbecue grills, restrooms, park benches, large grassy lawn, children's playground, volleyball, tennis and basketball courts, horseshoe pits and a seasonal concession stand
ACTIVITIES: boating, sailing, paddling, swimming, picnicking, volleyball, basketball, tennis, horseshoes, family and group creative fun (use your imagination!)

How to get here:

Turn right off First Avenue (a one-way street going north) onto Bridge Street, then cross over Sand Creek and go under the railroad bridge until you reach the spacious, looped public parking area. If traveling south through downtown Sandpoint, you'll have to go as far south as Pine Street (a one-way street going east) and circle around to First Avenue and head north again until the next right on Bridge Street. Getting here by bike or foot is easier.

- - - - - - - - - - - - - - - - - - - -

History of the Lake Pend Oreille Yacht Club
Although now headquartered in Bayview (see Area 1, chapter 4), the Lake Pend Oreille Yacht Club originated in Sandpoint in the mid-1970s. One of the club's founders was Gary Pietsch, a former newspaperman and printshop owner born and raised here.

"We wanted to have sailboat races and there seemed to be an interest, and a lot of people didn't know how to sail," Gary says. "The best way to generate enthusiasm for sailing was to have a club." Gary eventually became commodore, assuming duties similar to an organizational president. Races were held nearly every weekend in the summer and after work on Wednesdays. In the beginning, prizes included "bragging rights" only, with race ribbons, glassware, trophies and cups awarded as the club's membership grew. There were close to 100 members in those days including sailors from Sandpoint, Hope, Glengary Bay and Bayview. The really exciting races were the ones from Sandpoint all the way down to Bayview.

Even though Gary traded his sailboat for a tugboat in 1987, he still enjoys sailing on other people's boats.

"Sailing Lake Pend Oreille is something you never forget," Gary says. He recalls one voyage from Sandpoint to Bayview that took only four hours, at six or seven knots – a really fast trip. He laughs heartily remembering another one of those "white knuckle times," sailing a big wind with both his son and daughter on deck, the boat heeling over at least 20 degrees. His late wife, Carol, was below deck and saw only water out the cabin window. She yelled up to ask if they knew what they were doing. Gary quipped: "Hell no, but we're sure having fun!"

Bayview to City Beach Swim

Sandpoint is home to the Long Bridge Swim (see page 111) where hundreds of people take to the water every August and swim almost two miles to Dog Beach. But imagine swimming the length of Lake Pend Oreille from Bayview north to Sandpoint. During summer 2007, 11 buff swimmers, ranging in age from 13 to 59 years and selected by Eric Ridgway, the Long Bridge Swim founder, did exactly that. It took them only 17 hours as they swam in a relay arrangement with each swimmer doing three rounds in the water.

Beginning at Buttonhook Bay in the afternoon, the swimmers made it to City Beach just in time to see the sunrise over the Cabinets. The night portion of the swim was reported to be the most memorable hours in the water with some of them feeling like they "were swimming into nothing." A glow stick affixed to the goggles of each swimmer following a lead kayak, also aglow, was the only light along the 36-mile course.

But perhaps the person most exhausted from this historic swim was Sandpoint businessman, Ernie Belwood. He captained his houseboat, which was the expedition's base of operation. By the time the swimmers reached City Beach, Belwood had been awake for 28 hours straight.

In subsequent years, this core group of swimming aficionados undertook more historic, unprecedented swims. In July 2008, the "Crazy Lake Swimmers" departed from Kramer's Marina in Hope, swam across the mouth of the Clark Fork River, then south along the east shoreline of Lake Pend Oreille into the southern-most point at Buttonhook Bay. After jumping off the rope swing there, they headed back north along the western shoreline of the lake to City Beach and back to Hope, completing an 84-mile circumnavigation over two days and two nights of continuous swimming.

The following year in August, their attempt to swim from City Beach to Buttonhook Bay and back, a swim of about 68 miles, was blown apart by excessive winds that threatened the accompanying houseboat. They changed course after swimming about 10 miles, and instead headed west down the Pend Oreille River almost all the way to Laclede. This contingency-plan swim encompassed about 44 miles. This same group of swimmers plan to continue to splash around different courses in these exceptionally clean lake waters with the majestic mountains surrounding them wherever they go.

Fish Tales: Bluebacks for Breakfast, Lunch and Dinner

Sandi (Haugse) Belote couldn't eat fish for a very long time after working for her parents at Sandpoint's former Pastime Café. Leonard and Helen Haugse owned what was the most popular downtown restaurant at the time. It was the early 1960s, and Sandi was in high school. Those years also marked the peak of commercial fishing in Lake Pend Oreille for kokanee salmon, or bluebacks as the locals call them.

The Haugses lived at Talache and had contracted with a fisherman there to catch enough fish to serve in his Sandpoint café all year-round. The man took the challenge to heart and filled his small boat with hundreds of bluebacks that he caught seasonally fishing near the shore between Maiden Rock and Garfield Bay.

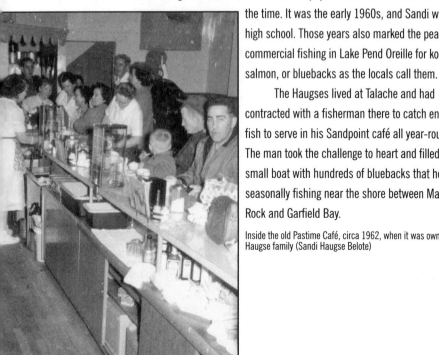

Inside the old Pastime Café, circa 1962, when it was owned by the Haugse family (Sandi Haugse Belote)

Sandi recalls helping her mom clean countless buckets of those fish, literally hundreds of kokanee a day, which her dad would then freeze in the giant lockers of the restaurant until needed. The Pastime offered bluebacks on the daily menu – breakfast, lunch and suppertime – a popular meal for tourists and locals. Sandi soon tired of eating the tasty fish, or any fish for that matter.

"I didn't like the bluebacks much," she now recalls, but it wasn't just the hours of tedious work. The silvery salmon also got in the way of Sandi's social life during high school. Her close friend, Ginger Evans, whose dad smoked tons of kokanee for shipping by rail to cities east and west of Sandpoint, also had chores in preparing the fish for smoking. The two young women had to have all the fish processed before they could go to a school dance or a movie at the Panida Theater. The Evans Smoke House still can be found at the southwest corner of Lakeshore Drive and U.S. Highway 95 near the Long Bridge – a reminder of the once-abundant fishery that existed here.

Points of Sail
By Cate Huisman

Wind and Sailors:

Sandpoint is home to the companionable bunch of the Sandpoint Sailing Association (www.sandpointsailing.com), with headquarters at the city-owned Windbag Marina (south of the breakwater, with the orange windsock). This group races on most Thursday nights and Saturday mornings in summer and always welcomes newcomers. The Windbag Marina is the only place on the lake besides Bayview where a sailor might find replacement gear – a modest collection of lines and hardware is for sale in a small shack on the dock.

Although local sailors in Sandpoint are enthusiastic and friendly, the waters off Sandpoint City Beach are fickle, especially in summer. Both the wind's direction and its velocity can change rapidly. In general, waters closer to Sandpoint and the shore are calmer, and there is more wind and more chop as you sail north and west toward Kootenai Point. Across the lake, as you pass Contest Point, the wind can drop

The Windbag Marina at City Beach, home of Sandpoint Sailing Association

off rapidly as you come in the lee of the south shore (see Area 2), so the northern shore is favored by sailors. There tends to be more wind in the spring and fall, so get your boat in the water as early in spring as you can, and keep it in until the lake drops out from under you in the fall.

Anchorages:

A small boat could anchor behind the breakwater at Windbag or in the mouth of Sand Creek and be well protected, but the water is shallow in both places, and lots of motorboat traffic goes up the creek. Boats also can anchor north of the jetty, as long as they are inshore from where the jetty doglegs and out of the fairway for the Seasons at Sandpoint marina. Moorage for sailboats is not available at Sandpoint Marina, farther up Sand Creek, as it is inaccessible to sailboats due to a low bridge. Note also that gas is not available to sailboats in Sandpoint because the gas dock is at Sandpoint Marina, although gas stations and the Sandpoint Marina are within walking distance for a sailor with a gas can.

Launching and Hauling:

The approach to Sandpoint's two very good launch ramps is in the shallow, weedy mouth of Sand Creek. Don't be fooled by the depth you observe at the ramps; the approach through the creek can be much shallower, and it is imperative to post a bow watch to get around the bar off City Beach and into the creek. In the fall, when the water level is dropping rapidly, you can launch from City Beach one day and then find it's too shallow to return there a few days later.

 SAND CREEK

This tributary flows into Lake Pend Oreille at the south end of Sandpoint City Beach. Traveling upstream by paddlecraft from City Beach takes you beneath the Cedar Street Bridge and north. Often there is ice skating here in winter.

FACILITIES: public docks at Sandpoint City Beach
ACTIVITIES: kayaking, canoeing, fishing from shore and bridges

How to get here:

The mouth of Sand Creek is at Sandpoint City Beach; public access is at the docks or boat launch. The boardwalk along the west side of Sand Creek is accessible by foot from a path leading down from Bridge Street, and boats can tie up along the boardwalk while they dine or shop downtown.

Sandpoint Wooden Boat Festival

If you like the aesthetics of an old wooden Chris-Craft, then this is your event. Held in early July after Independence Day at The Old Power House, Sandpoint Boardwalk and Sandpoint Marina along Sand Creek, the festival allows you to see some of the most beautiful classic wooden powerboats in the Inland Northwest. The weekend event also offers family activities, beach barbecue, treasure hunts and more. A popular favorite with the public when it comes to judging the boats is one award-winning boat named *Aphrodite*. Now, there's a beauty!

Wooden Boat Festival (Chris Bessler)

Lore Along the Shore: Kalispel History

Even during aboriginal times, Sandpoint had sandy beaches. Today's City Beach and Sand Creek were culturally important to American Indians as a late spring camp and summer village site of the Upper Kalispel. Called, *Qp Qepe*, the name translates from the Salish language as the "place of sand." The creek was fished for food by the villagers and, after David Thompson's arrival in 1809, native peoples trapped beaver here for trade.

As recently as the 1940s, the Upper and Lower Kalispel bands, now living on Indian reservations in Montana and Washington states, were joined by the Bonners Ferry Kootenai people to camp at traditional Kalispel sites in

Mrs. Yellow Eagle (Mary Masseslow), right, and her daughter with beadwork items at their feet. Kalispel tribal members sold beaded moccasins, bags and other items to tourists (Northwest Museum of Arts & Culture/Eastern Washington State Historical Society, Spokane, Washington. Digitally restored, for authorized publication, per financial support of the Kalispel Tribe of Indians)

Sandpoint. There are non-Indians here in Sandpoint who still remember the native people playing their traditional gambling game called the stick game. The unique style of drumming and singing of ancient songs heard so long ago on the sandy shores of Sandpoint still resonate today within the walls of the tribe's tule house in Usk, Washington. Even though Kalispel tribal members don't frequent this area much today, it remains an important part of their heritage.

DOG BEACH

Found on railroad and Idaho Transportation Department right-of-way as well as private land, this is a day-use, no-fee area.

What's it like?

Despite being sandwiched between U.S. Highway 95 and the railroad trestle, this site with good shade trees offers respite from the hot summer sun and a sandy beach. Dog Beach gets its name from the fact that this is a public beach that people can legally bring their unleashed dogs for play and a swim. Despite all the canine visitors, the area is surprisingly clean. The Sagle-to-Sandpoint Community Trail passes by the beach: to the north downtown Sandpoint is just a short distance; to the south the paved trail parallels the vehicular, two-mile span of the Long Bridge crossing Lake Pend Oreille.

FACILITIES: sandy beach, park benches, walking/ biking/rollerblading paved trail
ACTIVITIES: swimming (for people and dogs), picnicking, walking, biking
How to get here:

A gravel parking area on the north end of the Long Bridge in Sandpoint provides access to the paved community trail. Follow the trail several hundred yards south to the beach. A major highway reconstruction project is under way, which affects the northern end of the Long Bridge into town. Construction is expected to last until 2012. Access to Dog Beach will be maintained; however, keep in mind you'll be going through a construction area, so please use caution as you and your four-legged, best friend go to the beach.

Anecdota: Long Bridge Swim

A long-distance, open-water swim is something that Shawna Parry had never done before, let alone one that was nearly two miles long. A lover of freshwater, she decided to do the Long Bridge Swim. Shawna and her husband, Laird, relocated to the Sandpoint area from Seattle. Shawna says the 2006 swim was a way for her to experience "the spirit of community" in their new home in a unique and exciting way. She did a little training in the Sandpoint Athletic Club pool and in the lake at City Beach and Sunnyside, and she procured a used wetsuit to wear. When the hot August Saturday morning arrived, she was ready.

Long Bridge Swim spectators and participants at the starting point, south end of the Long Bridge (Rebecca Holland)

At the south end of the Long Bridge, Shawna and hundreds of other swimmers – girls and boys, women and men, mothers and daughters, fathers and sons, ranging in age from 8 to 84 – donned bathing caps with their swim numbers painted on. Swimmers came from as far away as the East Coast, but most swimmers were from Idaho, Washington and other Western states. The swimmers stood in the water or just onshore waiting for the customary loud blast of the bullhorn that marks the beginning of one of the longest freshwater, free-style swims in the Northwest. The Long Bridge Swim is largely a noncompetitive swim with many participants hoping just to make it to the other side of the lake, as safely and quickly as they can. Other swimmers have different, more competitive aspirations.

A Sand Creek Surprise

This is a true Sand Creek story I'd like you to know,
It all really happened just six days ago.

Two curious boys down at the rope swing,
Wondering what the last day of summer vacation would bring.

One boy saw what looked like a tooth,
The other boy said, "Let's pry it loose."

A girl in the water yelled, "I found a shovel!"
The boys both hollered, "Pass it up on the double!"

They scratched and they dug using much vigor,
As the group of onlookers grew, the object got bigger.

They pulled and they pushed without any luck,
'Til one of the boys got a rope from Dad's truck.

They hooked it to the rope and gave it a tug,
But as hard as they pulled the thing wouldn't budge.

So some of the onlookers came to their aid,
They all heaved and hoed then out came the blade.

They gazed at their find with really wide eyes,
Amazed by its age and its enormous size.

This story is true and it just goes to prove,
That Sand Creek is something we don't want to lose.

It's a wonderful place to come down to play,
And it's still unveiling its treasures today.

–John Breckenridge Jr.
Sandpoint, Idaho

(One of the curious boys who unearthed a giant, circular saw blade from
early 20th century logging days)

The first mile was the hardest, Shawna admits. She did the crawl, breaststroke and backstroke to keep going. Unzipping her wet suit top allowed her more breathing capacity. She made sure to wave assurances that she was fine in the water to her husband and friends walking the Long Bridge as spectators. Even though the one-mile marker seemed so far away, Shawna says, "I never had the feeling I couldn't make it." There was always a community volunteer in a safety canoe or kayak close by if she needed help or an allowable brief rest.

Once past the halfway point, Shawna says the rest of the swim was easy to the end. Striding out of the water at Dog Beach, she gave a knowing smile to the woman next to her in her late 60s. Shawna finished faster than half of the people swimming that day. Only five swimmers, ages 8 to 13, did not complete the course. It took Shawna, then 58, one hour and 16 minutes to do the swim. The fastest swimmer that year was a 49-year-old man from Montana who crossed the lake in just under 35 minutes. Wow!

Will Shawna Parry attempt to do the Long Bridge Swim again? "But of course," she says without hesitation, and she has every year since.

Comeback Bay

This part of the lake between the south end of the Long Bridge and the railroad trestle is a broad expanse of water called Comeback Bay. Fry Creek is the tributary that winds inland, which also is known as Sagle Slough where it widens and has private docks. This is a good wildlife viewing area for waterfowl. Besides ducks and Canada geese, an occasional common loon or grebe can be seen. The land on either side is private property, but it's possible for canoeists and kayakers to enter Fry Creek from Comeback Bay and paddle as far south as is possible until the creek becomes too narrow and shallow. Fishing off the bridge along Bottle Bay Road where it crosses the creek/slough is also popular, but safe parking along the roadside is sparse.

Aerial view of Comeback Bay (Jerry Luther)

Lore Along the Shore: Railroading at the Lake's Outlet

Though still a large body of water, Lake Pend Oreille begins to take on a riverine look to the west of where the railroad bridge spans the lake. This is the narrowest part of the lake, being less than a mile wide and less than 30 to 40 feet deep. The original Northern Pacific crossing was a wooden trestle replaced by a new structure in 1904 (its replacement began in 2008). In the middle of the span, a feature was designed to pivot to allow large boats through, but it has not been used since the 1940s. A railroad ghost town, Ventner (aka Venton or Ventor), had a post office and was located on Fry Creek.

Northern Pacific Railroad bridge over Lake Pend Oreille with steam engine pulling a passenger train
(Bonner County Historical Society)

PUBLIC ACCESS ▶ BOTTLE BAY

There are only private beachfront homes and residential lots along the lakeshore northeast from Sandpoint, but there is one privately owned facility whose amenities are available to the public — Bottle Bay Resort and Marina.

What's it like?

Bottle Bay is a long, bottle-shaped bay that still has many of the lake cabins that were built back in the days of commercial whitefish and kokanee fishing. On the west lip of the bay is Sourdough Point, a private residential area that used to be a winter settlement of fishermen who toughed out the harsh, cold months surviving on sourdough bread and smoked fish. The Bottle Bay Resort and Marina, built by then-commercial fish-processor Bill Zinter, still offers several amenities to the public for year-round enjoyment. Many boaters come from Sandpoint, moor up long enough to enjoy a rainbow trout dinner or glass of wine at the resort's fine restaurant and lounge, and then cruise back to town. Some folks spend the night, a close-to-home getaway.

FACILITIES: boat launch for resort patrons, overnight (for fee) moorage, sandy beach, docks, full-service restaurant and lounge, vacation cabin rentals, kayak and canoe rentals, boat fuel

ACTIVITIES: lodging, boating, sailing, fishing, paddling, swimming, scuba diving

How to get here:

About a mile south of Sandpoint's Long Bridge, turn east at Bottle Bay Road and follow for 11 miles. Look for resort signs on paved road, turn left and down steep hill to water's edge. The resort is also accessible by boat.

Points of Sail
By Cate Huisman

Wind and Sailors:

As you sail east from Sandpoint along the south shore, Gold Hill splits the wind from the south, and it can be quite strong coming out of Bottle Bay, especially toward the mouth of the bay. There is often little wind between Contest Point and Anderson Point. If you go beyond Bottle Bay and around the corner past Anderson Point, this southerly can kick up a big chop if it's been blowing awhile. Northerlies coming down the Purcell Trench are less common but can come at any time of year, and also can be quite strong.

Anchorages:

Anchorage in Bottle Bay is best far up in the bay, where you are most protected from the winds that cross the peninsula, although halfway in is usually sufficient and may be as far as a deeper-draft boat can go. From Bottle Bay to Anderson Point, there are no protected anchorages nor public access. In general, in the northern half of the lake, the bottom is mud and a Danforth anchor will hold. For more on sailing past Anderson Point and beyond to Garfield Bay, see Area 2, chapter 5.

Launching and Hauling:

There is a ramp at Bottle Bay if you pay a launch fee. It becomes increasingly difficult to use (and ultimately unusable) as the water drops in the fall.

— — — — — — — — — — — — — — — — —

Tour on Wheels:
Bottle Bay Loop

You can do it by car for sure, but if you are a cyclist, this is the quintessential paved ride in the Sandpoint area. It offers a fine road tour over asphalt with numerous options along the way for swimming, picnicking and sightseeing through open stretches of northern Idaho farmland. More than 26 miles in length with some hilly sections, this ride is an adventure in its own right. Do not underestimate the length, potentially dangerous potholes and oncoming traffic, especially around hairpin and other curves. In high summer, pack plenty of water and get an early start.

Begin in Sandpoint by crossing the Long Bridge on the community bike path. At 2.5 miles you'll notice the Bottle Bay Road turnoff to the left. This is where you end the loop on the return journey. Instead, proceed another 2.3 miles parallel to U.S. Highway 95 and turn left on Sagle Road. Follow it past the elementary school, through open pastures, hairpin turns and a few thrilling hill climbs. If the climbs and descents don't take your breath away, then the scenery surely will. Pass Talache Road and, several miles later, the Garfield Bay Road "Triangle Junction" on your right and stay on Sagle Road until you reach Bottle Bay Road (at 13.8 miles) and then make a hard left turn. Lake Pend Oreille will eventually come into view on your right through the trees. At 19 miles is the Gold Hill Trailhead (public vault toilet but no water). After that, watch out for sports cars and SUVs on the winding, curvy Bottle Bay Road. At 24 miles, you pop back out onto Highway 95, turn right and return to Sandpoint on the bike trail and over the Long Bridge. What an adventure!

Length: 26.5 miles (as a loop from Sandpoint)

Difficulty: moderate to difficult (due to length of the ride and a few hilly sections)

Safety Concerns: potholes, narrow roadways with thin shoulders, several blind curves, cars and other cyclists

Road Type: paved/asphalt

Road Conditions: good (be aware of seasonal changes in the asphalt)

Attractions: Bottle Bay (sportsman access on the north side of the road roughly four miles past the Bottle Bay Road – Sagle Road junction)

Facilities En Route: The unincorporated community of Sagle provides numerous provisions. Beyond that, the only public restroom is at the Gold Hill trailhead.

THIRD AVENUE PIER

Managed by the City of Sandpoint, this is a day-use, no-fee area. Hours are from 9 a.m. until 9 p.m.

What's it like?

This out-of-the-way spot is a great neighborhood place to take a dip on a hot summer day or for anglers to drop a line in the water. At night it is so very pleasant to sit on the dock alone or with a friend and gaze at the moon. It is a very small park nestled in one of Sandpoint's main residential sections and is worth seeking out since it is only a few blocks from downtown's bustling main street — First Avenue.

FACILITIES: dock, picnic table, benches, small sandy beach

ACTIVITIES: swimming, picnicking, fishing

How to get here:

From Pine Street in Sandpoint, turn south on Third Avenue until you get to the lake. Parking is limited since it is along residential streets. Walking here or biking is easy from downtown, so you might consider leaving your car there and enjoy a stroll or ride.

Lore Along the Shore: Seneacquoteen

The earliest ford across the Pend Oreille River, used by indigenous peoples, was at Seneacquoteen, (*Sin yaq' tn* in the Salish language), 15 miles downstream from the present-day Long Bridge. With white settlement Seneacquoteen became a town and ferry crossing. Then in 1910 the first "Long Bridge" was built across the lake from Sand Creek to Sagle Slough supported by more than 1,500 cedar pilings. That bridge was replaced in 1934 with another wooden structure; at the time both were called the longest wooden bridges in the world. A concrete bridge was built in 1956 and later converted into a community trail when another two lanes were built for vehicular traffic in 1981.

Lore Along the Shore: The Long Bridge

By Marianne Love

In the summer of 2006, Sandpoint contractor Skip Pucci honored the 50th anniversary of Sandpoint's third Long Bridge with a little sprucing up – replanting trees and putting in new flowers in the planters. After all, he's held a personal interest in the span since before it opened.

On Friday, June 22, 1956, Pucci and some friends took off on their bikes toward Superior Street and crossed the lake on the old wooden span that was soon to be replaced, bound for Gold Hill. Leaving their bikes at Dan Deshon's gravel pit, the boys climbed halfway up the mountain and found a perch where they could watch the first cars roll across Sandpoint's new bridge.

Meanwhile community dignitaries and bridge contractors met for lunch at Ponderay's Fairview Club. Later, at 2:30 p.m. on that sunny summer day, Miss Sandpoint Carol Barlow, with princesses Joanne Pennington (Kelly) and Shirley Hendrickson (Parker), snipped the ribbon, opening the way for Sandpoint Chamber of Commerce President James Brady to lead a caravan across the new structure that had cost nearly $2 million. That same week, the oft-heard "click-clack" from vehicles crossing the world's longest wooden bridge – the second Long Bridge that exited Sandpoint from First Avenue since its dedication by Governor C. Ben Ross in 1934 – went silent. That 2-mile-long structure was closed and later demolished by a Spokane firm. The first wooden bridge across Lake Pend Oreille had been completed in 1909. The "Wagon Bridge" cost about $50,000 and was also heralded as the longest wooden bridge in the world.

Long Bridge No. 3 departed dramatically from its two predecessors. Designed by Al J. Sachse, an engineer with the Idaho State Highway Department,

The third and fourth Long Bridge as seen from the air during the Long Bridge Swim on August 1, 2009 (Jerry Luther)

the project featured 6,445 feet of hydraulically dredged fill on its northern approach to Sandpoint's Superior Street. Riprap material came via dump trucks from a quarry west of Great Northern Road.

"I'd take them (the drivers) water and lemonade, and they'd give me a ride," Pucci said. "I'd make the rotation to and from the quarry with them."

According to a state report published in 1956, the foundation for the 5,879-foot-long bridge included 1,132 composite timber/concrete-filled pilings from 54 feet to 128 feet long. They were driven to penetrations as far as 100 feet below the ground. Pre-cast 80,000-pound concrete spans, transported by barge from City Beach, were lifted by a crane from pontoons. Pucci's father Geino worked on the forms and panels for the spans and later helped with the bridge guardrails.

The bridge served motorized traffic for 25 years. It began to deteriorate from unexpected, increased weight loads of larger, heavier vehicles. The fourth bridge, the one presently used for motor traffic, opened on September 23, 1981, at a cost of $11.4 million. After it opened, the third bridge was turned into a pedestrian path and was dedicated September 26, 1981, just below Pucci's present office in The Old Power House.

His interest in bridge No. 3 continues to this day; he has maintained the cement planters since the 1980s.

Miss Sandpoint Carol Barlow addresses the crowd during the dedication of the third Long Bridge, at its dedication on June 22, 1956. It was rededicated as a pedestrian bridge in 1981 (Bonner County Historical Society)

The Festival at Sandpoint at Memorial Field, an annual event in August (Jerry Luther)

WAR MEMORIAL FIELD AND LAKEVIEW PARK

Bonner County manages the boat launch and docks, and the adjacent park is maintained by the City of Sandpoint. Both are day-use only, with no fees. But the field is also home to nighttime athletic activities – baseball and football – for Sandpoint High School's "Bulldogs" and also to the evening concerts produced by the Festival at Sandpoint every August.

What's it like?

This is one of Sandpoint's most popular public areas. The ample parking lot to the east of the ball field is typically crowded with cars and boat trailers all summer long. The boat launch that extends from there is paved and there are two docks for boats. Kayakers and canoeists sometimes put in here and paddle downstream to Dover, but this is a busy powerboat area, so be aware. There's a gravel bike and walking path along the riverbank that takes you to Lakeview Park and the arboretum. A covered picnic area near the boat launch has two tables. A recent upgrading to the boat launch area in 2008 includes placement of benches along the bank.

But the most meaningful upgrade to the Memorial Field boat launch deserves special recognition. It is a project that was spearheaded by the late Gary Parker that brought together several government agencies and conservation groups. Gary's vision was to protect Lake Pend Oreille's water quality in a two-fold way. First, runoff from the concrete boat ramp and adjacent parking lot was diverted into a series of adjacent swales inoculated with a fungus that organically digests water pollutants such as oil and gasoline, rendering them harmless. Second, more than

650 riparian plants and shrubs, many of them native to our area, were planted along 500 feet of riverbank to demonstrate the importance of a vegetative buffer from the water – a great ecological improvement over a grass lawn that usually requires chemical fertilizers and herbicides to keep it green. Gary's contribution to our lake will be a model of sustainable resource management throughout the region for many generations to come.

To the west of the ball field bleachers is Lakeview Park, the Native Plant Arboretum and Bonner County Historical Museum. There are tennis courts and several picnic tables, a playground, a covered group shelter and a large grassy area beneath towering ponderosa pines to enjoy several family activities. Consider a game of catch, frisbee or tag – fun! Paths through the park are paved, making it easy for moms with strollers or for kids on bikes. The Bonner County Historical Museum is located on the park grounds – just look for the train caboose and large waterwheel out in front of the building. The Kinnikinnick Chapter of the Idaho Native Plant Society manages the arboretum surrounding the museum, which is a good place to learn about the native flora of the countryside surrounding Lake Pend Oreille. There are also several pairs of nesting osprey in this area, and it is thrilling to watch an adult bird spear a large fish with its talons and bring it back to the nest to feed the fledglings.

FACILITIES: concrete boat ramp, two docks, covered picnic tables, benches, gravel and paved paths, tennis courts, basketball court, playground, group shelter, restrooms, arboretum, museum and gift shop
ACTIVITIES: boating, picnicking, fishing, biking, walking, historical tours, wildlife viewing, learning about native flora and trees

How to get here:
The parking areas, boat launch area, and park and museum is accessed from town via Boyer Avenue (runs north and south) or Ontario Street (runs east and west), both accessible from U.S. Highway 2 in Sandpoint. There is ample parking for cars including those with boat trailers to the east of Memorial Field. Another parking lot is located on the west end of the park at the museum and arboretum grounds. It is accessed from Ella Avenue off of Ontario Street. Additional parking is along residential streets.

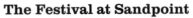

The Festival at Sandpoint

One of the outstanding events of summer on Lake Pend Oreille takes place annually at Memorial Field during the first two weeks of August. The Festival at Sandpoint is an extraordinary celebration of music that attracts thousands of visitors and has done so since 1982. It is truly a community event as hundreds of local residents volunteer their time and energy to make the festival happen.

The Spokane Symphony Orchestra performs every year at the Festival at Sandpoint (Duane Davis)

Nothing is quite like listening to the Spokane Symphony Orchestra perform a Beethoven symphony or Mozart piano concerto while lying on a blanket under the stars, sipping a glass of wine and enjoying some exquisite supper purchased from one of Festival Street's restaurant booths, all while watching a full moon rise over Gold Mountain and the lake. Or maybe you'd rather rock in the bleachers with a slice of pizza in one hand and a cold beer in the other as Lyle Lovett and his band wakes up the entire neighborhood. The variety of musical stars in concert will keep you coming back night after night, year after year. A Family Concert is held on a Sunday afternoon that includes music by the Spokane Youth Symphony, lots of creative activities, jugglers, clowns and a musical instrument "petting zoo" for the kids to enjoy.

Surprisingly, wildlife viewing is another highlight of the festival since at least three pairs of

122   Legendary Lake Pend Oreille

breeding ospreys have their nests at the tops of field lights. Sometimes ospreys' cries synchronizes perfectly with the live music and other times it seems to punctuate an awesome performance.

━ ━ ━ ━ ━ ━ ━ ━ ━ ━ ━ ━ ━ ━ ━ ━ ━

Bonner County Historical Museum and Native Plant Arboretum

While at Lakeview Park you'll want to spend some of your time indoors at the Bonner County Historical Museum. For a small admission fee you can learn about the history of the region while touring the exhibits on Glacial Lake Missoula, the Kalispel Tribe of Indians, explorer David Thompson, the railroad and steamboat eras, and early pioneer settlement. The museum also has on exhibition in a shoreline diorama an authentic reproduction of the unique sturgeon-nose Kalispel canoe (see story on page 192). In addition to its

exhibits, the museum houses an extensive research archive of historic materials, including photographs, and a gift shop where books on the human and natural history of the area are featured as well as books by local authors.

Adjacent to the museum is the Kinnikinnick Chapter of the Idaho Native Plant Society's Native Plant Arboretum that features native plants, shrubs and trees from several different habitats of the Lake Pend Oreille region. Maintained by volunteers, the arboretum is open year-round and is free to the visiting public. It is a good place to first identify many of the wildflowers and shrubs that are detailed elsewhere in this book under the heading of "Wildflower Notes."

Native Plant Arboretum at Lakeview Park (Sean Haynes)

Anecdota: Back to the Future

One of Pat Moon's earliest boating memories helped shape his philosophy on life. His family owned a 10-foot aluminum boat with a 3-horsepower outboard motor and Pat, at age 8, was allowed to take the boat out alone and freely go anywhere from their dock at Rocky Point in Dover, as long as he remained in sight of his parents. This remarkable freedom came with an expectation of taking responsibility for one's actions, and it engendered self-respect as well as a respect for the life in and around the lake. With such liberties, Pat came to know and deeply love Lake Pend Oreille, the surrounding countryside and its people.

What an adventurous environment in which to grow up! Pat would pick up his friend Kevin Cogswell on a nearby dock and they would go from Rocky Point across to Springy Point and back to what Pat calls the "Dover Bluffs." He says back in the 1960s, Dover was a mill town and some of the kids that lived there were tough characters, so they had to be careful not to get ambushed. With the boat eventually full of young boys, they would go to any number of little beaches and swim and explore. By the time Pat turned 10, his family had a bigger boat with a 10-horsepower motor that expanded his horizons. "I could go anywhere," Pat says, "but if I didn't tie up the boat right when I got back, I was in trouble."

Bud Moon with son Pat Moon, at age 10, with a Kamloops trout near Rocky Point, circa 1968 (Duane Davis)

In those days he and his friends would camp on the shores and have the kind of natural-world experiences that author Patrick McManus writes about in his humorous books. When Pat Moon became a teenager, he ventured farther from home, taking to the river in the family boat for a springtime fishing trip to Morton Slough or to Muskrat Point to hunt ducks and geese.

Besides the Moon's aluminum boat, there was the barge, a rickety raft that had a cabin on top, which his younger brother, Pete, "owned."

It was given to Pete by a neighbor at Rocky Point. The log deck rode barely above the surface, and if there were four or five kids on it, a corner would usually slip underwater. Pat considers this watercraft and the adventures they had on it his Huckleberry Finn stage of life. Their dad, Bud, put the small outboard motor on the raft, and they would go slowly along. The kids would take turns diving off of the deck and swimming alongside. It would take them an hour and a half to go from Rocky Point to pick up a friend across the lake at the end of the Long Bridge. "Then we'd go someplace else and pick up a fourth person and go camp somewhere along the shoreline," says Pat. He says area landowners were neighborly and very tolerant of boys who wanted to play on their lakefront beach. "The world was different then. People respected elders. Everyone knew everyone else, so you didn't get away with anything."

In the winter, the kids built snow forts along the shoreline and would ice skate until their toes got cold or until they would build a bonfire on shore to warm themselves. Pat remembers one particular, exhilarating moonlit night when the ice in the protected bays was as smooth as glass and he skated for hours on end. Once, when he was a little older, he cross-country skied along the shoreline halfway to Laclede.

One of the other highlights of being a boy growing up on the water was the large, new dock with a high-dive springboard that his dad built one summer. During summer vacation all the kids of the neighborhood would come over to swim, dive and play games on the dock all day long. They could also visit rope swings that locals maintained along the shoreline from Springy Point to Laclede. These were great for swinging out over the lake and dropping into the cool water on a hot summer day. "It was a carefree and simple life," Pat says. "I didn't realize until I grew up just how great I had it."

Once Pat got married and moved to Sagle, he would take his family by canoe on Sunday afternoons and paddle from Springy Point to Dover Bluffs. Nowadays, he and his family only go paddling in the spring and fall because of all the boating activity on the lake and river. With all the new lakeshore and riverbank developments, Pat says he feels more like a tourist these days than a native son.

Another rite of passage was, of course, fishing. His dad would motor downriver towards Priest River, and together they would catch 14- to 18-inch rainbows all day long. Today the trout are replaced by lunker smallmouth bass, Pat says; but back then, there weren't many bass around.

Today Pat Moon has nine grandchildren. He acknowledges with a heavy sigh that times have definitely changed. With the restrictive atmosphere of today's private properties and gated lakeshore communities, boys and girls have less freedom to explore this wilderness of water called Lake Pend Oreille. There are far fewer places to discover the inside and outside of one's self, or to develop philosophies on the good life.

Sandpoint

Old lady Weil
came here rough as an Iowa cob,
but the years pushed against her like waves,
wearing her skin smooth as the beach
she hobbles down to town.

And old man Deshon
sits in his sixty-four Ford
counting his four missing fingers,
remembering when he
set chokers with one hand.

So many dreams have drowned
in this lake …
The fish get bigger each year.
And tonight, a young logger
takes old lady Weil's granddaughter
out on the point,
holds her, raising his arm
with four good fingers
toward a fish rising
to swallow the white lure of the moon
knotted to a string
buoyed to the rest of their lives.

—William Studebaker
Idaho's Poetry: A Centennial Anthology, 1988
Permission to reprint granted by Judy Studebaker

"Sometimes I think I know how the Indians must have felt," Pat says. "I've lost (access to) all the hunting spots, picnicking spots, fishing spots we had as kids." Now there are too many houses along the shore and a real loss of the rural character that this area once had.

"The ancient Celts believed that in some places, the veil between heaven and earth was thinner than in other spots. Time should be spent looking for those places and catching glimpses of the beauty and joy of heaven. Sadly, people today want to put their homes in such places," Pat says. He would like to see what's left of paradise be preserved. Many of us who have lived here long enough to appreciate the lake's unique and remarkable values agree with him.

One of the boardwalks on Dover Bay's trails (Courtesy Dover Bay)

PUBLIC ACCESS ▶ DOVER CITY BEACH AND PARK

Managed by the City of Dover, this is a day-use, no-fee area that is adjacent to the new Dover Bay waterfront community and to the west of its marina.

What's it like?

Rocky Point is a rugged spit of land at the eastern edge of this area and Tank Hill is the small, hump-like hill that rises along the shore at Dover Point. Much of the inland area here is wetlands. In 2005, building began on the Dover Bay residential waterfront community that transformed the old mill site, 285 acres and over a mile of shoreline, into a major development with a 274-slip marina, hundreds of homesites, condos, bungalows for vacation rental, common open space, boardwalk, a waterfront village area with a café, market and fitness center, and nine miles of paved trails that connect to the Sandpoint-Dover Community Trail.

The public access area is the Dover City Beach and Park, sandwiched by the resort and located west of the marina at the end of a narrow sandy stretch of land next to Brown's Bay Inlet. The public can moor at the marina for access to the resort's restaurant and shops. Boat gas is available at the Dover Bay Marina dock as are canoe and kayak rentals. The Dover Bay community set aside Verwolf Vista Park at the top of Tank Hill and maintains a public hiking trail leading to it. The Balto Dog Park opened in 2009 and features a boardwalk for diving dogs, fire hydrants and a wash-down area with a solar-heated hose system.

Dover Bay is now the site of the annual Concerts-on-the-Lawn, free concerts held every Sunday in July, sponsored by Pend Oreille Arts Council. The community also puts on Dover Bay Days in July and participates in other special events such as Sandpoint Winter Carnival.

FACILITIES: dock, picnic tables, benches, sandy beach, paved bike trails, restrooms, dog park
ACTIVITIES: boating, swimming, paddling, picnicking, fishing, walking, biking

How to get here:

Dover is three and a half miles west of downtown Sandpoint along U.S. Highway 2. Turn south at the Dover Bay turnoff, go west past the Discovery Center on Railroad Avenue to Dover Bay Way and turn left. Follow to Lakeshore Drive and turn right. Dover City Beach and Park is at the end of this road next to City Hall.

– – – – – – – – – – – – – – – – – –

Lore Along the Shore: Dover's Lumber Legacy

The Dover Lumber Company operated here in the early days and the small town that sprung up eventually assumed that name. World War II and its need for supplies and the subsequent post-war baby boom housing demand renewed the life of the slumbering local timber industry. Jim Brown Jr. moved to Sandpoint from Spokane in 1940. He established Deadhead Logging Co. along Sand Creek and retrieved logs that had absorbed too much water and sank to the bottom, called "sinkies." From there, Brown's lumber empire took off, eventually expanding to 15 mills under a new name, Pack River Lumber Company.

One of the company's mills was at Dover and operated at the same site where today's

Dover Bay continues to unfold. Besides producing lumber, the Dover Mill served as a research facility for Brown, who

Dover Mill in 1963 during Pack River Lumber Co.'s heyday (Bud Moon)

was always looking for production efficiency with logs. In the 1950s, the mill began producing particleboard, which locals called "tenex," by compressing wood shavings under steam-operated pressure and applying a resin coating. One of Brown's daughters, Sandpoint resident Bobbie Huguenin said the process was the first of its kind in the timber industry. The Dover Mill employed hundreds of local people for four decades before closing in the early 1990s.

Brown and his Pack River Lumber Co. diversified and influenced a rapidly growing recreational and tourist industry in the Sandpoint area by helping to found Schweitzer Mountain Resort and, later, acquiring sole ownership of the resort, which it held until 1998.

Wildlife Viewing: Osprey

Along Lake Pend Oreille, the Clark Fork River and the Pend Oreille River high in the treetops or on tall poles decked with man-made platforms, you'll see the large stick nests built by ospreys. As seasonal residents that return to northern Idaho in April from a winter spent in Central or South America,

ospreys (*Pandion haliaetus*) are a raptor that continue to recover from their brush with near-extinction because of our country's former and ubiquitous use of DDT. Breeding adults return to the same nest year after year, repairing it if necessary due to winter damage. Wayne Melquist, an osprey biologist who surveys local nests in Clark Fork and along the Pend Oreille River, and bands chicks for research

Ospreys return to the same nest year after year (Duane Davis)

purposes, says that certain nests he has seen are constructed with amazing detail for comfort. He says some are like five-star hotels in the bird world! Ospreys live in extended families with the offspring building their nests in close proximity to their parents.

Ospreys feed primarily on fish, hence their common name – fish hawks. Along the Pend Oreille River, watch for these fish-eating hawks in action. Due to habitat loss, there are numerous man-made platforms all the way to Albeni Falls, right along Highway 2.

I could write pages about the osprey both because it is a significant wildlife species in the watershed and because it is one of my favorite birds – a powerful symbol of the need to care for our water, wildlife and the rest of our environment. To me, ospreys are messengers, so I pay attention.

There is so much to learn about this bird of prey, that I recommend reading an excellent book that follows the bird's life cycle and its amazing comeback from the brink of extinction. Published by Algonquin Books of Chapel Hill (copyright 2001) and written by naturalist and lyrical writer, David Gessner, *Return of the Osprey: A Season of Flight and Wonder* chronicles nearly every aspect of this raptor. Even though he writes about ospreys at Cape Cod on the East Coast, you can certainly refer to this book as you watch wildlife here. Since ospreys with their nearly 6-foot wingspan, dive fully into the water to catch their prey – unlike eagles that drown if they get submerged – the osprey's forceful and swift dives are something amazing to behold. Gessner's book will give you a more enticing glimpse into this species than I could ever provide here.

PUBLIC ACCESS ▶ **WATERLIFE DISCOVERY CENTER**

A cooperative project of Idaho Fish and Game, the Idaho Fish and Wildlife Foundation and the local community, which includes several sportsmen groups, this habitat education and interpretive area on the southern bank of the Pend Oreille River is a grassroots work-in-progress that began taking shape in the mid-1990s.

What's it like?

This self-guided educational center encompasses the historic Sandpoint Fish Hatchery, built in 1909, which is still used as a summer redistribution facility for rainbow trout. An interpretive center for the site features an indoor classroom and interactive exhibits for teaching about the health of aquatic ecosystems. This educational center aims to connect students and families with the natural world and their roles in it. In addition to the opportunity to learn about the fish and aquatic species of the Pend Oreille River and its tributaries, this area is also an opportunity to learn about other creatures who make their homes here – white-tailed deer, moose, muskrat, mink, river otters, bald eagles, ospreys and many species of waterfowl, woodpeckers and songbirds.

Construction and remodeling of the historic building began in 2003. Currently the property consists of 3.5 acres of developed interpretive exhibits and 6.5 acres of forested wetland with trails, benches and interpretive signs. The riparian trail meanders through wetlands, a cedar grove and mature forest habitat. On the river itself, there is a boat dock for visitors coming by water.

WaterLife Discovery Center (Mark Taylor)

The WaterLife Discovery Center eventually will include overlook bridges, wildlife viewing platforms, underwater fish-viewing windows, and a wetland pond to house native threatened bull trout. There will be information on how to identify the many species of fish and waterfowl in the Pend Oreille region, as well as local plants, and exhibits about insects that tell how bugs are studied as indicators of stream health. One of the local volunteers wants to feature amphibians and reptiles. The center, in its various stages of completion, is a perfect place for teachers to bring students and parents to bring children for an informative tour of natural habitats and processes to help understand how lifestyle choices can affect the world around us. It is also a place to showcase the North American Wildlife Conservation Model, which has shaped the way wildlife is managed and enjoyed on this continent.

FACILITIES: boat dock, boardwalk, benches, interpretive signs, hiking trails, picnic tables, large parking area for RVs and buses

ACTIVITIES: boating, hiking, fish and wildlife viewing

How to get here:

Turn west on Lakeshore Drive at the south end of the Long Bridge from Sandpoint on Highway 95. The WaterLife Discovery Center is 1.5 miles from the highway and is located on the south bank of the Pend Oreille River at the mouth of a small stream.

Wildflower Notes: Trillium and Twinflower

Along the riparian (streamside) wooded trail of the WaterLife Discovery Center in early springtime, look for one of the first-blooming native wildflowers of the area – *Trillium ovatum*, also called wake-robin. A member of the lily family, it can be found along the stream bank and also on the open forest floor. A single-flowered plant, it has three ovate or egg-shaped leaves towards the top of the non-branching main stem, three petals and three sepals almost as long as the petals. As the flower ages, it turns from white to rosy pink. The plant is edible and can be boiled like greens. The root was used by Native Americans to aid in childbirth.

Come early summer, after the trilliums have finished blooming, another wildflower springs up in the shady and wet places along the WaterLife Discovery Center trail. Twinflower (*Linnaea borealis*), is a member of the honeysuckle family. Its delicate beauty was a favorite of Carl Linnaeus, the father of modern botanical taxonomy, for whom it was named. A low-growing evergreen plant that bears a pair of white or pink bell-shaped blossoms on each branch of oval leaves, it flowers from June to July. The fragrant flowers form sticky fruits that hasten seed dispersal.

Trillium, shown at top, and twinflower (Jay Mock)

Wildlife Viewing: Bald Eagles in Black Cottonwood Trees

Back in the 1990s a friend and I lived in a small cabin off Lakeshore Drive adjacent to Murphy Slough. It was an area teeming with wildlife – deer, moose, beaver, muskrat, mink, ducks, heron, raccoon and the occasional bear. Perched high in the huge, native black cottonwood trees were bald eagles lured by spawning fish from the hatchery down the road, and I remember becoming ecstatic the morning of one January day as I counted 19 eagles! Come spring, bald eagles also used the black cottonwoods in which to build their nests, and I learned that it is a valuable tree to cavity nesters like woodpeckers and other species of birds and wildlife that make their home in riparian areas.

Black cottonwoods are usually found growing in wet soils along rivers in the West, and the Pend Oreille River is no exception. A remarkable giant of a tree, the black cottonwood can reach 150 feet high and live well over a century. The wood and bark was used by American Indians to make tools and baskets and it was also used medicinally in several ways. Lewis and Clark documented the tree during their journey of discovery. Unfortunately, because of the tree's ubiquitous cottony fluff that helps disperse its seeds, and because its enormous branches can rot and fall in strong winds, the black cottonwood is sometimes considered a nuisance tree by landowners. Instead of admiring this forest giant, people will cut and remove the tree from their property. Not only does this deprive birds like the bald eagle of a valuable home, but it also subjects stream banks to erosion and instability. While you watch for wildlife in and around the black cottonwoods of this area, please consider that it is far better to be in awe of the tree's special contribution to the life of the forest than as a wood or waste product.

Bald eagles in a black cottonwood in winter (John Chaplin)

▶ **SPRINGY POINT**

Managed by the U.S. Army Corps of Engineers, this is a large, modern campground open between mid-May and early October. There is a fee for overnight camping and campsite use is limited to 14 days. Reservations are recommended, especially for July and August; phone 877-444-6777 or visit www.recreation.gov to reserve your campsite.

What's it like?

A quiet cove protected by a spit of sand, Springy Point provides excellent swimming and

The cove at Springy Point (Chris Bessler)

beachcombing. The river is downhill from Lakeshore Drive, and the mature woods are peppered with dozens of good campsites. The picnic area is down near the ample stretch of beach. People in kayaks and canoes sometimes put in here and paddle across the river to Dover or east and west along the southern riverbank. This spot is often crowded with summer visitors.

FACILITIES: concrete boat ramps, dock, swimming area and sandy beach, picnic area with tables, 40 non-electric and pull-through campsites for RVs up to 32-feet-long, toilets, showers, potable water, large parking area, dump station

ACTIVITIES: camping, boating, paddling, fishing, swimming, picnicking, wildlife viewing, bird-watching

How to get here:

Turn west on Lakeshore Drive at the south end of the Long Bridge from Sandpoint on Highway 95. Follow Lakeshore Drive three miles to the Springy Point Campground.

- - - - - - - - - - - - - - - -

Tour on Wheels:
Dufort Road Loop

This excellent jaunt offers a great loop ride through classic northern Idaho countryside and riverbank with a spicy ride along U.S. Highway 95 on the return until you reach the Sandpoint-Sagle Community Trail.

Turn west onto Lakeshore Drive just after the Long Bridge and continue another 12.5 miles

134   Legendary Lake Pend Oreille

Hayfield under harvest on Dufort Road (Ben Olson)

to the junction of Lakeshore Drive and Dufort Road. Turn left (east) onto Dufort Road and proceed approximately six miles to the junction of Dufort Road and Highway 95. Turn left (north) and follow Highway 95 approximately 5.5 miles back to Sandpoint.

Length: Approximately 31 miles (as a loop from Sandpoint)

Difficulty: moderate, fairly flat

Safety Concerns: narrow shoulders, traffic along Highway 95 (note: no bike path between Sagle and Dufort Road turn-off)

Road Type: paved asphalt but with 3.6 miles of unpaved but rideable road on Lakeshore Drive before reaching Dufort Road.

Road Conditions: good to excellent

Attractions: Springy Point Recreation Area, Round Lake State Park and Morton Slough

Facilities En Route: Public restrooms and potable water can be found at Springy Point and Round Lake State Park; snacks and other provisions can be purchased in the town of Sagle on Highway 95 south of Sandpoint.

Part of the proposed shoreline trail along Pend d'Oreille Bay (Tina Friedman)

 PEND D'OREILLE BAY

A proposed two-mile public waterfront trail is in the planning stages on mostly private property and a little city-owned property.

What's it like?

The original French spelling of the lake's name is used on this bay. A large sweep of private and city-owned, undeveloped shoreline beyond the Seasons at Sandpoint private residential resort parallels the railroad tracks to Ponder Point. The trail skirts the Elks Golf Course on the east side of the railroad tracks and passes through undeveloped private property and land owned by both Sandpoint and Ponderay. From shore, Pend d'Oreille Bay affords one of the most spectacular views from Sandpoint across the lake towards the Cabinet Mountains. To learn more, visit www.pobtrail. org. The bay itself is popular with paddlers and sailors.

How to get here:

There is no developed trailhead, but trail users can park at City Beach and take the bike lane along Sandpoint Avenue in front of the Best Western Edgewater Resort. Go past Seasons at Sandpoint to the end of the road and past the city water plant. Formal permission to use the existing private, waterfront trail is necessary and available on an annual basis by calling (866) 877-3995 or submitting a form under the "Invitation" tab at www.penddoreillebay.com. Please respect the privilege of using it by leaving it better than you found it.

Good Neighbor Trail

Pend d'Oreille Bay Trail, a pedestrian waterfront trail, is a little bit of heaven along Lake Pend Oreille between downtown Sandpoint and the city of Ponderay. It's hard to believe, but not that many years ago it was a tangle of vegetation and junk known as "Bum Jungle." I never went down there but could easily imagine the makeshift camps of transients waiting to hop the next train.

Ross and Hazel Hall in Sandpoint, 1977

In the early 1990s, one of the landowners, the Ross Hall family, hired Leo Addison to help them clear their part of the trail of trash and tree limbs. Today from the Sandpoint water treatment plant to the end of the Hall family property – nearly 1.5 miles – the public can walk, bike or cross-country ski. This splendid bit of urban wildness is a great stress-reliever during your lunch hour or as a long walk after work with your dog. It is "policed" by a whole network of friends and is an example of old-fashioned good neighborliness. How lucky we all are!

One fall day, Wade Jones and his son Cameron came out to help Leo work on the trail. During work breaks, they watched a pileated woodpecker enjoy an insect meal at the base of an old tree on the forested side of the trail. They gazed out across Pend d'Oreille Bay and the lake to see spectacular sunrays shining over the Green Monarch Mountains – the kind of view that once only a few hobos enjoyed. Wade walks the trail an average of 275 days a year and regularly sees waterfowl and other wildlife: swans, geese, bald eagles, moose, deer, beaver and otter. Over the years, he's also picked up hundreds of golf balls.

Although the Halls have been generous in providing formal access through their property, other landowners have offered informal access. Some people tend to think that Black Rock is public access because there is a dock and a picnic bench there. But it's actually private property. Those who do use the trail with permission must mind the signage that identifies areas not open to the public.

However, there is a grander vision for this area, the seeds of which were planted decades ago by the Halls and other landowners. As Sandpoint and Ponderay continue to develop, this undeveloped waterfront between the two towns should be permanently protected.

A committee to begin studying and negotiating at least a pedestrian trail with landowners was formed after the City of Sandpoint acquired 600 feet of waterfront just south of the old Humbird Lumber mill site adjacent to the city water treatment plant. At the time of publication, the demand and support for the Pend d'Oreille Bay Trail is growing, thanks in part to the work of Friends of the Pend d'Oreille Bay Trail (www.pobtrail.org).

With waterfront property values so high, a variety of reasons exist for the stakeholders to want to protect this priceless gem, but I like this rationale best: "Because your soul and my soul need to be refreshed," Ross Hall Jr., the son of the late renowned photographer, says. "We expect to enjoy it in perpetuity, but it'll take some work."

- - - - - - - - - - - - - - - - - -

Lore Along the Shore: Smelting at Black Rock

Two miles north along the shoreline from Sandpoint City Beach is the site where the Panhandle Smelting and Refining Company operated in the early 1900s. The company received ore from several lake locations by steamboat and it was processed in the smelter here. Black Rock, which remains at the water's edge, was the smelting company's slag pile. (The shoreline here has since been stabilized to prevent erosion.) With the increasing productivity of mining around the lake, the company established the town of Panhandle in 1905. It became a supply point for many of the small mining communities around the lake. The name eventually was changed and the village incorporated in 1968 as the city of Ponderay. Ponder Point is a relatively recent name given to the point of land forming the northern edge of Kootenai Bay.

Panhandle Smelting and Refining Company, 1908 postcard (Bonner County Historical Society)

Schweitzer Mountain Resort offers chairlift rides in summer

Tour on Wheels:
Schweitzer Mountain Road

Schweitzer Mountain Road's claim to fame is the distinction of being the region's highest paved road. Its many switchbacks wind up through thick forests and overlook the lake and the town of Sandpoint far below. The road services Schweitzer Mountain Resort and numerous homes and climbs to a breathtaking height of 4,800 feet in elevation, which puts one roughly at eye level with the surrounding peaks, offering views that stretch far into western Montana. From Schweitzer Mountain Village, take the chairlift to the top of the mountain for 360-degree views including into British Columbia, Canada.

This 11-mile road is actually popular with bicyclists – but it's not easy! If biking up from the valley floor, take plenty of water, as there is none until you get to the mountain village. Keep in mind that you are consistently climbing up the mountain with an elevation gain of more than 2,000 feet. It is recommended to park your car at the gravel lot at the railroad tracks at the base of the road. From the gravel lot, cross the railroad tracks and wind through a short residential section before beginning the steady climb up switchbacks all the way to the top.

Length: approximately 22 miles round-trip

Road Type: paved

Road Conditions: excellent to good

Facilities En Route: None until you reach the village

Attractions: Schweitzer Mountain Village at the very top of the road has a number of shops and restaurants that are open year-round. Lodging is also available.

Directions: Travel north of Sandpoint on U.S. Highway 95 and turn west onto the Schweitzer Cut-Off Road and proceed one-half mile to Boyer Road at the "T" intersection. Turn right and follow this road for another mile. Turn left onto Schweitzer Mountain Road and proceed to the top.

Kootenai Bay

From Ponder Point to Kootenai Point, the entire lakeshore is private frontage. However, Boyer Slough is a popular paddle route for canoes and kayaks from Sandpoint City Beach.

– – – – – – – – – – – – – – – – – – –

Paddle Route: Boyer Slough

Going northeast from Sandpoint City Beach by canoe or kayak, and crossing Pend d'Oreille Bay, it is two and a half miles one way to Boyer Slough. The mouth of the slough opens to the north out of Kootenai Bay between Ponder Point and Kootenai Point. As it is the shallowest part of the lake, it is best experienced at full pool. This is a fairly open expanse of water, and it can be rough if there's a strong south or west wind. Launch at Sandpoint City Beach or at the south end of Pend d'Oreille Bay's shoreline and paddle for up to four hours round-trip.

– – – – – – – – – – – – – – – – – – –

Lore Along the Shore: Kootenai Bay

Platted in 1885 just a few years after the Northern Pacific line was finished, the land around Kootenai Bay served as a Northern Pacific railhead. The town was named Kootenai after the railroad established a station there. That name was most likely chosen because it was the southern end of the main trail that went to the Kootenai River. In the early years of the 20th century, Kootenai also became home to one of the nation's largest lumber mills – the Humbird Lumber Company. It was said to be the fastest-growing town in Idaho at the time. Ruins from the mill can be seen along the shoreline.

The area around today's Boyer Slough was a summer village site of the Upper and Lower Kalispel bands of Indians. The Kalispel would camp here and meet and trade with the Kootenai people. In the 1860s, what was originally called Mud Slough became a steamboat landing – Kootenai Landing – as miners moved north to British Columbia and gold strikes in Canada. Two ancient trails of travel crossed at Boyer Slough: the north-south Kootenai Trail from southwestern Washington to the Canadian mines; and the east-west Road to the Buffalo, which largely follows state Highway 200 and connected the Montana plains, where buffalo were plentiful, with the Columbia River country where salmon spawned every year.

140   Legendary Lake Pend Oreille

Humbird Lumber Company and the *Pend d'Oreille*, 1915 (Dick Himes/Ross Hall Collection)

The rocky promontory that separates Kootenai Bay from Oden Bay is called Kootenai Point. The dilapidated remains of a boardwalk can still be seen when the lake is at low pool.

— — — — — — — — — — — — — — — — — —

Points of Sail
By Cate Huisman
Wind and Sailors:

Be careful sailing along the shore north and east of Sandpoint to Kootenai Point. In contrast to the southern end of the lake, this area is quite shallow, and a century ago it was home to numerous piers for canneries, sawmills and steamboats. Look out for old pilings a few feet under the surface, virtually all of which are unmarked and uncharted.

Anchorages:

Along the north shore there is little to duck behind if the wind picks up too much. From a distance it may appear that there are docks at Sunnyside, but as you sail closer you realize there are only derelict, old pilings. Perch Bay, northwest of Sunnyside, can provide some respite; however, watch out for the reef at the entrance, marked with an orange marker. Fisherman Island also provides protection for shallow draft sailboats, although only those with the shallowest draft can actually sail behind it – there is 18 inches of water over the bar between it and the "mainland" at full pool. You can anchor temporarily on one side or the other, depending on the wind direction.

To the east of the Sunnyside peninsula, you can drop the hook about 100 yards past the launch dock at Hawkins Point and 100 yards offshore, where you will be partially protected and a

Danforth anchor will hold in the mud bottom. A boat with a shoal-draft keel can go farther up into Pack River Flats near the railroad trestle; it's very shallow (1 to 4 feet) and the bottom is obscured by weeds, but it's easy to push off the mud if you hit.

Launching and Hauling:

The dock and launch ramp at Hawkins Point are fully exposed to south winds coming up the lake and west winds coming off Sandpoint, so launching and hauling here can be exciting.

Fish Tales: Tollboms – Fishin' Buddies

A sign hangs on the wall of Ward Tollbom's art gallery in downtown Sandpoint that says "Fish Stories Told Here." Boy, was I lucky enough to catch some real whoppers the day I stopped by.

Ward's dad, Stewart Tollbom, came here from Sweden in 1915 and was a good role model for northern Idaho adventuring, especially when it came to fish. Even though I was looking for summertime stories, I just can't resist sharing the one about his dad ice fishing off Contest Point. It was a late winter day and he stayed out too long. The waves became swells and changed conditions so quickly that he had to jump from one melting ice block to another to get back to town. See what I mean?

Thankfully, Ward's boyhood wasn't quite as breathtaking as that. But, boys will be boys, and from about 9 years old through high school, he and his buddies fished any place that was in reach of their bikes as often as possible. They would cast off Contest Point, Sand Creek, the old Cedar Street Bridge, down the end of Main Street and over the railroad tracks to Berry Creek in springtime for brookies and from Chuck Slough for spawning suckers. They also fished from Sandpoint City Dock – the most popular fishing spot in town, located where the jetty next to the Windbag Marina is today. At City Dock the boys would spend all day fishing when the kokanee were running in the spring. Some days they would only catch a few, but other times they would catch 150 or more, and occasionally a nice cutthroat trout.

"Or I could tell you about the time I hooked onto the Pend Oreille Paddler off City Dock when I was fishing for kokanee," tempts Ward, and another fish story begins. "We used to put a piece of corn on a hook and a weight. It would drop to the bottom to draw the fish in. If the kokanee weren't biting, you'd wait for whitefish. Every now and then you'd give it a jerk and see if you had a fish on. And one time I gave it a jerk and it was a solid stop. I jerked and jerked and couldn't get my hook loose from whatever it was snagged on and finally decided I would have to cut my line.

142   Legendary Lake Pend Oreille

I tightened my drag and pulled as hard as I could to break my line and whatever it was started coming up to the surface. I raised it three, four feet off the bottom, slowly and gradually; and all of a sudden there were three big surges as the thing pulled away and my hook came out straight. Whatever I hooked onto nonchalantly swam away undisturbed. Obviously it was very, very big," says Ward who was 15 years old at the time.

Age has mellowed Ward. He no longer swims much at City Beach. "The water is too cold and wet," he claims. Nowadays, he is a watercolor artist and paints fish, as well as birds and other wildlife. With his hallmark incredible detail and beauty, he paints some of the least colorful and least painted fish in Lake Pend Oreille — lake trout, or mackinaw, and bull trout. His original paintings are rarer than hens' teeth, which is the reason he named his art gallery and frame shop, Hen's Tooth Studio.

But Ward still loves to go fishing. Today his favorite fishin' buddy is his grown-up, married daughter, Delci Hoehn. Ward says, "For years she wouldn't be caught dead with me, as a teenager mostly. Now the contrast is so nice and rewarding that it's just a very pleasant thing." They've been fishing together now for several years.

Ward Tollbom and daughter Delci Hoehn (courtesy photo)

As for Delci, she loves the time on the lake angling with her dad. She's always up for it. "I don't feel at home unless I'm by the water," she says. "I have to be around this lake." Since her husband, Josh, is not big on the outdoors, she comes back to Sandpoint at least once a week from Coeur d'Alene where they live, to help her dad at the shop, see her family and, depending on the weather and if the fish are biting, go fishing. As a kid, Ward Tollbom remembers going out with his dad and fishing for cutthroat and rainbow trout in Kootenai Bay. Now he and Delci, with her little dog Bunny, go there and fish for smallmouth bass from Ward's 14-foot aluminum boat. "It's out on the lake and it's gorgeous," says Delci, even when it's wet, cold and windy like the time a storm came up and they had to motor up Boyer Slough and take shelter under a bridge and got totally soaked. ...

Looks like this fish storytelling business has become a family tradition.

As for the changing environment of Lake Pend Oreille, Delci worries about that a lot. "Some people don't even want you fishing in front of their homes and docks. It's sad." She feels the whole ambience of the area is changing and wants to see more areas around the lake protected for public access. As for Ward, "I'd like to see it like it was when I was a kid," he says. "My dad probably felt the same way."

Wildflower Notes: Kinnikinnick

A member of the Heath family, kinnikinnick, or bearberry, (*Arctostaphylos uva-ursi*) is a low, matted plant with smooth, leathery leaves that were a substitute for tobacco for native peoples. They also used the plant medicinally to treat sexually transmitted diseases. The small pink lantern-shaped flowers of late spring mature into bright red berries in summer, and as the Latin name reflects, bears do indeed eat the ripe berries. Look for the plant in open places in the mountains.

Kinnikinnick, or bearberry
(Billie Jean Plaster)

Oden Bay Segment of the Pend Oreille Wildlife Management Area

Before construction of the Albeni Falls Dam, Oden Bay was a natural meadow that attracted wildlife and was a place where the Kalispel Indians would camp. Today the Oden Bay segment of the Pend Oreille Wildlife Management Area contains about 300 acres of protected habitat for thousands of waterfowl that teem across the bay's shallow waters, as well as for shorebirds and other wildlife. A small parking area exists for up to six vehicles where the Sunnyside Road crosses Raymond Slough just before Perch Bay Road on your right. The surrounding undeveloped forestland is popular for wildlife watching or for hiking the trail through open meadows and the woods to the lakeshore. It's possible to haul a car-top kayak or canoe down the bank of the slough in order to paddle out to the lake, but there is really no official launch site here. Paddling from here to the small, unnamed islands south of Perch Bay and to Fisherman Island is delightful. Look for the eagle's nest on Fisherman Island, and watch out for Canada geese flying low over the road to get to the north side of the slough.

Wildflower Notes: Lupine

Dotting the forest and meadow landscape from the lowlands to the mountains beginning in June is a lovely but poisonous, blue-purple flower, the blue-pod lupine (*Lupinus polyphyllus*) – a member of the pea family. The name comes from lupus, which means wolf-like. It is a misnomer because as a legume, this plant doesn't "devour" or deplete the soil, it actually enriches poor soil by fixing nitrogen from the air. The fruit and seeds, however, are toxic to livestock and a bad idea for humans to eat as well, even as survival food, because of its alkaloids. These wildflowers can grow

Lupine, a member of the pea family (Duane Davis)

from 8 inches to more than 3 feet tall and they may vary in color. Their palmate leaves are arranged in whorls, like spokes on a wheel. It grows along roadsides, streams and moist meadows of this area.

FISHERMAN ISLAND

This is a rustic site for day use only managed by Idaho Fish and Game.

What's it like?

Off the western shore of Sunnyside, this small island was once popular with fishermen who went there for bull trout and char. No camping is allowed. Access is by boat only; put in down the road at Sunnyside Access or Hawkins Point and paddle back west and northwest around the peninsula until you see the island. Watch out for the shallows that create two islands at high water. The island is a popular destination for full moon paddles on the lake in summer months (see story on page 153). There are also bald eagle and osprey nests on this and the other small, unnamed islands from here north to Perch Bay, also known as Shaw Bay. Western grebes also are known to build their floating nests in the area, which make them vulnerable to powerboat activity. This general area has been designated an Important Bird Area by Idaho Fish and Game in cooperation with the Audubon Society, so remember to bring your binoculars for a close-range view.

Fisherman Island (Linda Lantzy)

FACILITIES: gravel beach, porta-potty
ACTIVITIES: boating, paddling, fishing, swimming, wildlife viewing

Wildlife Viewing: Mergansers on a Log

During summer quiet, along the lake's shoreline where the fishing is good, you are apt to find a driftwood log with young, auburn-headed common mergansers bunched so tightly together that they look like bristles on a brush. It's hard to count them even with binoculars. Sixteen? No, 17 … I think. There are also two adult females resting together a little farther up on the log. Are they the mothers of this large brood or babysitters while the birds' parents are out on the lake fishing for food?

Juvenile mergansers sun themselves on a log (Karen DIngerson)

The juvenile mergansers' ivory breasts when facing the golden sun of early morning or late afternoon turn the color of creamery butter tailored into a gray-brown suit of speckled plumage. Then there's that crest of reddish-brown feathers that sweeps back like a wild head of hair.

Occasionally, when a bird falls off the log or is pushed accidentally by a sibling, the youngster will literally leap out of the water and use its orange feet to snag the log and pull itself back up. Sometimes that sharp, fish-eating beak can help with the process.

A sandpiper, a shorebird with a nest nearby, swoops past scolding the birds. One of the juveniles tries to swipe at the small bird with its sharp beak, missing it. The adult birds are patient with all the activity below them and they say little. But there's squawking from more than a few of the youngsters on the crowded log as the birds preen one another, stretching and wrapping their long necks around the body of another.

Once the merganser adults have sunned long enough, maybe 15 to 20 minutes, they'll slip silently back into the water and the entire brood will immediately follow, jumping down in a series of smooth plops to quietly paddle after them in single file on their watery march to the next stop.

Now it's easy to count them ... yes, there are 17 juveniles!

Not all of a young merganser's watery life is so regimented, however. They enjoy playing tag in their nursery area, chasing one another this direction and that, literally running across the water's surface like a schoolyard full of children during recess.

Whether they're fishing, frolicking or playing follow-the-leader, mergansers are a native species of waterfowl on Lake Pend Oreille that are a joy to watch.

- - - - - - - - - - - - - - - - - - - -

Anecdota: The Tie that Binds

Author's note: In the time between writing this story and production of this book, Dale Selle passed away in 2007. He was highly respected for his knowledge of local history.

In their boyhood, Dale Selle and his cousin Will Hawkins would blaze a long trail through late-winter snow from their family homestead at Sunnyside to an overlook high above Fisherman Island. Their mission was to catch a spectacular view of Lake Pend Oreille

Will Hawkins, left, and Dale Selle playing as children at Sunnyside (courtesy photo)

toward Sandpoint.

Along the way, riding stick horses, they would joust at tall stalks of mullein plants with imaginary swords. Some days they would dress up as Indians for the adventure. As Dale tells it: "We never sat still. We roamed those hills all the time – up and down, up and down."

Today Dale is a grandfather and Will has passed on. Although they no longer own all the land they once did, many members of the Hawkins clan still call Sunnyside home. It is one of the few places on the lake where you'll still find family so strongly connected to place.

John George Hawkins, Dale's great-grandfather, acquired the land in 1884 after helping to build the long wooden railroad trestle over the Pack River Bay. Today the former pastureland floods and recedes with the operation of the Albeni Falls Dam. Known as the Pack River Flats, its rocky shoreline is excellent for bass fishing in summer, and in spring and fall the muddy river delta is a paradise for migrating waterfowl.

In 1943, Dalton Hawkins took over the care of the Sunnyside homestead and deeded parcels to extended family members, and the Hawkins family donated 20 acres of lakefront and 40 acres of woodlot to the state of Idaho. Now anyone can freely share in what's known as Hawkins Point and Sunnyside Access – two of the three public access sites on the peninsula. If your family enjoys swimming there on the weekends, or if you're one of the kayakers who paddle from here to Fisherman Island, be grateful to the Hawkins family. Please show respect as any guest would.

According to historic newspaper clippings, Sunnyside's formerly all-private shoreline was one of the most popular swimming areas on Lake Pend Oreille. However, today only a few landowners continue to welcome visitors to enjoy their lake frontage, requesting that visitors simply care for and treat it well. It's a rare privilege these days, Dale admits. Fisherman Island, managed by Idaho Fish and Game, used to allow camping, but too many people abused the privilege and so it is now only a day-use area.

It is Lake Pend Oreille that makes the Hawkins family ties to Sunnyside especially strong, Dale says. Beach parties over the years involving family members favored campfire sing-alongs to entertain the children and storytelling that went very late into the night. Because of its southern exposure, the weather at Sunnyside is often mild and the winds are typically calm. So canoeing in the moonlight remains a longstanding, romantic family tradition, Dale says.

But it's the clarity of the lake that Dale will never forget. Back in the 1950s, the water was crystal clear, the rocky bottom was squeaky clean, and you could see 20 to 30 feet down. In those days, the kids would play pantomimes and other guessing games underwater. Dale Selle expects that the days of a pristine lake will likely only live on in memory. However, if visitors and new landowners were to imagine a life of such pure, watery magic, who knows what might happen?

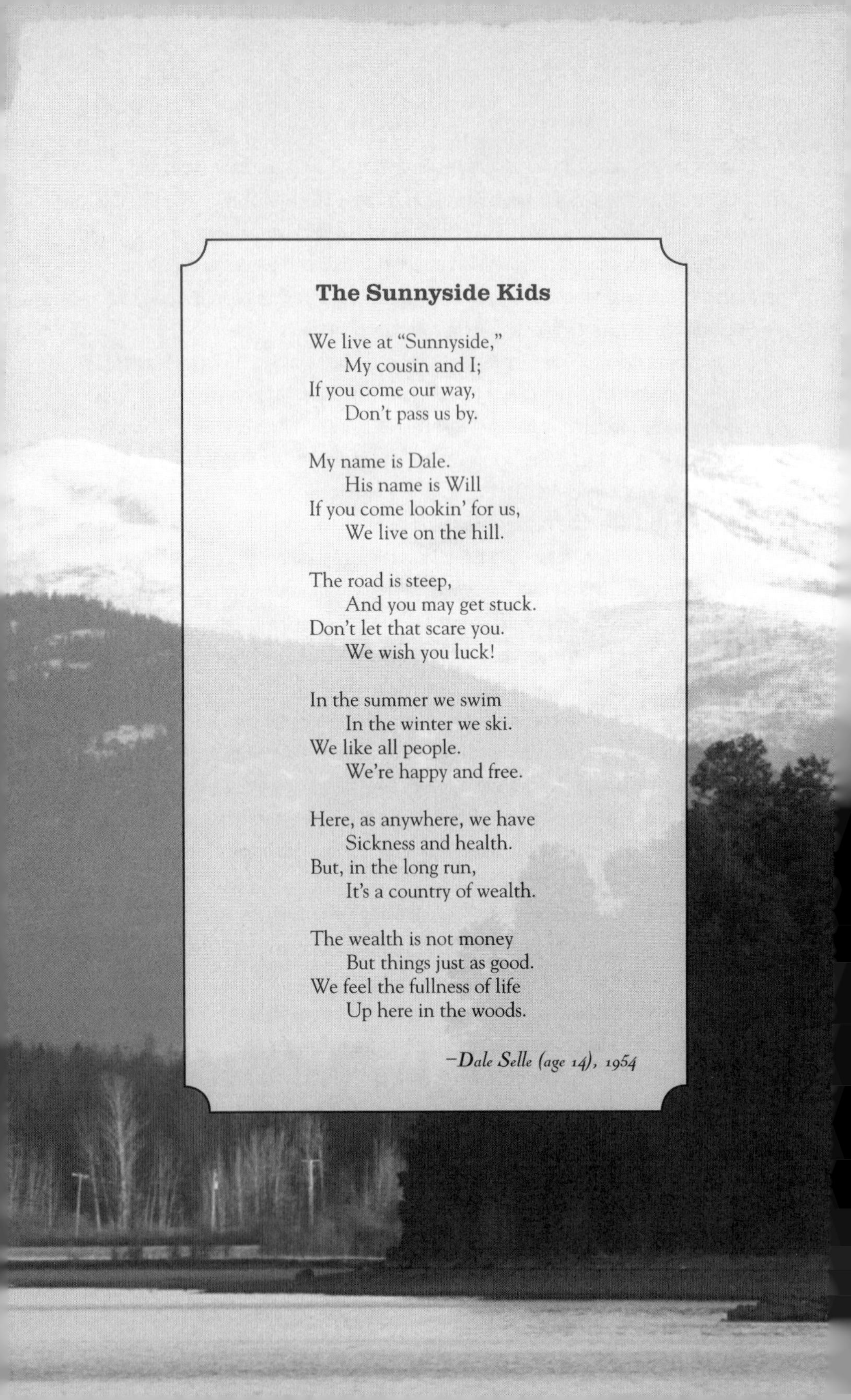

The Sunnyside Kids

We live at "Sunnyside,"
    My cousin and I;
If you come our way,
    Don't pass us by.

My name is Dale.
    His name is Will
If you come lookin' for us,
    We live on the hill.

The road is steep,
    And you may get stuck.
Don't let that scare you.
    We wish you luck!

In the summer we swim
    In the winter we ski.
We like all people.
    We're happy and free.

Here, as anywhere, we have
    Sickness and health.
But, in the long run,
    It's a country of wealth.

The wealth is not money
    But things just as good.
We feel the fullness of life
    Up here in the woods.

—Dale Selle (age 14), 1954

SUNNYSIDE ACCESS

Managed by Idaho Fish and Game, this is a day-use only, no-fee area.

What's it like?

One half mile of lakeshore parallels the main dirt and gravel road providing access to a rocky beach and a small boat ramp. It is a pleasant, sunny place to relax with a fishing pole or to splash around in the water. Parking is limited.

FACILITIES: boat ramp, rocky beach, vault toilet
ACTIVITIES: boating, fishing, swimming, picnicking on the beach

How to get here:

Turn south off Idaho State Highway 200 at Sunnyside-Oden Bay Road and go about six miles on Sunnyside Road, which goes from pavement to dirt and gravel. Located one-quarter mile west of Hawkins Point on Sunnyside Road, this primitive site offers a boat ramp suitable for small boats. The park is also accessible from Highway 200 on the east end of Sunnyside Road near the Pack River Flats. Please respect surrounding private property.

HAWKINS POINT

Managed by Idaho Fish and Game, this is a day-use only, no-fee area.

What's it like?

Before Sunnyside Road turns north to wind its way back to Highway 200 on the west side of Pack River Bay, you encounter this well-maintained public access site to Lake Pend Oreille. There is a good turnaround and parking for five or six vehicles with trailers. This is also the launch site for full moon paddles to Fisherman Island. At one time a train trestle crossed the bay from Trestle Creek to this point. A historical monument honors the Hawkins family who homesteaded Sunnyside and donated this land to the state for everyone to enjoy.

The boat ramp at Hawkins Point (Chris Bessler)

FACILITIES: concrete boat ramp, dock, restroom, historical monument

ACTIVITIES: boating, paddling, fishing, swimming

How to get here:

See directions for Sunnyside Access above.

- - - - - - - - - - - - - - - - -

Lore Along the Shore: Railroading and Pioneers at Sunnyside

Sunnyside was an important steamboat landing, and a steamboat repair facility flourished here for years. Many of the pilings can still be seen along the shoreline. The Northern Pacific Railroad originally followed the shoreline around the broken, forested uplands, but after it was moved farther inland, the old railroad grade became the Sunnyside Road.

The Sunnyside Peninsula was homesteaded by two families: the John George Hawkins family (in 1882) and the William Ashley family (in 1886). Over the years, descendents married one another and many of their families still live on the original homestead (see Anecdota on page 148). The lakeshore and upland public access area known as Hawkins

Willie Ashley, age 10, at the Ashley ranch on the old Pack River Meadows during a flood in June or July, circa 1900

Point was gifted to the state by the families and in 1982, a monument was erected at the site to commemorate the 100th anniversary of the Hawkins pioneer settling in the area.

Full Moon Paddlers
By Gary Hassler

Lake Pend Oreille is nearly twice as deep as Scotland's famous Loch Ness and rumored to be home to a lake monster that rivals Nessie. Nevertheless, knowledge of this creature, called the Pend Oreille Paddler, didn't keep me from joining a local kayak tour for a full moon paddle. When dealing with a lake monster, you don't have to paddle faster than the creature, just faster than the person next to you.

Since I am a novice paddler, I studied a book on kayaking prior to the trip. Kayak strokes take less effort than one would think. In the basic forward stroke, the top hand pushes forward while the bottom hand guides the paddle, lightly gripping it. The author compared a paddle stroke called a "sculling brace" to spreading peanut butter on bread, and explained how to make a "wet exit." Learning how to escape a capsized boat is always valuable to know.

On the night of the full moon, we met at dusk at Hawkins Point on Sunnyside to kayak to Fisherman Island and back. The touring company provided all the necessary equipment. For astronauts, takeoffs and landings are considered the most dangerous; it's much the same for novice kayakers.

"Most dumpings happen getting in or out of the boat," said our guide. (He didn't mention attack by lake monsters, but since that occurrence is rarer than a blue moon, I wasn't worried.) Twelve boats launched from shore without incident. Paddlers included myself and another newspaperman, a photographer and his wife, a family of four with young children, a filmmaker from California, and a sprinkling of young women as every monster film requires. Fully mustered, we paddled out to watch for the moonrise above the Cabinet Mountains. Some of us were cruising along smoothly, others struggled with the proper paddling form only to be corrected by the gentle coaching of a guide.

All of a sudden, the moon arose from behind the ridgeline, casting a ribbon of sparkling light across the water. We saw the moon as we had never seen it before. Words fail to describe the beauty of the moment. Photos were insufficient. To experience such a night truly requires being there. Yet, the paddle was just beginning. As we kayaked out into open water toward Fisherman Island, each kayaker switched on a white strobe strapped to their person. We looked like a swarm of fireflies. "Those lights are great; you can track the advance of the lake monster by watching them go out one-by-one," I remarked to one guide who chuckled heartily. At Fisherman Island, I coasted smoothly to land ashore and enjoyed the satisfaction of reaching our destination under my own power.

"Why did we come down here?" asked the little girl who had stayed in her boat instead of exploring the island. "So we can paddle back into the moon," a guide calmly replied. The rest of us understood completely. The return to Hawkins Point was silent except for a few exclamations of "I can't believe how beautiful it is," and "Can't we just stay out here?" We all took our time paddling back, not wanting the journey to end.

On shore the most common remark was "I've got to do this again!" It's a brilliant idea even if lake monsters might be lurking about.

- - - - - - - - - - - - - - - - -

Tour on Wheels:
Sunnyside Loop

This is an excellent choice for those who want an easy loop ride with immediate lakeshore access, well-maintained dirt roads (despite a few potholes here and there) and great views of Lake Pend Oreille. Some of the best and sunniest gravel beaches in northern Idaho lie along this ride. They call it Sunnyside for a reason!

Length: 12 miles if doing just the loop. Add an additional 12 miles if riding from the town of Sandpoint.
Difficulty: easy
Road Type: mixed pavement and dirt/gravel
Road Conditions: fair to good (some potholes)
Facilities En Route: bathrooms, beach access points. No public sources of potable water.
Attractions: easy access to one of Lake Pend Oreille's best stretches of rock/gravel beaches, wildlife viewing at Hawkins Point overlooking the Pack River Flats and excellent views toward the escarpment of the Green Monarch Mountains

How to get there:

From Sandpoint, drive (or bike) Idaho State Highway 200 east for approximately six miles. Turn right at the sign for Sunnyside-Oden Bay Road. Or you can drive this far to bike the loop and park along the road near the railroad underpass. (Note: this is where the loop ends).

Go under the railroad underpass and follow Sunnyside-Oden Bay Road to the left. The first part of the road is an almost two-mile-long, straight stretch with the lake off to your right. Keep pedaling! Once you cross Raymond Slough, immediately to your right is the first public access point. A maintained trail winds through the surrounding undeveloped forestland to the lakeshore.

Cyclist on Sunnyside Loop (Chris Bessler)

This area is part of the Oden Bay Segment of the Pend Oreille Wildlife Management Area and a great spot for wildlife viewing.

Continue down the Sunnyside Road past Perch Bay (all privately owned properties) a mile and a half farther and you will see Fisherman Island offshore to your right. The next stretch of roadway changes to gravel and dirt but offers excellent riding close to the lakeshore. The sunny southern exposure of this stretch gives "Sunnyside" its name.

Traveling another mile or so along the shoreline brings you to Sunnyside Access. One half mile of public lakeshore parallels the main dirt and gravel road, providing access to a rocky beach and a small boat ramp. It is a perfect place for a swim. Parking is limited, but there is a porta-potty. Another quarter of a mile down the road is Hawkins Point, another public access area with a boat launch, parking and vault toilet.

From Hawkins Point, it's just over six miles back to Highway 200 continuing along Sunnyside Road just west of the Pack River Flats area. Turning left on Highway 200, it's another two miles back to the beginning of the loop at the railroad underpass parking area and Sandpoint is six miles west from there.

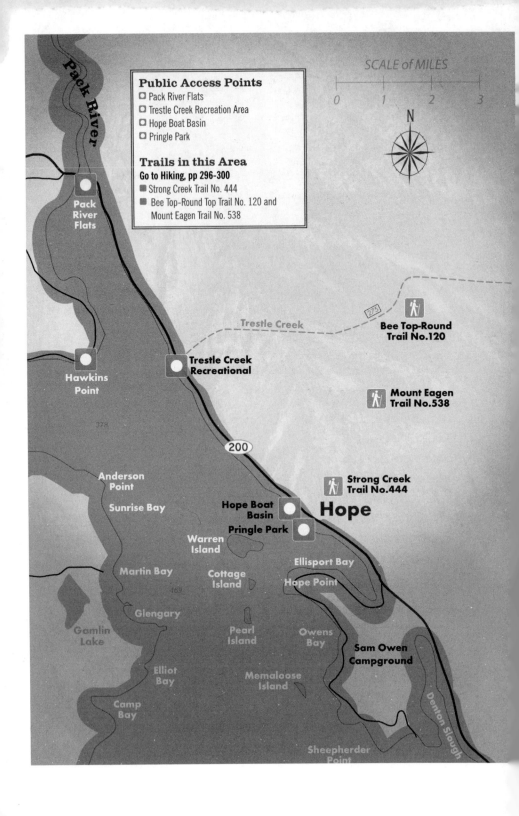

SCALE of MILES

0   1   2   3

N

Public Access Points
☐ Pack River Flats
☐ Trestle Creek Recreation Area
☐ Hope Boat Basin
☐ Pringle Park

Trails in this Area
Go to Hiking, pp 296-300
■ Strong Creek Trail No. 444
■ Bee Top-Round Top Trail No. 120 and
   Mount Eagen Trail No. 538

Pack River

Pack River Flats

Trestle Creek

275

Bee Top-Round Trail No.120

Hawkins Point

Trestle Creek Recreational

Mount Eagen Trail No.538

378

200

Anderson Point

Sunrise Bay

Hope Boat Basin

Strong Creek Trail No.444

Hope

Pringle Park

Warren Island

Martin Bay

Cottage Island

Ellisport Bay

Hope Point

469

Glengary

Gamlin Lake

Pearl Island

Owens Bay

Sam Owen Campground

Elliot Bay

Memaloose Island

Camp Bay

Denton Slough

Sheepherder Point

CHAPTER SEVEN

AREA 4, PACK RIVER TO HOPE

OVERVIEW

*T*raveling east, past the Sunnyside Peninsula, you reach the Pack River, the main waterway that drains the eastern slopes of the Selkirk Mountains and the western slopes of the Cabinet Mountains. It is one of two rivers that feed the lake, the other being the Clark Fork. Born from a high alpine lake on the Selkirk Crest, the Pack River flows many meandering miles before it reaches Lake Pend Oreille. North of the highway the estuary once was a wild and essential habitat to herds of elk and deer, and frequented by moose and beaver feeding in the brushy wetland shallows. Today these wetlands have been curtailed by residential and golf course development.

But, for now, south of the highway is still largely undeveloped. Known locally as the Pack River Flats, and officially as the Pack River Wildlife Management Area, it is both home and haven to a rich biodiversity of wildlife, especially waterfowl. The entire delta is a prime spot for watchable wildlife, which is why this is a popular paddle area for canoeists and kayakers.

Past the flats and beyond the train trestle, the view looks southeast towards Hope, the area's several islands and an expanse of water all the way to the steep and majestic Green

Pack River Delta seen from Idaho State Highway 200 (Linda Lantzy)

Monarch Mountains. At Trestle Creek there are both public recreation facilities and private resorts. This is also a popular area for scuba divers since a train derailment into the lake in 1904 left several railcars underwater to explore.

Idaho State Highway 200 from Trestle Creek to Hope's Ellisport Bay is one of the prettiest stretches of road anywhere in Bonner County. It curves and climbs against the mountainous shoreline providing spectacular views of the breadth of Lake Pend Oreille. In addition to Trestle Creek, there are two more public access areas: the Hope Boat Basin under the highway bridge west of Hope; and Pringle Park at the west end of Ellisport Bay and adjacent to the former Litehouse Restaurant, which spawned Litehouse Foods. There are several highway turnouts on this section of road, some of them looking southwest down the long body of Lake Pend Oreille. These turnouts are ideal for creating memorable photographs of your trip to northern Idaho. The backdrop is breathtaking! There are also several interpretive signs along the way as part of the Pend Oreille Scenic Byway, including information about the Ice Age floods and geology of the area, wildlife and native Kalispel and Kootenai Indian traditional culture.

A business route off Highway 200 near mile marker 46 goes alongside the hill to Hope and East Hope and then loops back again to Highway 200 near the Hope Memorial Community Hall. This alternative route offers some amazing views of three of the lake's islands with the Bernard Slide miles behind them at the southern end of the lake. The view is so expansive it seems you can actually see the curvature of the earth! It is also one of the best places to watch and photograph our famous Pend Oreille sunsets.

Aerial view looking west over the hillsides of East Hope (Jerry Luther)

Several restaurants and marinas are located in the Hope-East Hope area as well as condominium resorts and the historic Hotel Hope. Across from the Hope Post Office is a small city park that has interpretive signs and a monument to Canadian fur trader and surveyor David Thompson, who arrived in 1809 and established Kullyspel House, a trading post on the peninsula.

Traveling by water, this area is easily accessed by powerboat or sailboat from Hawkins Point boat launch on Sunnyside Peninsula, or across the lake from Glengary Bay. It's a little longer boat trip or sail from Bottle Bay or Garfield Bay and a fair distance from Sandpoint. You will find several marinas in Ellisport Bay with an array of amenities and services for both boaters and sailors. The only boat repair station on this side of the lake is at Hope Marine Services. Hope Marine Services, Holiday Shores Resort/East Hope Marina, and Kramer Marina all have moorage opportunities, including for large houseboats. The only floating restaurant on the lake, appropriately named by locals as "The Floater," is located at Hope Marine. The restaurant deck is another place to watch spectacular sunsets, this time looking northwest to Schweitzer Basin and the Selkirk Crest.

As for trails in this area, one of the longest trails in the region – 19 miles in length – is the Bee Top to Round Top Trail 120. Other trails in this area of the west Cabinet Mountains connect to Trail 120, including Strong Creek Trail No. 444 with its trailhead in Hope and fantastic views of the lake. Trail No. 444 is also open to motorbikes and ATVs.

This is one of the most beautiful and popular scenic areas on Lake Pend Oreille, so plan on spending some time here, even if it's just for a Sunday drive.

Area 4: Pack River to Hope   159

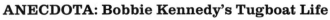

ANECDOTA: Bobbie Kennedy's Tugboat Life

There are aspects of living on and around Lake Pend Oreille that most of us never really think about, or simply take for granted. Like who drove all those pilings that make up the area's marinas and bridges? And how did the power and telephone cables reach the residences on Warren Island? And who rescues boats stranded by violent storms that move through the area tossing vessels up on shore as if they were Neptune's playthings?

Tugboats, barges and cranes. Their influence and mechanical appeal created a unique lifestyle and a lifetime of hard physical work that Bobbie Kennedy says he wouldn't trade for a

Bobbie Kennedy aboard the tugboat *Josephine* circa 1978, top, and with child star Bobby Vinton (center) above, and friend Deena McFarland in the 1950s (courtesy photos)

million bucks. He liked spending time on the lake, and becoming a tugboat operator was what he always wanted to do, ever since he first took the helm of his dad's tugboat when he was only 8 years old. Then at age 10, with just a little assistance, Bobbie drove his first piling. Maybe there is some ancestral connection with Irish shipbuilding that is in Bobbie's blood, or the influence of his granddad's life spent on the coast of Nova Scotia before emigrating to the West. But after nearly 50 years of working on and off Lake Pend Oreille in one way or another, including as a former member of the Bonner County Sheriff's Marine Division, Bobbie Kennedy considers his life on Lake Pend Oreille as very special: "This is the best that it can get. Just growing up here was magical enough for me," he says.

In 1946 his dad, Fred Kennedy, built the first marina in the Sandpoint area where Sandpoint Marina is today. Fred also owned the Power House building next door. From here Bobbie soloed his first tugboat, hauling a huge barge across the lake when he was 15.

"A tugboat is an awesome piece of machinery.

It's not like an outboard. You become a part of it," says Bobbie. That kind of man-made power was evident in the log boom that measured 36 feet wide by a mile long – called a braile – that four tugboats would pull, hauling up to 2 million board feet of logs from the mouth of the Pack River to Albeni Falls. In good weather the trip took four days, and the crew would eat and sleep on the tugs. They had to negotiate four bridges along the way and then release all that timber to Diamond Match Company at Albeni Falls. The efficiency and speed of logging trucks replaced barges moving timber to sawmills, and the last log tow by tugboat was in 1960. That same year the Kennedy family got out of the marina business and focused on lake construction projects, eventually moving to East Hope and building a home on Ellisport Bay. In addition to construction work, they also managed a charter business with four fishing boats.

I still recall many mornings years ago driving west on Highway 200 from my home in Clark Fork and watching the Kennedys' small but mighty diesel tugboat noisily chugging along, hauling a gigantic crane on a big barge on its way to do work somewhere on the lake far from Ellisport Bay. Since Bobbie didn't marry until his late 50s, he often worked alongside his dad building log booms, bridges, marinas or laying underwater utility cables. They built and then hauled into place the floating restaurant at Hope Marine back when it was called The Golden Hind. They also worked together on the Albeni Falls and Cabinet Gorge hydroelectric dams and built the U.S. Navy's first dock at Cape

Josephine tows a U.S. Naval barge near Bayview off Cape Horn with test submarine *Shamu*, circa 1980 (courtesy Bobbie Kennedy)

Horn. Bobbie even hauled the Navy's quarter-scale model of the *Seawolf* class attack submarine down to Bayview, a trip that took almost five hours.

Storms were situations where the Kennedys' tugboats and equipment became rescue vessels. Bobbie still remembers negotiating 10-foot waves around Hope Point during the summer of 1991 to reach several marine vessels that washed ashore on Memaloose Island, a result of a sudden freak storm. Since Bobbie has had to do a lot of rescue work, he offers this advice for boaters choosing to spend the night on the wild shores of Lake Pend Oreille: Rather than parking your boat for the night on a beach, take a rope from shore and tie the boat off in deeper water, putting an anchor off the front and pointing the boat into the wind. Otherwise, he says, if a storm comes up during the night, you might find your boat under water in the morning.

In the years before Global Positioning Systems (GPS) and back before county navigation lights were placed on the lake, Bobbie learned from his dad to navigate at night using star constellations, mountain peaks against a dark skyline and a compass.

The Kennedys sold their tugboat business to Charlie Kramer in 1989. Fred retired to enjoy the lake on the *Lottie Mae*, named for his wife. It was a unique marine vessel to be sure – a 50-foot by 22-foot barge with a motor home welded on top. Before his death in 1999, Fred Kennedy could be seen chugging down to Bayview and back.

Today, Bobbie Kennedy, now married with family and in his mid-60s, still manages to keep busy working on various projects around the lake and still gets out on the water as often as he can. But now he only owns one small barge with two outboards and a powerboat for family recreation. He wonders if those magical years of living here have passed with the area growing so fast and with so much activity on the lake. He observes that people seem too busy to really enjoy a truly relaxing lifestyle. If you can sit a spell, Bobbie has plenty of other amazing stories about Lake Pend Oreille to share.

PUBLIC ACCESS ▶ **PACK RIVER FLATS**

Comanaged by Idaho Fish and Game and U.S. Army Corps of Engineers as the Pack River Wildlife Management Area. This is a day-use area only with access limited to non-motorized kayaks and canoes upstream of Highway 200, and only small car-top fishing boats downstream of the highway to the railroad trestle. This entire area is designated as a no-wake zone.

What's it like?

South of the highway the shallow mouth of Pack River broadens out into a large wetland that, because of the dams, now floods during summer high water and is characterized by a vast mud flat during spring and fall, just the opposite of its natural order. Before the dams were built at Albeni Falls and Cabinet Gorge, spring snowmelt would flood this vast meadow, and then dry out during summer. Kalispel Indians likely harvested edible camas bulbs here (see page 203), and in later years local farmers cut hay around the meandering river.

Despite the dams, the Pack River Flats is still home to white-tailed deer, moose, river otter, muskrat and beaver, and is both habitat and a migratory haven for many species of waterfowl. You can literally see thousands of swans, geese and ducks here throughout the year, especially during spring and fall migration. In winter, the Pack River Delta is home to thousands of redhead ducks, according to Ducks Unlimited. In summer there are nesting ospreys, bald eagles and great blue herons along the shoreline. You might even be lucky enough to see and hear the wail of a loon. Thanks to grants and local land donations, a restoration project returned hundreds of acres of the delta to its original habitat, especially productive for waterfowl.

Paddling on the Pack River

The square platforms on short posts seen here and there in the estuary are man-made nesting boxes that were installed some years ago for Canada geese. The more recent restoration work included creating islands that trap sediments, eventually producing marshes and enhancing nesting habitat for many species. Ducks Unlimited was the coordinating organization for this restoration project.

If exploring on foot, please avoid marshy areas and take care not to disrupt this fragile wetland ecosystem. Using binoculars will limit the need to wade or hike far from the roadside. Interpretive signs at the highway pullout will help you identify the birds and wildlife you might see. This is also a good fishing area for smallmouth bass.

FACILITIES: gravel bank access for cartop kayaks, canoes and small fishing boats only
ACTIVITIES: canoeing, kayaking, floating, bass fishing, wildlife viewing, bird-watching

How to get here:

Access from Idaho State Highway 200 is approximately 9.5 miles east of Sandpoint to the Pack River Bridge near milepost 38. Parking along the road here is tight. A safer parking area is the pullout less than a mile east of the bridge. A primitive launch site is a gravel bank at the last paved pullout just north of the east end of the railroad trestle.

Lore Along the Shore: Tribal Hunting and Fishing Grounds

The mouth of the Pack River and the shoreline from Trestle Creek to Hope were important hunting and fishing camps for the Upper and Lower Kalispel. Brush weirs were used in the Pack River Delta to take pikeminnows (formerly called squawfish) and suckers. This was also the site of one of their summer villages. From the hill overlooking the mouth of the river they would await the return of buffalo hunters from the east, while also hunting bear and deer there. Another bear hunting camp was between Trestle Creek and Hope with the animals hunted in the surrounding mountains.

At another location between Trestle Creek and Hope, called "trees standing on the edge of the water," the Upper Kalispel had an early spring fish camp for catching pikeminnows. In summer and fall they built stick weirs to catch

An unidentified Kalispel Indian woman fishes at Trestle Creek
(Bonner County Historical Society Collection)

whitefish, and they would also spear trout in the fall. About a mile from shore near Hope at the foot of a talus slope, the Kalispel built extensive deer fences for fall deer drives. The Pack River to Hope area and the lands around the Clark Fork Delta were two of the most important locations on Lake Pend Oreille to the tribe because of nature's abundance of fish and wildlife.

Paddle or Float Route: Pack River

Paddling or floating the Pack River north of the highway can be treacherous during spring because of swift current, icy snowmelt and log jams formed from trees that have washed down from the Selkirk Mountains to the northwest. Lives have been lost on this river in spring, which is hard to believe if you ply the waters during the summer. In summer the river is so shallow in the straight-aways that you might have to pull or push your canoe through sandbars.

Some people put their kayaks and canoes in the water near the Highway 200 river bridge and paddle upstream and back. Others will leave a shuttle car at the pullout just east of the river bridge on Highway 200 and backtrack by car via the Lower Pack River Road adjacent to the golf course, which winds around to the north and ends at a "T" and Rapid Lightning Creek Road. Turn right (east) and proceed until you reach the Pack River Bridge almost to the Pack River Store. Put in here and float back down to the Highway 200 bridge.

Either as a float trip downstream or as a paddle upstream, the Pack is a delightful way to spend the day, since this area of the waterway is limited to only non-motorized watercraft. On the hottest days of summer, numerous sandy banks double as swimming beaches and picnic grounds. And you're apt to see wildlife along the way. (Moose used to be frequent visitors to this area, but with development, there are fewer of the large animals to be seen.) The river is also a chance to test your navigational skills by paddling or floating through riffles and small rapids. The distance from the Pack River Bridge on Highway 200 to the bridge on Rapid Lightning Road is between four and five miles one way. Estimated paddling time is from two to five hours depending on the current, whether you are floating downstream or paddling upstream, and stops along the way.

Wildlife Through the Seasons
By Heather McElwain

From dawn until dusk, twilight to morn, with each new moon and passing season, Lake Pend Oreille is home to a diversity of wildlife. Animal trails and bird flyways guide both the everyday and the extraordinary like veins to a heart.

Before the sun climbs over the Cabinet Mountains on a spring morning, the lakeshore quickens with sights and sounds: Animals leave the water's edge under the cover of predawn light to seek more clandestine refuge. Hiding

White-tailed deer with fawn in summer (Duane Davis)

in shadows the sun hasn't yet warmed, a black bear shuffles from the rocky shoreline to dense hillside shrubbery. A red fox pads surefooted in a tall-grass meadow along the water. In the midday sun, eagles coil upward on thermals above the lake, as an osprey plummets talons first into a shallow bay and thrusts up clutching a twisting trout. When the sun disappears behind the hills, bronze-colored deer brazenly graze the greening lakeside lawns. The lone howl of a coyote echoes from a secluded cove while moonlight flickers on the roiling waves.

As summer's warmth awakens the earth, the lake slowly begins to mirror the shoreline's greening foliage. With an abundance of food in the basin, some animals and birds boldly emerge. Wild turkeys and Canada geese forage raucously in lakeside fields. Grouse rake through leaf-strewn forests close to shore. Snakes and salamanders bask on boulders along the water. Other animals leave cover more cautiously. A great horned owl lifts from a signpost near Trestle Creek and glides to a high bough of a ponderosa pine. A silhouetted raccoon scavenges in the moonlight. Often these creatures leave only a hint of their presence — an occasional track, a shed antler or feathers.

White-tailed deer in winter (Karen Dingerson)

Inevitably the air stiffens again, and autumn brings Northwest cloudscapes to shroud the sky. Squirrels scurry to stash seeds from fir and pinecones. As hillside grasses shrivel and parch, deer and bear visit ripened gardens and orchards to feed. Flocks of migratory birds descend upon the watery runway, a stopover on their winged voyage south. In the Pack River Flats, tundra or whistling swans seek aquatic delicacies in the seasonal mudflats. A solitary blue heron wades long-legged into the estuary inlet. Just offshore, coots huddle and sway en masse with the breakers.

Though such occurrences become commonplace after years on the lake, some remain unforgettable: a cow moose piggybacking her calf to Fisherman Island; the haunting bugle of the bull elk resounding above the Pack River Delta; and the rare wail of the common loon beckoning through the fog.

After the first snowfall, tracks expose unseen journeys to the water's edge. Heavily trod trails disappear into dense forests and up steep hillsides. As shallow bays freeze over, tiny footprints on a snow-dusted beach reveal river otters fishing from ice ledges. These impressions punctuate the shoreline and plot any movement to and from the lake.

Everywhere around Lake Pend Oreille, on island, bluff, point, delta, bay or slough, the sights and sounds narrate a primeval tale of the heart for all seasons, twilight to morning, dawn until dusk.

Fish Tales:
Pack River Delta – Angling for Bass

Tom Anderson and his buddy, a black Labrador retriever, spend a lot of summer mornings and evenings together. Ruger is a water-loving dog after all, so they board Tom's flattop bass boat and go fishing. As owner of Sandpoint Outfitters in Ponderay, Tom leaves his partner Calvin Fuller to mind the store while he goes angling for smallmouth bass in one of his favorite places – the Pack River Flats.

Smallmouth bass, a warmwater species, migrated here from Montana through the dams in 1992. They spawn in spring and live in shallow areas; but, when temperatures get below 40 F, they move into deep water and "just hang," Tom says. The fish lie dormant out on underwater shelves that drop 25, 50 to 75 feet, until June when they become active again as the water warms to 50 F or higher. As the fish prepare to reproduce, they become voracious eaters gobbling up perch, crappie, minnow and mysis shrimp. They eat a lot. Once the water warms to around 65 degrees, they'll spawn in 6 to 15 feet of water along rocky shorelines like that surrounding the south end of Pack River Flats. They'll rise to the surface at night and dive to the depths of the lake in the daytime. At Pack River the water is actually not very deep – 20 feet or less. Where largemouth bass like brackish, weedy water, the smallmouth species prefers rocks and stumps. Neither species free-range like the kokanee salmon.

Tom Anderson and canine friend bass fishing and, below, smallmouth bass

Tom says bass are a desirable fish to catch because you don't need a big fancy boat to catch them. You can fish from a 10-foot car-top boat, kayak, canoe or even from the rocky shore. In dollars or hours spent, Tom believes bass is the most valuable fishery anywhere.

Tom knows more than a little bit about fish. He was born in Spokane, but his dad and granddad lived in Bayview in the 1940s and 1950s where they were commercial kokanee fishermen. They had a smokehouse in their garage and Tom used to hand-line kokanee. "There wasn't a bar in downtown Spokane in the old days that you couldn't get a cold beer and smoked kokanee," Tom says. Before angling for bass Tom trolled for rainbow trout.

When it comes to protecting the bass fishery, "Why not be proactive?" he asks. Smallmouth bass are "fun to catch, beautiful fish to admire and interesting to get to know." Tom has learned where and how they live and reproduce, and although he'll keep a few perch for the dinner table, he practices catch and release with the bass he's lucky to land. Lake Pend Oreille could be a world-class smallmouth bass fishery if the species had more protection. Idaho's record bass is 8 pounds, 14 ounces with some of the bass being caught in Pend Oreille weighing between 6.5 to 7.5 pounds.

"We're getting close to a state record, and there's tons of food and great habitat for them," says Tom. "There's no need to kill them while the fish are spawning between May and July. There are 18 bodies of water in the state of Idaho that have protections for bass; I don't know why they can't do it here," he adds. "We surely don't want to be a day late and a dollar short."

Since so many people already fish for bass here, it really bothers Tom that some fishermen are catching 5- to 10-year-old females full of eggs. Bass can live 10 to 15 years, but it takes three to five years for the fish to reach reproduction maturity. Right now the regulations allow anglers to keep six fish longer than 12 inches, including spawning females.

If you are a bass fisherman angling for the first time in the Pack River Flats, or any other place on the Pend Oreille Lake populated by bass, consider following these conservation measures: Practice catch and release until the first of July, with a two-fish limit after that on fish 12 to 16 inches. Have fun, but be a prudent angler and help protect the bass fishery in Lake Pend Oreille.

– –

Tour on Wheels:
Pend Oreille Scenic Byway

When one daydreams of a leisurely drive along a picturesque waterfront with long views of rolling mountains and across open waters, they are dreaming of Highway 200 east of Sandpoint. Known locally as the Hope Highway, this 33.4-mile stretch of two-lane pavement is the only portion of state highway that skirts the very shores of Lake Pend Oreille.

The Pend Oreille Scenic Byway traces the northern edge of Lake Pend Oreille (Al Lemire)

This scenic drive traces the northern edge of Lake Pend Oreille from the Pack River Delta to the Clark Fork Delta and offers spectacular views of the lake surrounded by the Cabinet, Coeur d'Alene and Selkirk mountains. The pullout near milepost 44 provides one of the most amazing views of Lake Pend Oreille. The road curves and climbs along in places, so if you are biking, ride carefully. To learn more about this federally recognized National Scenic Byway, go online to www.byways.org.

Length: Round-trip it is 54 miles (to Clark Fork) or 66.8 miles (to Montana line) from Sandpoint with an optional scenic loop drive that travels east along Highway 200 to Montana Highway 56, north to U.S. Highway 2, west to U.S. Highway 95, and then south back to Sandpoint.

Road Type: paved

Road Conditions: excellent

Facilities En Route: A number of amenities lie along this stretch of highway past the towns of Ponderay and Kootenai. The towns of Hope and East Hope offer restaurants, cafes, a historic hotel, gas stations and marinas. You will also find services in the town of Clark Fork.

Attractions: Side-trip opportunities abound along this stretch of highway. It is advisable to take this journey slowly, stopping often. Swimming, wildlife viewing, fishing, golfing, hiking and biking are possible along this portion of highway. There are actually 13 special attractions and several helpful on-site interpretive signs at the many pullouts along the way between Pack River (milepost 39) and the Montana state line. The byway is well marked with highway signage.

Directions: From Sandpoint, take Idaho State Highway 200 east 24 miles to the town of Clark Fork, the final town in Idaho on Highway 200 and turn around there, or proceed another seven miles to the Cabinet Gorge Interpretive Site just west of the Montana state line.

TRESTLE CREEK RECREATION AREA

Managed by the U.S. Army Corps of Engineers, this is a day-use area only with no fee for public access. Private campgrounds and resorts are nearby.

What's it like?

Located southeast of the mouth of Pack River, this area is named for the original Northern Pacific Railway's 6,500-foot, curved, wooden trestle built in 1882 that extended from Hawkins Point on the Sunnyside Peninsula to this site across Pack River Bay just west of the creek. At low water, the old pilings of the trestle are still visible. The existing train crossing was built in 1904. Trestle Creek tumbles out of the Cabinet Mountains into the lake here and is an important spawning stream for bull trout and kokanee salmon in the fall.

Shaded by enormous black cottonwood trees – that during fish spawning season are crowned with bald eagles – the grassy lawn is a great place for a family picnic or for tossing a flying disc about. There's also a roped swimming area. The site is adjacent to the railroad tracks and does get momentarily noisy when a train goes by. A paved parking

Trestle Creek Recreation Area (Linda Lantzy)

area will accommodate up to a dozen vehicles including boat trailers. In addition to the public day-use facilities at the recreation area, there are campsites and RV spaces available at private campgrounds on both sides of the highway.

FACILITIES: concrete boat ramp, dock, public parking, rocky and muddy beach, swimming area, picnic tables, park benches, shade trees, large grassy lawn, vault toilet

ACTIVITIES: boating, fishing, swimming, picnicking, scuba diving

How to get here:

Paved access from Idaho State Highway 200 southeast of the Pack River bridge just past milepost 42, about 12 miles east of Sandpoint. The Trestle Creek bridge is at the bottom of a steep curve in the road. Turn right at sign and then turn left into the entrance of the recreation area after crossing the railroad tracks.

- - - - - - - - - - - - - - - - - - -

Scuba Diving: Underwater Train Cars

In September 1904, Bonner County's newspaper headlined this story: "Cars Fell Into the Lake: Bridge Breaks Through Bringing Mishap to a Gravel Train." It seems that the fill for the new crossing cut to replace the original 1882 railroad trestle across Pack River Bay hadn't quite settled in and the bridge gave way with a heavy trainload of gravel. Fortunately nobody was hurt. Of the seven rail cars that went into the lake four were recovered, but three cars fell into deep water and are still there, making for an intriguing and adventurous underwater exploration for scuba divers.

It is a popular scuba site in Lake Pend Oreille because you can dive into one of the railcars from the top. Since the train was hauling gravel, you are not likely to find any gold, but some pretty big bass might follow you closely, a thrill of a different kind.

Marilynne Robinson's *Housekeeping*

Pulitzer Prize-winning author Marilynne Robinson was born in Sandpoint. Her first novel, *Housekeeping*, is a story of two young sisters and their unusual family life in a small Northwest town on a great glacial lake that are reminiscent of Sandpoint and Lake Pend Oreille. Both are named Fingerbone. The novel was made into a movie by the same name, but it was filmed in Nelson, British Columbia, Canada. For many readers, though, this Hemingway Foundation/PEN Award-winning book is too imaginative to be captured on film. It's better to just float along in your canoe reading *Housekeeping* aloud to your partner like you would a book of poetry. It is a riveting tale at times – there's a spectacular train wreck derailing into the lake – and at other times what takes your breath away is simply the language; it is as exquisite and clear as the waters of Lake Pend Oreille itself. I highly recommend this book, which was originally published in 1980.

Tour on Wheels:
Trestle Creek to Lightning Creek

A challenging alternative to the more typical highway routes east of Sandpoint would be the mountaintop route up Trestle Creek Road off Idaho State Highway 200 all the way to Lightning Creek Road and then back down to Highway 200 at Clark Fork – a 35-mile loop ride that gains lots of elevation, about 3,000 feet – but is spread over a long distance.

Due to a dramatic flood in November 2006, 38 miles of backcountry roads in the 75,000-acre Lightning Creek drainage were washed out or severely damaged. At the time of publication, the U.S. Forest Service was undergoing restoration of Lightning Creek Road and developing trailheads at the end of the closed/obliterated roads and converting the roads into non-motorized trails, due to be finished by 2010. Trailheads will be established at East Fork Creek Road, Mud Creek Road and upper Rattle Creek Road (to provide access from Montana).

Most of the reconstruction effort under way in 2009 focuses on restoring nearly the entire length of Lightning Creek Road No. 419 to vehicle access, including construction of a bridge across the East Fork of Lightning Creek, which will allow a wider range of seasonal access into the entire Lightning Creek drainage. Road No. 419 will once again connect with Trestle Creek Road No. 275. The Lunch Peak Lookout and access to Darling, Gem, Moose, Estelle and Blacktail lakes trails are still open via Road No. 275. Once reconstruction of Road 419 is complete, access will be available from Clark Fork. One should check with the U.S. Forest Service for current road conditions and updates before heading into the backcountry; call Sandpoint Ranger District at 208-263-5111.

Roads closed due to the 2006 flood included portions of Lightning Creek, Porcupine, Rattle Creek, Auxor Basin and East Fork roads. Road No. 642 to Porcupine Lake will be converted to a motorized trail open to off-road vehicles 50 inches wide or less. Trail users will have to ford Lightning Creek, which may be difficult during periods of high water.

Length: 35 miles if completing the entire loop

Difficulty: moderate to strenuous

Safety Concerns: recreational traffic, sharp rocks, stream crossings or washouts if biking beyond gates

Road Type: dirt, gravel, asphalt

Road Conditions: fair to good

Facilities En Route: Vault toilet located at Huckleberry campsite, 4 miles from Highway 200 on Trestle Creek Road; otherwise none until return to Highway 200 in either Hope or Clark Fork

Attractions: The side trips along this route – Bee Top-Round Top Trail 120, Lunch Peak Lookout, Lake Darling, Gem Lake and the Moose Lake trail system – are all accessible and offer great day hikes. You can drive to Lunch Peak Lookout, a wonderful viewpoint of the surrounding mountains and Lake Pend Oreille. The lookout is also available for seasonal summer rentals through www.recreation.gov.

Directions: A good beginning place for mountain bikers is the Trestle Creek Recreation Area where you can leave your vehicle and ride from there. From here go west on the highway just a couple hundred yards to Trestle Creek Road No. 275. This is a dirt and gravel road that climbs high into the mountains and joins with Lightning Creek Road No. 419. This is a highly scenic route down a long valley with views of Scotchman Peak – the tallest mountain in the area at 7,009 feet – along the way. Once back on the pavement of Highway 200 at Clark Fork, it is about 11 miles west traveling back to the Trestle Creek Recreation Area.

HOPE BOAT BASIN

Managed by Bonner County, this is a day-use area only with no fee for public access.

What's it like?

This is the primary boat launch for powerboats because it offers quick and easy access to the lake right off the highway. There are two boat docks with a concrete ramp in-between. There's also a stretch of gravel beach here, a swimming area frequented by local Hope residents. Since it is under the highway overpass, though, it's more a place to take a quick dip on a hot summer day, rather than a place to lounge around because of all the noise and boat traffic.

Highway 200 overpass above Hope Boat Basin
(Linda Lantzy)

FACILITIES: concrete boat ramp, two docks, ample public parking, gravel beach, portable toilet
ACTIVITIES: boating, swimming

How to get here:

Access is from Idaho State Highway 200, 15 miles from Sandpoint, just past milepost 45 at the east end of the Hope overpass that curves out over the lake. Turn left off the highway onto the access road.

Lore Along the Shore: The Isles of Hope

There are four islands in this area of Lake Pend Oreille – all of them privately owned. Three islands are visible from Highway 200 and the hillside community of Hope – Warren, Cottage and Pearl. Warren is the largest and named in honor of General Charles S. Warren, a Civil War veteran who built a home there in 1890; although in 1909 he sold the island for $24,000 – a paltry sum by today's standards. Several people now own land at Warren Island, a fact that still mystifies elders of the Kalispel Tribe since use of these islands, once held in common by their ancestors, was important to the survival of everyone.

The Kalispel Indians called Warren "the big island" and culturally it was considered a landmark for them. Cottage Island was named "middle island." Here they stored dried berries, meat and fish for winter use. The Kalispel called Pearl Island the "island farthest out in the water," and it was a short-term spring fishing camp. I've heard a persistent notion that the Indians called the big island "the mother of twins" and the smaller islands, "the twins"; it's likely one of those romantic legends that non-Indians have projected onto native peoples.

View overlooking Hope showing Pearl, Cottage and Warren islands (Duane Davis)

The fourth island, Memaloose, is just off the southern shore of the Hope Peninsula, southwest of Hope Point and not visible from the highway. This island was a Kalispel Indian burial ground. Traditionally, tribal members would offer prayers and offerings near a special boulder on the island that was considered sacred.

Cottage Moon
By Dennis Nicholls

Voices float out from somewhere above me, from behind a curtain of maples. I pause, as though trying to make out what the voices are saying, but in fact, I am studying the ascent of countless steps climbing the brushy hillside to Larry and Karen's house. Tonight they are hosting a small party at day's end for friends, as a half moon hangs over Pend Oreille.

A perception of timelessness awakes inside me as we all sit on the cottage porch, following the antics of the ripples and moonlight playing on the lake's hospitable lap. Like silvery shards of fractured glass cast upon endlessly moving waters, the dim glow of the half moon reflects the mood of Pend Oreille, and hers matches ours. It is a quiet mood, full of reflection, contemplation. Well into the night, we share the camaraderie of friendship, seemingly as old as the moon itself.

We watch as boats ply the serene waters, but from our perch high above the shoreline there is no way to know if the people in them are strangers or acquaintances; if they are happy or sad; whether they see the moon as we see it and cherish its performance as it moves among the islands with them.

A thin veil of clouds joins our hushed party and shrouds the moon, diffusing its soft light across the waterscape. Pend Oreille's far side is swallowed up in the darkness, but only for as long as it takes the moon to shrug off the unwanted cloak. The clouds flee, the moon finds the islands once more and the dance resumes. We watch the display of moonlight and water until our eyes become too heavy to watch any longer.

The magical spell cast by the moon's sorcery over the waters tonight lulls me into peaceful oblivion. When the moon caresses the shores of Cottage Island and kisses the rocks at Pearl's watery edge; when its radiance glances off the dark boughs of tall timber towering above Warren's upland mounds and bathes the flanks of the Cabinets in a soft ecclesiastical glow, I can almost hear the applause of the stars overhead.

As the moon begins the long, slow descent toward Pend Oreille's western horizon, we each stir, as though awakened from dreams that leave you wishing you were still asleep. Descending down the wooden steps, we make our separate ways home, leaving Larry and Karen to put the moon to bed.

Whenever I drive by that brushy hillside with the long flight of stairs leading to my friends' house, my gaze turns to the south, to the islands out beyond the bay. If the winds whip the water into white-capped waves, I figure Pend Oreille is restless because she, too, is lonely without the moon.

The magic of the moon on Pend Oreille fades until night falls once again, and I find a few moments to contemplate the voices I hear: voices of friends, the voice of the wind and the quiet whispering of the lake urging me to come out and play, to dance once more with the cottage moon over Lake Pend Oreille.

-- -- -- -- -- -- -- -- -- -- -- -- -- -- -- --

Wildflower Notes: Serviceberry, Syringa and Ocean Spray

Many locals consider this sunny end of the lake to be the most beautiful. Those fond of gardening will see why this area is often referred to as the "banana belt" of Bonner County. The southern exposure is perfect for growing flowers.

It's also why you will see so many native, flowering shrubs along the hillsides in spring and summer. The sunshine and shallow, rocky soils give rise to a progression of three flowering shrubs that all show lovely white flowers. The first to bloom in late April and early May is Western serviceberry (*Amelanchier ainifolia*). As I speed past in an automobile, its blossoms remind me of kernels of popped popcorn against the green background of foliage. Those blossoms form delicious blue-black berries in the summer, an important traditional food in the American Indian diet. Native people would pound the berries and mix them with tallow from hunted animals and make pemmican, or make loaves or patties of the fruit. Serviceberries do make excellent jelly, but it's better to leave the fruit on the bush for the many birds, bears, chipmunks and other small animals that depend on them for food.

Serviceberry (Jay Mock)

Syringa (Jay Mock)

Some people mistake serviceberry for Lewis' syringa (*Philadelphus lewisii*), which blooms a month or so later in the area. It was collected first by Meriwether Lewis on his famous Western expedition, and the shrub has leaves and white flowers similar to serviceberry. Besides structural differences and blooming dates, the very obvious difference between the two shrubs is the smell of the flowers. Syringa, Idaho's state flower, is also known as "mock-orange." It typically blooms in this area from late June through July framing the turnouts along Highway 200. Its sweet orange-blossom aroma is best enjoyed standing next to the shrub and taking in deep whiffs of its fragrance. Please do not cut these bushes! Be a friend to nature and smell them right where they are and photograph, draw or paint them. The fruit of the Syringa is a woody capsule, not a berry.

Another native shrub that bridges the blooming dates of serviceberry and syringa in this area is ocean spray (*Holodiscus discolor*). Also known as creambush or ironwood, its stems were strong and ideal material for making arrows, spears, handles and root-digging sticks. But it is ocean spray's showy, white clusters of flowers that can be up to a foot in length that contribute to its name. It is a perfect complement to Pend Oreille's blue water.

Ocean spray (Jerry Pavia)

Wildlife Viewing: Bald Eagles

Bald eagles are commonly seen along the northeastern edge of Lake Pend Oreille from Sandpoint to Clark Fork. This perimeter region is home to active bald eagle nests and habitat for both immature and adult birds. It takes five years for an eagle to mature for breeding and to acquire its white head and tail feathers; mottled birds are considered juveniles and are sometimes confused with the golden eagle because of its coloring.

Bald eagle nests are used year after year by the breeding pair that typically mate for life. The adults add to the nest year after year, building it up to 9 feet in diameter where it can weigh several hundred pounds. Females lay one to three eggs in spring and both adults share incubation. Pearl Island is an eagle sanctuary, and March and April are prime incubation months for the birds there and elsewhere; so special attention to their privacy needs to be taken into account during this period. The eaglets grow rapidly and after several weeks the female will leave the nest to help fish. The eaglets will take their first flight around 12 weeks old, but less than half of them survive that first attempt.

The fledglings then spend the rest of summer learning to fish so they can survive the winter.

Primarily a fish-eater, bald eagles can't plunge underwater like osprey and can drown if their feathers get too wet. In addition to spearing fish just under the water's surface with their talons, they eat some carrion and also will skim the surface of the water for dead fish. They also prey on crippled coots and ducks. Even small mammals and pets have been taken by bald eagles. But be aware that it is unlawful to harm, kill or trap bald eagles. It is also illegal to be in possession of bald eagle feathers, talons or other body parts. Penalties from the U.S. Fish and Wildlife Service are stiff. Become aware of nesting areas and avoid disturbing bald eagles, their nests and brood at any cost.

- - - - - - - - - - - - - - - - - - - -

Points of Sail
By Cate Huisman

Wind and Sailors:

Opinion differs as to where sailing on the lake is best, but the area around Hope is one of the contenders, where winds from various directions converge around the islands offshore. The predominant summer wind is from the southwest, with more northeasters coming in the spring and fall. Summer heating also creates upslope and downslope winds coming out of Trestle Creek and Strong Creek. Mornings tend to be calmer than later in the day.

Sailboat passes Cottage and Pearl islands in Hope (Betsy Canfield)

If you've launched at Sandpoint and are sailing down the lake, you'll find that the usual summer southerly is stronger here (and its associated chop is bigger) because of the long fetch up from Bayview. Fortunately, this fetch also provides a long view; be ready to reef if you see darkening water or whitecaps down the lake.

The two miles of open water between Hope and Anderson Point across the lake can sometimes build up an uncomfortable chop for a small boat, but these conditions rarely last long. Just west of Hope Point are three small islands, Warren, Cottage and Pearl. Since they are private, you cannot land on them, but sailing among these islands is a real treat.

You'll see the most masts at Kramer's Marina in Ellisport Bay, which is home to a loose affiliation of experienced sailors known as the Lost Boys. Although most of the slips are long-term rentals, a side-tie might be available for a transient vessel, and it's worth spending an evening with whatever Lost Boys are around, as many of them have sailed far beyond the confines of Lake Pend Oreille. No club here has a weekly race, however.

This area has some hazards that are worth mentioning. Logs come down the Pack River in spring freshets and can be bobbing up and down on the surface or just under it. There are shoals off the islands, only the most prominent of which, off Pearl Island, is marked (Buoy A, which flashes white every 10 seconds). These are not sandy or muddy bars like those in the northern bend of the lake; they are pieces of bedrock hiding just a few feet under the surface when the lake is at full pool. There is an unmarked piling north of Cottage Island as well.

Anchorage:

Ellisport Bay provides the best anchorages in the area; far enough in, there is good protection from both northerly and southerly winds, although the bay gets shallow as you proceed in. Most of the logs have been removed from the bottom by a salvage operation, but there are submerged lines near the "mainland" shore; it's better to stay closer to the peninsula, just inside the bay. Getting out can be a challenge without a motor, so consider how much protection you want to trade tonight for ease in picking up the wind tomorrow.

It is possible to anchor among the islands, although they are all privately owned and there is no option to go ashore. Also, the converging winds pass between them and offer little long-term shelter, although they might offer temporary shelter until the wind switches direction. From here south along the lake, a Danforth is of little use; a Bruce, plow or CQR will hold best on the rocky bottom. If you're not the anchoring kind, several marinas in this area have public slips.

Launching and Hauling:

The launch ramp under the highway overpass at the Hope Boat Basin is inaccessible to all but the smallest of sailboats because of the low clearance; sailors can use the nearby Trestle Creek ramp instead. In the fall, this situation reverses itself, as the water falls too low to use the Trestle Creek ramp, but some sailboats can then make it under the overpass to access the Hope Boat Basin ramp. If all else fails, Kramer Marina has a crane and can haul boats of any size at any time of year.

Lore Along the Shore: Hope's Commercial History

In 1882 the Northern Pacific Railway constructed tracks along the shore of Lake Pend Oreille. The settlement of Hope was named for the veterinarian with the railroad who cared for the horses during construction, and who also cared for workers' medical needs. Chinese laborers were also instrumental in building the railroad line and Hope became home to these immigrants. The Chinese community flourished here into the 1920s.

In 1886, the Northern Pacific built one of the largest and most luxurious resorts in the region for $3,949.64. Called the Highland House, the 22-bedroom hotel was built on the bluffs above the lake's north shore with a breathtaking view overlooking the islands and the long stretch of Lake Pend Oreille all the way to Bernard Peak. Thirteen years later in 1899, due to a lack of population and clientele, the Highland House sold for one dollar. Eventually the structure was turned into a schoolhouse.

East Hope was home to a large sawmill at the water's edge, and the mill and logging crews lived in boarding houses built nearby.

Another hotel, built in 1898 as Hotel Jeannot, has been restored as the Hotel Hope. It is fascinating to read the hotel's guest register from several decades back to see who once stayed there. J.P. Morgan, Teddy Roosevelt, Gary Cooper and Bing Crosby are a few of the prominent people who have been guests at Hotel Hope.

Early days in Hope (Bonner County Historical Society)

Today, Hope is a resort community attracting celebrities, artists, literary figures and many retirees. Blessed with mild weather and natural beauty, the area's history includes a touch of virtually every element of white settlement from the past two centuries – steamboats, logging, mining, railroads, farms, fishing and general tourism.

Where Litehouse Dressing originated, the Litehouse Restaurant in Hope, from a vintage postcard (Ross Hall)

PRINGLE PARK

Managed by Idaho Fish and Game, this is a day-use area only with no fee for public access. Note: The adjacent property to the west, including the sand volleyball court, is private.

What's it like?

Located at the mouth of Ellisport Bay, this is a nice shady spot but a much smaller site than the Hope Boat Basin. The turnaround area is tight, but it offers quick and easy access to the lake. There is no beach, just muddy lake bottom. Parking is limited to only a couple vehicles.

FACILITIES: concrete boat ramp, dock, picnic table, vault toilet
ACTIVITIES: boating, swimming, picnicking

How to get here:

Access is from Idaho State Highway 200 about 16 miles east of Sandpoint. It is one mile east of the Hope overpass and Hope Boat Basin launch near milepost 46.

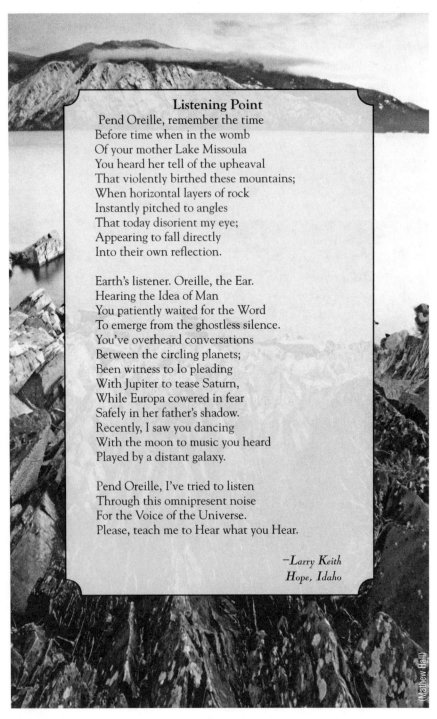

Listening Point

Pend Oreille, remember the time
Before time when in the womb
Of your mother Lake Missoula
You heard her tell of the upheaval
That violently birthed these mountains;
When horizontal layers of rock
Instantly pitched to angles
That today disorient my eye;
Appearing to fall directly
Into their own reflection.

Earth's listener. Oreille, the Ear.
Hearing the Idea of Man
You patiently waited for the Word
To emerge from the ghostless silence.
You've overheard conversations
Between the circling planets;
Been witness to Io pleading
With Jupiter to tease Saturn,
While Europa cowered in fear
Safely in her father's shadow.
Recently, I saw you dancing
With the moon to music you heard
Played by a distant galaxy.

Pend Oreille, I've tried to listen
Through this omnipresent noise
For the Voice of the Universe.
Please, teach me to Hear what you Hear.

—Larry Keith
Hope, Idaho

(Mathew Hall)

Visions of
Lake Pend Oreille

Stone stack at Green Bay's cobble beach (Patrick Orton)

Sailing in a Thursday evening regatta at Sandpoint (Mathew Hall)

Lincoln-loop flip from a climbing wall halfway between Garfield and Green bays (Patrick Orton)

Paddling past a seasonal creek between Talache Landing and Maiden Rock (Woods Wheatcroft)

Sunrise Bay boat launch at Idlewilde Bay, Farragut State Park (Mathew Hall)

View of the Clark Fork River Delta from Johnson Creek Road No. 278 (Jane Fritz)

Early evening scene from Trestle Creek area (Sandy Bessler)

The southern arm of the lake as seen from Bernard Peak viewpoint, looking north at sunset (Leland Howard)

Double rainbow over Gold Mountain seen from Third Avenue Pier in Sandpoint, looking east (Marie-Dominique Verdier)

Gazing east at the Green Monarchs from Grouse Mountain, south of Garfield Bay (Patrick Orton)

Late summer at Sandpoint City Beach (Marie-Dominique Verdier)

LIFEGUARDS ONLY
KEEP OFF

Moose one misty morning at Pack River Flats (Jon Shaver).

Ice skating on a brisk January day at West Oden Bay (Doug Marshall)

Twin strikes over Pend Oreille from the Long Bridge (Ryan McGinty)

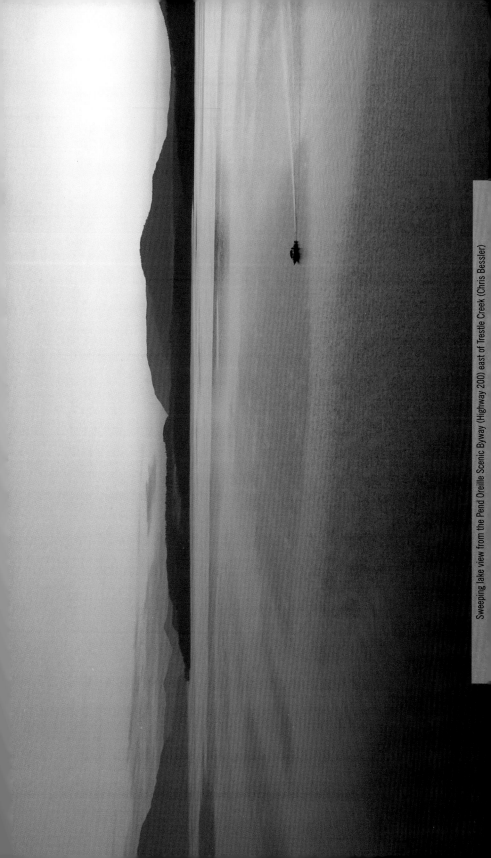

Sweeping lake view from the Pend Oreille Scenic Byway (Highway 200) east of Trestle Creek (Chris Bessler)

Bull trout (Ward Tollbom)

Cutthroat trout (Eileen Klatt)

Spawning kokanee (Eileen Klatt)

Kamloops trout (Eileen Klatt)

Ellisport Bay

This bay is the center of boating activity on this side of the lake. There are three private marinas – Hope Marine Services, Holiday Shores Resort/East Hope Marina and Kramer Marina. All three offer boat slips and moorings for powerboats, sailboats and even houseboats. Rentals and gas are available at Holiday Shores and Hope Marine, and the latter is the only business this side of the lake that services and repairs boats. There is a convenience store and cafe at Holiday Shores and a few fine restaurants in the area, including the renowned Floating Restaurant. There are also condominium resorts and even houseboats available for vacation rental. Charter boats for fishing and sightseeing are located here. Lake Pend Oreille Cruises, moored alternately at Kramer Marina and Sandpoint City Beach, offers a variety of group lake excursions.

Ellisport Bay in Hope (Woods Wheatcroft)

- - - - - - - - - - - - - - - - - - - -

Lake Pend Oreille Cruises: Circling the Islands

From Kramer Marina at Ellisport Bay, several couples and families join me as we board the tour boat, *Shawnodese*. Our guide and first mate Linda Mitchell passes out lap blankets to keep everybody warm this cool and cloudy autumn day in the open-air boat, a cross between the old steamboats that once navigated these waters in the early 1900s and an Alaskan fishing trawler. It can accommodate up to 30 passengers plus the crew. It was built by and is usually piloted by the boat's captain, Curtis Pearson, but today, Jim Sebero, a marine deputy for the Bonner County Sheriff's Department, is our skipper. As we cruise out of the bay, some of us get our binoculars ready to watch for bald eagles on Pearl Island, a protected sanctuary for the birds. Linda serves coffee and hot cocoa while Willy, her small dog and second mate, follows behind and easily makes friends with the passengers.

We scout the gray sky for the majestic white-headed raptors, but so far all we've seen — or rather heard — is a dozen or so "honkers," Canada geese. But we have faith that in this two-hour cruise we're bound to see at least a couple of eagles as we cruise past Hope Point and Memaloose Island on the south side of the Hope Peninsula. Linda is also our historian and purveyor of the trends of modernity. It's mind-boggling to learn that this small island, a former burial ground of the Kalispel Tribe and later settled by white pioneers, is presently for sale by its current owners for more than $16 million. The lakeshore properties in this area are some of the most expensive on Lake Pend Oreille, says Linda, and although that's interesting, we're here to see a more enduring treasure — the bald eagle.

As our captain pilots the boat toward Pearl Island and Linda talks about her other favorite subjects — explorer David Thompson and the local fur trade of the early 1800s, the Ice Age floods and how most of the water here in Lake Pend Oreille is fed by tributaries of the Clark Fork River, which flows into the lake just east of us — nature does not disappoint us. Finally one of the passengers spots an eagle flying low toward our destination. As we circle around, we hear an eagle cry from a ponderosa pine nestled in deep foliage towards the center of the small island. Linda tells us that she and Curtis discovered that nest more than six years ago. The adult eagles come back to it year after year to breed, adding new material to the existing structure. Its size is already larger than 6 feet in diameter and will likely get bigger. We linger offshore to watch the birds with binoculars. The one that was flying has landed in a snag not far from the nest. Its characteristic yellow beak and white hood and tail feathers reveal that it is at least a 5-year-old male or female. Eagles can live 25 years or longer, says Linda, and, unlike ospreys, both parents service the nest, and it's difficult to tell them apart.

Our sojourn continues on to Cottage Island and the much larger Warren Island. The history of these islands is colorful and a tad bawdy. It seems that the tiny cottage on the small island was actually a "crib," or brothel. It's also the oldest building on the Bonner County tax rolls, built in 1882 by Northern Pacific Railway. The *Henry Villard* steamboat would bring railroad workers here daily to utilize the services of the ladies. "If only those walls could talk," quips Linda. Warren Island has electricity from cable laid on the lake bottom from Hope but has only a few year-round residents. Linda tells us that Teddy Roosevelt stayed at one of the old cabins on this island during one of his famous hunting and fishing expeditions.

As we head back to port, the passengers — all visitors to the area except for me — say that the trip was enjoyable and worthwhile despite the chilly weather. The eagle watching was definitely a highlight of the tour.

Besides the cruise around the Hope Islands, Lake Pend Oreille Cruises also tours the Clark Fork Delta watching for wildlife. These tours occur only on weekends and one other day during the week in the spring and fall. During the summer the Shawnodese is moored at Sandpoint City Beach.

Linda admits she simply loves her job and then recounts her most memorable passenger, former First Lady Patricia Kempthorne whose husband, Dirk, was governor of Idaho at the time. During dinner a big storm came up, but Mrs. Kempthorne had a blast because she's an experienced sailor, says Linda. A glorious double rainbow over the Clark Fork Delta was enough to convince the First Lady to bring her husband back here from Boise for their 25th wedding anniversary, a tour that lasted five hours.

Anecdota: Trail 120 and a Horseback Jamboree

Pat (Shaffer) Holt is a fifth-generation Sandpoint native whose great-great-grandparents came here in 1892 as pioneers. She shares some of that true grit: She has been riding the mountain trails around Lake Pend Oreille on horseback for more than 30 years.

The Bee Top-Round Top Trail No. 120 from Lunch Peak to Lightning Creek is one of Holt's favorite trail rides. She insists that the view of the lake from the ridgeline is like that from an airplane. Riding the trail takes two days and so halfway across you need to camp overnight.

But one thing about Trail 120 that Holt will always fondly remember was the annual event that took place here and on other trails around the lake (the High Drive was another) for 10 summers beginning back in the late 1960s – the Pend d'Oreille Ride. Ed and Lorena Hawkins, longtime owners of the former Litehouse Restaurant in Hope, and their family, founders of the successful salad dressing company, organized and sponsored the ride.

Just imagine the scene: More than 200 riders – young and old alike – coming from miles around to spend three days and two nights together in the wilderness on horseback (without cell phones!). Then imagine Ed Hawkins and his son Doug doing *all* the cooking to feed all those people. Meals began at base camp on Friday night, usually a barbecue. Then they would prepare and serve a breakfast the following morning, a *hot* lunch along the way, and steak, potato and corn-on-the-cob supper, usually with strawberry shortcake for dessert, around the campfire on Saturday night. The following morning there would be another breakfast and then at the end of the trail, the riders would make their way to the Litehouse and share in a scrumptious Hawkins-style Sunday buffet.

Lorena remembers one ride in which a lot more riders showed up than had pre-registered, and they ran out of fried chicken planned for lunch. Ed frantically raced to Clark Fork and bought

The Hawkins family and their pack train rests on Trail 120 in this 1975 photo (Will Hawkins)

every chicken that Emma Rathbun had at the Mercantile, quickly cooked them up and saved the day.

But that's not all. Ed's nephew, Will Hawkins, who was the trail boss, would plan each ride and organize a family ride down the trail in advance of the guest ride to plan meals and camping stops, as well as do any necessary trail work, such as removing downed trees and widening the trail in places. Then during the Pend d'Oreille Ride, Will and his father, Dalton Hawkins, would haul in all the camping gear for the riders and grain and hay if needed, and sometimes even water, for the horses. Holt remembers one special supper while camping at Auxor Basin, near the Round Top Mountain Lookout. What a starry, starry night that must have been!

Will Hawkins, the trail boss, planned and organized the annual horseback jamborees (courtesy Hawkins family)

Friends of the Hawkins family gathered one more time for one last horseback ride on the ridgeline in the early 1980s to honor and to thank Ed and Will Hawkins for all those wonderful sojourns. Sadly, both men have passed on. That was the last summer the whinnies of so many horses and the laughter and songs of so many people were heard along Trail 120. Those days really *were* the good old days.

Tour on Wheels:
Strong Creek to Wellington Creek

For a rough and challenging ride, hearty mountain bikers tackle the Strong Creek Trail, which is actually an old road in Hope. That means the grade is manageable on a bike, but there are times it gets quite steep. Also the elevation gain is more than 3,500 feet to Wellington Saddle, where the road goes over the ridge and descends Wellington Creek to Lightning Creek Road. A major flood event in 2006 washed out many stream crossings on Lightning Creek Road. Construction to repair the road began in 2009. The entire length of this loop is dirt and gravel, except for the final few miles on Highway 200 back to the town of Hope. It is perhaps one of the most difficult bike rides in the region.

Length: approximately 35 miles, but much of the route may be gated

Difficulty: very difficult

Safety Concerns: sharp rocks, trees across the road, stream crossings

Road Type: mostly dirt and gravel

Road Conditions: fair to washed out stream crossings

Facilities En Route: In Hope there are stores and restaurants. Water can be taken from numerous streams along the way but should be filtered.

Attractions: There are primitive campsites at Wellington Saddle and the Bee Top-Round Top Trail 120 crosses the road here. A side hike (or singletrack ride) is possible to Round Top, the highest summit on this divide overlooking the lake.

Directions: A good place to begin this ride is near the Hope Post Office. Take the paved road that ascends the hill to the west, then turn sharply right toward the cemetery. Proceed past the cemetery onto Strong Creek Road. A barrier blocks the road about a mile or so beyond the cemetery but the roadbed continues and is in pretty good shape. You will pass through deep woods with lots of shade, which you will appreciate, because the road begins to rise steeply. It crosses the creek after a couple miles and switchbacks up the mountainside. Views of the lake become increasingly fabulous. Once at the top of the ridge, after about nine miles from the post office, this is a great place for a long breather. Ardent mountain bikers may follow Trail 120 east or west for some excellent singletrack riding. The road was closed to vehicles beyond this point to Lightning Creek after the major flood event in 2006, but it was being restored at the time of this publication (see Tour on Wheels: Trestle Creek to Lightning Creek, page 172). Once back on pavement, a good alternative to Highway 200 is about two miles west of Clark Fork traveling the old highway all the way to Hope.

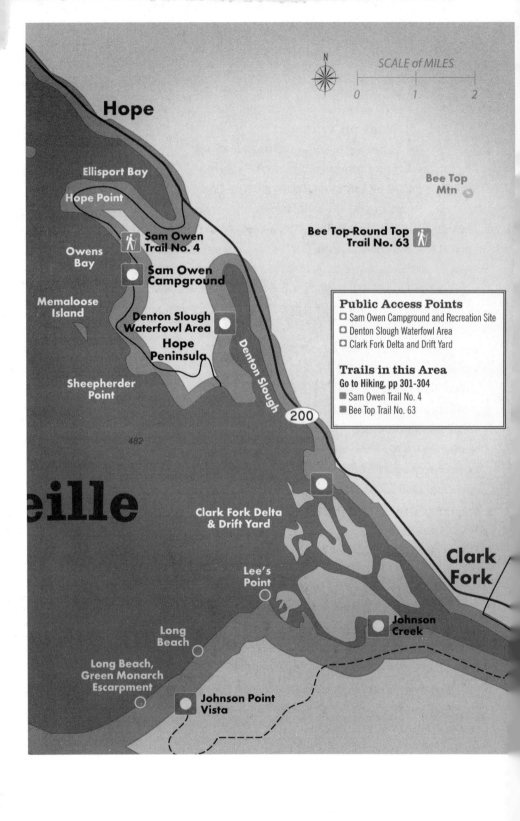

N

SCALE of MILES

0   1   2

Hope

Ellisport Bay

Hope Point

Owens
Bay

Memaloose
Island

Sheepherder
Point

482

Sam Owen
Trail No. 4

Sam Owen
Campground

Denton Slough
Waterfowl Area

Hope
Peninsula

Denton Slough

200

Bee Top
Mtn

Bee Top-Round Top
Trail No. 63

Public Access Points
☐ Sam Owen Campground and Recreation Site
☐ Denton Slough Waterfowl Area
☐ Clark Fork Delta and Drift Yard

Trails in this Area
Go to Hiking, pp 301-304
▇ Sam Owen Trail No. 4
▇ Bee Top Trail No. 63

eille

Clark Fork Delta
& Drift Yard

Lee's
Point

Long
Beach

Long Beach,
Green Monarch
Escarpment

Johnson Point
Vista

Clark
Fork

Johnson
Creek

CHAPTER EIGHT

8

AREA 5, HOPE PENINSULA TO
CLARK FORK DELTA

OVERVIEW

A little east of Hope, past all the activity of Ellisport Bay, Idaho State Highway 200 becomes rural and sparsely populated once again all the way to the town of Clark Fork. You are still on the Pend Oreille Scenic Byway, and three more special attractions are worth visiting: the Sam Owen Campground and Recreation Site on the Hope Peninsula, Denton Slough Waterfowl Area and Clark Fork Delta and Drift Yard. Interpretive signs at byway turnouts provide fascinating information.

Peninsula Road, also known as Sam Owen Road, gives you access to the Hope Peninsula – also a home to wildlife. The David Thompson State Wildlife Preserve is a safe area (no hunting allowed) for deer, Canada geese and other wildlife, so drive slowly on its winding roads because animals wander freely. And as tempting as it may be, please do not feed the wildlife; help them stay wild. This area, also referred to as Beyond Hope, is both a residential and recreation area. There are RV resorts on the peninsula and at least one fine eatery and marina at Beyond Hope Resort. But the highlight for visitors to the area is the Forest Service-managed Sam Owen Campground and Recreation Site, rated as one of the top 100 national campgrounds in the

Cyclists peddling past Denton Slough on the old highway (Chris Guibert)

country. It is a beautiful, 65-acre park that has 78 campsites, a swimming beach, boat launch, group pavilion, handicapped accessible hiking trail and an interpretive site about Thompson, the first white man to visit the area in 1809. Thompson's trading post, Kullyspel House, was built somewhere in the vicinity and was the first trading post in the Inland Northwest.

Back on the highway, get ready for the ride of your life, for this is remarkable lakeshore. For almost five miles from Peninsula Road to Clark Fork, except for only a few homes, this is largely undeveloped private land. In the many years that I have lived here and the hundreds of times that I have driven this stretch of road, I have been so grateful for the shoreline's relatively unspoiled natural beauty, especially at night. The night sky, except for when the moon is brightly shining, is actually dark. Few scenic places exist where light pollution has not seeped in and this is one of them. It's partly because as you drive parallel to the shore, the land across the lake from you is public, mostly Forest Service land. There are no lights simply because it is a wild place.

One of the more amazing experiences a person who treasures wildness can have in northern Idaho, without hiking far into the backcountry, is simply to pull off the highway onto the access road at the Clark Fork Drift Yard and get out of your car. Just listen to the soft murmurs of Canada geese on the water or the wail of a loon as you gaze in awe at the full moon poised above the Green Monarchs or watch for northern lights or meteor showers to dance across the night sky. Sometimes when the water is glassy you can even see stars reflected on the lake's surface.

This area is the genesis site for the Kalispel Tribe and one of their most culturally important

Legendary Lake Pend Oreille

Clark Fork Delta and Drift Yard at sunset (Jerry Luther)

places. The Kootenai have ties here as well. Although I've never had it verified by a Kootenai tribal elder, I once read that the tribe believed when a Kootenai died, his or her soul went to the sun and came back to earth between Hope and Clark Fork at Lake Pend Oreille. This area is indeed sacred to many other people, including me. The place once known by locals as "Indian Meadows," (see page 205) which is now mostly underwater, was a traditional site of large tribal gatherings. Throughout this chapter, I will share some of the remarkable history as well as the contemporary connections that the Kalispel people have with this part of Lake Pend Oreille. When you visit, please be respectful, take nothing you find, and leave no trace of your visit.

The whole family can enjoy hiking the short, easy trail honoring Sam Owen with a trailhead just across from Sam Owen Campground. The other trail in this area is designed with the serious hiker in mind: Bee Top Trail 63 veers off Bee Top-Round Top Trail No. 120 on the high ridges above the town of Clark Fork, with a panoramic vista of the pastoral setting of the Clark Fork River Delta and Lake Pend Oreille.

Another reason to visit this resplendent part of Bonner County is to see wildlife. The marshes and wetlands around Denton Slough and the Clark Fork Delta are part of the Lake Pend Oreille and Clark Fork Wildlife Management Areas and home to a tremendous diversity of waterfowl, fish-eating birds and mammals. It is one of the most vital wildlife areas on the lake and critical habitat to thousands of migratory waterfowl including tundra swans. There are 15 rare animal species, as well as three rare plant communities found living here. Some of the interesting bird species to watch for include western grebe, osprey, blue heron and common loon. You might see a moose up to his neck in Denton Slough munching away on aquatic vegetation or have a beaver slap his tail on the water, startling you as you kayak along in the delta.

The Clark Fork Delta is a paddler's paradise. There are sloughs and backwaters to explore where you literally can get lost. You can launch at either Denton Slough or the Clark Fork Drift Yard boat launch, commonly used by fishermen and waterfowl hunters. Remember to bring your binoculars for watching wildlife and for a closer look at the numerous birds that depend on this area for food, shelter and the rearing of their young. This area is shallow, and the shoreline is home to many creatures, so unless you have a boat with a small electric motor, it's smarter to put in your powerboat, sailboat or personal watercraft elsewhere on the lake, and enjoy that vicinity rather than disturbing the wildlife here.

Anecdota: Paddling a Kalispel Canoe

The first time I met J.R. Bluff, a Kalispel tribal member, was in 1991 at an environmental education camp for American Indian youth held in Clark Fork. We were both camp counselors, but I was the one that had the responsibility of organizing canoe trips to a tribal sacred site in the Clark Fork Delta.

I called upon several friends with canoes to help. The first evening's paddle went smoothly, but the next trip was a near disaster. The lake was unusually rough from a storm that had just moved through. It was brisk and windy as June can sometimes be.

Suddenly, I realized two girls in a small, peapod-like vessel had capsized. They had lifejackets on, but they were in very cold water. Not knowing what to do, I sat in my cedar canoe on shore, frozen with panic. J.R. kindly told me to get out of the stern, which I did, and taking my canoe he paddled out to rescue the students. Not only did he save the girls from hypothermia, he taught me a lesson about preparedness when it comes to being responsible for others on the water.

Several years passed before I saw J.R. again at a Kalispel powwow on his reservation in Usk, Washington. We laughed about how so many years before he had rescued a novice canoeist — on land. Since then we have both grown more proficient in our life's work: I as an environmental writer and oral historian and he as a tribal leader and now assistant director of the tribe's culture program. We both have become more adept at canoeing, too. Now he regularly takes tribal youth canoeing on Lake Pend Oreille as part of his cultural work for the tribe.

J.R. Bluff on his maiden voyage in a Kalispel canoe (Robert C. Betts, Vanguard Research)

So it seems perfect that J.R. Bluff was the first Kalispel in 65 years to paddle a traditional Kalispel canoe again on Lake Pend Oreille. The Kalispel were a canoe people, but with acculturation, a different way of life on the reservation took hold and canoe making became a lost art. A skilled boatbuilder in the Sandpoint area (who wishes to remain anonymous) had researched their unique, sturgeon-nose design and built a canoe out of traditional natural materials. It is quite different from other Indian canoes. When Kalispel leaders saw the canoe on display at the Bonner County Historical Society Museum in Sandpoint, where it still is today, they asked the boatwright to help them build another canoe for the tribe in 2000.

J.R. and Francis Cullooyah, director of the tribe's culture program, were both involved in the process of making the second canoe, beginning

Kalispel Tribe member J.R. Bluff (foreground) peels bark from a white pine tree with two helpers to build a traditional canoe. The tribe's cultural leader, Francis Cullooyah, looks on, upper right (Robert C. Betts, Vanguard Research)

with stripping the bark from a huge, 50-inch-circumference, live, western white pine tree. The bark had to be removed as a single piece and be longer than 20 feet. Before pioneers logged the hillsides bare around Lake Pend Oreille, western white pine was the predominant species here, and these trees were giants. In making the Kalispel canoe, the rough outer tree bark becomes the inside of the canoe and the smooth inner bark becomes the outside surface of the boat. The skeletal structure is cedar, and it is lashed together with chokecherry bark. It has a nose of birch bark, and the seams are sealed with pine pitch. It is a very handsome vessel on the water and as it ages the outer bark surface turns a reddish gold color.

J.R. talks about his first paddle in a Kalispel canoe as if he were riding a new horse for the first time. It took a few minutes before he and the canoe got comfortable with each other. "I am a Kalispel," he remembers saying out loud to his waterborne steed.

He paddled the pine bark canoe out from the Hope Peninsula near Memaloose Island on an April day where snow lingered on the Monarchs before him and geese honked as they flew past low to the water. Sitting on an elk hide in the stern of the canoe, J.R. paddled quietly into open water and thought about his ancestors. He had read once that people in Hope would see Indian canoes out on the water here every morning. He realized that he was rekindling a strong connection to his past. Sitting in the canoe, the teachings of his elders about gratitude came flooding back to him; of how the canoe was at once a simple thing and also at the very heart of his people's survival.

"Every time I think of Pend Oreille Lake, I think of Indian Meadows and the life of the camp," J.R. says. "When I'm out there (on the water in a canoe), I'm always visualizing the families that came down and camped – this was a shared area. Even though times were tough and we had to gather meat to make it through the winter, the smiles on the faces of the kids running around, the women working hard, the men out fishing and hunting ... we were just a common people following nature, and basically sharing everything with everyone. We need to keep rekindling our connections with the Kalispel places off the reservation.

"Being on the water in a Kalispel canoe was a very special feeling," J.R. continues. "We were here and are still here today. Everything is still alive. It gives you that extra energy to get back to your regular daily living and say 'I'm going to do something better.' There are a lot of people who have paid the price for me to be here, and I have to be sure to keep their memories alive and our heritage and culture strong in the best way I can," he says. This part of the Kalispel past certainly has been reawakened as J.R.'s intentions are to carry on the tradition of canoe making as part of the tribe's culture program.

►**SAM OWEN CAMPGROUND AND RECREATION SITE**

Managed by the Idaho Panhandle National Forest, this 65-acre park is a fee-based campground and recreation area on the Hope Peninsula at Owens Bay. Seventy-eight campsite units are available from late April through late September. The campground gets crowded during the height of summer beginning around July Fourth. Reservations can be made for 47 of the campsites, with 31 available on a first-come, first-served basis. Camping is limited to 14 days for up to eight people per campsite. Although there are no electrical hookups, the units can accommodate RVs up to 40 feet in length. A group picnic site, with a covered pavilion also can be reserved for events such as weddings, memorials and reunions. A fee is charged for day-use of the beach and picnic area, but a season pass is also available.

Sand volleyball court on the beach at Sam Owen Campground (Linda Lantzy)

Reservations are accepted year-round up to 240 days in advance of your stay. To make campsite reservations, call toll-free 877-444-6777, TDD 877-833-6777 or 518-885-3639 for international. Or go online to www.recreation.gov. A campground manager/host is on-site during the camping season.

Private campgrounds and several RV resorts are also in the vicinity. Beyond Hope Resort, the closest to Sam Owen Campground, has visitor slips for boaters coming to dine at their restaurant and lounge. Pontoon boats, canoes, kayaks and pedal-boats are also available to rent. Fuel, additional moorage and boat rentals are available at Hope Marine Services, and Holiday Shores Resort/East Hope Marina on the other side of the peninsula at Ellisport Bay.

What's it like?

Voted in the top 100 of 1,700 campgrounds nationwide, this is a great place to spend vacation time on Lake Pend Oreille. You can swim, boat, fish, barbecue, picnic, bike and hike all from one setting. This is truly a campground set in the woods with several acres of old western red cedars, ponderosa pines and Douglas firs to camp among and to shade you from the hot summer sun. There is a large, grassy picnic area and a long stretch of sandy-gravel beach along the southern shore of the peninsula. There are also a sand volleyball court and horseshoe pits in the day-use area.

The boat launch and dock, for loading only, is also available to non-campers for a fee, and there is ample parking for cars with boat trailers. Kids on bikes, roller blades and skateboards can safely enjoy riding the four and a half miles of paved roads that loop in and around the campsites. For history buffs, there is a new David Thompson Interpretive Site near the restrooms. The entire family can also be entertained and educated about local lore, wildlife and other fascinating subjects around a campfire most summer weekend evenings in the amphitheater.

According to Joe Willard, a longtime camp host and manager, Sam Owen Campground has been spruced up over the past several years, so it's a good idea to reserve your camping space by the Independence Day holiday. Sam Owen Campground becomes a temporary community with so many people returning year after year, and Willard tries to nurture that sense of unified enjoyment as if the camp was home to one big extended family. If it's privacy you seek, this is not where you want to be during peak summer. The record stay is a couple that has returned every year for 55 years in a row! But before and after the busy summer weekends the park usually has plenty of space for spontaneous weekend campers and travelers.

Forest Service Sam Owen Trail No. 4 is across Peninsula Road from the entrance of the park and is wheelchair and stroller accessible. The easy, mile-long round-trip trail leads to Sam and Nina Owen's gravesites. This was the couple that became the benefactors of the land that was developed into the campground. Sam Owen Campground is also a wonderful place to cross-country ski in the winter if there's enough snow, although it is officially closed for the season. The park in winter is about as peaceful as it gets around here.

FACILITIES: concrete boat ramp with loading dock, sandy gravel beach, campground for tents and RVs (no electric hookups) with paved access, campground host, covered pavilion for group use, ample parking, picnic tables, cooking grates and grills, firewood, drinking water, RV dump station, flush restrooms, amphitheater, historic interpretive site, walking trail, volleyball sand court, horseshoe pits
ACTIVITIES: camping, boating, swimming, fishing, picnicking, hiking, wildlife viewing, volleyball, horseshoes, historical site

How to get here:

Access from Idaho State Highway 200 is about 21 miles east of Sandpoint. Just past East Hope near milepost 48, turn south on Peninsula Road (also called Sam Owen Road) and slow down for deer on this winding, narrow road, because the peninsula is a wildlife preserve. Go about one mile (stay left when the road forks) until you see the Sam Owen Campground signs. Turn right into the entrance and stop to pay your fee. Private resorts, a marina, RV parks and private residences are farther down Peninsula Road.

Lore Along the Shore: Sam and Nina Owen
By Marianne Love

Nina Smith Owen, born in 1876, came to Hope, Idaho, from Sweden as an 11-year-old with her mother and three sisters to join their father, Charles Smith, who had come seven years earlier. Mr. Smith cared for the beautifully landscaped grounds

Seated upper right, Nina and Sam Owen, shown in August 1923 with a group who was looking for the long-lost site of Kullyspel House (Bonner County Historical Society Collection)

and rowboats at the Highland House, built by the Northern Pacific Railroad in 1885. The Highland House was touted as the Pacific Northwest's first resort to attract wealthy Easterners. Smith was also a fishing and hunting guide, but apparently his advice fell on deaf ears when General William Tecumseh Sherman visited in 1884; Sherman couldn't snag a single fish in the lake or in Strong Creek, which at the time teemed with trout. The Smith family embraced the elegance at the Highland House and eventually purchased the resort from the railroad after only a couple of years. They rented out rooms for the next five years.

"What awed the family was an oasis of luxury in a wilderness populated by Indians and wild animals," Nina Owen told *Spokesman-Review* reporter Jim Parsons in a 1958 interview. Nina misunderstood the sociability of Kalispel Indians who camped at the nearby Indian Meadows when they would arrive uninvited and come into their house without knocking. Afraid, she and her sisters would go hide in their bedrooms.

After completing her education, Nina taught school in a one-room schoolhouse at Boyer (now Kootenai). "One day Sam Owen rode up on his horse and asked the way to Bonners Ferry," the newspaper revealed. The couple eventually married in 1897 and moved to the Hope Peninsula where Sam built a log cabin and planted the first apple orchard in the territory. Sam and Nina Owen donated 35 acres of their homestead to the U.S. Forest Service in 1940, and this was developed into what today is the Sam Owen Campground. A short trail across the road from the campground entrance takes casual hikers up to a double gravesite for Nina and Sam Owen overlooking the forest above Lake Pend Oreille.

- -

David Thompson Interpretive Site

David Thompson was a fur trader for the Canadian North West Company. He also was a surveyor and mapmaker in search of a Northwest Passage and the route to the Pacific by way of the Columbia River. He and his men first saw Lake Pend Oreille when they arrived on horseback on September 8, 1809, from the "Lake Indian Road" (Kootenai Indian Trail from Canada) most likely at present-day Boyer Slough.

In his journal Thompson wrote of that event: "A fine day, but very cold Night – Ice was formed – but the leaves are yet every where very green ... At 7 ¼ Am set off...Co S20E 6M to a Rill of water which we followed down S40E 1 ½ M to the Lake."

Thompson named this lake Kullyspel Lake, after the Kalispel Indians whom he befriended in his fur-trade relations. Somewhere in the vicinity, he and Finan McDonald built the first trading post in the Inland Northwest – the Kullyspel House; but, it proved not to be a profitable site because the Kalispel only came to this area in spring and summer and most beaver trapping is done during winter. So Thompson built another trading post, Saleesh House, upriver near present day Thompson Falls, a tribal winter village site. The lake name was eventually changed to the French words meaning "ear pendant," Pend d'Oreille. Thompson bestowed the name Saleesh River to the Clark Fork and Pend Oreille rivers, marking a major canoe route for all the tribes that were linguistically related to each other as Salish speakers.

Thompson returned to his home in the East and to his Cree Indian wife Charlotte in April 1812, and he never came back to Lake Pend Oreille. But he recognized the intrinsic value of the Lake Pend Oreille watershed and what its future might be like. His memoir, *The Travels of David Thompson*, written in his later years, included this recollection: "The impression of my mind from the formation of the country and its climate, its extensive Meadows and fine Forests, watered

198   Legendary Lake Pend Oreille

The currently accepted site of the Kullyspel House, on private property on Hope Peninsula, contains rock piles that are presumably the remains of the building's chimneys (Dann Hall)

by countless Brooks and Rills of pure water, that it will become the abode of civilized Man, whether Natives or other people."

For more information on David Thompson, read Chapter 14 by Dennis Nicholls. You also can visit the new interpretive exhibit in the beach house display window located near the restrooms at Sam Owen Campground. The Bonner County Historical Society installed the exhibit in 2007 in anticipation of the bicentennial commemoration of Thompson's exploration of this area.

— — — — — — — — — — — — — — —

Points of Sail
By Cate Huisman

The tiny dock at Sam Owen Campground is barely big enough for a dinghy. There is no protection at all, but you can anchor temporarily offshore in a gravelly sloping bottom. However, it's the kind of anchorage that requires constant surveillance – the crew can go ashore and explore, but the captain will have to stay with the ship. Overnight sailors can use one of the three marinas on the other side of the peninsula at Ellisport Bay: Kramer Marina, Hope Marine Services and Holiday Shores Resort/East Hope Marina. The most masts are seen at Kramer Marina.

Although a look at the chart suggests that it might be fun to explore in Denton Slough or among the islands at the mouth of the Clark Fork River, a sailboat is not the best vessel for this purpose. The slough is weedy and shallow, and unless you're in a flat-bottomed scow and you like hopping over the side a lot, don't think about sailing in the river delta. The backwaters are full of wildlife and tempting, but the area is also full of shifting bars and less than 2 feet deep in many places. Log booms or riprap block much of the access by boat in this estuary, and numerous submerged tree stumps are just below the surface as well. Better to poke around in a dinghy.

DENTON SLOUGH WATERFOWL AREA

Comanaged by the U.S. Army Corps of Engineers and Idaho Fish and Game as part of the Lake Pend Oreille and Clark Fork Wildlife Management Areas. This is a day-use area only with no fee for public access.

Canada geese at Denton Slough (Jay Mock)

What's it like?

There is a narrow strip of land between the highway and the water that is screened with trees that help to curtail some of the noise from the highway and the railroad tracks north of the road. The turnout off the highway at the west end of the slough is up the bank from the water and has interpretive signs describing the wildlife and waterfowl that can be found on the slough. This is a breeding area for western grebes, ospreys and heron. At the east end of the slough is a turnoff that makes a hard right and follows a short dirt road to a parking area with a tight turnaround that will accommodate four to six vehicles. A portable toilet is at this end of the slough. A muddy bank is accessible at either end (you have to portage a short distance at the west end) for kayaks, canoes and small boats (electric motors only recommended) that can negotiate the thick native aquatic vegetation and shallows along the shore.

A lot of anglers fish from shore for largemouth bass, yellow perch and crappie, and some of these same folks camp and build campfires. Campfires are neither allowed nor acceptable, especially building fires so close to the water; they only pollute the water and upset the delicate balance of this valuable wildlife habitat. Other properties around the slough are private and need to be respected.

FACILITIES: muddy banks for launching kayaks, canoes and small fishing boats, portable toilet, wildlife interpretive signs

ACTIVITIES: kayaking, canoeing, fishing, wildlife viewing, bird-watching

How to get here:

Access is from Idaho State Highway 200, just over 20 miles east of Sandpoint past milepost 50. There are two turnouts – at the west and east ends.

Wildlife Viewing: Western Grebes

The grassy meadows, near the site of summer encampments of native peoples, were called various names by the area's white settlers, but the name that stuck was a combination of railroad man Dennis Thornton's first and last name – Denton. After the Albeni Falls Dam flooded the meadows, it became known as Denton Slough.

Western grebes perform a courting display at Denton Slough (Jay Mock)

Today Denton Slough is habitat to many fish-eating birds, waterfowl and mammals. Thousands of ducks – American wigeon, gadwalls, pintails, redhead, greater and lesser scaup, green-winged teal and mallards – and grebes, mergansers, tundra swans and Canada geese use the slough during migrations.

But Denton Slough is especially noted for being the breeding and nursery area for a rare and sensitive colony of long-necked, resident western grebes. The western grebe is not a diving duck; it is a piscavore, or fish-eating species of bird. This is the elegant water bird that you've likely seen in nature programs on television. Pairs of adult birds gracefully dance across the water's surface during their remarkable courting display with their long necks arched in a beautiful curve. After the dancing and the graceful head bobbing while singing their distinctive crik-crik cry, they mate and begin building their nests directly on the water. Using their beaks, the birds dive underwater and pull up native milfoils and pondweeds and gather them into a deep and large floating nest in which to lay their eggs. Once hatched, the chicks remain in their watery nursery, fed first by the adults and then learning to fish on their own, until fall migration.

Depending on the growth of aquatic vegetation, the birds can be on nests anywhere from June to August. This makes them very vulnerable to strong winds and predators like bald eagles (who also nest nearby), ravens and otters. Nature can be harsh: Several years ago a group of grebe watchers, myself among them, saw dozens of nests with females incubating eggs destroyed over two days time. One of our members saw an otter going nest to nest. It was a devastating loss!

In addition to natural events, these breeding grebes are also extremely vulnerable to boaters. I've encountered (and gently educated) at least one Jet Skier racing in and out of the slough right through a chain of nests. But these birds are even more wary when the boats approach slowly. A nesting female will typically leave her nest when a canoe or kayak gets closer than 150 yards, leaving the eggs or chicks not only open to predation but also cold or heat depending on the weather. The birds are not great flyers so they scoot away from boats. The constant drone of nearby traffic and trains does not disturb these birds, while an angler or paddler can spell death.

I find the best way to enjoy the western grebes here is to watch them with binoculars from shore; this is true for most wildlife watching. Keep your distance. This colony of grebes has been experiencing a decline in nesting success at Denton Slough since 2005, a situation most likely due to human disturbance more than anything else. The birds also have been moving into the Clark Fork Drift Yard, a place where they don't encounter boats but are more vulnerable to wind, waves and predators. They are now on Idaho Fish and Game's list of Species of Special Concern.

In addition to the western grebe are other species of grebes on Lake Pend Oreille, including the horned grebe, pied-billed grebe and red-necked grebe. Western grebes are often mistaken for common loons. Although from different groups, these two species of piscavores share some things in common: long, sharp bills for spearing fish; diving completely underwater and coming to the surface somewhere else; and carrying their young on their backs. This is in addition to lobed toes on legs placed far to the rear of their bodies (rather than webbed feet) making it difficult to walk on land, solid bones to help them dive, and those haunting, red eyes, which help them to see their underwater prey at greater depths.

The best practice to ensure the survival of this breeding colony is to stay off Denton Slough altogether or keep your kayak or canoe out past the slough into the mouth of the Clark Fork River and around the peninsula. There are plenty of other places on Lake Pend Oreille in which to play and fish; but by all means watch their unique antics for as long as you can, especially after dawn and before dark. They are truly remarkable creatures.

Wildflower Notes: Camas

When only native peoples lived around Lake Pend Oreille, each spring the lovely blue flowers of the edible, bulbous camas plant would color the landscape so abundantly that grassy meadows like those around the Hope Peninsula and Clark Fork River Delta appeared as water.

Common or blue camas (*Camassia quamash*), a member of the lily family, was such an important food source to the Kalispel that they became known as "Camas People." The camas

plant's bulb, about the size of a woman's thumbnail, provided a staple food for the tribe. The nutritional value of the starchy bulbs exceeds brown rice. Native women would dig the bulbs in early to midsummer with a specially made tool, a digging stick, and then roast the peeled bulbs underground with heated stones and between layers of black lichen. They would form them into loaves and cakes and store them for winter use. The interpretive historic trail at Pioneer Park along the Pend Oreille River in Newport, Washington, just west of Oldtown, Idaho, offers a glimpse of the Kalispel's ancient food preservation system including the archaeological remains of camas ovens.

Common camas in bloom (Jerry Pavia)

Today tribal members still roast and preserve camas bulbs in the traditional ways. However, with the introduction of non-native grasses and herbaceous plants for livestock after white settlement, the camas has been out-competed and their numbers greatly reduced. It's also important to know where the edible plants grow and the difference between the edible blue camas and the poisonous white-flowered death camas (*Zigadenus elegans*). This is because the plants often grow together and bulbs are dug after the flowers have bloomed and died away. As a valuable ethno-botanical plant to the Kalispel people, camas is best left alone for native gatherers to harvest.

Fish Tales: Ospreys, Eagles and Great Blue Herons

I spoke with a woman from Clark Fork in 2006 whose husband had spent 50 years catching fish from the shore at Denton Slough. Yellow perch and crappie live in the slough, and largemouth bass like to hang out there and spawn in the warm, shallow water, eating crawdads and other fish species.

But to ospreys, bald eagles and great blue herons, the bass is just another fish on the food chain. Denton Slough and the Clark Fork Delta are home to more than 20 nesting pairs of ospreys, blue heron rookeries, and a few resident bald eagle nests. It is also an important wintering area for hundreds of bald eagles that migrate here during fish spawning season.

Ospreys (*Pandion haliaetus*) are also sometimes called fish-hawks. Chocolate brown and white in color with a bandit eye band, you can see them sitting in snags, atop their high and impressive treetop or bridge-top stick nests, or flapping or hovering with their 4- to 6-foot wingspans high above the water from early April until late September as the birds' keen eyes scan below the water's surface for fish. Once it spots its prey, an osprey will dive, wings tucked and feet first, fully plunging underwater to capture it. Then with its clever-toed talons, it will turn the fish around so that when the osprey rises from the water, shakes its body of excess water like a dog, and flies home to its nest, the fish will be pointing in the same direction as flight, essentially reducing wind resistance.

Unlike ospreys, bald eagles can drown if their wings get wet. They skim the surface of the water, spearing their fish with those mightily sharp talons. Sometimes you will see an eagle try to steal a fish from an osprey in flight. The aerial battle can sometimes result in the fish accidentally being dropped. Even though eagles are bigger than ospreys, the latter defends its catch with the persistence of any good fisher.

Another bird looking for a meal of fish to eat is the great blue heron. Its hunting behavior is that of standing completely still in the water for long periods of time, displaying a demeanor of ultimate patience. But if a fish swims near, the 4-foot-tall bird with gangly legs moves as quickly as lightning to catch its prey in its long bill. Herons nest and roost in trees along the shore in this area. When startled, they utter a loud, prehistoric sounding grak, grak. They are very wary and rarely let people get too close. Sometimes in spring you can see a dozen or more standing in the shallow waters of the delta as the lake level rises. They fly high with their neck folded back on the shoulder – quite an impressive sight.

CLARK FORK DELTA AND DRIFT YARD

Comanaged by the U.S. Army Corps of Engineers and Idaho Fish and Game as the Clark Fork and Pend Oreille Wildlife Management Area, this is largely a day-use area with no fee for public access and camping allowed up to three days. Much of the area is closed between April 1 and May 15 each year to protect nesting waterfowl, in particular Canada geese. Please ensure the success of waterfowl breeding by respecting the gate across the access road when you come to it.

What's it like?

This huge, grassy wetland is newly improved with a large meadow maintained for camping and group gatherings. Its large parking area can accommodate 20 cars or more. This spot accesses the Clark Fork River Delta, valuable wildlife habitat, particularly to nesting waterfowl and songbirds. On the right-hand side, near the highway is the Drift Yard, a series of log booms built in the river by the U.S. Army Corps of Engineers. Also called "the boneyard," its purpose is to catch and collect stray logs and driftwood that wash downriver during spring runoff so that they don't float into the lake and create hazards for marine vessels. Periodically, the Corps piles the wood on a gravel pad next to the booms and burns all that wood; so if you are a collector of driftwood, by all means grab an interesting, water-worn piece for your garden or yard.

Adjacent to the Drift Yard and booms lie the Clark Fork River Delta and Lake Pend Oreille. Recently, riprap barriers have been built to curtail erosion of the delta. The mouth of the river is two miles wide, dotted with islands, and braided with channels and backwaters.

FACILITIES: concrete boat ramp, dock, large parking area, handicapped accessible vault toilet
ACTIVITIES: boating, canoeing, kayaking, fishing, wildlife viewing, bird-watching, camping

How to get here:

Access is from Idaho State Highway 200, about 21 miles from Sandpoint, just past Denton Slough. The Clark Fork Drift Yard dirt access road is on your right before the highway bridge that curves up and to the left.

Tribal Gatherings at Indian Meadows

The day after David Thompson's arrival at Lake Pend Oreille on September 8, 1809, Kalispel Indians in canoes escorted the expedition to the grassy meadows in the Clark Fork River Delta east of present-day Denton Slough. Here

Thompson's party came upon a large Indian encampment with dozens of families representing the three tribes present – Kalispels, Coeur d'Alenes and Kootenais. The native peoples were very friendly and invited Thompson and his men to camp for the night, probably because they had already received word of their coming. As Thompson relates in his memoir, he was given "dried Salmon and other Fish, with Berries and the meat of an antelope." In his journal, Thompson called the gift "a handsome present."

The encampment at Indian Meadows, 1898 (Leiberg photo, Bonner County Historical Society Collection)

This northern shoreline of the delta continued to be an important traditional fishing and camping site for Upper and Lower Kalispels in spring, summer and fall until the early 1940s. A few old-timers from Clark Fork and Hope still remember the large Indian encampments that took place at the mouth of the Clark Fork. Families from a number of tribes around the area – Spokane, Bitterroot Salish, Kootenai, Coeur d'Alene, Nez Perce and others – would join the Kalispel at this traditional site, which white settlers called Indian Meadows. The Kalispel name for this place is *ncm cin'* which means "banks and waters are dark." The Kalispel referred to Lake Pend Oreille as *ctq w t ne t q* or "big water." The Indians would spend time fishing for whitefish, pikeminnow, bull trout and cutthroat trout and dry their catch on sticks at warming fires near their sleeping lodges. They even went night fishing with torches to fish for char or bull trout. Their horses would graze on the grasses in the long meadow of what today is Denton Slough. They would also hike or ride horses up into the surrounding Cabinet Mountains to hunt deer, bear, woodland caribou and mountain goats, and to pick baskets of huckleberries.

My friend, the late Henry SiJohn, spoke fondly of these times. Each summer as a boy until he was 15 years old, he traveled along with all of the Kalispel grandfathers and grandmothers to the Clark Fork Delta. Henry's relatives would pack up their tents and belongings and travel by horse and wagon from Plummer where they lived on the Coeur d'Alene Reservation. It would take them three days to get here. Henry's mother and grandmother were always very emotional when they arrived.

"They missed this place so badly," Henry would recall. "When they got here we'd unpack the tent and before we'd even put it up, they would sit on the tent and cry and wail for about 15 to 20 minutes while everybody just stood around and waited until they got through." He used to say their strong feelings were both in appreciation for being able to return again to this special place, and in bittersweet remembrance of earlier days. The last summer Henry spent at the edge of the Clark Fork Delta was 1932. His eyes welled up with tears and his voice quivered as he recalled those years spent here; he believed it was as close to a utopian lifestyle that any person could live. They would visit with old friends, make new acquaintances, and barter for goods. Even weddings would take place. Henry said that every summer was like returning home. "And when you return home," I remember him saying, "everything is good."

But when Henry spoke of the destruction of their traditional meadows with the building of Albeni Falls and Cabinet Gorge hydroelectric dams, the tears in his eyes were from sadness. The dams flooded their traditional lands, killing native "tule" bulrushes, cottonwoods and old-growth cedar. Important religious sites and ancient rock petroglyphs were submerged. "Nothing can ever replace what we had," Henry said.

But in 1999 the Kalispel, Confederated Salish and Kootenai and Coeur d'Alenes returned to this site once more. For the first time in 50 years, a tribal gathering at the Clark Fork Drift Yard took place led by Kalispel elder and spiritual leader, Francis Cullooyah. Tribal elders from several tribes, native drummers, singers, dancers and a couple hundred non-native locals celebrated what this place continues to represent to tribal people today. The gathering was blessed by the animals, as well: a bald eagle and a pair of ospreys circled overhead, and to punctuate a brilliant red sunset at the end of the ceremonies, the wail of the common loon was heard.

Although changes to their traditional lands have persisted, the Kalispel still bring their tribal youth here to experience their cultural traditions. You might encounter them paddling a canoe like their ancestors did, or fishing or hunting for dinner, or picking huckleberries in the surrounding mountains. The tribe has worked hard to keep their traditions alive; their heritage is a priceless legacy for the youth and a grateful acknowledgment to the elders who persisted in preserving what it means to be Kalispel. As they say, "In the future, we hope for a wonderful life."

To learn more about the Kalispel, see chapter 13, "Land of the Kalispel," on page 333.

--- --- --- --- --- --- --- --- --- --- --- --- --- --- --- --- ---

Sensitive Archaeological Sites

On the shoreline of Lake Pend Oreille are complexes of ancient petroglyphs, or rock engravings, carved most likely by the ancestors of native peoples of this area thousands of years ago. The images of bear paw prints, circles and arcs are not only significant culturally to the Kalispel and Confederated Salish and Kootenai tribes, but are protected by federal law. It is a felony to tamper, deface or in any way damage these archaeological sites. Even the oils in your skin can harm the rock art if you touch it.

There are also Indian artifacts that sometimes appear in low water. If you come upon an arrowhead or any other artifact, the most respectful thing to do is to leave it where it is and cover it with earth. If it is a significant find – such as a grinding stone or spearhead – it is important to contact the Cultural Resource Department of the Kalispel Tribe in Usk, Washington. These cultural materials are valuable to the integrity of Kalispel tribal heritage. Some artifacts also have religious importance and need to be handled in special ways.

The rocky outcroppings on Lake Pend Oreille are considered part of tribal sacred geography, or geomancy. To the Kalispel people, the entire physical universe was imbued with a spiritual power that could be experienced throughout their natural environment, from old tree snags to mountain peaks to petroglyphs to lakes. Spiritual revelations and guidance were received from guardian spirits in these places in the past as well as in the present day. The Kalispel culture is dynamic and continues to unfold. The transformational power and interconnectedness of nature and the people's relationship with their sacred geography transcends time. The spiritual presence at these sites is palpable to many non-natives as well. Please respect the petroglyph sites if you come upon them.

Paddle Route: Clark Fork Delta

Greater than 90 percent of the water that flows into Lake Pend Oreille comes downriver from Montana bringing with it a lot of sediments, historically with springtime floods. For more than 50 years, the Cabinet Gorge Dam has operated a hydroelectric project seven miles upstream. The result of these sediment deposits is the forming of channels, backwaters and islands that all together provide a rich habitat for waterfowl and wildlife.

The Clark Fork Delta is a paradise for kayakers and canoeists to explore and one of the few places on Lake Pend Oreille where you can experience such a diversity of nature. There are numerous songbird and waterfowl species, herons, grebes, loons, ospreys and bald eagles. The delta estuary is complex, and it's easy to lose your way in the backwaters if you aren't paying attention to your self-chosen route. This actually happened to me once, catching me out in my canoe past sunset with no flashlight – not a smart move on my part – making it difficult to find the boat ramp in the dark.

Launch at the concrete boat ramp next to the small, concrete block U.S. Army Corps of Engineers building at the end of the Drift Yard access road. There is ample parking here as well as a portable toilet. Paddling time can be one to several hours of your choosing.

Author Jane Fritz in her cedar canoe, paddling in the Clark Fork Delta

At the Water's Edge

Sun up, and the luminescence reflected
on the water danced among ripples
left by a mallard at the water's edge.

It was a silent flight, but for the rhythmic
oscillation of wings and one soulful
cry from the startled duck.

Then silence descended, only the silence
was neatly folded into the breath
of wind that sighed through sedges and moss,

as though looking for a place to rest
among the grasses and shrubs crowding
the rocky shoreline, hiding the nest.

Across the placid surface, calmly basking
in the early morning serenity,
the drake motionlessly studied the intruder.

By its side, in a flutter of ruffled
feathers, landed its mate, rankled at leaving
the nest to whatever fate came with the sun.

The delta, wide and green, a watery
home of marsh and creeks and islands,
transforms the river into a lake.

A force that pushed rocks and mountains far apart
once cradled ice that choked the canyon
until a torrent tore the world asunder.

Now awash in golden beams, and immersed
in foam from the gorge that channels
the flow from the divide to this resting place,

the river laps protectively at the nest
that belongs to worried mallards who patrol
just out of reach upon the bosom

of the lake. A matriarch, it has embraced
their ancestors; it will nurture their descendants,
as long as the sun rises and sets beyond its shores.

So slowly I move away, mired
in mud and muck to the knees, quietly
hoping I have not disturbed the family
on the lake, beneath the sun, at the water's edge.

—Dennis Nicholls

Beargrass along Scotchman Peak Trail No. 65, top, and a close-up of the lily-like bloom, above (Jolanda Van Ooyen)

Wildflower Notes: Beargrass

While hiking the high country of the Cabinet Mountains in July or later, you might be dazzled by a population of blooming beargrass (*Xerophyllum tenax*). Consider yourself very lucky, because beargrass usually only flowers once every five to 10 years and the plants often bloom together, covering a slope with club-shaped, white flower clusters that resemble an oversized bottle brush. The flowering stalk can be from 2 to 4 feet tall. Their lily-like fragrance, which perfumes the air, only adds to this remarkable floral experience. The plant's roots are edible and the large clumps of long and wiry, grass-like and sharp-edged leaves are quite distinctive. Native peoples gathered the coarse leaves as they provided plenty of fiber for weaving baskets, clothing and making rope. Mountain goats eat the tough evergreen leaves in winter. Other large game, including bear, eat the succulent flowers. Beargrass is the official flower of Glacier National Park.

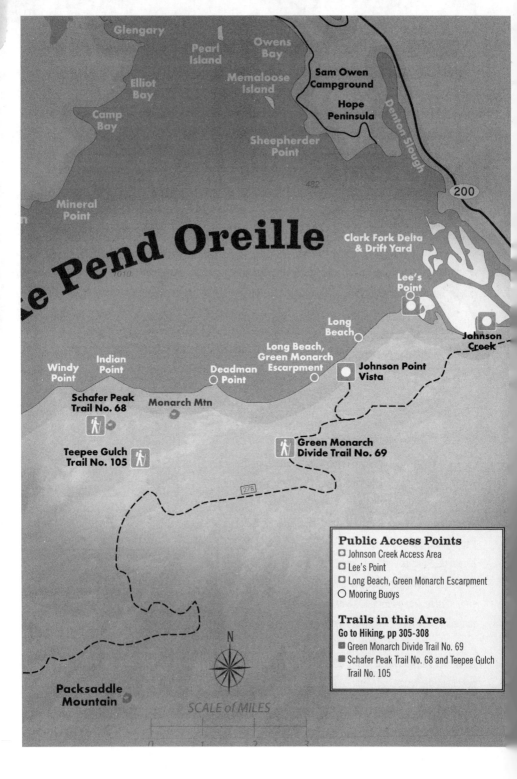

Glengary

Pearl Island

Owens Bay

Elliot Bay

Memaloose Island

Sam Owen Campground

Camp Bay

Hope Peninsula

Denton Slough

Sheepherder Point

482

Mineral Point

200

Clark Fork Delta & Drift Yard

Pend Oreille

1010

Lee's Point

Long Beach

Johnson Creek

Long Beach, Green Monarch Escarpment

Johnson Point Vista

Windy Point

Indian Point

Deadman Point

Schafer Peak Trail No. 68

Monarch Mtn

Teepee Gulch Trail No. 105

Green Monarch Divide Trail No. 69

278

N

Packsaddle Mountain

SCALE of MILES

0   1   2   3

Public Access Points
☐ Johnson Creek Access Area
☐ Lee's Point
☐ Long Beach, Green Monarch Escarpment
○ Mooring Buoys

Trails in this Area
Go to Hiking, pp 305-308
■ Green Monarch Divide Trail No. 69
■ Schafer Peak Trail No. 68 and Teepee Gulch Trail No. 105

CHAPTER NINE

AREA 6, JOHNSON CREEK TO GREEN MONARCHS

OVERVIEW

he northern end of the Coeur d'Alene Mountains drop steeply into Lake Pend Oreille southwest of the Clark Fork River Delta and are collectively known as the Green Monarchs. They create a dramatic band of cliffs and steep, forested slopes that are as primitive and remote as they are captivating. Spectacular vistas of Lake Pend Oreille can be seen high above the water at the Johnson Point Vista or from the high mountain hiking trails of this area.

Excellent views of the lake can be seen from trails connecting high atop the Green Monarchs, one that undulates on its way to the summit of Green Monarch Mountain and another that leads to Schafer Peak.

This area is for those who want to experience the lake's wilder nature. The rugged and relatively unspoiled lakeshore draws people to this area of the lake mainly because it is public land. Managed by the U.S. Forest Service as part of the Kaniksu National Forest, the shoreline is accessible only by boat. However, there are very few places here where you can actually land any size of watercraft, despite nearly eight miles of shoreline, which stretch from the mouth of the river to Windy Point.

Many people come here with a desire to escape civilization, but during the months of July and August you'll likely have to contend with large powerboats and personal watercraft,

The author 's canoe at "Loon Beach" (Jane Fritz)

especially traveling the river channels, which can be downright dangerous if you are in a canoe or kayak. But if you are lucky enough to paddle out into the lake and find one of the sparse, pebble beaches unoccupied that lie below the Green Monarch escarpment, it will offer rustic tent camping (sometimes just enough space for your sleeping bag), a primitive picnic site, deep water to swim in and a place to experience the fury of wind, water and whitecaps. You may camp in one place as long as 14 days.

More people come here to fish off the Monarchs than to camp or explore. When the weather is decent, a dozen or more fishing boats can be seen trolling the shoreline miles angling for lake and rainbow trout. If you're camped overnight, prepare to be awakened as early as 4:30 a.m. by boat motors and people talking (voices really carry over water). Power boaters usually arrive by midday from the Hope marinas, Johnson Creek Access Area, or across the lake's deep, open expanses from Garfield Bay. Traveling over open water is far too risky for a canoe or kayak except from within the delta. Paddling closer to shore is much safer.

Weather is another wildcard. Good weather conditions are critical while boating in this area. But even if the sky is clear of clouds, high winds can suddenly and unexpectedly blow through this region from the southwest – the predominant wind direction on Lake Pend Oreille. Other times the winds will funnel downriver from the Clark Fork River and hit you from the southeast. Wind currents will sometimes do both if you are in the delta or crossing the small bay from Lee's Point in a kayak or canoe. I capsized my canoe halfway across the bay one early July afternoon when it would have been smarter to wait at Lee's Point for calmer winds and water. The most important advice I can give about this area of the lake is to always be prepared for dangerous weather. Give yourself ample time to get to your destination and let someone know how far you plan to go. Start early in the morning, pack a tent, sleeping bag and extra food, water and clothing, all in watertight bags, and expect to spend several hours exploring. Remember, the lake is your only passage back to where you started.

I've been told that the Fourth of July holidays are one of the stormier times to be on the lake. My own experience bears that out. Years before my exciting capsizing incident of sudden strong winds, I had another close call. I was sleeping peacefully on a small Green Monarch beach when a sudden, unexpected storm hit. Temperatures plummeted 30 degrees, and large waves crashed ashore pulling my canoe back into the water and lodging it against a partially exposed rock outcropping 10 yards out. Somehow I was able to swim to the canoe and pull it back to shore, a Herculean task, and then spent 12 hours sleeping under it, waiting for one storm after another to pass over before I could negotiate my way back to Johnson Creek. This is not an area for the faint-hearted or inexperienced boater.

There are three visible landforms at the foot of Green Monarch Mountain: Deadman Point, Indian Point and Windy Point. The latter is the final landform on this wild side of the lake. Around Windy Point is where the lakeshore turns southwest toward Bayview. You've now come full circle on Lake Pend Oreille.

Anecdota: The Lake's Song

It had been a severe winter and by the end of April the snow had melted in the lowlands, but spring runoff had not begun in earnest from the mountaintops.

I had returned to the Clark Fork Valley after spending winter in a distant big city. Whenever I roam, I celebrate my return with a canoe sojourn to my special place on Lake Pend Oreille at the base of the Green Monarchs, a varied-colored pebble beach that I call Loon Beach because of the rare black and white birds that sometimes fish offshore. Others know it as Sacred Woman's Beach. If the lake were a woman's body, this would be the place to find her heart.

In the 30 years I have lived in northern Idaho, I have canoed to this place more than a hundred times. Once I spent five days here in solitude, camping as simply as one can: no fire; nights warmed by a down sleeping bag and my nylon half-dome tent; sparse, simple meals; and water heated for tea using my backpack stove. Solitude isn't really accurate, though. I was surrounded by and observed a multitude of non-human creatures, but the only humans were the fishermen who would troll past my camp arriving just past dawn and leaving just before sunset. On rainy days I was usually the only human around. It is a wild setting to be sure.

I have a special routine when I visit Loon Beach. It begins with picking up trash, pulling invasive knapweed and dismantling any fire rings that people have built because the ash contributes to water pollution. Once the beach is restored to its usual beauty, I'll say a prayer of thanksgiving for the opportunity to return once more to this magical place on the lake, and then I go for a ritualistic swim.

Author Jane Fritz relaxing at "Loon Beach"

Every visit here surprises. On this first day of May the water is icy cold, so as I step in, I'm left breathless except that an unfamiliar song rises up from within me. Unexpectedly, I find that as long as I sing this chant, I don't feel the cold. If I stop for even a moment, the frigid water chills me, so I keep singing. I wade deeper and deeper, singing all the while, amazed as to why I still feel warm. When I take the plunge and return to shore, I feel blessed and clearly welcomed home again.

A Kalispel Indian elder told me years ago that songs are one of his tribe's ways of traditional healing. Maybe the Lady of the Lake understood my need to be in this special place, to return once more for rest and healing, and to come away renewed. Mystery, it seems, is just another facet of this great gem of a lake that is both fully alive and so full of life.

JOHNSON CREEK ACCESS AREA

Comanaged by the U.S. Army Corps of Engineers and Idaho Fish and Game, this is the southern access point to the Clark Fork Delta and Lake Pend Oreille. There is no fee for access and use of this area. Camping is limited to three days.

What's it like?

The Clark Fork River Delta – its islands, channels, backwaters and wetlands – is accessible from the Johnson Creek Access Area. The delta is the richest natural habitat on Lake Pend Oreille for myriad species of songbirds, waterfowl and mammals. Also known as the Clark Fork Wildlife Management Area, this area is best experienced by kayak, canoe or small fishing boat.

This is also the best launch point to get to the lake and the Green Monarchs. From Johnson Creek, the south fork of the river, adjacent to the largest island in the delta – Derr Island – comprises two channels. If you are in a powerboat with anything but an electric motor, it's better to travel the straight-ahead route down the primary south fork channel from Johnson Creek. This is also the quickest and shortest route to the lake if you are in a hurry to get to big water to catch fish. But this channel must be traveled slowly without creating a wake; it is a no-wake zone. Please keep in mind that shoreline disturbance caused by boat wakes can be detrimental to wildlife – especially during the times of day when they are most active, before both dawn and sunset. Wakes also cause riverbank erosion.

Johnson Creek Access Area (Patrick Orton)

The second route is a wilder, quieter, winding channel that branches off to the far left of the primary south fork channel a short distance downriver from the launch. It also is a no-wake zone. It hugs Jakes Mountain, a jagged, angular mountain red with lichen that rises steeply from the water's edge. This channel is very popular with paddlers because of its wild beauty and the wild creatures that can often be seen very close at hand – from bear to osprey to beaver.

This is not the ideal route for powerboats, although people do come this way (I once rescued with my canoe a family of four who had run their boat aground at one of the sharper bends in the channel). Personal watercraft should avoid this channel as it is a no-wake zone. In addition, common courtesy asks powerboaters to slow down when encountering a single, non-motorized vessel or a whole flotilla of kayakers or canoeists, an action dictated by the narrow width of the channel and the possibility of swamping their small watercraft.

The gravel parking area at Johnson Creek will accommodate a dozen vehicles. And since this is the end of the road, typically during the summer months there will be someone camping overnight. Camping here is limited to three days. There is no potable water available here or even a trash can. Please remember to pack your trash back home with you.

FACILITIES: two concrete boat ramps, dock, picnic table, limited space for camping, parking area, two vault toilets

ACTIVITIES: boating, paddling, fishing, picnicking, camping, wildlife viewing, bird-watching

How to get here:

From downtown Clark Fork, turn south off Idaho State Highway 200 on Stephen Street by the gas station. Cross the railroad tracks and follow the road to the left over the river. At the south end of the bridge, turn right on Johnson Creek Road and go about two miles west until you see the dirt road turn-off on the right. Watch for the public access sign. Follow this road to the parking lot.

Johnson Point Scenic Viewpoint

High above the Johnson Creek Access Area is a scenic, gravel, back-road route – the Johnson to Lakeview Road No. 278, more familiarly known as the High Drive. It climbs high into the Green Monarchs and eventually drops down to the community of Lakeview at the southern part of the lake. There is more written about the High Drive in Area 1, page 60.

Four miles up Jakes Mountain you'll see a sign that indicates a turnout to the right, which leads to the Johnson Point scenic viewpoint. A dirt road winds for another half mile or so until it reaches a pullout. This affords one of the most expansive views of Lake Pend Oreille from its eastern shore.

There are numerous wildflowers to photograph here as well, and be careful not to run into a bear like I did my first summer in northern Idaho when I went foraging for huckleberries here. Hint: Make noise! Huckleberries and fireweed, two edible flora of this high mountain terrain, are discussed on page 230-231 of this chapter.

Paddle Route: Clark Fork River Channels

There are three main channels of the Clark Fork River Delta — north fork, middle fork and south fork. There are numerous songbird and waterfowl species here, as well as heron, grebes, loons, ospreys and bald eagles. The delta is a wildlife paradise for kayakers and canoeists. Take care if you are paddling the river channels during spring runoff, as a very swift current typically develops. Swimming in the river at this time of year also can be dangerous.

Paddler in the Clark Fork Delta
(Mathew Hall)

The far southern channel of the south fork of the river from the Johnson Creek boat launch is my favorite paddle route of any on the Lake Pend Oreille watershed. After three decades of sojourns in every season except the heart of winter, I can attest that no two trips are alike. It is a resplendent place to find peace and quiet as well as to see more wildlife than anywhere else on the lake. I encourage paddlers to go quietly and without haste. If you do, you will likely be rewarded with a close encounter with a wild creature or two. I once passed a mountain goat drinking at the shoreline of Jakes Mountain, which I call Red Mountain because of the red lichen on the rock face. Another September paddle, I floated quietly past a black bear only a few yards away foraging in an old crabapple tree on one of the smaller islands. One fall sojourn, I surprised a mother otter and her three juvenile offspring playing on the branches of a fallen tree that was half on the bank and half in the water. Once she realized my cedar canoe wasn't a log floating by, she sent her youngsters scurrying for cover and then climbed onto the tree branch closest to me and proceeded to growl and threaten. She really startled me, and so I paddled away quickly, apologizing for my disturbance.

The distance from the Johnson Creek launch site to Lee's Point and the lake, along either of the south fork channels, is less than two miles one way. But if you explore the delta, you can rack up several miles of paddling. It typically takes me less than an hour to make it to Lee's Point along the far southern channel depending on how long I linger. I always have my binoculars ready and use them, so I guess you could say I take a leisurely paddle. But once you make it to the county dock, you can tie up your craft, have a picnic on the beach or take a swim and paddle back to

Johnson Creek either as a loop along the middle fork of the river to the primary south fork channel, or back the way you came. Since the estuary is full of backwaters, it's a little tricky to know where to find the south fork channel from the middle fork, but I've always turned right near a very large tree rising above the shoreline shrubbery.

▶ **LEE'S POINT**

Managed by Bonner County, this is a camping area, boat dock and swimming area in a primitive setting. Public access is by boat only and there is no fee.

What's it like?

The south fork of the Clark Fork River together with stormy Lake Pend Oreille deposited sediments and stones to create a spit of land that used to be thickly covered with tall cottonwood trees and undergrowth of native shrubs and wetland plants like cattails. But severe storms in recent years have carved away some of the stony spit or reshaped it enough that there are fewer places to pitch a tent than before. Also, beaver in the area have cut down numerous trees and windstorms have knocked down additional trees. But despite the occasional tree-limb debris, it is still a popular beach that opens lakeside first to a small bay and then to the Monarchs and the wide expanse of Lake Pend Oreille.

Lee's Point (Laura White)

This is an area perfect for enjoying the lake's famous sunsets and summer moonrises over the river. Sometimes you get this far from Johnson Creek and around the dock jetty and the lake is all roiling with whitecaps and big winds. All of a sudden Lee's Point becomes your turnaround point for a speedy trip back to the boat launch; or, you might choose to tie up to the dock and wait out the storm on land watching weather come dancing across the lake from the southwest. I've seen rough water here about as often as calm water.

The boat dock provides a sheltered overnight tie-up for sailors who typically arrive from the Hope area. There is primitive camping here for a couple tents and there is also one picnic table and fire ring, but no fresh water. Another backwater behind the stone spit is lined with cattails that create an ideal breeding habitat for waterfowl. During migration in spring and fall, common loons sometimes use the small bay for feeding.

FACILITIES: boat dock, stony beach, picnic table, fire ring and vault toilet
ACTIVITIES: boating, camping, swimming, kayaking, canoeing, fishing, picnicking, wildlife viewing, bird-watching

How to get here:

Access is by boat only from Johnson Creek Recreation Area along the south fork of the Clark Fork River or from other points on the lake like Hope or the Clark Fork Drift Yard.

- - - - - - - - - - - - - - - - - - -

Lore Along the Shore: Kalispel Culture

In Kalispel mythology, Rock was the big chief. Chief Rock, with Coyote's help, gave all the fish, wildlife and plants a good home here in the delta. And so it is still today.

Chief Rock also was the chief that wed Pend Oreille Lake (a man) to Priest Lake (a woman). The female lake was nice and gentle, but the male lake was very mean and caused many people to drown. Grandparents would warn their children to get to shore quickly if they saw a vision of a large animal like an elk swimming in the lake that suddenly went underwater, because a storm would surely arise. These spirits were as important as the physical

Kalispel Chief John Big Smoke and son Baptiste fish in a traditional canoe at the mouth of CCA Creek where it empties into the Pend Oreille River (Bonner County Historical Society)

world to the people. Because of the dangerous nature of Lake Pend Oreille, the Kalispel people wouldn't cross the lake here in a single canoe, but traveled in twos or threes, sometimes tying the canoes together with a length of cedar for more stability in rough water. They also might leave offerings for safe passage.

The Kalispel fished the delta by building brush and stick weirs for whitefish and also catching bull trout and pikeminnow with set hooks and line, sometimes at night using torches. There was a summer village and fishing camp in this area that they called a "curve in the side of the mountain." After 1875 it became a vision-questing site after someone saw an underwater spirit elk and the resulting storm. The people also hunted in these rugged, steep mountains for deer, mountain goats and bear.

Kalispel ancestors adapted to the dynamic conditions of the environment caused both by nature and human behavior. They adjusted the location of their campsites, sometimes yearly, due to the changing nature of the shoreline caused by variable spring runoffs, winter storms and the availability of trees to use as fuel. The Clark Fork River was part of the "rope" that bound together the different tribal villages and groups who lived east as far as the Flathead Valley in Montana, along Lake Pend Oreille and west down the Pend Oreille River as far as Canada. This rivers-and-lake corridor is still used by modern-day Kalispel to visit relatives east and west, but today the people travel by automobile instead of canoe, foot and, in later days, horseback.

- -

Points of Sail
By Cate Huisman

Wind and Sailors:

In summer an east wind comes down the mouth of the Clark Fork in the wee hours of the morning. Outside the river, wind sources along the Green Monarchs include Packsaddle Mountain, which generates a morning breeze, and winds wrapping up from Cape Horn, out from Clark Fork, and down from the Pack River. Note that the point on the corner of the Monarchs, where the shoreline reorients itself from east/west to north/south, is called Windy Point.

There are few obstructions along the shore, and in a light wind you can glide silently and close to the land to observe wildlife.

Floating or slightly submerged logs can be a hazard anywhere, but the area around the mouth of the Clark Fork may have more of them than any other part of the lake, particularly after a period of heavy rain.

Anchorages:

The county dock, also known as Lee's Point, at the south edge of the river mouth, right behind the navigation light No. 7, is well-protected behind a spit, and anchoring is possible in about five feet of water (in summer) or off the exposed outer side of the spit if you can handle whatever chop and wind is apparent. The bottom is mud here, and a Danforth will hold. The county also has a mooring buoy at Lee's Point.

Along the Green Monarchs there is no protection and the shoreline is steep. The county maintains four mooring buoys, all fully exposed, along this shore, but it is suggested that boaters not count on them, especially during severe storms.

Launching and Hauling:

A trailer-hauled boat with a bow watch can proceed up the channel behind the navigation light, up the south fork channel, to the launch ramp in Johnson Creek. It can be windy in this channel, but there is no chop.

- - - - - - - - - - - - - - - - - - - -

Wildlife Viewing: Uncommon Common Loons

One of my favorite Salish legends is about an encounter between Coyote and Loon. Told to me by Spokane tribal elder Pauline Flett, the story takes place at the edge of a deep lake and the theme is similar to other tribal loon legends of the Northwest and Alaska: The loon is a healer, restoring eyesight to those who are blind. Of course, I always imagine the lake in the story as being Lake Pend Oreille where loons once were numerous, nesting on the edges of the shoreline, in marshy wetlands, or on small grassy islets in the Pack River or Clark Fork deltas. They've likely been here since the last ice age. Alice Ignace, a beloved Kalispel who was a major culture-bearer of her tribe, told me that on certain spring nights her ancestors would find it difficult to sleep because the loon's mystical-sounding calls were so prevalent.

Common loon (courtesy U.S. Fish and Wildlife Service)

Of course all that beautiful loon music was in the years before the huge log drives, the building of the railroad, powerboats and shoreline development. It was long before the dams were built. Today, either hearing a loon's wail echo out across the water or seeing one is uncommon. The birds are shy and elusive and tend to stay out in the middle of the lake away from people, only coming closer to shore at dawn or after dusk when things quiet down. The common loon, a piscavore but in its own family, *Gaviidae*, rarely breeds here anymore mainly because of the fluctuating water levels caused by the dams. Biologists, who leg-band birds for research, find that Lake Pend Oreille is more often a stopping place during the loons' long seasonal migrations between the Arctic and Pacific Ocean. The common loon is the species most typically seen and heard on our lake, although there have been the occasional sightings of Arctic, red-throated and yellow-throated loons.

In recent years, there has been some effort to reverse the decline of the nesting loons on Lake Pend Oreille. Although sedge or cattail marshes are the loon's favorite native habitat, loon platforms – small floating manmade bits of landscape – have been placed in this area of the Clark Fork Delta and in Denton Slough with the hope of encouraging a breeding pair to stay and nest.

Common loons are a goose-sized bird that sit deep in the water and dive deeply for its prey, usually fish. Its average territory is about 100 acres of lake. It also needs a long "runway" for taking flight, gathering speed with its feet before liftoff. Once in the air they fly up to 100 miles per hour. Males and females are identical in appearance with the male being slightly larger. Although a drab gray-brown in winter, the bird's summer plumage is distinctive in black and white dress. It's head, neck and dagger-like bill are solid black with white, vertical bars called a "necklace" circling its throat. It has a solid white breast, and white spots also dot its black back, like stars scattered across a night sky. The eyes of the adult loon are deep red which help them see underwater. Like grebes, loons have a solid bone structure making them superb divers, but on land they are clumsy because their feet are positioned far back on its body. They go ashore only to mate, lay and incubate eggs. Their brood, of one or two chicks, will ride about on the adult's back.

The common loon's other distinctive feature is its voice. It has four different calls: yodel (a territorial call done only by the males), wail (similar to a wolf howl and used to locate its mate across distances), tremolo (a quavering laugh that is actually its alarm call that humans or predators are getting too close) and hoot (uttered when in close proximity of each other).

If you think you have positively identified a loon on the lake (or even more so, a nest site) please protect the area from boat use, stay at least 150 yards away, and learn what activities stress the birds. Loons can coexist with humans if certain precautions are taken. If you are positive that you see one and that it isn't a red-necked or western grebe, document the location and time of day and contact Idaho Fish and Game at 208-769-1414. The loon has been around for 60 million years; so let's do our part to help keep this mystical, mysterious healer of a bird around Lake Pend Oreille for a long, long time.

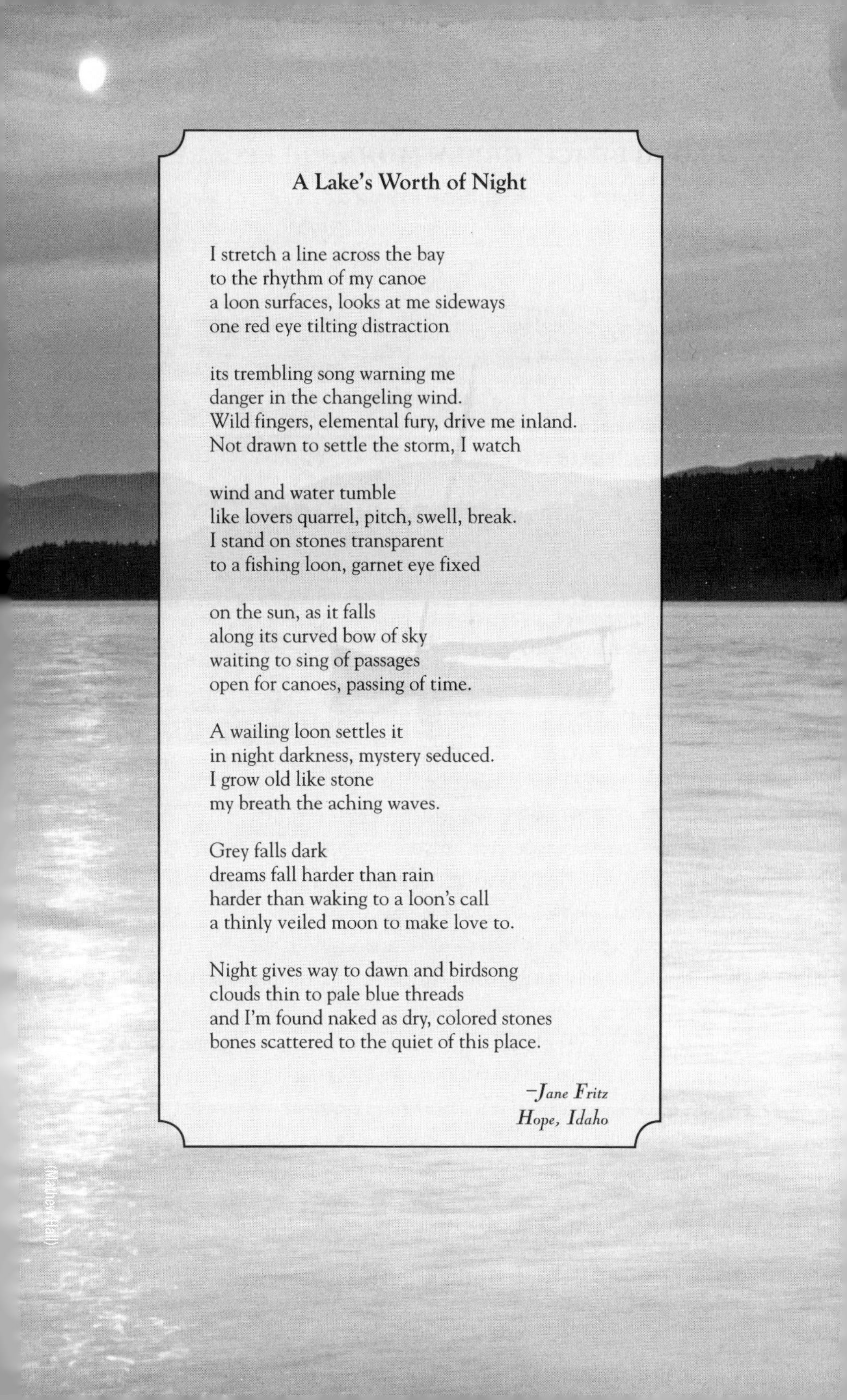

A Lake's Worth of Night

I stretch a line across the bay
to the rhythm of my canoe
a loon surfaces, looks at me sideways
one red eye tilting distraction

its trembling song warning me
danger in the changeling wind.
Wild fingers, elemental fury, drive me inland.
Not drawn to settle the storm, I watch

wind and water tumble
like lovers quarrel, pitch, swell, break.
I stand on stones transparent
to a fishing loon, garnet eye fixed

on the sun, as it falls
along its curved bow of sky
waiting to sing of passages
open for canoes, passing of time.

A wailing loon settles it
in night darkness, mystery seduced.
I grow old like stone
my breath the aching waves.

Grey falls dark
dreams fall harder than rain
harder than waking to a loon's call
a thinly veiled moon to make love to.

Night gives way to dawn and birdsong
clouds thin to pale blue threads
and I'm found naked as dry, colored stones
bones scattered to the quiet of this place.

—*Jane Fritz*
Hope, Idaho

▶LONG BEACH, GREEN MONARCH ESCARPMENT

Managed by U.S. Forest Service, there is no fee for public access. Camping is allowed for up to 14 days.

What's it like?

A long, narrow stretch of stony/sandy beach characterizes the shoreline below Green Monarch Mountain. Long Beach is a popular primitive camping area and is one of the more beautiful sites on the lake to enjoy a near wild experience. The beach runs for nearly a mile and features some pockets of sand. It looks northwest across the lake and at times you feel like you have landed in paradise, especially at sunset when all the fishing boats go in for the evening. It can feel like you have Lake Pend Oreille all to yourself. But you are never alone: This is also home to wildlife on the water and in the mountain forests above you. A deer walking at night with the clip-clop sound of their hooves on stones might startle you awake in your

View of Long Beach from the Green Monarchs (Jim Mellen)

tent. During the early dawn or after dusk, loons and mergansers often fish parallel to shore, close enough for a great view with your binoculars. You might also be lucky enough to hear the wails of the common loon at night, the bird calling for its mate.

Swimming in the deep, cold water – cold even in August – is also a thrill. But remember that the steepness of the mountains is mirrored underwater. In other words, not far from shore it is hundreds of feet deep, so take care when swimming.

Campsites here are rustic and unmarked, but there are a few fire rings spaced along the beach for building campfires away from the water and for keeping nutrients out of the lake. There are also a couple of vault toilets at Long Beach but no potable water. It is important to minimize human impacts to this sensitive, natural area, so please help keep the beach clean and take any trash home with you for disposal. Practice that catchy phrase: Pack it in, pack it out.

People will paddle several miles to the primitive beaches below the Monarchs from the Johnson Creek boat launch, but more often there seem to be powerboats coming here from various places, sometimes even bringing their noisy radios and boom boxes. It's not the wilderness experience of former days, at least during the summer months. Since the lake is deep here close to shore, anchoring a boat is either not possible or will leave your vessel unprotected to sudden weather, but you can use the mooring buoys that the county has placed offshore. Otherwise, only motorboats capable of rocky beach landings are suitable for this area of the lake.

You will likely see up to a dozen or more fishing boats, including charter boats out from Hope and Garfield Bay trolling parallel to the shoreline, fishing like the loons. This is one of the most popular fishing spots on the lake for trophy-size fish. Anglers arrive early and leave before suppertime when solitude and serenity once more replaces the low hum of motors. Several miles of open, deep water must be crossed to reach other parts of the lake. The landmarks to the west of this stretch of beach that mark the rocky, steep mountain terrain are Deadman, Indian and Windy points. If you leave civilization behind and just embrace the wild here, your time will be memorable.

FACILITIES: primitive campsites, fire rings, two vault toilets, stony and sandy beach
ACTIVITIES: camping, boating, fishing, swimming, wildlife viewing, bird-watching

HOW TO GET HERE:

Access is by boat only, with the closest launch sites at Johnson Creek, Garfield Bay, Hope and Hope Peninsula.

— —

Lore Along the Shore: Monarch Landmarks

Early prospectors in these mountains called their diggings the Green Monarch Mine. The mineshaft is still visible among the trees and shrubs that have grown up around its dark entrance, which today is blocked. The mine's name was later applied to the entire mountain and to the ridgeline that also includes Jakes Mountain and Schafer Peak. A forest fire swept this mountainside in October 1991, originating around Windy Point at Kilroy Bay.

The landmarks along this very steep, rugged, rocky section of the Monarchs carry memorable names: Deadman Point refers to an incident here that claimed the life of an Indian. According to accounts, an avalanche crashed down the exceedingly steep slope and buried him alive. Indian Point is named for the same man, and just east of this rocky point is an interesting crack in the cliffs, which beckons closer examination. But beware of falling rocks! Windy Point is where the east-west lakeshore makes a directional turn to the south-southwest, exposing this point to the harshest elements the lake can muster. The wind slashes the shoreline here when it whips across miles of open water.

Fish Tales: Charter Boat Fishing for the Big Lunker

Ed Dickson and I are sitting inside his luxurious 32-foot Carver. It's a big and bulky marine vessel that Ed says can handle a slow troll and big waves. We're on the boat at the dock at Hope Marine Services, because today is a cold, early November day. I can only imagine what it might be like to go fishing with him some hot and sunny August afternoon. Ed's been in the charter business on Lake Pend Oreille for 17 years. I picture us trolling the shoreline under the shadow of the Monarchs near Deadman Point, then suddenly catching the drag of a huge mackinaw (lake trout) or a 20-pound, colorful Kamloops rainbow trout.

With fisheries in the lake certainly in flux, more of Diamond Charters' activity these days is as a recreation and sightseeing service. Ed believes the days of the deep, big-water charter captain have come and gone. Nowadays he's more likely to take visitors on a tour of the lake, stopping awhile at some sheltered cove of deep, clear water so his guests can go swimming. He still takes a lot of people fishing, but younger generations of anglers simply want to fulfill a desire to experience what it's like to catch a fish – any size fish – and they want to do it quickly. Just seeing a wild fish is a thrill for many people these days, Ed says.

The reasons why the big predator fish are declining are complex, but it relates to what trout eat, introductions of non-native species into the lake and competition for food. Bigger fish eat smaller fish. Forgive me here for my reduction of nature's life cycles, but fisheries come and fisheries go.

There's a lot of debate about whether good or bad management practices are being followed, and Ed definitely has his point of view. For instance, he would like to see the Kamloops fishery return to what it once was – world record. Even in the 1990s, just about every other day he would catch a 15-pound or bigger rainbow trout. He admits to being spoiled by catching so many big fish back then. Today he still catches eight to 12 fish a day, but they're just a whole lot smaller. Ed fears the big rainbows have all been fished out and he says the lake is inundated with small lake trout as well, so he also is promoting more catch and release with his customers. Ed also likes to persuade his customers that their goal should be to bring home a fresh fish or two at the end of the day for dinner rather than a whole cooler full of them. He explains what he wants for his charter anglers is for them to see what a great opportunity it is to catch fish, not focus on the number of fish caught.

"It's a great pastime," he says. "For that little moment when your pole goes off and your line screams out a little bit ... your heart gets to soar when you get to tangle with a wild fish. That's really the whole purpose of fishing."

At this point, whether anyone will be catching big rainbow or lake trout in the future is anybody's guess. While fishery biologists work on management solutions, Ed suggests that perhaps the lake's fisheries should play out for the immediate future without human intervention. He says maybe that's what it will take to bring this amazing resource back into balance. Either way, if you're inclined to charter a fishing boat out toward the Monarchs to try your hand at snagging one of those famous Lake Pend Oreille lunkers, you better do it now.

Ed Dickson, right, weighs in a rainbow trout caught by Steve Hiscock. The 20-pound, 4-ounce fish won second place in the 2006 K&K Derby
(courtesy photo)

Storm Warnings

I've encountered a lot of weather out on Lake Pend Oreille in my canoe, but usually I'm close enough to get to shore quickly and stay there. But what do you do when you're out fishing on a powerboat and a big storm comes up from the southwest?

Charter boat captain Ed Dickson says normally in those situations everyone in a powerboat goes to shore, but once he and a friend stayed out during a big storm with pouring rain and huge winds, only because they were catching big fish. Every time they ran into 10-foot waves, the poles would go off and they would land another 15- to 22-pound rainbow. They caught seven lunkers before reaching Windy Point. From there they decided to head for home and managed to perch on 16-foot waves that they literally surfed all the way back to Hope. (Another charter boat was out there that same day, but had engine problems; this captain swears the waves were 20 feet high!)

At times, this lake can be life threatening for mariners. Winds predicted to be 20 to 40 miles per hour can quickly become 60 miles per hour and turn what were 8-foot waves into 10-foot waves. There are at least 50 "lost souls" as Ed calls them, people who have drowned, whose bodies have never been recovered, and that doesn't include the Kalispel Indians whose oral histories surely add to that number.

Ed says he has great respect for Lake Pend Oreille and its weather. He also has seen a lot of waterspouts on the lake. He says they start out as tornadoes, dropping into the water after first tearing up enormous bull pine trees and tossing them around on land. He's been out on his boat in at least 14 of these type storms. He once witnessed a guy who ran out on the dock to help tie up Ed's boat get tossed 30 feet out into the water by one of those wild winds. A friend of Ed's was in a 36-foot boat trying to make it in and was spun around 360 degrees before he got into the marina. Enough said? Watch out for weather.

- - - - - - - - - - - - - - - - - - -

Wildflower Notes: Huckleberries and Fireweed

There are two wild plants in these high mountain forests that are good to know because they are edible. The first is fireweed, *Epilobium angustifolium*, a member of the evening primrose family, that can grow up to 7 feet high with a spire of hot-pink flowers. It is a valuable forage plant for deer and elk, as well as favorite forage for grizzly bear. To the human palate, the young leaves are like spinach and the young shoots like asparagus, so it may be eaten raw in a salad or boiled as a potherb. The pith of the stems also are

Fireweed, found in abundance at Schweitzer Mountain Resort

used in soup. The flowers are a colorful addition to salads, and the entire raceme can be cooked like a vegetable. The leaves also make a delicious tea. Fireweed's name comes from its habitat – disturbed soil like that found in burned areas. The plants will grow thickly, spreading from persistent underground stems to quickly mask with color and beauty the unsightly burned or clear-cut areas of the mountains.

Huckleberries, *Vaccinium membranaceum*, are delicious berries and a highly prized, wild, blueberry-like fruit, but more tart, which grow abundantly on small leafy bushes in this area. Most

locals are secretive about their favorite picking sites, but if you hike any of the mountain trails in this area, you are bound to come across some of these delectable shrubs dotted with dark purple to black berries. They are often eaten on the spot, but if brought into camp they can be added to fruit salads or pancake batter.

If you manage to get any quantity home with you, they can be cooked into pies, muffins or cobblers and made into delicious jam and syrup. The dried leaves of the shrub, which turn red or purple in autumn, also make a delicious tea. Both the berries and the leaves are high in vitamin C. Keep in mind that huckleberries are also a primary food for bears, so be

Huckleberry (Autumn Oscarson)

sure to make noise while picking to scare them away. Kootenai Indian stories tell of more romantic days not that very many years ago ... the bears would pick on one side of the bush and the elders pick on the other. That way everyone got their fill!

Granite Point Crags: A Rock Climber's Thrill

Once a desirable area for free climbs up above Lake Pend Oreille, the Granite Point Crags has lately grown mossy, and climber hardware left there in the 1980s has rusted with lack of use. But it is still a remote and beautiful area for rock climbers to explore even if it needs some care. It is important to climb here with an adventurous spirit.

Located at the foot of Green Monarch Mountain, access to the crags is by motorboat. Six miles, directly across the lake, is the Garfield Bay boat launch or you can follow the eight miles of shoreline from the Johnson Creek launch. Many of the climbs can be made directly from your boat if one of the four public mooring buoys is available. Otherwise the lakeshore is too steep here for anchoring your boat. The exception is a wall that is near a small cove where you can land your boat and make a short hike uphill to the wall.

Several climbs are possible here on rock walls with interesting names like Flying Squirrel Buttress and Foreboding Buttress. For details and climbing maps, I recommend checking out Thaddeus Laird's guidebook, *Climber's Guide to North Idaho and the Cabinet Wilderness*, also published by Keokee Books.

Opposite page: Rock climbers Ben Porietis, John Winton, Jason Munske and Sandy Chio at Granite Point Crags
(Doug Marshall)

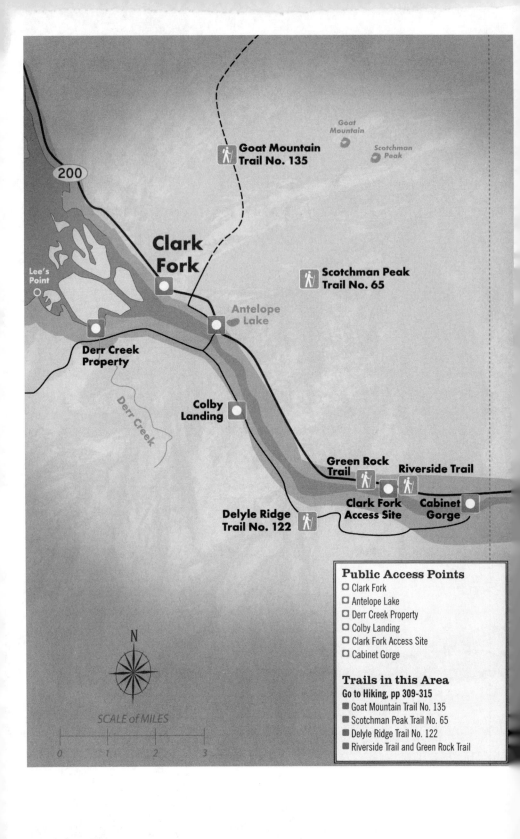

200

Goat
Mountain

Scotchman
Peak

**Goat Mountain
Trail No. 135**

**Clark
Fork**

**Scotchman Peak
Trail No. 65**

Lee's
Point

Antelope
Lake

**Derr Creek
Property**

Derr Creek

**Colby
Landing**

**Green Rock
Trail**   **Riverside Trail**

Clark Fork   **Cabinet
Access Site**   **Gorge**

**Delyle Ridge
Trail No. 122**

N

SCALE of MILES

0   1   2   3

Public Access Points
☐ Clark Fork
☐ Antelope Lake
☐ Derr Creek Property
☐ Colby Landing
☐ Clark Fork Access Site
☐ Cabinet Gorge

Trails in this Area
Go to Hiking, pp 309-315
■ Goat Mountain Trail No. 135
■ Scotchman Peak Trail No. 65
■ Delyle Ridge Trail No. 122
■ Riverside Trail and Green Rock Trail

CHAPTER TEN

AREA 7, CLARK FORK TO CABINET GORGE

OVERVIEW

*T*raveling east from Sandpoint along Idaho State Highway 200, the last town you pass through before the Idaho-Montana state line is the small community of Clark Fork. A variety of services are available here, including restaurants, coffee and retail shops, groceries, lodging and RV parks.

Named for Captain William Clark of the Lewis and Clark Corps of Discovery, the "Clark's Fork of the Columbia River" flows for more than 400 miles through western Montana on its way to Lake Pend Oreille. Most of the shoreline on either side of the river east from Clark Fork to the state line is privately owned. Traveling east, there are only two public access points on the river before reaching the Cabinet Gorge Dam, a hydroelectric project.

Despite limited water access, there are remarkable points of interest along this stretch of the river to discover. Scotchman Peak, the highest mountain in the region at 7,009 feet, is a spectacular destination for hiking in the West Cabinets and home to shaggy, white mountain goats. Looking like a great woman lying on her back, the peak is visible from the center of town and the western stretch of the river before Antelope Mountain blocks the view. Antelope Lake, a small high mountain lake perfect for family fishing, is less than a mile from Highway 200. If you linger

The Clark Fork River at sunset from the walking bridge (Chris Bessler)

awhile at the wildlife viewing area near Derr Creek, you might see elk or peregrine falcons perched on the cliffs to the south. From October through June, fish can be seen at the Cabinet Gorge Fish Hatchery, built to augment the wild kokanee population in Lake Pend Oreille. Lastly, there is the Cabinet Gorge Dam, built in 1952 to generate hydroelectricity, visible from a viewpoint off Highway 200 close to the state line.

It's a lovely drive into Montana and beyond, and if traveling by water, this area is limited in its accessibility to boats coming from the Johnson Creek Access Area and Hope boat launches. Because of the dam, powerboats can't go too far upriver. The Clark Fork Access Site along the north side of the river, managed by Avista Utilities, is a launch site only for kayaks, canoes and other cartop boats.

But be advised that boating is not recommended at all when Lake Pend Oreille is being filled from early May to the first week of July, since the current can be as fast as 10 to 12 knots and rip currents occur. Since greater than 90 percent of the water in the lake comes from the Clark Fork watershed, and upriver dams and Flathead Lake significantly contribute to its flow, the river can be dangerous. Sea kayakers and experienced whitewater canoeists are the most appropriate folks to take to the river after July 1, and I recommend paddling very close to shore.

Swimming is best done in some of the sheltered coves and backwaters of the river because of its powerful current. Children should be watched with an eagle's eye since drownings do occur.

Historically, there have been many significant floods in this part of the watershed and at least one or two after the dam was built. In 1996, students were let out of the local high school to help sandbag the riverbank to protect the small town of Clark Fork. Flooding is possible when you consider the measure of snowmelt that comes from the surrounding high mountains adding to upstream water management practices.

Because of the wild tributaries that feed the river, this area is also good for catching native fish, especially from the bank. Sections of the river are ideal for fly fishing for cutthroat, brown and rainbow trout. Bull trout are among the fish species also found here. However, this native fish is listed as a threatened species under the Endangered Species Act, so any bull trout accidentally caught must be released.

There are private RV resorts along the Clark Fork River and a large motel at the east end of the town of Clark Fork, but no developed public campgrounds exist in this far eastern end of Bonner County.

Two of the trails in this area, Goat Mountain and Scotchman Peak trails, have some of the most spectacular views from the north side of the lake, while Delyle Ridge Trail features magnificent views of vast river delta feeding the lake from its south side. At the Clark Fork Access Site, a shoreline trail contains five spurs down to the river for fishing and swimming and also meets up with a singletrack uphill loop.

Anecdota: River of Rainbows

As a teenager, the first cast that Christian Thompson made with his fly rod in the Clark Fork River became a rite of passage. Fishing was in his blood, a tradition among the men in his family, like hunting big game. His dad, Terry, had fished the Clark Fork all his life, while his grandfather Milton preferred fishing the big lake. That transition from salmon eggs on a hook – the way he fished as a kid – to the art of enticing a trout to rise to the surface from the river's depths and snatch a feathered muddler on the end of his dancing fly line took considerable skill and grace. The magic and intensity of that first communion with the river and its aquatic life not only made his dad proud, the experience has stayed with Christian all his life.

"You cast out there and the sun is reflecting off the water and you see the fly floating down the river, and as it finally trails off at the end of the riffle, all of a sudden you see this huge body of the fish roll over and sink your fly. Your heart jumps and you pull your fly rod up taut into the air and the next thing you know you have this rainbow leaping out of the water. The river is flowing fast and a 16-inch trout feels like it weighs 30 pounds, and you're fighting to get that fish into the bank," he says.

There's excitement as well as adventure in trying to fly fish the Clark Fork, but most people don't have the patience. Sometimes you have to stand thigh deep in the river in your waders and cast for hours until you snag a fish. Christian recalls one October day when he chose to go fishing alone instead of elk hunting with his dad, a break from family tradition. Fishing his favorite mile of the river between the Cabinet Gorge Dam and the delta, he caught not only the two biggest fish of his lifetime but also created for himself a lifelong philosophy about fishing.

"I was fishing with a streamer pattern that I tied myself because I was really into tying my own flies. I fished for six hours and caught only two fish. Ah, but the fish I had caught! The first one was a rainbow and it was over 20 inches. It was a pretty intense moment and it took me a long time to bring that fish in. Then I let it go. It seemed like the right thing to do at the time and not more than 30 minutes later I caught an 18-inch cutthroat (trout)," he says. It was an exhilarating experience of being on his own and fishing his own way. What was his dad's response? "Tie me more flies!" Terry exclaimed. For Christian it was another fly-fishing rite of passage.

Returning the fish to the river was also a break from tradition since Christian grew up in a family where fishing was also a means of putting food on the table. But today fishing is more about recreational pursuits than providing subsistence. With that in mind, he sees it as his responsibility to the larger fishing community to release most of the fish he catches. He wants to protect those big

Christian Thompson with a cutthroat trout

fish in the river so other people can have similar exciting experiences while fishing.

"I love to eat trout and I do keep them; but I'm mindful of how many I keep and the limit that the law says I can keep. But that's not what governs my choice; it's what is the decent thing for me to do for the next person. I love my community, too," he says.

With the construction and operation of the Cabinet Gorge hydroelectric project, the Clark

Fork River is more nuanced than it was before. It is always changing, and Christian says it takes time to get to know the river and get a feel for its ebb and flow. If you fish and don't catch a single thing one day, it doesn't mean there are no fish there. It's like getting to know a person; it's just one day in the river's life and some days are better than others. The river will give more to someone who is patient and willing to let it be what it is. He also feels it is important for river anglers to know the history of the area and to contribute in some meaningful way to the natural environment so that it lasts. He loves the river and wants generations after him to love it, too.

Although public access to the Clark Fork River is limited, Christian believes that it shouldn't stop someone from fishing it. Respect for private lands and landowners go with the territory, he says. He always asks for permission to fish. Good stewardship of our lands and rivers starts by having good relationships with local landowners, he believes, and he's never had anyone say no to his request to fish even with "no trespassing" signs posted. It's also important to show reciprocity, he says, whether it's sharing your catch or simply sharing a story afterwards of how the day went. The bonus is that you just might create a relationship that could last a lifetime.

"It isn't privacy that protects and sustains the land, it is community," Christian believes. "We need to understand this quickly as things are developing so fast. We have to work together to maintain the resources. So don't act as if you have a right to be on that land. Be kind and humble about it." Christian Thompson is optimistic that new landowners settling here will be that way, too. He says the fishing will only get better if the river's future care is grounded in respect.

 ▶ **CLARK FORK**

Incorporated in 1912, this historic community on the Clark Fork River was first an important railroad camp in 1882 with the building of the Northern Pacific Railroad. It also prospered as a center for lead and silver mining in the early 1900s with three major mines — Lawrence, Hope and Whitedelf — whose production activities continued into the 1950s. The area around Clark Fork also was timbered with enormous, old-growth trees, and so logging became another prominent industry here with a series of sawmills built, beginning in 1891. The town still has the flavor of its early beginnings, and descendents of some of the original pioneer families still live here. The town's traditional July Fourth holiday celebration becomes a sort of reunion for anyone who has ever lived or worked in Clark Fork and is the centerpiece of the community's yearly events.

What's it like?

Clark Fork is at the eastern edge of the Clark Fork River Delta and is base camp for hikes into the western Cabinet Mountains. Scotchman Peak, the highest mountain in our region, is visible from the center of town and its trailhead access is just north of town. There is no public boat access to the river here, however. An aging fish hatchery on Spring Creek managed by Idaho Fish and Game that raised several species of native trout between the 1930s and 1990s is being revitalized for kokanee spawning, a project of the volunteer-directed Lake Pend Oreille Idaho Club.

Clark Fork has two public parks, one with a ball field north of town, and the other south of the highway. The latter is a relatively quiet place for a picnic with a table shaded by old willow trees. It's located off Railroad Avenue adjacent to the railroad tracks.

You can walk or bike from the center of town down to the river and across the old railroad bridge, which is now a footpath and bike trail. From April to September osprey pairs build their nests on top of the bridge and raise their young, so walk quietly, especially when directly

The old bridge over the Clark Fork River, converted to a pedestrian bridge in 2007 (Chris Bessler)

beneath them, and try not to disturb the birds. Some folks drop their fishing line into the river from the bridge, but in shallow water all I've seen swimming there are northern pikeminnow. Bald eagles sometimes grace the branches of cottonwood trees along the riverbank, especially when fish are spawning.

FACILITIES: automotive repair, gas, propane, groceries, restaurants, retail shops, laundromat, RV park and lodging

ACTIVITIES: hiking, biking, fishing, picnicking

How to get here:

Clark Fork is located 27 miles east of Sandpoint. To access Forest Service hiking trails, turn north on Main Street at the Chevron gas station. Turn south off Highway 200 on Stephen Street by the town's other gas station to get to the south side of the river. Directly after you cross the railroad tracks, bear left until you reach the old railroad bridge. Once you cross the river you can make a hard right onto Johnson Creek Road to points southwest or continue on the paved road east to Montana.

ANTELOPE LAKE

Managed by Idaho Fish and Game as "Family Fishing Waters," which operates under a different set of regulations, Antelope Lake allows limited primitive camping and there is no fee for use. Avista Utilities maintains the site, which is two-thirds owned by the utility, and the remainder by Bureau of Land Management.

What's it like?

East of the town of Clark Fork, up Antelope Mountain, is a picturesque little lake that is designated as Family Fishing Waters, one of six in Bonner County that includes Round Lake, Jewel Lake, Bull Moose Lake near Priest Lake, Kelso Lake and Granite Lake. Family Fishing Waters provide a great setting with simplified rules for memorable fishing trips for families, children and first-time anglers. Only electric motors are allowed in Antelope Lake; otherwise, the season is year-round, the limit for catching trout using standard fishing gear is six fish of any length of rainbow, brook and cutthroat trout. Primitive camping is allowed here, but there are very few sites and no other facilities. Remember to practice Leave No Trace ethics. Float tubes for fly-fishing are perfect for this lake.

FACILITIES: a few primitive campsites, limited parking
ACTIVITIES: car-top boating with electric motors only, fishing, camping, swimming

How to get here:

From downtown Clark Fork, go 1.2 miles east to a dirt road that is north off Highway 200 just past milepost 56. Follow this road up the hill for almost a mile (0.8 mile) to the lake. The access road is rough and best traveled using a short wheelbase SUV with four-wheel drive or a horse. Since there's limited parking available at the lake, unless you're camping it's actually best to park off the highway and hike the road. It climbs 1,800 feet in elevation, but children usually can handle the trek.

DERR CREEK PROPERTY

Managed by Idaho Fish and Game, this is a wetland and wildlife viewing area that is along Derr Creek, a tributary to the Clark Fork River. It is southeast of the town of Clark Fork on the south side of the river. There is no fee for access.

What's it like?

This is a wetland area where you can watch for wildlife, waterfowl and songbirds. Peregrine falcons nest on the rocky cliffs to the south of the area. This is also a calving area for elk. Comprising 240 acres, sometimes the area is flooded, although in summer, there are mainly large potholes of water. There are no established trails; nonetheless, it is a good area to explore on foot. The small gravel parking area can accommodate several cars. There are no other facilities here. Be sure to bring binoculars and a camera.

FACILITIES: gravel parking area
ACTIVITIES: wildlife viewing, bird-watching

How to get here:

From downtown Clark Fork, turn south off Highway 200 on Stephen Street by the gas station. Turn right directly after crossing the railroad tracks and proceed south over the river bridge and follow the road as it curves to the east. Go about a mile or so until you see the gravel road turnoff to the right. Watch for the public access sign. Follow this road a quarter mile to the parking lot.

--- --- --- --- --- --- --- --- --- --- --- --- --- --- --- --- ---

Wildlife Viewing: Peregrine Falcons

This rarely seen bird of prey, or raptor, is featured on the Idaho quarter. It's because a nonprofit organization – The Peregrine Fund of the World Center of Birds of Prey – in Boise, Idaho, was instrumental in the falcon's recovery from near extinction.

In 1970, the peregrine falcon was listed as a federal endangered species as only 39 pairs of the birds were known to exist in the Lower 48 due to pesticides – the primary cause for the species losing 80 to 90 percent of its former numbers. Ending the use of DDT was a critical factor in the bird's recovery.

The Peregrine Fund overcame naysayers and incredible odds by implementing experimental breeding programs. Only a handful of peregrines had ever successfully bred in captivity and none had been successfully released to breed in the wild. The first successful hatches occurred in 1973 and the first release occurred in 1974. By 1999, with more than 4,000 captive-raised peregrines released in 28 states – including here along the steep, rocky cliffs on the south side of the Clark Fork River – the bird was removed from the endangered species list.

Historically a desirable bird for falconers to hunt with, the adult male of the species is a strikingly handsome bird with its slate blue-gray back and white throat and long narrow, pointed wings. Peregrine falcons are roughly crow-sized birds but with a wingspan of nearly 40 inches.

They hunt other birds while in flight – songbirds, starlings, pigeons, blackbirds, jays, shorebirds and waterfowl, and rarely take mammals or reptiles. The flight of the peregrine after prey, with its fast pursuit and spectacular dives, are stunning. Speeds have been clocked faster than 200 mph! The peregrine falcon uses its feet and curved, sharp talons to capture its prey and then uses its sharp, hooked beak to kill what it has snared.

They don't build nests, but lay their eggs usually near water and in a hollow on an inaccessible rocky cliff ledge. Like an eagle, the home of a peregrine is called an aerie. The young falcons fledge five to six weeks after hatching and, like ospreys, the birds will migrate to Central or South America, although sometimes peregrines south of Canada don't migrate and instead remain in their home habitat.

To release captive-bred peregrines, young birds are placed in a special box on top of a man-made tower or cliff ledge. The birds are fed through a chute so they can't see their human benefactors. When they are old enough, the box is opened and the young peregrines begin testing their wings. Gradually, the feeding is reduced and the young falcons

Peregrine falcon (painting by Ward Tollbom)

learn to hunt on their own. This process is known as hacking. A hack site on the cliffs south of the Clark Fork River near Idaho Fish and Game's Derr Creek property proved successful for reestablishing peregrines in our area. Sometimes the falcons can be seen in this area performing their aerial acrobatics.

An endangered species success story, there are now estimated to be about 1,200 breeding pairs of peregrine falcons in the Lower 48.

PUBLIC ACCESS ▶ COLBY LANDING

There is access to the river here through a railroad easement. This is the closest access point to fish the river from the town of Clark Fork, about 1.75 miles from the bridge. Look for the old black-and-white railroad sign and turn left, cross the tracks and proceed until you reach the river.

Fish Tales: A Routine Fishing Trip
By Patrick F. McManus

For 20 years we had a place on the Clark Fork River near the town of Clark Fork. Nothing seemed to go right there. There were always problems. It was one of the few places in the world where I felt at home.

One day I got a call from a Portland TV producer that he was bringing a crew up to do a feature on me. I told him my friend Dave Lisaius and I would meet him and his crew in Spokane, and they could follow us up to our fishing spot on the Clark Fork. The producer said that sounded great, just the sort of angle he was looking for.

So Dave and I met them and started off toward the Clark Fork. I was driving my old truck, with my canoe strapped to the top. As we were passing a tire company in the vicinity of Sandpoint, we heard the distinct sound of a flat tire thumping along at the rear of the truck. As it turned out, the spare was also flat. Usually, two of my tires go flat only when I'm far back in the mountains, but in this case I had pulled right into the parking lot of a tire company. I explained to the TV crew that this sort of thing usually doesn't happen to me, but that I would buy a new tire from the tire company and get the other one repaired. The producer didn't react well to this news, apparently because he was working under certain time limits. I had heard of time limits before, but this was the

Author Patrick McManus on the Clark Fork River
(Billie Jean Plaster)

only one I had ever experienced firsthand. It made me nervous. I ran into the tire company and told them what I needed. The manager said it would be two hours before they could get to me. I went out and told the producer this, and he started to jump up and down. I suggested they start shooting our fishing trip right then, even though there wasn't any water in sight. He said, "OK, we might as well." Soon they had the TV cameras out and were about to start shooting footage of me pretending to change a tire, with the tire company in the background. At that point, the tire company manager came running out, and said to stop filming, he could take care of me right then. Soon we were on the road again.

Presently we arrived at our fishing spot. It wasn't the fishing spot I had planned on but a different one, because I had gotten distracted. Finally, though, we got the canoe launched on some section of the Clark Fork. It was then that I discovered we had forgotten the paddles. I say "we," for the reason that Dave is supposed to remind me of the paddles. I told the producer this wasn't a serious problem, because Dave and I often used pieces of driftwood for paddles. The producer stopped jumping up and down, and his crew got out the cameras and started shooting footage of Dave and me paddling around with the pieces of driftwood.

After awhile we caught a fish. It was about 7 inches long. An hour or so later we caught another one, but it was small. So far the fishing trip had been pretty routine for Dave and me, but I could tell that the TV producer hadn't had much experience with fishing. I personally find fishing to be a relaxing activity, but the producer seemed on the verge of a nervous breakdown. Dave commented on that himself and wondered if perhaps the man had drunk too much coffee that morning. I suspected, however, that the producer simply hadn't fished a great deal. This turned out to be the case.

Several weeks later the TV station sent me copies of the feature, and it was wonderful. In the final segment, the announcer turns to the producer and says, "I understand this is the first time you've ever gone fishing, John." And John says, "Yeah. But never again!" So it was just as I suspected.

Lore Along the Shore: The Town of Cabinet

The road along the south side of the river was the original road to Montana, part of the Yellowstone National Highway. The settlement of Cabinet, built along this road, sprung up during the construction of the Northern Pacific Railroad in 1882. Also known as Cabinet Landing, steamboats brought men and supplies here from the southern end of the lake. Chinese laborers were among those who helped build the railroad and they remained here after its completion. According to local historian Nancy Renk, one of the construction supervisor's wives called Cabinet "a conglomeration of dirt, saloons, drunkenness and debauchery," perhaps an apt description since the settlement had 33 saloons. All that remains today is the cemetery.

But it was wildfire, not the wild life, that found residents of Cabinet taking refuge on sandbars in the river during the summer of 1910. All of northern Idaho had been exceptionally dry with virtually no rain after March. By mid-July nearly 3,000 fires were burning. But the tinderbox exploded on August 20 when the fire swept across the Clark Fork Valley and the flames jumped the river in certain places from the south bank. Eighty-five people died in the northern Idaho fires.

After the 1910 fire, farmers moved in buying burned-over land. Finnish immigrants settled here and some of the buildings, barns and saunas that they built are still evident in the valley. In the winter, these settlers hand-lined for whitefish for subsistence along the Clark Fork River all the way to Denton Slough.

Swinging bridge and ferry across the Clark Fork River at Cabinet, circa 1930
(Truman Shawver/Bonner County Historical Society Collection)

▶ CLARK FORK ACCESS SITE

PUBLIC ACCESS

Managed by Avista Utilities, this is the newest public access area on the Idaho portion of the river. Adjacent to the north bank, located directly off Idaho State Highway 200, this is a day-use area only and there is no fee for access. Part of this site was a former Veterans of Foreign Wars campground, but camping is no longer allowed. Trails are closed to motorized vehicles, including all terrain vehicles and motorcycles.

Kayakers near the Clark Fork Access Site (Patrick Orton)

What's it like?

This 40-acre site is a recently redeveloped recreational opportunity on the river and borders Bureau of Land Management land on the east end. The site is across the road from a rock quarry, and there are paved entrances at both the east and west ends. From Highway 200, two parking areas can accommodate eight to 10 vehicles at both the west and east ends. Another paved entrance at midpoint can hold up to three vehicles. A small gravel launch ramp at the west entrance is accessible only to kayaks, canoes, rafts and other small cartop boats.

There are two hiking trails on-site that also are open to mountain bikers. The Riverside Trail goes upstream for almost two miles. From the west end, the first one-half to two-thirds of a mile is an old roadbed, but then the trail parallels the river through a beautiful forest of big fir, ponderosa pine, larch and cedar trees. Along the way are five side trails down to the water as access for anglers and swimmers. The Green Rock Trail branches off the shoreline trail about one mile in and becomes a singletrack uphill loop for another three-quarters of a mile. A portion of the Riverside Trail is wheelchair accessible from the west entrance with a developed vista point two-thirds of a mile from the parking area. The east entrance offers limited wheelchair accessibility.

There are a few nice, sandy stretches of beach here along the riverbank. But swimmers need to be aware that the river is shallow for a foot or two out from the edge of the sand and then drops off a ledge, becoming deep water with a swift current. Children should be watched carefully. This is also a nice spot for a picnic, but there is no potable water available.

This is a perfect place for shoreline fly fishing for cutthroat, brown and rainbow trout. But watch out for poison ivy that grows here at the edges of the parking areas and at trailheads.

FACILITIES: gravel boat launch, picnic tables, sandy stretches of beach, information signs, hiking trails, parking area, vault toilet

ACTIVITIES: paddling, fishing, swimming, picnicking, hiking, biking, cross-country skiing

How to get here:

From downtown Clark Fork, follow Idaho State Highway 200 for another five miles. The site is just past the River Delta Resort. The west entrance is directly off a newly constructed section of Highway 200 between mileposts 60 and 61, two miles west of the state line. The east entrances are accessed via the old highway. The entire site is located across the highway from a privately owned rock quarry with steep cliffs, a visible landmark.

— — — — — — — — — — — — — — — — —

Paddle Route: Lower Clark Fork Water Trail

Launching from Avista's Clark Fork Access Site, paddling upstream is just too risky because of the Cabinet Gorge Dam, a half-mile to the east. But downstream, you can paddle with the current all the way down to Johnson Creek Access Area, the Clark Fork Drift Yard, or points farther west along the north shore of Lake Pend Oreille. But I don't recommend paddling this seven-mile stretch of river between May and early July as water currents can range between 10 to 12 knots. It's too wild unless you are a helmeted whitewater kayaker and like living dangerously.

After July 1, only experienced paddlers should travel downstream as the ride varies depending on weather and river flows. It's also very important to be well prepared: Wear protective clothing and shoes, a type V-PFD (personal flotation device), take dry bags and an extra paddle. After July 1, because of the dam's power-peaking activity, the flows can still range from 33,000 cubic feet per second (cfs) to 52,000 cfs in the course of a single day. This doesn't make it too difficult to maneuver the south fork of the river when you finally reach the delta, but the upper middle fork — the main stem of the river — often has a much stronger current. Less-experienced paddlers can have difficulty navigating this section, especially during high flows.

There is also a line of log pilings connected with heavy steel rope in the middle fork of the river that diverts floating logs and debris into the U.S. Army Corps of Engineers Drift Yard at

248   Legendary Lake Pend Oreille

the end of the north fork of the river. You can cross over this floating fence in your vessel at the place where the south fork channel begins. There's a 20-foot-wide gap here, which gives you paddling access to the river's south and middle forks. But if you paddle to the right of the pilings by accident, because of river flow, you'll want to stay in the north fork channel another three miles to its end. Turning around and paddling back upstream against a strong current is very difficult. Also be aware that powerboats and personal watercraft often travel up and down this area of the river too fast and wakes can also cause difficulties in keeping your boat from capsizing. The large, 97-acre island to the south of the

The Clark Fork Water Trail takes paddlers through the picturesque Clark Fork drainage (Patrick Orton)

north fork of the river is called Carter's Island and is managed by Idaho Fish and Game as part of the Pend Oreille Wildlife Management Area. Derr Island and Yonkers Island are privately owned.

Estimated paddling time for the seven miles from the Clark Fork Access Site to the Clark Fork Delta is from two to five hours depending on the current and whether you choose to float downstream to a shuttle car at Johnson Creek Access Area or just west of the Clark Fork River bridge. There's a small gravel launch under the bridge that crosses over the river to Derr Island (there's room for at least one car). Otherwise, to return to your launch site, make a loop in the delta and paddle back upstream to where you started — a very, very long canoe trip.

Cabinet Gorge Fish Hatchery

Built in 1982 and managed by Idaho Fish and Game, the Cabinet Gorge Fish Hatchery's sole purpose is to increase the population of naturally occurring landlocked kokanee salmon in Lake Pend Oreille. Millions of kokanee eggs, which are spawned in Granite Creek on the southeast shore of the lake in December and January each year, are brought to the hatchery to be raised. When they are at least 2 inches long, the salmon fry are then released back into Lake Pend Oreille at Granite Creek, so they will physically remember their birth waters, a strategy called thermal marking. When the fish are adults they will return to spawn at Granite Creek, thus completing their life cycle.

In the creek next to the hatchery, you can see wild Kamloops spawning in April and wild kokanee spawning November and December. Around the hatchery, there are other wildlife to see including ospreys, wintering bald eagles, wood ducks, otter, whitetail deer and moose.

The hatchery is open to visitors for guided tours year-round, seven days a week, although there are no fish to see from early July to September. Cutthroat trout also are raised here. Phone 208-266-1431 for tour information.

Kokanee fry at Cabinet Gorge Fish Hatchery (Patrick Orton)

Wildflower Notes: Wild Rose and Elderberry

Two eye-catching native shrubs that can be seen as you drive along the river deserve a closer look since they have value as wild foods.

The wild rose (*Rosa woodsii*), whose five petals are light pink to deep rose in color, blooms in late May or early June. This prickly stemmed and toothed, leafy shrub is dotted with many delicate flowers that have a lovely, sweet fragrance. Most parts of the plant are edible: The petals make a pleasant tea and can be added to salads; the round, scarlet-red rose hips – the fruit of the flower appearing in late summer and staying on the bush late into winter – can be eaten fresh, dried for tea or made into jam or jelly. Rose hip jelly is as pretty a color as the flower itself. It's the pulp of rose hips that is eaten; the seeds can irritate the digestive tract and also contain cyanide, which can be destroyed by cooking or drying. The young leaves, shoots and buds of the wild rose are also edible – raw or cooked. High in several vitamins, you only have to eat three rose hips to get as much vitamin C as eating an orange – a great trail snack to try when out hiking.

There are three species of elderberry in our Western region, and the blue elderberry (*Sambucus cerulea*) is the shrub most commonly seen growing along the roadways that

250   **Legendary Lake Pend Oreille**

parallel the Clark Fork River. In springtime, the elderberry shrub with its opposite branches and toothed leaves is dotted with many flattop clusters of creamy white flowers that form dull blue fruits in late summer. Both the flowers and berries are edible, but the leaves, stems and roots are poisonous. The berries were sometimes eaten raw by native peoples, but it's recommended that they be cooked or dried to destroy any possible toxic compounds. The flower clusters can be gathered, dipped in batter and fried like fritters, or used to make tea or wine. I once made a delicate tasting wine out of the flowers that was semi-dry and very pleasant. I've also made wine out of the berries, as well as jelly and elderberry pie, one of my favorites. In addition to their value as food, elder flowers and berries are also valuable as herbal medicines, the berries being particularly known for their antiviral properties in treating influenza.

Wild rose, top (Duane Davis)
Elderberry, above (Billie Jean Plaster)

CABINET GORGE

This canyon holds a significant place in geologic history; it is where ice dams formed backing up Glacial Lake Missoula (see "Carved by Glacial Ice and Floods," page 252). Built within the chasm today is a hydroelectric dam operated and owned by Avista Utilities of Spokane, Washington. This is a day-use area fully accessible to wheelchairs. There is no fee for access.

What's it like?

As the last point of interest along the Pend Oreille Scenic Byway, interpretive signs at the gorge overlook help explain the ice age incident. The viewpoint overlooking the river is open daily from 6 a.m. to 8 p.m., May to October, and provides quite a show of thundering whitewater and rapids during spring runoff. Looking downstream you get a feel for the former beauty of the canyon; looking upstream are the turbine housings and concrete walls of the Cabinet Gorge Dam. There is a paved path up to the canyon rim that is fenced for safety and security. There is also a historic display of a turbine runner, removed from the powerhouse in 2001, to give visitors a glimpse into the inner workings of the dam. Tours of the powerhouse are available through special arrangement with the utility company in Spokane;

Area 7: Clark Fork River to Cabinet Gorge 251

phone 509-495-8759. Osprey nests
are visible in some of the surrounding trees
and these birds of prey are often seen
fishing the churning waters of the river
below the dam.

FACILITIES: interpretive signs, paved loop
trail to overlook, parking areas for cars and large
RVs, vault toilet
ACTIVITIES: sightseeing, wildlife viewing

How to get here:

The viewpoint is located on a side road
south of Highway 200 seven and a half miles
east of the town of Clark Fork. The turnoff to
this road is near mile-marker 62. A parking
lot and turnaround for RVs is located just

Cabinet Gorge canyon (Patrick Orton)

before the overlook on the left-hand side of
the road. Parking for passenger vehicles is at the overlook on the right. The Idaho-Montana state
line is one-half mile east of Cabinet Gorge.

- -

Carved by Glacial Ice and Floods

About 11,000 years ago, the last ice age in the Pleistocene epoch ended in
this region leaving behind today's vast and deep Lake Pend Oreille and its
surrounding landscape – the result of glacial ice and floods that are among
the greatest known to have occurred on Earth.

In a fascinating book on the subject, *Glacial Lake Missoula and its Humongous Floods*,
author David Alt ponders what kind of wildlife may have roamed here before massive floods
washed them away – mammoths, giant beavers and oversized bison – and whether or not this
catastrophic spectacle was witnessed by the ancestors of the Kalispel Tribe. "We can only imagine
what they felt," he writes.

The oral tradition of local tribes indeed recounts great floods that occurred long before the
white man arrived. Several years ago, Spokane elder Pauline Flett told a traditional story on public

Cabinet Mtns
Coeur d'Alene Mtns
east
Antelope Mtn
Clark Fork R.
Green Monarchs Ridge
Lake Pend Oreille

Site of the ice dam: topography left behind at the Clark Fork Delta, the heart of the Ice Age floods (Bruce Bjornstad)

radio's, "A Prairie Home Companion" (with her telling it in Salish and Garrison Keillor retelling it in English), about a boy and a girl escaping the complete devastation of an enormous flood by climbing to the very top of Mount Spokane. As the legend goes, once the waters receded, the young couple discovered salmon stranded in shallow rock basins, a fish they had not seen before.

The melting waters from the glacial ice sheet, responsible for scouring the region and carving away at mountains, originated to the east in present-day western Montana and formed the enormous Glacial Lake Missoula. As deep as 2,000 feet, Lake Missoula's natural drainage to the sea encountered a finger of ice from the Cordilleran Ice Sheet that formed in the Purcell Trench between the Cabinet and Selkirk mountain ranges and was blocked by a 3,000-foot-thick ice dam that formed here in the Clark Fork Valley near the present-day Idaho-Montana state line. (At the south end of Lake Pend Oreille, the ice may have been as much as 5,000 feet thick!) When the ice dam broke, it unleashed waters that rushed through the basin at speeds exceeding 65 mph and at a volume 10 times that of all the rivers in the world today combined. It roared through the frozen basin that would become Lake Pend Oreille and across the Rathdrum Prairie and Spokane Valley, before spilling south into the Channeled Scabland.

The dramatic episode that emptied Glacial Lake Missoula in a matter of a few days and shaped the topography of the area took place more than once (it is estimated that perhaps

Labels on image:
Cabinet Mtns
Packsaddle Mtn
Coeur d'Alene Mtns
Cape Horn Peak
glacier-faceted slope
Jokulhlaup Point
Lake Pend Oreille
Scenic Bay
Idlewilde Bay
Bayview
Farragut State Park
Outburst Plain

Site of the floods' outburst plain, where water roared through at the southern end of Lake Pend Oreille (Bruce Bjornstad)

as many as 100 such floods took place every 40 to 140 years during the last glacial cycle, between 13,000 to 18,000 years ago). Eventually the ice receded northward far enough so that the floods ceased and Lake Pend Oreille remained. Geological evidence of these roaring waters can be seen on both sides of the Clark Fork River. These floods also created the scablands of Eastern Washington.

Studying the ice age floods helps scientists better understand natural cycles of climate change on Earth as well as geologic processes on Mars where landforms are strikingly similar to the scablands.

In 2001, the National Park Service submitted a report to the U.S. Congress proposing an Ice Age Floods National Geologic Trail that would be an interconnected network of trails and roads with interpretive centers extending across parts of Montana, Idaho, Washington and Oregon. Legislation to create the national trail moved slowly until Congress finally approved it in March 2009. A nonprofit educational organization, the Ice Age Floods Institute, with a chapter in the Sandpoint area, worked for years to promote the trail. An interpretive site will likely be built in this area as part of a series of sites along floods' routes. This remarkable geologic story, known to so few Americans, will be an exciting one to tell across the region. Look up www.iafi.org to learn more.

Unidentified Kalispel at the north fork of the Clark Fork River in the 1930s (Bonner County Historical Society)

Lore Along the Shore:
Kalispel Life at Cabinet Gorge

The Kalispel Indians traveled along the Lower Clark Fork River by canoe and later by horseback along trails on the north side of the river. The people fished and camped where tributaries entered the river. A fall encampment was near present-day Clark Fork on Mosquito Creek. They hunted deer and woodland caribou in the surrounding mountains and gathered many plants including hemp near Antelope Mountain and an abundance of elderberries along the river. When they traveled west to Lake Pend Oreille from their winter villages in Montana near present-day Thompson Falls and Plains, they would have to portage around Cabinet Gorge during high water. But at other times of the year they would canoe through the gorge and back again. Fishing upstream of the canyon, they used dip nets to catch whitefish and spears to take other species like char or bull trout.

Today the north side of the Lower Clark Fork River is still a transportation route for the Kalispel, as they travel to visit their relatives and friends on the Flathead Reservation of Montana.

Cabinet Gorge Hydroelectric Dam

Of the eight hydroelectric facilities owned and operated by Avista Utilities, Cabinet Gorge Dam is the second largest in generating capacity at 263.7 megawatts. It produces more than a million megawatt hours of electricity a year, satisfying the annual energy needs of nearly 100,000 households in the region.

Completed in 1952, it was constructed to help meet a critical energy shortage in the Northwest in the late 1940s and early 1950s. Built in only 21 months, 1,700 men and women laboring around the clock excavated millions of cubic yards of rock blasted from the canyon walls and poured 240,000 cubic yards of concrete in its place. At 208 feet high, the dam regulates eight spill gates that hold back 105,000 acre-feet of water in the 20-mile-long Cabinet Reservoir.

Most of the Cabinet Reservoir lies within Sanders County, Montana, and the surrounding area offers boater access, camping and wildlife viewing opportunities. Recreational sites managed by the U.S. Forest Service include Big Eddy Day Use Area, Bull River Campground and Triangle Pond Day Use Area. The community of Noxon, Montana, manages the Pilgrim Creek Park Recreational Area.

A display of a turbine runner at the Cabinet Gorge overlook, top, and a view of the dam (Patrick Orton)

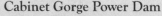

Cabinet Gorge Power Dam

The river is born of the ice packs
In the Rockies' eternal peaks,
Where countless seeps form streams that rush
To the tryst they pledge to keep.

It has carved its way since the earth was young,
Weathering ageless stone,
Where it cut a gorge through the Cabinet Range
Which blocked its journey home.

Man looked at the gorge and dreamed a dream,
As he has since he took man's form,
When he fashioned a club to protect himself
And a shelter to keep him warm.

So he took his drills and his dynamite,
And his mammoth combustion tools,
And he proved "the impossible" isn't so –
While the skeptics talked of fools.

So he rived and shaped the native rock
To the structure of his dream,
And he trapped with a copper switch the strength
That surged in the rampant stream.

Now the gorge is blocked and the river held,
And the power works man's will –
But the peaks that rear toward a million stars
Worship creation still.

–Paul Croy
Pioneer Pencil Dust, 1976

(Michael White)

CHAPTER ELEVEN

U

HIKING, MOUNTAIN BIKING AND HORSEBACK RIDING TRAILS

By Dennis Nicholls with Jim Mellen

A system of more than three dozen trails of varying conditions exists around Lake Pend Oreille, providing ample opportunities for enjoyment by foot, mountain bike and on horseback. Many of these trails lead to majestic viewpoints of the lake and surrounding countryside or to the lake itself.

The trails are organized here according to the same seven areas described in Part I of this book. Note that some trails are designated "Family Fun Hikes." These are generally suitable for all ages and a good place to take young children and older relatives, as long as they are in reasonably good health.

Directions to trailheads are fairly precise, but it's always best to check with the U.S. Forest Service (USFS) for changes and updates before you head out. Particularly helpful is the Kaniksu National Forest map, available at the Sandpoint Ranger District office, located at U.S. Highway 2 and Ontario; phone 208-263-5111.

Most of the descriptions that follow are self-explanatory. But a word on what I mean by the sweat index for hiking. This level of difficulty is based on three factors: distance, elevation gained and the condition of the trail. I'm also assuming that the hiker is in fairly good health and has some experience hiking. Of course, it is my purely subjective rating. As for the mountain bike sweat index, it is based on the International Mountain Biking Association rating system.

Key to the difficulty ratings:

Easy – means that practically anyone of any ability can tackle this trail.

Moderate – this is a hike or biking experience that will cause you to breathe heavily and break a sweat.

Difficult – at this level you're working hard, sweating a lot, and afterwards you'll be weary enough to take a nap on the beach or in your sleeping bag.

Strenuous – this is the kind of hike that will test your endurance as well as tax your strength.

Area 1: Bayview

Legendary Lake Pend Oreille

Trails in this area:

Scout Trail No. 37

Squirrel Cache Trail

Shoreline Trail

Highpoint Trail, Buttonhook Bay

Chilco Peak Trail No. 14

Kick Bush Gulch Trail No. 113

Dixie Queen Trail No. 677

Branch North Gold Creek Trail No. 111

Packsaddle Mountain Trail No. 76

Falls Creek Trail No. 229 and Minerva Ridge Trail No. 84

Granite Creek Trail No. 71 and Granite-Packsaddle Trail No. 611

Bayview-Blacktail Trail No. 230

Evans Landing Trail No. 64

Maiden Creek Trail No. 321

Talache-Blacktail Trail No. 117 and Little Blacktail Trail No. 231

At the far southern tip of Lake Pend Oreille, Farragut State Park has more than 40 miles of trails for hikers and bikers to explore, including more than 20 miles also open to equestrian use. In 2006, park staff developed the Corral equestrian day use and camping area and the Buggy Trail on the north side of the park to meet growing horse and llama use. Horses are not permitted on the south side of Highway 54 inside the park. For those hikers and bikers who like a challenge, take the Highpoint Trail to the Scout Trail and hike up Bernard Peak (5,143 feet) and look back across the lake at Farragut State Park.

The park encompasses land that was deposited during the last glacial period 10,000 years ago. The outflow and impact of this water on its way to the ocean can still be seen on the escarpment of Bernard Peak. The

Trail break at Farragut State Park (Chris Guibert)

escarpment is 500 feet higher than the current surface of Lake Pend Oreille; these waters rushed westward, leaving behind a large "glacial gravel bar" between Cape Horn and Bernard Peak forming the peninsula that is now the park. A diverse biological community exists in this scenic forest-and-lake setting.

Most of the land on the eastern side of Lake Pend Oreille is Forest Service-managed public land. This side of the lake has the most rugged shoreline: From Bernard Peak to the Green Monarchs, the mountainsides often plunge steeply into the depths of the lake. The centerpiece of this side of the lake is the looming hulk of Packsaddle Mountain (6,405 feet), which is the magnet to the many trails weaving through the forests from stream bottoms to ridgetops. The views of the lake from its multiple rocky pinnacles are distant but awesome.

The Bitterroot and Coeur d'Alene mountain ranges converge here. Both are heavily timbered, but many logging roads also exist and some slopes have been heavily harvested for lumber. After the Kalispel Indians, trappers and prospectors were the next to explore these slopes, and loggers soon followed. The result is an extensive network of roads and clear-cuts, but more than 50 miles of trails still offer solitude in the woods here. From the exquisite, old-growth cedar forests in Branch North Gold Creek to the old lookout on Delyle Ridge in Area 7, there is a guarantee of superb hiking.

Framing the deep waters of the lake on the west shore is a string of low hills that separate Pend Oreille from the main valley of the Purcell Trench. From Gold Hill to Cape Horn Peak, these uplands are what forced the waters of the Ice Age floods westward down the Pend Oreille River and south through the twin outlets of Scenic and Idlewilde bays.

These hills are heavily timbered, easily accessible and have been extensively managed by private and Forest Service activities. The Maiden Creek and Evans Landing trails lead to the lakeshore. Other trails, such as Talache-Blacktail Trail No. 117, offer scenic vistas. All three of those also allows motorbikes, so be cautious if you choose them for non-motorized exploration.

— — — — — — — — — — — — — — — — —

Scout Trail No. 37

Destination: Bernard Peak
Best Suited For: hiking, mountain biking, horseback riding
How Much Use: A Little * A Little More * A Lot * A LOT MORE * Excessive
USGS Map: Bayview **GPS:** N47 57 24 W116 34 55 or N47 56 42 W116 33 41

What's it like?

Heavy timber cover characterizes most of this trail, but along the way there are four viewpoints that offer a good look out over the surrounding terrain and the south end of the lake. Once abandoned and overgrown, this trail was reconstructed by Boy Scouts in 2002 and is now called Scout Trail. From the trailhead on South Road in Farragut State Park, the trail meanders through dense forest to a series of rocky outcrops and ledges. It climbs among the trees, brush and rocks, coming to a spur trail to the first overlook after a mile and a half or so. To get to Highpoint View requires a difficult scramble among big granite boulders. On top there really is not much of a view of the lake, but to the south and west and out over the park the views are great.

Twenty to 30 minutes past this point is another short spur trail to a viewpoint that focuses on Mount Spokane to the west and the forested terrain to the south. The trail drops downhill from here and enters an area that has been selectively logged. Following skid trails, the trail comes to a fork with a sign. Go left to the Lake Viewpoint and what is really the best view from this trail. Buttonhook Bay and Idlewilde Bay are far below, and off in the distance you can see Baldy Mountain and Schweitzer Mountain near Sandpoint. Packsaddle Mountain on the east side of the lake is visible, too. The trail from the Twete Road trailhead joins just beyond this point and is typically the place where mountain bikers set off on this trail. Walking, it will take an hour or more to get to the next viewpoint, which features views of Roman Nose and up the lake all the way to Mineral Point and Kirby Mountain. Nearing the top, the trail enters a stunning forest of old-growth grand fir. It then gains a high ridge and crosses the access road that can be driven to the top. A lookout once stood here; there are good views south to Chilco Peak and beyond. Walk a couple hundred feet down the south ridge for views to the Cabinet Mountains far to the east.

Trailhead: Turn east off U.S. Highway 95 onto Idaho State Highway 54 at Athol and go four miles to the entrance to Farragut State Park. After purchasing a day-use permit, go a couple hundred yards beyond the visitors' center and turn right onto South Road. Go about one-quarter mile to the parking area for the Highpoint Trail. Another way to get on this trail is to take Highway 54 to the traffic circle at the west entrance of the park, turn right (south) and take Goodhope Road about two-thirds of a mile to Twete Road, turn west and go about 2.75 miles to the trailhead.

Trail Length: 8 miles one-way

Trail Condition: good

Elevation: start (Highpoint Trailhead at Farragut State Park) – 2,400 feet; end – 5,156 feet – 2,756 net gain

Estimated Duration of Hike: 4 to 6 hours up, 3 to 5 hours down

Sweat Index: difficult

Mountain Bike Sweat Index: difficult

Best Features: views of the lake, Farragut State Park, Mount Spokane and distant peaks

Availability of Water Along the Trail: Several small brooks cross the trail and some of them may have a trickle of water late in summer.

Stream Crossings: nothing significant

Campsites: There is camping available at Farragut and a primitive site at the top of Bernard Peak.

- - - - - - - - - - - - - - - - - - - -

Three popular trails within the boundaries of Farragut State Park that are briefly described below include Squirrel Cache Trail, Shoreline Trail and Highpoint Trail.

Squirrel Cache Trail, Farragut State Park
This is a Family Fun Hike

Destination: Highpoint and Shoreline Trails

Difficulty and Length: easy, 1.2-mile loop, not handicap accessible

Best Suited For: hiking, biking

Best Features: interpretive signs, meadow and forest habitats, wildlife

Mountain bikers on Squirrel Cache Trail
(Richard Heinzen)

Shoreline Trail, Buttonhook Bay, Farragut State Park
This is a Family Fun Hike

Destination: Eagle Boat Launch, Beaver Bay Beach, Blackwell Point

Difficulty and Length: easy, 1.5 miles one-way

Best Suited For: hiking, mountain biking

Best Features: follows shoreline of Idlewilde and Buttonhook bays to reach Highpoint Trail

Highpoint Trail, Buttonhook Bay, Farragut State Park

This is a Family Fun Hike

Destination: Bernard Peak

Difficulty and Length: easy first two miles; rocky and steep for third mile

Best Suited For: hiking, mountain biking (only until point No. 47)

Best Features: excellent viewpoints of the southern end of the lake

---

Chilco Peak Trail No. 14

Destination: North Chilco Peak, 5,635 feet

Best Suited For: hiking, mountain biking, horseback riding

How Much Use: A Little * A Little More * A Lot * A LOT MORE * Excessive

USGS Map: Bayview, Lakeview **GPS:** N47 54 18.4 W116 30 53.0

What's it like?

This trail is open to motorized users but is a great hike as well. Most of it traverses a steep hillside covered with timber. After one mile or so a spur trail heads up to the summit of North Chilco Peak, a big rocky summit. Once out of the trees and on this exposed mountaintop, the views are exceptional. The remains of a lookout are still here, but you will find yourself engrossed in looking in every direction at the vast expanse of mountainous country reaching to every horizon.

Trailhead: At milepost 449 on U.S. Highway 95, just across from Silverwood Theme Park about 18.5 miles north of Coeur d'Alene, turn east onto Bunco Road. Go just over seven miles to the end of the pavement and continue on Bunco Road No. 332. Go six miles to the junction with Road No. 385 and look for a pair of concrete pillars on either side of the trail on the south side of the road. There is no sign for the trail.

Trail Length: approximately 1.5 miles one-way

Trail Condition: good

Elevation: Start – 4,212 feet, a sign at the summit says 5,635 feet – 1,423 feet net gain

Estimated Duration of Hike: 1.5 to 2 hours up, 1 to 2 hours down

Sweat Index: moderate

Mountain Bike Sweat Index: moderate

Best Features: expansive views from the Selkirks to the Cabinets and south across the Coeur d'Alene

Mountains, including views of three ski areas – Schweitzer Mountain, Silver Mountain and Mount Spokane

Availability of Water Along the Trail: none

Stream Crossings: none

Campsites: A primitive site is located near the trailhead off Road 332.

Kick Bush Gulch Trail No. 113

Destination: Kick Bush Gulch, Bunco Road No. 332

Best Suited For: hiking

How Much Use: A LITTLE * A Little More * A Lot * A Lot More * Excessive

USGS Map: Lakeview **GPS:** N47 57 30.4 W116 26 15.6

What's it like?

From Road 278 the trail strikes off into the brush and climbs moderately steeply to the first stream crossing. From there it switchbacks up a steep bank and joins an off-road vehicle trail that originates on private property. It continues for maybe a mile, then the trail becomes narrow with brush pressing in tightly on both sides. At mile marker 2, a spring bubbles to the surface next to the trail. The trail winds through a beautiful cedar forest along the stream, then climbs rather steeply to the top of a spur ridge from which you can catch glimpses of Packsaddle Mountain. Near the Coeur d'Alene-Pend Oreille Divide, the trail crosses the gated Road No. 1358, makes a steep, rutted ascent up and over a summit, and then follows the ridgeline to Road 332. From the main ridge there are distant views of Lake Pend Oreille. This would be a challenging excursion on a mountain bike and the trail is quite narrow for horses.

Trailhead: At milepost 449 on U.S. Highway 95, just across from Silverwood Theme Park about 18.5 miles north of Coeur d'Alene, turn east onto Bunco Road. Go just over seven miles to the end of the pavement and continue on Bunco Road No. 332. Between mile markers 5 and 6 turn onto Road No. 278 and follow it just over 10 miles to where Kick Bush Gulch crosses the road and the trailhead. The parking area is a turnout with room for one to three vehicles.

Trail Length: about 5.5 miles one-way

Trail Condition: fair

Elevation: start (at Road 278) – 2,400 feet, end (at Road 332) – 5,000 feet –2,600 feet net gain

Estimated Duration of Hike: 3 to 4 hours up, 2 to 3 hours down

Sweat Index: difficult

Mountain Bike Sweat Index: not suitable

Best Features: nice, forested walk alongside a beautiful stream

Availability of Water Along the Trail: Most of Kick Bush Gulch flows year-round and is close to the trail much of the way.

Stream Crossings: five crossings and one spring; several may be dry later in the year

Campsites: none

Wild notes: White-tailed deer shed their antlers each winter in December or January, and though they are a treasure for many "horn hunters" there are animals in the forest that depend on antlers for food. Mice, squirrels and chipmunks gnaw on shed antlers for the essential minerals they contain.

— — — — — — — — — — — — — — — — —

Dixie Queen Trail No. 677

This is a Family Fun Hike

Destination: North Gold Creek, Bunco Road No. 332

Best Suited For: hiking, mountain biking, horseback riding, ORVs

How Much Use: A Little * A LITTLE MORE * A Lot * A Lot More * Excessive

USGS Map: Lakeview, Minerva Peak, Faset Peak, Packsaddle **GPS:** N47 58 38.4 W116 25 24.2

What's it like?

This trail, like its close neighbor Trail 111, begins as a wide, off-road vehicle (ORV) route suitable for motorbikes and ATVs. The trail forks about one-third mile from the road to the right and Trail 111 continues straight ahead. In this broad meadow is where Trail 677 fords Branch North Gold Creek, a perennial stream. Only a couple hundred feet from the trailhead you might notice an old bridge crossing the creek off to the right. It is in a poor state of repair and is not suitable for use by anyone other than hikers, but it does offer a shortcut. The old roadbed this bridge connects to ties in with Trail 677 in a flat meadow after several hundred yards. The ORV trail continues for nearly two miles to an old dilapidated cabin. This is as far as the family fun hike goes. After that the trail becomes narrow and brushy. It stays close to the creek for a couple miles, then begins to switchback up a steep hillside through some nice open, brushy meadows. Here it is possible to see deer or elk. From the upper slopes, the southern end of the lake comes into view. The lower parts of this trail are great for mountain bikes, but the upper reaches are narrow, steep and rugged. However, this could make for a terrific loop ride with Trail 111 for experienced bikers.

Trailhead: At milepost 449 on U.S. Highway 95, just across from Silverwood Theme Park about 18.5 miles north of Coeur d'Alene, turn east onto Bunco Road. Go just over seven miles to the end of the pavement and continue on Bunco Road No. 332. Between mile markers 5 and 6, turn onto Road No. 278 and follow it about 12.5 miles to where North Gold Creek crosses the road and the trailhead. There is minimal parking here, though a spur road a hundred yards or so from the trailhead will accommodate several vehicles.

Trail Length: 6 miles one-way

Trail Condition: fair to excellent

Elevation: start (at Road 278) – 2,620 feet, end (at Road 332) – 4,600 feet – 1,980 feet net gain

Estimated Duration of Hike: 3 to 4 hours up, 2.5 to 3.5 hours down

Sweat Index: easy to the cabin; difficult beyond that

Mountain Bike Sweat Index: easy to the cabin; strenuous after that

Best Features: historical old cabin, wildlife and views of Bayview on Lake Pend Oreille

Availability of Water Along the Trail: North Gold Creek has water in places, but it also has dry sections and may only have a trickle in late summer.

Stream Crossings: none

Campsites: A primitive campsite can be used near the old cabin and there is an established primitive campsite with a fire ring and a makeshift corral about 200 yards from the trailhead on a spur road.

Alternate Hikes: Trail 677 shares a trailhead with Trail No. 111.

– – – – – – – – – – – – – – – – – – – –

Branch North Gold Creek Trail No. 111

This is a Family Fun Hike

Destination: Branch North Gold Creek, Packsaddle Mountain Trail No. 76

Best Suited For: hiking, mountain biking, horseback riding, ORVs

How Much Use: A Little * A Little More * A LOT * A Lot More * Excessive

USGS Map: Minerva Peak, Packsaddle **GPS:** N47 58 14.0 W116 24 26.9

What's it like?

Only a few hundred feet from the trailhead are the remains of an old cabin next to the trail. About one-third mile from Road 278, Trail 111 forks from Dixie Queen Trail No. 677 and goes on for two miles along an old roadbed that is now utilized as a route for off-road vehicles (ORVs) as well as for hikers, bikers and horse riders. It passes through several old clear-cuts, which are now growing in nicely. These openings provide good views of the surrounding mountainsides. But just beyond the first stream crossing, where the creek flows in the trail for a hundred feet or more early in the spring, and across two more minor crossings, the trail enters a magical forest of giant cedars and hemlocks. This old growth continues for several miles past a primitive campsite at the first bridge. A half-mile farther the trail climbs up onto the mountainside a ways. Along this stretch you'll encounter another old cabin adjacent to the trail, and the family fun hike takes you at least this far. The trail then dips back down to the creek and crosses it on a second bridge. The third bridge marks the end of the trail for all-terrain vehicles. Near mile marker 3 is a trail junction. This is where Trail 191, abandoned, fades into the forest in a northwesterly direction. The trail becomes rough and steep as it ascends through a narrow, steep-sided canyon for maybe a half-mile, then it winds through a changing forest to its junction with Road 2238.

Trailhead: At milepost 449 on U.S. Highway 95, just across from Silverwood Theme Park about 18.5 miles north of Coeur d'Alene, turn east onto Bunco Road. Go just over seven miles to the end of the pavement and continue on Bunco Road No. 332. Between mile markers 5 and 6, turn onto Road No. 278 and follow it about 12.5 miles to where North Gold Creek crosses the road and the trailhead. There is minimal parking here, though a spur road a hundred yards or so from the trailhead will accommodate several vehicles.

Trail Length: 6 miles one-way

Trail Condition: excellent

Elevation: start (at Road 278) – 2,620 feet, end (at Road 1073) – 4,550 feet – 1,930 feet net gain

Estimated Duration of Hike: 3 to 4 hours up, 2.5 to 3.5 hours down

Sweat Index: easy if going to the second cabin; difficult if going all the way to the end

Mountain Bike Sweat Index: easy to the first bridge; strenuous after that

Best Features: historic cabins, old-growth forest

Availability of Water Along the Trail: The trail is close to Branch North Gold Creek most of the way.

Stream Crossings: There are more than a dozen, but most are easy; a few may be dry and the three major crossings all have sturdy bridges (that may wash out from time to time).

Campsites: There is an established primitive campsite with a fire ring and makeshift horse corral about 200 yards from the trailhead on a spur road. A hunter's camp is located at the first stream crossing with a bridge about two miles up the trail.

Alternate Hikes: This trail shares the trailhead with Trail 677. Abandoned Trail 191 has a junction with this trail near the three-mile mark. It is no longer maintained, but hunters still use it. On the saddle between Branch North Gold Creek and Granite Creek, this trail connects to Packsaddle Mountain Trail No. 76 at the junction of Roads 2238 and 1073.

Wild Notes: Trail 111 passes through some exquisite old-growth forest dominated by giant cedars. Notice that some of these have large, rectangular holes in them – often hundreds. These holes are carved out by pileated woodpeckers – the largest woodpecker in the Rocky Mountains, close to 2 feet tall. Other animals benefit from these holes for nesting spots, such as flying squirrels, birds and some small owls. (See page 59.)

- - - - - - - - - - - - - - - - - -

Packsaddle Mountain Trail No. 76

This is a Family Fun Hike

Destination: Packsaddle Mountain, 6,405 feet

Best Suited For: hiking, mountain biking, horseback riding, motorbikes

How Much Use: A Little * A Little More * A LOT * A Lot More * Excessive

USGS Map: Packsaddle Mountain **GPS:** Lakeview N48 01 33 W116 25 26 (lower) N48 01 33 W116 22 25 (upper) N48 01 011 W116 20 42 (from Road 1073)

Trail No. 76 with Packsaddle Mountain in view (Chris Guibert)

What's it like?

Packsaddle Mountain is the dominant feature on the east side of Lake Pend Oreille. A wonderful network of trails converges on this mountain, but only Trail 76 goes over the top. From the upper trailhead it is two miles to the top from Road 1073. The trail passes through a clear-cut, then enters a forest of spruce and fir and skirts a boulder field. It switchbacks up the steeply ascending mountainside to the remarkable subalpine summit. Several rocky pinnacles punctuating small grassy meadows interspersed with clumps of dwarfed fir trees characterize Packsaddle Mountain. On the highest point are the remains of an old lookout. The middle trailhead offers the

Legendary Lake Pend Oreille

shortest route to the top (about a mile or so), though it is a long drive to get there. Off-road vehicle enthusiasts utilize this trailhead, since a portion of the trail here will accommodate motorbikes and all terrain vehicles. Several good campsites can be found at the end of Road 1050. From the lower trailhead, where parking is scarce, it is a grueling, relentless climb above Tumbledown Creek on a southwest aspect. That means on a hot summer afternoon this is really not the route to take. But the trail passes through beautiful brush fields and meadows and offers a good chance of seeing elk, deer and bear. In June look for diminutive splashes of pink from the common clarkia, which is actually not a very commonly seen wildflower. Mountain bikers will find this trail to be extremely difficult to negotiate going up, and it could be a hair-raising ride coming down. The family fun hike is from the east end of the trail.

Trailhead: There are three ways to get on Trail 76: In downtown Clark Fork turn southwest off State Highway 200 onto Stephen Street next to the gas station. The road crosses railroad tracks and bears left to the bridge over the Clark Fork River. At the south end of the bridge, turn right. Continue about 2.5 miles to Johnson Creek Road No. 278. Cross the cattle guard and creek and follow this road seven miles to Johnson Saddle. To get to the upper trailhead, go straight on Road 1066 from Johnson Saddle for four miles to Road 332, then follow it south about three miles to Road 1073. Take it almost two miles to a saddle and the trailhead. There is plenty of parking here. To get to the lower trailhead, stay on Road 278 from Johnson Saddle for approximately 22 miles to the junction of Road 1050. Take 1050 about three miles to the trailhead. A wide spot in the road here accommodates a couple of vehicles. To get to the middle trailhead, stay on Road 1050 all the way to its end, about eight miles beyond the lower trailhead, where there is plenty of parking.

Trail Length: 6 miles altogether (from lower to upper trailheads); 2 miles from the east end of the trail to Packsaddle Mountain.

Trail Condition: good

Elevation: start (at Road 1050) – 3,080 feet, end of Road 1050 – 5,240 feet, Packsaddle Mountain – 6,405 feet, end (at Road 1073) – 4,550 feet

Estimated Duration of Hike: from 1 to 3 hours up, depending on your starting point

Sweat Index: moderate from the upper and middle trailheads, difficult from the lower trailhead

Mountain Bike Sweat Index: not suitable

Best Features: mountaintop, views of the lake and fabulous mountain views all around

Availability of Water Along the Trail: Several springs are located near the top of Packsaddle close to the trail, but they could be dry later in the summer (beware, there is none between the lower and middle trailheads).

Stream Crossings: none

Campsites: Primitive camping can be enjoyed at the upper and middle trailheads and at the top of Packsaddle.

Alternate Hikes: Trail 84 connects to this trail about a mile above the middle trailhead and just below the summit. It provides access to Trails 229 and 611 and a variety of terrific open loop hikes.

Wild Notes: About half a mile from the lower trailhead an invasion is taking place. Dalmatian toadflax, a noxious weed, took hold in 2001 or 2002 and is spreading across a large brush field. Pulling this weed may help bring this infestation under control. Dalmatian toadflax, which resembles a snapdragon, has a beautiful yellow flower, but it is an aggressive non-native and every effort should be made to eradicate it from this site.

--- --- --- --- --- --- --- --- --- --- --- --- --- --- ---

Falls Creek Trail No. 229 and Minerva Ridge Trail No. 84

Destination: Packsaddle Mountain, 6,405 feet
Best Suited For: hiking, mountain biking, horseback riding, motorbikes
How Much Use: A Little * A Little More * A Lot * A LOT MORE * Excessive
USGS Map: Minerva Peak, Packsaddle Mountain **GPS:** N48 03 37.7 W116 24 09.4

What's it like?

From the site of an old mining operation long ago abandoned, Trail 229 continues as a narrow road for about a half-mile before it becomes too difficult for even a jeep to follow. But ATVs use it for another half-mile perhaps, and then it narrows further to a hiker's trail. The ascent is easy for almost two miles altogether before the first of 30 switchbacks loops the trail up the mountainside. Heavy timber frames the trail most of the way, but at times, there are some great views of the open slopes of Minerva Ridge. With binoculars it is sometimes possible to spy wildlife feeding in the vast meadows across Falls Creek. Once on the high flanks of the mountain, the trees thin out, it becomes very brushy and the path then joins Trail 84, which climbs a half-mile to a junction with Trail 76 and the last lunge to the summit of Packsaddle Mountain.

Trailhead: In downtown Clark Fork turn southwest off Highway 200 onto Stephen Street next to the gas station. The road crosses railroad tracks and bears left to the bridge over the Clark Fork River. At the south end of the bridge, turn right. Continue about 2.5 miles to Johnson Creek Road No. 278. Cross the cattle guard and creek and follow this road seven miles to Johnson Saddle. Stay on Road 278 for another 14 miles to its junction with Road 1088. Take 1088 about 2.5 miles to the end of the road at an old mine site and the trailhead. This road is narrow and brushy in places (at times it is like driving through a green tunnel).

Trail Length: 4.8 miles one-way

Trail Condition: good

Elevation: start (Trail 229 near Falls Creek Mine) – 3,200 feet, junction with Trail 84 – 6,000 feet. Trail 84 (at junction with Trail 76) – 6,160 feet – 3,205 feet net gain

Estimated Duration of Hike: 2.5 to 3.5 hours up, 2 to 3 hours down

Sweat Index: difficult

Mountain Bike Sweat Index: not suitable after the first 2 miles, which are easy

Best Features: mountaintop and views of the lake

Availability of Water Along the Trail: Falls Creek has water about midway along the trail.

Stream Crossings: There are six or seven crossings, but several are dry much of the summer; the others are minor.

Descending Minerva Ridge (Chris Guibert)

Campsites: Camps can be set up in a couple places along Road 1088, and there is a good site at the end of the road; also, there is a primitive site less than a mile up the trail.

Alternate Hikes: This trail connects to Trail 84, which ties Trail 611 to Trail 76. Note that Trail 84 beyond its junction with Trail 611 has been abandoned. It can still be followed, but it becomes increasingly obscure. However, a little bushwhacking will take you out onto a fabulous ridge covered with open meadows for possible views of wildlife and magnificent vistas of the surrounding terrain.

- -

Granite Creek Trail No. 71 and Granite-Packsaddle Trail No. 611

Destination: Peep-A-Day Ridge, Minerva Ridge

Best Suited For: hiking, mountain biking, horseback riding

How Much Use: A Little * A Little More * A LOT * A Lot More * Excessive

USGS Map: Packsaddle Mountain **GPS:** N48 05 05.8 W116 21 22.4

What's it like?

Unlike its tributary, Dry Gulch, Granite Creek flows year-round. Trail 71 follows along it for a couple of miles, crossing the stream once by way of a sturdy footbridge. This trail is in heavy timber most of the way, but once beyond the fork with Trail 611, it climbs a brushy hillside sporting some nice ponderosa pines. Once on the ridgeline, Trail 608 comes out of Dry Gulch and joins the combined trail. Trail 71 continues up the ridge, making several switchbacks. At the third switchback from the trail junction is a rocky outcrop that offers a fine view of Packsaddle Mountain, but the best view is near the end of the trail. A jagged pinnacle of rock just above the trail provides an unobstructed view of upper Granite Creek and the stony turrets of Packsaddle across the valley. Trail 611 forks from Trail 71 a mile and a half from the trailhead and dips down to Granite Creek, which must be waded to get across, or by walking across the creek on a slick log. Trail 71 continues to climb steadily for 2.5 miles and 2,000 feet to Minerva Ridge and a junction with Trail 84. From the top, a mountain biker could follow Trail 71 all the way to Road 278, although it is narrow and steep in places.

Trailhead: In downtown Clark Fork turn southwest off Highway 200 onto Stephen Street next to the gas station. The road crosses railroad tracks and bears left to the bridge over the Clark Fork River. At the south end of the bridge, turn right. Continue about 2.5 miles to Johnson Creek Road No. 278. Cross the cattle guard and creek and follow this road seven miles to Johnson Saddle. Stay on Road 278 and go about 10 miles to the trailhead where Granite Creek crosses the road. There is scarce parking here, though a wide spot a hundred feet farther will accommodate a couple of vehicles. The top portion of this trail can be reached by taking Road 1066 from Johnson Saddle four miles to Road 332, then following Road 332 about 2.5 miles to gated Road 2401 and taking that to its end and the trail.

Trail Length: 4.3 miles one-way

Trail Condition: good

Elevation: start (Trail 71 at Road 278) – 2,738 feet, junction with Trail 611 – 3,200 feet, end (at Road 2401) – 4,650 feet. Trail 611 (junction with Trail 71) – 3,200 feet, junction with Trail 84 – 5,140 feet

Estimated Duration of Hike: 2 to 3 hours up and 2 to 3 hours down

Sweat Index: difficult

Mountain Bike Sweat Index: strenuous

Best Features: views of Packsaddle Mountain from near the top of the trail

Availability of Water Along the Trail: closely follows Granite Creek, a perennial stream, for about 2 miles

Stream Crossings: one minor crossing that is dry much of the year and a second crossing over

Granite Creek using a footbridge

Campsites: There are primitive sites along Road 278 from Granite Creek to Toms Gulch, and a primitive site is located about 1.5 miles up the trail just before the footbridge.

Alternate Hikes: Trail 611 forks from this trail and connects to Trail 84 on Minerva Ridge. Trail 608 joins it on Peep-A-Day Ridge a mile or so from the top. These connector trails make for some great loop hikes.

Bayview-Blacktail Trail No. 230

Destination: along the flanks of Three Sisters Peaks, Cape Horn Peak
Best Suited For: hiking, mountain biking, horseback riding, motorbikes
How Much Use: A Little * A Little More * A Lot * A LOT MORE * Excessive
USGS Map: Cocolalla, Bayview **GPS:** N48 03 34.3 W116 33 28.6

What's it like?

Virtually the entire length of this trail passes through areas that have been extensively logged. The trail crosses numerous logging roads and skid trails. This activity has enhanced the area for wildlife and birds. Listen for the blending of birdsong as you walk along this trail. Moose are frequent visitors here, too. The trail spends much of its time on the west side of Three Sisters Peaks, so views of the lake are sparse until near the south end of the trail. About two miles from the north trailhead is a faded metal sign indicating Trail 233 to Careywood, but the trail no longer exists. Another mile farther is an old decaying Forest Service sign indicating Little Blacktail Road is three miles to the north and Cape Horn Peak is four miles to the south. The views of the lake from near the south trailhead are quite good. Mostly used by motorized recreationists, this trail is also a good route for mountain bikes.

Trailhead: Near milepost 457 on U.S. Highway 95 about 17 miles south of Sandpoint, turn east onto Blacktail Road (Blacktail Road makes a loop and joins Highway 95 near milepost 457 and near milepost 463). Proceed 2.6 miles to Little Blacktail Road. Turn east again and travel just about two miles to a fork in the road where there is a hiking sign. Go right about 0.1 miles to the north trailhead. The parking area will accommodate three to five vehicles. The south trailhead is accessed from Highway 95 near milepost 456 by turning southeast onto Bayview Road next to the Careywood Post Office. Travel about 4.5 miles to Perimeter Road adjacent to Farragut State Park then go east about two miles to the Bayview Post Office. Turn left beside the post office onto Cherokee Road (Road No. 297) and follow it as it switchbacks five miles up Cape Horn Peak. Look for a fork in the road and take the left fork 0.2 miles to the trailhead. The parking area is small and has a tight turnaround. It will accommodate up to three vehicles. Road 297 is narrow, steep and rough. High-clearance vehicles are advised.

Trail Length: 7 miles one-way

Trail Condition: good

Elevation: 2,700 feet to 4,200 feet undulating – 1,500 feet net gain

Estimated Duration of Hike: 3.5 to 4.5 hours either way

Sweat Index: moderate

Mountain Bike Sweat Index: moderate

Best Features: views of the lake and of Mount Spokane, wildlife

Availability of Water Along the Trail: none

Stream Crossings: none

Campsites: none

Evans Landing Trail No. 64

This is a Family Fun Hike

Destination: Evans Landing, Lake Pend Oreille

Best Suited For: hiking, horseback riding

How Much Use: A Little * A Little More * A Lot * A LOT MORE * Excessive

USGS Map: Talache, Cocolalla **GPS:** N48 04 09.2 W116 32 39.4

What's it like?

A multitude of switchbacks make for a gentle grade along this trail. Beginning at the top of Kreiger Creek, the trail climbs modestly for a couple hundred yards before clearing the crest of the divide that separates Cocolalla Lake from Lake Pend Oreille. It is downhill from here through a thick forest of Douglas fir, larch and grand fir. Root disease, bark beetles and mistletoe have combined to create several openings along the way that offers sweeping vistas of the lake. Though the slope becomes extremely steep closer to the lake, the builders of this trail kept the descent (and the subsequent ascent when returning to the parking area) manageable. The last few steps, however, are tricky as the trail is worn and rutted just above the lakeshore. Before 1985, when this trail was constructed, Evans Landing was accessible by boat only. The remains of an old cabin are tucked behind a couple of old ponderosa pines and nearby there is a picnic table on the edge of the stony beach, plus a vault toilet. Mountain bikes are permitted, though the ascent back up is challenging.

Trailhead: Near milepost 457 on U.S. Highway 95 about 17 miles south of Sandpoint, turn east onto Blacktail Road (Blacktail Road makes a loop and joins Highway 95 near milepost 457 and near milepost 463). Go 2.6 miles to Little Blacktail Road, turn east again and go another 2.6 miles past one trail sign to East Ridge Road where a second trail sign indicates the way to this trailhead. Take a right on East Ridge Road, go a half mile and turn left onto a short spur road. Proceed to a parking area where the road splits. It will accommodate five to 10 vehicles.

Trail Length: 2 miles one-way
Trail Condition: good
Elevation: start – 3,080 feet, end (lakeshore) 2,061 feet – 1,019 feet net loss
Estimated Duration of Hike: 1 to 2 hours down, 1 to 2 hours back up
Sweat Index: moderate
Mountain Bike Sweat Index: difficult
Best Features: primitive picnic area on the shores of Lake Pend Oreille, historical site
Availability of Water Along the Trail: none until reaching the lakeshore
Stream Crossings: none
Campsites: There is a primitive site by the lakeshore at Evans Landing.

Maiden Creek Trail No. 321

This is a Family Fun Hike
Destination: Lake Pend Oreille, Maiden Rock
Best Suited For: hiking, mountain biking, horseback riding, motorbikes
How Much Use: A Little * A Little More * A Lot * A LOT MORE * Excessive
USGS Map: Talache, Cocolalla **GPS:** N48 07 02.4 W116 32 21.3

What's it like?

The story goes something like this: An Indian maiden had been scorned by her lover and was distraught. In a fit of despair, she stepped to the edge of a cliff and threw herself into the tumultuous waves crashing on the rocks far below. To this day, you can still see the form of the maiden framed in the pitted rock from out on Pend Oreille's roiling surface. Maiden Rock was the name given to one of the lake's most prominent geologic features by the early settlers. It is the final stony obstacle on a long flight of rocky ledges tumbling crazily from the summit of Blacktail Mountain and the last step is a drop-off – nearly vertical for a couple hundred feet. The trail to this magical spot on Lake Pend Oreille's western shore is fairly short, though quite steep. It cuts through a dense forest in a deep notch between two mountains to where the waters of Maiden Creek first gurgle to the surface in a small spring next to the trail. The trail then follows the creek steeply downhill to the lake. The climb back up is much more demanding than going down.

Hikers take a break at trail's end, Maiden Rock (Chris Bessler)

Trailhead: From Sandpoint, take U.S. Highway 95 south approximately 11 miles to milepost 463. Turn east onto Blacktail Road, which rises at a sharp angle from the highway across from Tri Con Bolt (Blacktail Road makes a loop and joins Highway 95 near milepost 457 and near milepost 463). Go 1.5 miles to Butler Creek Road No. 230. Turn left and travel three miles to the trailhead. The parking area will accommodate three to six vehicles. This is a rough and rutted road passing through private property.

Trail Length: 2 miles one-way

Trail Condition: good

Elevation: start – 3,230 feet, end (lakeshore) – 2,061 feet – 1,169 feet net loss

Estimated Duration of Hike: 1 to 2 hours down, 1 to 2 hours back up

Sweat Index: moderate

Mountain Bike Sweat Index: not suitable

Best Features: At the beach are picnic tables, fire rings, a pit toilet and a fabulous view of Maiden Rock.

Availability of Water Along the Trail: The trail crosses the spring that gives birth to

Maiden Creek.

Stream Crossings: one minor crossing

Camping: primitive camping opportunities at the beach

Alternate Hikes: Talache-Blacktail Trail No. 117 and Little Blacktail Mountain Trail No. 231 share the trailhead with Maiden Creek.

Wild Notes: This trail offers a cool opportunity to see exactly where a creek is born. Maiden Creek surfaces as a small spring less than a half mile from the trailhead right next to the trail. Its waters are cold and refreshing as they encounter the sky and air for the first time.

Talache-Blacktail Trail No. 117 and Little Blacktail Trail No. 231

Destination: Butler Mountain, 4,893 feet, Talache Landing on Lake Pend Oreille

Best Suited For: hiking, mountain biking, horseback riding, motorbikes

How Much Use: A Little * A Little More * A Lot * A LOT MORE * Excessive

USGS Map: Talache **GPS:** N48 07 02.4 W116 32 21.3

What's it like?

The trail over Butler Mountain has long been used by off-road vehicles (primarily motorbikes), resulting in some rather steep sections, which began to experience erosion. The Forest Service in cooperation with the Idaho Off Road Vehicle Association has rebuilt portions of the trail to a gentler grade with numerous switchbacks. Virtually all of Trail 117 is in heavy timber, but a few small meadows afford excellent views to the west, and the ridge connecting Blacktail Mountain to Butler Mountain offers filtered views of the lake. What you don't see on the forest map is a loop trail that descends Butler Mountain into Hickman Creek. It ties in with a logging road, then an off-road vehicle trail rises sharply through a logged area and accesses a system of ridges and bald knobs laced with open meadows adjacent to state lands. From the highest point along this ridge is perhaps one of the most spectacular views of Lake Pend Oreille anywhere. There is also a glimpse of Cocolalla Lake and a terrific bird's-eye view of the city of Sandpoint. The trail drops into a saddle where it rejoins Trail 117. It can be followed down Bimetallic Ridge, across Talache Creek, back upslope for half a mile then down to the trailhead two miles above Talache Landing, or climbed back to the mountaintop, completing a wonderful loop of perhaps five or six miles. Mountain bikes are permitted, but much of this trail system is steep and rutted and poses a stiff challenge to the mountain biker. This trail is heavily used by motorized recreationists.

Trailhead: From Sandpoint, take U.S. Highway 95 south approximately 11 miles to milepost 463. Turn east onto Blacktail Road, which rises at a sharp angle from the highway across from Tri Con Bolt (Blacktail Road makes a loop and joins Highway 95 near milepost 457 and near milepost 463). Go 1.5 miles to Butler Creek Road No. 230. Turn left and travel three miles to the trailhead. This is a rough and rutted road passing through private property. The parking area will accommodate three to six vehicles. This trail also can be accessed from Talache Landing by turning off Highway 95 about six miles south of Sandpoint east onto Sagle Road. Just shy of a mile, cross two sets of railroad tracks and go .4 miles to Talache Road. Take it past Shepherd Lake and Mirror Lake for 6.2 miles, the last two of which are gravel. At the second Talache Loop Road junction a dirt track goes down to the lake and another dirt track bears right and leads past several houses. There is a Trail 117 sign at this junction. Go right for a quarter mile to a fork and another trail sign. Continue to the right for 1.7 miles to the trailhead. The parking area will accommodate two to four vehicles. This last stretch of road is extremely steep and rough. High clearance 4WD vehicles are suggested.

Trail Length: 6 miles one-way

Trail Condition: fair to excellent

Elevation: start – 3,230 feet, near top of Butler Mountain – 4,850 feet – 1,620 feet net gain

Estimated Duration of Hike: 3 to 4 hours each way

Sweat Index: difficult

Mountain Bike Sweat Index: strenuous

Best Features: views of Lake Pend Oreille

Availability of Water Along the Trail: none from the Butler Creek trailhead to the top of Butler Mountain; Talache Creek crosses the trail about three miles above Talache Landing.

Stream Crossings: At one point Talache Creek actually flows in the trail for a distance of about 50 feet in the spring.

Campsites: none

Precautions: This is an off-road vehicle (ORV) trail so hikers and mountain bikers need to be alert for motorized recreationists.

Alternate Hikes: In Butler Creek, this trail shares a trailhead with Maiden Creek Trail No. 321 and Little Blacktail Trail No. 231. The reconstruction of ORV trails into Hickman Creek and onto the open ridges near the old Hope and Faith Mine and back up Butler Mountain has opened up a wonderful loop for hikers and bikers as well as ORVs. It is possible to travel 12 miles or more on these trails.

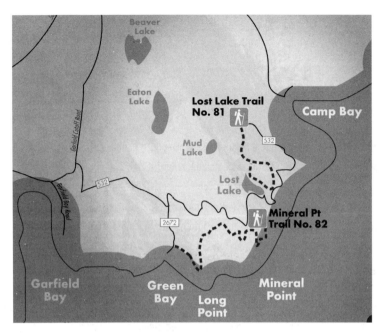

Area 2: Garfield Bay
Trails in this area:

Lost Lake Trail No. 81
Mineral Point Trail No. 82

The trails in this section are popular with hikers, mountain bikers and horseback riders. Lost Lake Trail is easy and so very enjoyable, offering wonderful opportunities for experiencing forest wetlands and the possibility of seeing moose, osprey and waterfowl. Mineral Point Trail has a lot to offer: vistas of the lake towards the Green Monarchs and south to Talache Landing, Maiden Rock and the Three Sisters Peaks; a self-guided interpretive loop trail; groves of old-growth cedar and ponderosa pines; dazzling displays of mountain wildflowers on rocky outcrops; and exploration at the water's edge at Green Bay. A new trail connected the two in 2007, opening access to a fine loop.

Lost Lake Trail No. 81

This is a Family Fun Hike
Destination: Lost Lake

Best Suited For: hiking, mountain biking, horseback riding

How Much Use: A Little * A Little More * A LOT * A Lot More * Excessive

USGS Map: Talache, Hope **GPS:** N48 11 43.4 W116 23 36.2

What's it like?

The simplest way to experience this beautiful, easy forest trail is to begin from the end of Road 532 and follow the trail into a mesmerizing grove of 60-foot alders dotting a forest wetland. A brief ascent climbs to a broad, flat ridge and a fork in the trail. You can go either way because the trail makes a loop down by Lost Lake, which becomes visible through the trees. A quiet approach may well reward you with a view of a moose or the resident waterfowl. An osprey nest is perched atop a giant ponderosa pine snag next to the lake. A couple of benches are located near the lake for relaxing moments of solitude. This, along with Mineral Point Trail No. 82, is a popular trail for mountain bikers. It is easy enough for beginners to learn the art of singletrack riding. In 2007, a new trail was constructed with the help of the Pend Oreille Pedalers, a local bike group, connecting the Mineral Point Trail 82 with Lost Lake Trail 81. This 2.2-mile addition makes it possible to hike or bike from Green Bay to Lost Lake, offering some fabulous vistas of Lake Pend Oreille with several well-placed benches along the way.

Trailhead: From U.S. Highway 95 about six miles south of Sandpoint, turn east onto Sagle Road and follow it 7.2 miles to Garfield Bay Road. Take it 1.4 miles to Garfield Bay and the Garfield Bay Cutoff Road, which bears left and uphill. Go 1/3 mile to Mineral Point Road No. 532 and turn right. This is a narrow dirt road. Take it 4.5 miles to the end of the road. The parking area will accommodate five to seven vehicles. You might notice about 1.2 miles before the end of the road another signed access to this trail. It leads to the same loop by Lost Lake.

Trail Length: 2.3 miles (part of it is a loop)

Trail Condition: excellent

Elevation: 2,456 feet to 2,536 feet – 80 feet net gain

Estimated Duration of Hike: 1 to 2 hours

Sweat Index: easy

Mountain Bike Sweat Index: easy

Best Features: wildlife at Lost Lake

Availability of Water Along the Trail: none

Stream Crossings: a couple of small boggy areas

Campsites: none

Wild Notes: The pair of osprey at Lost Lake has chosen a giant ponderosa pine snag for their nesting site. They will use bridges, manmade platforms and telephone poles for places to build nests, but in nature they most like big snags close to water. The same pair will come back year after year to that nest to raise their young.

- - - - - - - - - - - - - - - - - -

Mineral Point Trail No. 82 (Jake's Trail)

wheelchair accessible restroom and picnic area
This is a Family Fun Hike

Destination: Green Bay on Lake Pend Oreille, the Brent K. Jacobson Memorial Monument or Lost Lake
Best Suited For: hiking, mountain biking, horseback riding
How Much Use: A Little * A Little More * A LOT * A Lot More * Excessive
USGS Map: Talache, Hope **GPS:** N48 10 51.8 W116 23 17.6 (middle) N48 10 35 W116 24 11 (lower)

View from Mineral Point Trail looking west toward the Clark Fork Delta (Chris Bessler)

What's it like?

In early 1989 Brent "Jake" Jacobson, a U.S. Forest Service law enforcement officer, was tragically killed while in the line of duty. Six months later the Forest Service constructed Mineral Point Trail No. 82 in his memory. From the middle trailhead, a short, easy, wheelchair-accessible footpath leads to several picnic tables and benches overlooking Lake Pend Oreille and the Green Monarchs. In 2007, a new trail was constructed with the help of the Pend Oreille Pedalers, a local bike group, connecting the Mineral Point Trail 82 with Lost Lake Trail 81. This 2.2-mile addition makes it possible to hike or bike from Green Bay Campground to Lost Lake, offering some fabulous vistas of Lake Pend Oreille with several well-placed benches along the way. The trailhead is now

Hiking, Mountain Biking and Horseback Riding Trails   283 in the middle of the trail. Heading to Green Bay from that trailhead, just beyond the picnic area is a monument erected in memory of Jacobson and another bench for quiet contemplation beneath a majestic ponderosa pine. The trail carries on from there, dipping in and out of several draws holding groves of big old cedars. The ridges harbor some fantastic, giant pine trees. In spring the rocky outcrops and small meadows sport dazzling displays of wildflowers. The best views of the lake are from an open hillside above Green Bay looking south to Talache Landing, Maiden Rock and the Three Sisters. The lakeshore at Green Bay offers ample opportunity for exploration along the water's edge. Trail 82 makes for a fine mountain bike excursion, not too easy but just challenging enough to make it thrilling.

Trailhead: From U.S. Highway 95 about six miles south of Sandpoint, turn east onto Sagle Road and follow it 7.2 miles to Garfield Bay Road. Take it 1.4 miles to Garfield Bay and the Green Bay Cutoff Road, which bears left and uphill, with a road sign that's not easy to see. Go a third of a mile to Mineral Point Road No. 532 and turn right. This is a narrow dirt road. Take it 1.2 miles to its junction with Green Bay Road No. 2672 and follow that narrow road – a rough, steep 0.8 mile – to the parking area and lower trailhead at Green Bay; or continue on Road 532 another 1.9 miles and turn right onto Road 532A, a spur road that leads just over 0.5 mile to the middle trailhead. Each parking area accommodates up to eight vehicles. There are vault toilets at either trailhead.

Trail Length: 5 miles one-way (2.5 miles to Green Bay or 2.5 miles to junction with Lost Lake Trail 81)
Trail Condition: excellent
Elevation: 2,100 feet to 2,500 feet, undulating – 400 feet net gain
Estimated Duration of Hike: 1 to 2 hours each way
Sweat Index: moderate
Mountain Bike Sweat Index: moderate
Best Features: access to Lake Pend Oreille, great views of the lake, old-growth ponderosa pines and cedars, memorial plaque to Brent K. "Jake" Jacobson
Availability of Water Along the Trail: none
Stream Crossings: none
Campsites: Green Bay Campground is located at Green Bay, a short walking distance from the parking area for the lower trailhead. There are picnic tables, fire pits and vault toilets.

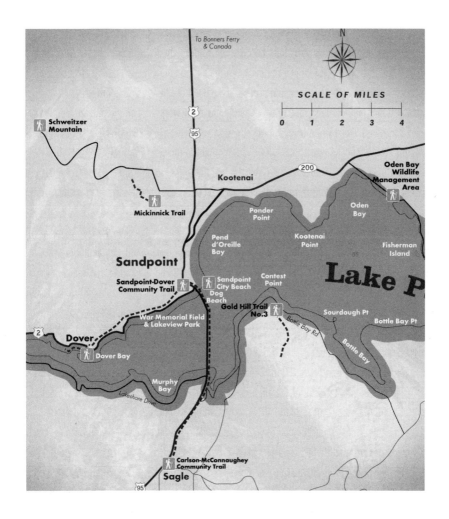

Area 3: Greater Sandpoint
Trails in this area:

Sandpoint-Dover Community Trail and Carlson-McConnaughey
Community Trail (Sagle-Sandpoint-Dover Community Trails)

Gold Hill Trail No. 3

Pend d'Oreille Bay Trail

Dover Bay Trails

Mickinnick Trail No. 13

Schweitzer Mountain Resort

Oden Bay Segment of Pend Oreille Wildlife Management Area

Connecting downtown Sandpoint to the small community of Sagle adjacent to the Long Bridge is the Carlson-McConnaughy Community Trail. Paved and wide enough for strollers and wheelchairs, it undulates gently once it crosses Lake Pend Oreille. It is popular for cyclists, joggers, mothers and children, and anyone wanting an easy walk through the outlying countryside around Sandpoint. Once you cross the bridge, you're not far from the Gold Hill Trail off of Bottle Bay Road that affords spectacular scenic views of Sandpoint to the west from the Gold Hill viewpoint. You access the lower trailhead about 4.5 miles down Bottle Bay Road from U.S. Highway 95 to the paved parking lot. The Gold Hill Trail is popular with mountain bikers, hikers and horseback riders.

Connecting downtown Sandpoint to the small community of Dover is the bike path that is part of the Sagle-Sandpoint-Dover Community Trails. Paved and adjacent to the bike path that goes to some of the area's schools, it is popular for students, cyclists, joggers, mothers and children, people walking their dogs, and anyone wanting a flat and pleasant three-mile walk from Sandpoint to Dover. It runs parallel to U.S. Highway 2 and connects to nine miles of trails at Dover Bay, which wind through wetlands and lead to Verwolf Vista Park atop Tank Hill.

The Pend d'Oreille Bay Trail is a proposed two-mile-long shoreline trail that begins just north of Sandpoint City Beach.

In the Selkirk Mountains north of Sandpoint, a new Forest Service trail climbs high on a ridge north of Sandpoint, Mickinnick Trail, providing the most extraordinary views of the Pend Oreille River, Lake Pend Oreille, Sandpoint and the Cabinet Mountains to the east. It traverses various habitats, from timber to open meadows, passing splendid arrays of wildflowers in the spring and summer months. It's a perfect place for a day hike close to town.

North of there, Schweitzer Mountain Resort has numerous hiking and mountain biking trails with sweeping views of Lake Pend Oreille. Hikers and bikers can even choose to hitch a ride up on the Great Escape chairlift. Down in the valley at Sunnyside, a short walking trail takes hikers through the woods to the lakeshore at Oden Bay.

- - - - - - - - - - - - - - - - - -

Sagle-Sandpoint-Dover Community Trails

wheelchair accessible
This is a Family Fun Hike
Destination: Paved trail connects the communities of Sagle, Sandpoint and Dover.
Best Suited For: hiking, biking, strollers, inline skates and wheelchairs
How Much Use: A Little * A Little More * A Lot * A LOT MORE * Excessive
USGS Map: Sandpoint **GPS:** N48 16 17.0 W116 32 44.7

What's it like?

The realization of a dream to build non-motorized trails connecting the close-knit communities at the north end of the lake came about in the late 1990s with the construction of wide, paved trails connecting Sagle to Sandpoint and Sandpoint to Dover. These asphalt paths quickly became popular for bicyclists, joggers and anyone wanting an easy, quiet meditative walk through the outlying countryside around Sandpoint. The Sandpoint-Dover Community Trail, which parallels U.S. Highway 2, is essentially flat while the trail to Sagle, Carlson-McConnaughy Community Trail, which parallels U.S. Highway 95, undulates gently once across The Long Bridge.

Pend d'Oreille Bay Trail

The Pend d'Oreille Bay Trail is a proposed shoreline trail that will begin at Sandpoint City Beach and extends to Ponderay. In 2009, this waterfront trail was in the planning stages on mostly private and a little city-owned property, and access requires permission from the private property owners. The trail includes the site of a proposed park on the old Humbird Mill site next to the city's water treatment plant. Plans call for the trail to eventually reach Ponder Point in Kootenai, linking three communities. From Pend d'Oreille Bay, visitors may see one of the most spectacular views from Sandpoint across the lake toward the Cabinet Mountains.

(Sean Haynes illustration)

To learn about efforts to make this a public trail, visit www.pobtrail.com, the Web site for Friends of Pend d'Oreille Bay Trail, a community partnership committed to establishing a public waterfront trail along the Lake Pend Oreille shoreline. Formal permission to use the existing private, waterfront trail is necessary and available on an annual basis; call (866) 877-3995 or submit a form under the "Invitation" tab at www.penddoreillebay.com. To learn more about this proposed trail, see chapter 6, pages 136-138.

Trailhead: In Sagle the trail begins on the east side of U.S. Highway 95 near the highway's junction with Monarch Road on the east and Gun Club Road on the west (technically the trail extends farther south to Sagle Road). It ends at a parking area for Dog Beach at the north end of the Long Bridge. In Dover the trail begins on the east side of town on the north side of Highway 2. It continues into downtown Sandpoint to the junction of Fifth Avenue and Larch Street.

Trail Length: approximately 6 miles one-way from Sagle to Sandpoint, approximately 3 miles one-way from Dover to Sandpoint

Trail Condition: good, all paved, but watch out for root damage on the Sandpoint-Sagle Community Trail south of Bottle Bay Road

Elevation: approximately 2,180 feet

Estimated Duration of Hike: These pathways can be followed for anywhere from a few minutes to a few hours. This community trail is designed for casual walking, pedaling, rollerblading or pushing a stroller.

Sweat Index: easy to moderate

Mountain Bike Sweat Index: easy

Best Features: paved path, great views over the lake from the Long Bridge

Availability of Water Along the Trail: none

Stream Crossings: none

Campsites: none, but motels and other accommodations abound in the area

--- -- -- -- -- -- -- -- -- -- -- -- -- -- -- --

Gold Hill Trail No. 3

This is a Family Fun Hike

Destination: Gold Hill, 4,042 feet, Contest Mountain Road No. 2642

Best Suited For: hiking, mountain biking, horseback riding

How Much Use: A Little * A Little More * A Lot * A LOT MORE * Excessive

USGS Map: Sandpoint, Elmira, Sagle, Talache **GPS:** N48 15 44.4 W116 29 34.3 (lower) N48 14 42.6 W116 29 51.1 (upper)

What's it like?

There are 40 switchbacks along this trail from the bottom to a pair of benches situated on a rocky knob overlooking Sandpoint and the Pend Oreille River. The view is awesome and well worth the three miles up to that point. The trail switchbacks frequently up a steep hillside through a dark forest of Douglas fir, cedar, grand fir and larch alongside Gold Creek, which is barely a trickle most of the summer, to the first wooden bench perched on a rock shelf. The view through the treetops of Trestle Creek and Scotchman Peak is inspiring. Beyond that overlook, though, the trail enters a no-less inspiring forest of birch, maples and alders that extends for several hundred vertical feet up the mountain. The brilliant green vegetation carpeting the forest floor, the crowded shrubs and the sighing leaves overhead make for a fabulous reflective hike. As though passing through a gateway, the hiker leaves that forest through a pair of large old trees, one a ponderosa pine and the other a Douglas fir, and gains the first of several rocky openings that provide unparalleled vistas of Sandpoint and the Pend Oreille River. Mountain bikers like to begin at the upper trailhead and descend the mountain along the trail's many switchbacks. The grade is generally pretty mellow, but some switchbacks are tight and steep.

Gold Hill Trail, with its iconic view of Sandpoint (Duane Davis)

Trailhead: About three miles south of Sandpoint, near milepost 471 on U.S. Highway 95, turn east onto Bottle Bay Road and follow it about four and a half miles to the lower trailhead. There is a paved parking lot with a pit toilet and room for six to 10 vehicles. To get to the upper trailhead, turn off Highway 95 onto Sagle Road about six miles south of Sandpoint and go six miles to Contest Mountain Road No. 2642. Follow it approximately six miles to the upper trailhead.

Trail Length: 3.7 miles one-way
Trail Condition: excellent
Elevation: start – 2,133 feet, end – 3,655 feet – 1,522 feet net gain
Estimated Duration of Hike: 2 to 3 hours up, 1.5 to 2.5 hours down
Sweat Index: moderate
Mountain Bike Sweat Index: difficult
Best Features: spectacular views of Bottle Bay, the city of Sandpoint, Schweitzer Mountain and the Selkirks, and the Pend Oreille River

Availability of Water Along the Trail: none (although Gold Creek might be a trickle alongside the lower part of the trail in summer)

Stream Crossings: none but a few small boggy areas

Campsites: none

--- --- --- --- --- --- --- --- --- --- --- --- --- --- --- ---

Dover Bay Trails

majority wheelchair accessible

This is a Family Fun Hike

Destination: points at Dover Bay, including Dover City Beach and Park, Dover Bay Marina, Verwolf Vista Park, Walson Wetland Park and Community Park

Best Suited For: hiking, biking

How Much Use: A Little * A Little More * A Lot * A LOT MORE * Excessive

What's it like?

Rocky Point is a rugged spit of land at the eastern edge of this area and Tank Hill is the small, hump-like hill that rises along the shore at Dover Point. Much of the inland area here is wetlands. In 2005, building began on the Dover Bay residential waterfront community that transformed the old mill site, 285 acres and over a mile of shoreline, into a major development with a 274-slip marina, hundreds of homesites, condos, bungalows for vacation rental, common open space,

One of the bridges on Dover Bay's public trail system (Laura White)

boardwalk, a waterfront village area with a café, market and fitness center, and nine miles of paved, gravel and boardwalk trails that connect to the Sandpoint-Dover Community Trail. Dover City Beach and Park is sandwiched by the resort and located west of the marina at the end of a narrow sandy stretch of land next to Brown's Inlet Bay. The public can moor at the marina for access to the resort's restaurant and shops. Boat gas is available at the Dover Bay marina dock as are canoe and kayak rentals. The Dover Bay community set aside Verwolf Vista Park at the top of Tank Hill and maintains a public hiking trail leading to it. The Balto Dog Park opened in 2009 and features a boardwalk for diving dogs, fire hydrants and a wash-down area with a solar-heated hose system.

Trailhead: Take U.S. Highway 2 west from Sandpoint for 3 miles and turn left on Fourth Avenue at Dover, following the signs to Dover Bay.

Trail Length: 9 miles

Trail Condition: excellent

Elevation: start 2,062 feet – 2,162 end – 100 feet net gain

Estimated Duration of Hike: Recreationists can choose to spend any amount of time, up to all day, on the trails, at the beach and parks, or on the estuaries at Dover Bay.

Sweat Index: easy

Bike Sweat Index: easy

Best Features: spectacular views across Pend Oreille and from the top of Tank Hill, wetlands and waterfront access

Availability of Water Along the Trail: Pend Oreille River is accessible at Dover City Beach and Park, and the trails cross the wetlands and skirt around the estuary.

Stream Crossings: none

Campsites: none, although vacation rentals are available

--- --- --- --- --- --- --- --- --- --- --- --- --- --- --- --- ---

Mickinnick Trail No. 13

Destination: A ridge between Syringa Creek and Little Sand Creek north of Sandpoint, Idaho, and south of Schweitzer Mountain Resort, called Greenhorn Mountain by some

Best Suited For: hiking

How Much Use: A Little * A Little More * A LOT * A Lot More * Excessive

USGS Map: Sandpoint **GPS:** N48 18 38.8 W116 34 05.1

What's it like?

A cooperative effort on the parts of a private landowner, the City of Sandpoint and the Forest Service made this new trail a reality. The trail is a result of a donation of 160 acres from Mick and

Nicky Pleass to the Forest Service made just before Mick's passing. The name comes from their names and the native kinnikinnick plant that grows here. The proximity of this trail to Sandpoint and the terrific views from all along its winding ascent have already made this a well-used and popular trail. But the trail is a fairly steep grade all the way to the end, which is more demanding on the knees coming down than going up. The trail climbs high onto a ridge north of Sandpoint and provides extraordinary views of the Pend Oreille River to the southwest and Lake Pend Oreille, Sandpoint and the Cabinet Mountains to the east. Traversing various habitats, sometimes the trail is in timber and at other times open meadows. It navigates among giant boulders and through forests of huge cedars, ponderosa pines, and other evergreen and deciduous trees. Wildflower lovers will love this hike, and those wanting to marvel at the magnificent, scenic setting of the town of Sandpoint will want to go as high as they possibly can, as the views get better with each step up.

Trailhead: From Sandpoint, follow the signs on U.S. Highway 95 north toward Schweitzer Mountain Resort. At the light turn left (west) on Schweitzer Cutoff Road, go one-half mile to North Boyer Road and at the "T" turn right at the Mormon church. Go one mile, turn left onto Schweitzer Mountain Road and go one-half mile to Woodland Drive. Turn left and go one-half mile to trailhead on right with vault toilet and parking.

Trail Length: 3.5 miles one-way

Trail Condition: new

Elevation: trailhead – 2,150 feet, end – 4,300 feet – 2,150 feet net gain

Estimated Duration of Hike: Viewpoints are plentiful along this trail, so hikers can go for just about any length of time they choose, from an hour or two up to an entire day.

Sweat Index: difficult

Mountain Bike Sweat Index: not suitable

Best Features: unequaled views of Sandpoint, Pend Oreille River, Lake Pend Oreille, the Cabinet and Monarch mountains

Availability of Water Along the Trail: Several small, seasonal streams carry water early in the summer, but don't expect any later in the year.

Stream Crossings: nothing significant

Campsites: none

Alternate Hikes: Someday this trail might tie in with a trail coming from Baldy Mountain, which would total about 9 miles one-way.

Schweitzer Mountain Resort

Some Trails are Family Fun Hikes

Destination: various points at Schweitzer Mountain Resort, including Schweitzer Peak, Colburn Lake and Picnic Point

Best Suited For: hiking, biking

How Much Use: A Little * A Little More * A LOT * A Lot More * Excessive

USGS Map: Sandpoint **GPS:** N48 22.08 W116 37.399

What's it like?

More than 20 miles of trails line the slopes at Schweitzer Mountain Resort, from family-friendly hikes to expert mountain bike trails. From Schweitzer Village, take the Great Escape high-speed quad chairlift to the top of the mountain for 360-degree views that reach into British Columbia, Canada. Hikers and bikers can then descend 1,700 vertical feet back to the village via either the intermediate Beargrass Cruiser or expert-rated Pinch Flat Downhill bike-only trails, or the foot-traffic-only Nature Trail. Starting from the village, hikers and bikers may head out directly on numerous multiuse trails to explore the areas west and north from there. Take in the sweeping views of the mountains

Schweitzer's famous view of Lake Pend Oreille (Ryan McGinty)

and Lake Pend Oreille from Picnic Point or sit by the serene waters of Colburn Lake, a glacial lake in the Outback Bowl. Opened in 2009, Beargrass Cruiser is 5 miles long and has 46 switchbacks; this mellow downhill trail has a 6 percent grade all the way down from Schweitzer Peak to the Village. Schweitzer has also built two bike parks, one mid-mountain and one at the base, with numerous wooden features for adrenaline-bound downhillers. In August, Schweitzer hosts mountain bike races on Wednesday evenings; the Twilight Bike Races are open to all and emphasize fun with post race parties each week. In winter, the mountain grooms 32 kilometers of cross-country ski trails and a snowshoe trail; Schweitzer also sponsors a number of cross-country skiing and snowshoeing events. Pamphlets and trail maps are available at the Schweitzer Mountain Activity Center inside Selkirk Lodge. Look up www.schweitzer.com or phone 208-255-3081. If you're interested in horseback riding, book a guided ride with Mountain Horse Adventures (www.mountainhorseadventures.com) through the Activity Center or call 208-263-TROT (8768).

Trailhead: From Sandpoint, follow the signs on U.S. Highway 95 north toward Schweitzer Mountain Resort. At the light turn left (west) on Schweitzer Cutoff Road, go one-half mile to North Boyer Road and at the "T" turn right at the Mormon church. Go one mile, turn left onto Schweitzer Mountain Road at the welcome sign. Follow that road for 9 miles, staying in the center lane at the "chicken foot," to reach Schweitzer Village. The Schweitzer Mountain Activity Center is on the left inside Selkirk Lodge.

Trails and Lengths (where available)

Bike trails (bike traffic only): Beargrass Cruiser, 5 miles; Moffitt's Edge, Moffitt's Revenge, Pinch Flat Downhill, The Collector

Hike trails (foot traffic only): Stewart's Loop; Summit View Loop; Nature Trail, 2.5 miles

Multiuse trails (shared trails): Bear Ridge, 0.5 mile; Boomerang, 1.2 miles; BSR, 0.25 mile; Cloudwalker, 1.1 miles; Colburn Lake; Cougar Gulch, 1 mile; Coyote Canyon, 2.4 miles; Huckleberry Hill, 0.6 mile; Lower Grr, 0.9 mile; Moose Trot, 0.5 mile; Morris Mile; Overland, 5 miles; Rolling Thunder, 0.7 mile; Screech Owl, 0.9 mile; Upper Grr, 1.2 miles; and Wolf Ridge, 1 mile

Trail Condition: fair to excellent

Elevation: lowest point – 4,250 feet, Schweitzer Village – 4,700 feet, Highest point – 5,200 feet

Estimated Duration of Hike: from an hour or two up to an entire day

Sweat Index: easy to difficult

Mountain Bike Sweat Index: moderate to strenuous

Best Features: breathtaking views of Lake Pend Oreille and the Cabinet and Selkirk ranges, services and other activities in Schweitzer Village, bike parks, huckleberry picking

Availability of Water Along the Trail: Water can be found at small streams, Colburn Lake, Summit Activity Center and in Schweitzer Village.

Stream Crossings: nothing significant

Campsites: RVs may park in the Gateway Parking Lot for a fee in winter and free in summer, and lodging is available in Schweitzer Village and at other sites on the mountain.

Oden Bay Segment of the Pend Oreille Wildlife Management Area

Destination: Raymond Slough at Oden Bay
Best Suited For: hiking, biking
How Much Use: A Little * A Little More * A LOT * A Lot More * Excessive
USGS Map: Sandpoint **GPS:** N48 18 20.1 W116 25 41.8

What's it like?

Part of the Pend Oreille Wildlife Management Area, this is a great spot for wildlife viewing. The Oden Bay segment contains about 300 acres of protected habitat for thousands of waterfowl that teem across the bay's shallow waters, as well as for shorebirds and other wildlife. A small parking area exists for up to six vehicles where Sunnyside Road crosses Raymond Slough just before Perch Bay Road on your right. A maintained trail winds through open meadows and surrounding undeveloped forestland from the parking area to the lakeshore. It's possible to haul a car-top kayak or canoe down the bank of the slough in order to paddle out to the lake. Paddling from here to the small, unnamed islands south of Perch Bay and to Fisherman Island is delightful. Look for the eagle's nest on Fisherman Island, and watch for Canada geese.

Trailhead: From Sandpoint, head east on Idaho State Highway 200 for six miles and turn right onto Sunnyside Road. Follow it under the railroad overpass, then veer left and continue to a small parking area for up to six vehicles where Sunnyside Road crosses Raymond Slough just before Perch Bay Road on your right.

Trail Length: quarter mile
Trail Condition: good
Elevation: approximately 2,060 feet
Estimated Duration of Hike: 10 minutes one-way
Sweat Index: easy
Mountain Bike Sweat Index: easy
Best Features: wildlife viewing, lake access
Availability of Water Along the Trail: The trail runs along Lake Pend Oreille for its entire length.
Stream Crossings: none
Campsites: none

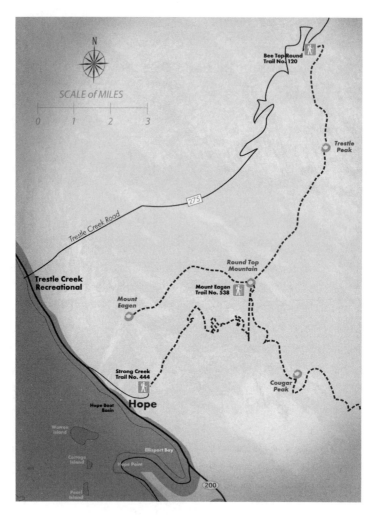

Area 4: Pack River to Hope
Trails in this area:

Strong Creek Trail No. 444

Bee Top-Round Top Trail No. 120 and Mount Eagen Trail No. 538

Rising more than 4,000 feet above the Pack River Flats and Ellisport Bay are the spectacular ramparts of the Cabinet Mountains. There used to be forest fire lookouts on three of the peaks — Round Top, Bee Top and Scotchman Peak — but all that remains now are some concrete, wire and rotted wood. Several trails in these mountains provide magnificent views of the lake, including one of the longest trails in the region — Bee Top-Round Top Trail 120. It was once a National Recreation Trail, but because the south end crosses private property where there is no legal easement, the trail lost this designation. Nonetheless, at 19 miles in length and with spectacular views of the lake, Trail 120 offers some of the best panoramas this side of heaven. It is also a very popular horseback trail. Other trails in this area of the west Cabinet Mountains connect to Trail 120, including the popular Strong Creek Trail No. 44 and Mount Eagen Trail No. 538.

— — — — — — — — — — — — — — — — —

Strong Creek Trail No. 444

Destination: Round Top Mountain, 6,149 feet, Bee Top-Round Top Trail 120

Best Suited For: hiking, mountain biking, horseback riding, ATVs, motorbikes

How Much Use: A Little * A Little More * A LOT * A Lot More * Excessive

USGS Map: Mount Pend Oreille, Elmira

GPS: N48 15 35.0 W116 17 07.2

The splendid view from Trail 444 in winter (Jim Mellen)

What's it like?

Miners explored a lot of this country years ago, then left the road in place for future users. It is now maintained as a trail suitable for a variety of uses, including mountain bikes. About four miles from the bottom, between the fifth and sixth switchbacks after crossing Strong Creek, there is an old mine shaft adjacent to the road. It is interesting to look at but extremely dangerous to enter. The trail climbs steadily through dark timber, some of it old-growth cedar, along the stream to the more-open upper slopes, switchbacking nine times from the stream crossing up 2,200 vertical feet to a saddle between Round Top and the Auxor Mine. Views on the way up are filtered by heavy timber, which is punctuated by some nice Douglas fir, larch and white pine. Nearing the top, views improve of Lake Pend Oreille, which stretches out below in its entire glorious splendor.

Trailhead: The trailhead in the town of Hope is a bit obscure. Turn north off Idaho State Highway 200 onto Centennial Avenue next to Hope's Memorial Community Center. Take a left onto the old highway and go about one-quarter mile to the post office. Main Street, a narrow, one-lane paved road, veers right uphill in front of the post office. Follow it a couple of hundred yards and take a sharp right on Grandview uphill toward the cemetery; continue past the cemetery on a dirt road beyond the sign that says "Road Closed 3/4 Mile Ahead" to the trailhead. There is a narrow, steep turnaround and parking for only two or three vehicles.

Trail Length: 7.3 miles one-way

Trail Condition: fair to good

Elevation: start – 2,700 feet, end (junction with Trail 120) – 5,710 feet – 3,010 feet net gain

Estimated Duration of Hike: 4 to 5 hours up on foot, 3 to 4 hours down; a great 1- to 2-hour ride up on a bike and less than an hour down

Sweat Index: difficult

Mountain Bike Sweat Index: strenuous

Best Features: fantastic views of the lake, historic mines, old-growth timber

Availability of Water Along the Trail: A couple of small streams cross the trail near the beginning, and Strong Creek flows year-round and parallels the first couple miles of the trail. There are several small springs within a mile and a half of the top.

Stream Crossings: The only major crossing of Strong Creek is about two miles from the trailhead and can be a tricky rock hop if the water is high.

Campsites: There are several primitive campsites at the top of the ridge at Auxor Basin, and a couple of primitive sites can be located on the way up.

Alternate Hikes: At the top, this trail, which is actually an old roadbed all the way up, ties in with Auxor Basin Road 489, which accesses the old Auxor Mine. Road 489 provides a route to Lightning Creek Road No. 419. This may be one of the best mountain biking trails around the lake. Trail 120, a non-motorized trail, crosses this old road on the ridgetop and provides easy access to Round Top Mountain a mile away.

- - - - - - - - - - - - - - - - - -

Bee Top-Round Top Trail No. 120 and Mount Eagen Trail No. 538

This is a Family Fun Hike (Wellington saddle to Round Top)

Destination: Round Top Mountain, 6,149 feet, Trestle Peak, 6,320 feet

Best Suited For: Hiking, mountain biking and horseback riding

How Much Use: A Little * A Little More * A LOT * A Lot More * Excessive

USGS Map: Mount Pend Oreille, Elmira **GPS:** N48 21 01.2 W116 13 19.7

What's it like?

From almost anywhere along this trail there are outstanding views of Lake Pend Oreille, but especially from Round Top Mountain (6,149 feet) and Cougar Peak (6,004 feet) and the fabulous beargrass meadows that flank the southwest slopes facing the lake. From the trailhead at Trestle Creek Road 275 the trail climbs gently past giant spruce trees onto the west side of the ridge. From here there are great views of Trestle Creek all the way down to the lake. Near Trestle Peak it crosses a shallow saddle onto the east side of the ridge and stays there all the way to its junction with Strong Creek Trail No. 444. To reach the highest point along this ridge system requires just a brief, off-trail climb to the top of Trestle Peak (6,320 feet) for magnificent views in every direction.

Views of the lake are outstanding from Trail 120
(Jim Mellen)

The easiest way to get to the most glorious lake views is to take the long, rough drive to the end of Auxor Basin Road No. 489 and then hike the short distance to Round Top, or follow the trail southeast for a couple of miles into a vast meadow on the side of an unnamed summit. In places along this trail are beautiful subalpine forests with wood rush and beargrass and huckleberry carpeting the forest floor. Mountain bikers can enjoy the trail for several miles from Wellington Saddle toward Bee Top, though the farther from the saddle the more difficult the trail becomes. The trail from Trestle Creek begins as an easy mountain bike trail, but after approximately three miles it becomes less suitable for bikes.

Trailhead: The most popular starting point on this trail is reached by turning off Idaho State Highway 200 about 12 miles east of Sandpoint onto Trestle Creek Road No. 275, between Pack River and Hope, and traveling approximately 12.5 miles to the trailhead, which is located on a switchback about a mile past the junction of Lunch Peak Road No. 1091.

Trail Length: 19 miles one-way (about 8 miles from Trestle Creek Road 275 to Auxor Basin Road No.

Hiking, Mountain Biking and Horseback Riding Trails 299

489 and Strong Creek Trail 444); 1 mile from road 489 to Round Top; 6 miles from road 489 to Porcupine Lake Trail No. 114; 8 miles from road 489 to Bee Top Ridge Trail No. 63

Trail Condition: fair to good; some damage from 2006 flood

Elevation: start (north end at Road 275) – 4,980 feet, junction with Round Top spur trail – 5,960 feet, junction with Bee Top Trail No. 63 – 5,538 feet

Estimated duration of hike: Depending on the destination, this trail can be traveled for anywhere from two to 12 hours one-way.

Sweat Index: easy to moderate

Mountain Bike Sweat Index: Although difficult, much of this trail offers some fabulous singletrack action.

Best Features: unparalleled views of Lake Pend Oreille, the City of Sandpoint and the west Cabinets

Availability of Water Along the Trail: There are several small brooks and springs in the first mile from Road 275, but after that there is no water for miles. A spring bubbles across the trail about 4 miles southeast of Wellington Saddle.

Stream Crossings: nothing significant

Campsites: There is a primitive Forest Service campground at Porcupine Lake a couple miles below the Bee Top-Round Top Divide. About five miles off State Highway 200 on Road 275 is a primitive Forest Service campground. At the end of Auxor Basin Road No. 489, there are several primitive but well-used campsites. Also, at the Road 275 trailhead there are several well-established campsites.

Precautions: Trail 120 at its southern end has no right-of-way across private property, so taking it beyond the junction of Bee Top Trail 63 is not advised.

Alternate Hikes: This trail also can be reached by taking Strong Creek Trail No. 444 from the town of East Hope. Trail 444 is an old road all the way to the top and ties in with Trail 120 at the Wellington Creek Road. It is a popular route for mountain bikers. Bee Top Trail 63 provides easy access to the summit of Bee Top Mountain (6,212 feet). A spur trail less than one-quarter mile in length, No. 538, accesses the summit of Round Top and the site where a forest fire lookout tower once stood. This trail used to go all the way out to Mount Eagen, but it is no longer maintained and is in poor condition.

Wildlife Sighting: Most people expect to see moose along streams and rivers munching on willows and the lush vegetation of riparian areas, but moose in these mountains also frequent the ridgetops.

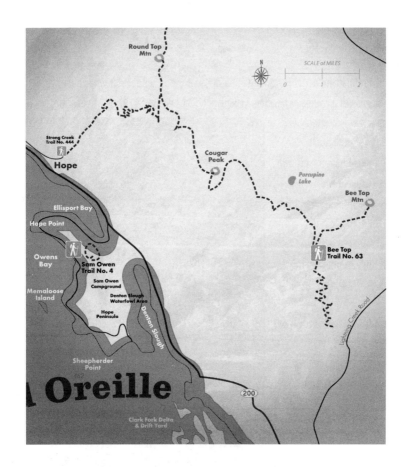

Area 5: Hope Peninsula to Clark Fork Delta
Trails in this area:

Sam Owen Trail No. 4

Bee Top Trail No. 63

— — — — — — — — — — — — — — — — — —

Sam Owen Trail No. 4

wheelchair accessible

This is a Family Fun Hike

Destination: monument to the memory of Sam and Nina Owen

Best Suited For: wheelchair users, strollers, hiking, mountain biking

How Much Use: A Little * A Little More * A LOT * A Lot More * Excessive

USGS Map: Hope **GPS:** N48 13 01.6 W116 17 14.2

What's it like?

The first half-mile of this trail has a hardened surface suitable for wheelchairs and strollers. It goes to a couple of benches looking out over Lake Pend Oreille through the surrounding trees. The forest is primarily beautiful Douglas fir and ponderosa pine interspersed with meadows carpeted with wildflowers in spring. Beyond the benches the trail has a dirt surface and makes a loop up a small hill through the forest. A spur trail accesses the gravesite of Sam Owen (1865-1949) and his wife, Nina (1876-1963). They homesteaded on the Hope Peninsula and late in life deeded the property that is now the Sam Owen Campground. This is a good path for beginner mountain bikers.

Deer are plentiful on the Hope Peninsula, a wildlife preserve (Jane Fritz)

Trailhead: About two miles east of Hope on Idaho State Highway 200, turn south onto Peninsula Road and travel approximately a mile and a half to Sam Owen Campground. The trail is across the road from the campground entrance, next to a small parking area that holds five or six vehicles. Be careful when crossing the road.

Trail Length: 1 mile round-trip

Trail Condition: excellent

Elevation: 2,100 feet to 2,200 feet

Estimated Duration of Hike: 1 hour

Sweat Index: easy

Mountain Bike Sweat Index: easy

Best Features: historical monument at the gravesite of Sam and Nina Owen, wildlife, views of Lake Pend Oreille

Availability of Water Along the Trail: none

Stream Crossings: none

Campsites: Sam Owen Campground (a fee area) is right across the road from this trail.

Precautions: Look both ways before crossing the road from the parking area to the start of the trail.

Bee Top Trail No. 63

Destination: Bee Top, 6,212 feet

Best Suited For: hiking, horseback riding

How Much Use: A Little * A LITTLE MORE * A Lot * A Lot More * Excessive

USGS Map: Clark Fork **GPS:** N48 13 07.5 W116 10 20.8 (connects to Trail 120)

View from the Bee Top-Round Top Trail
(Chris Bessler)

What's it like?

Getting to Trail 63 is a bit tricky, or just a lengthy undertaking, but once there what a grand hike this is out to Bee Top. Aside from a moderate climb of about 300 feet at the beginning, the trail follows this narrow, gently undulating ridge out to a perch on Bee Top's rocky knob that affords a view sure to make you gasp in awe. You can glimpse Still Lake in a small basin on the north side and see far up Lightning Creek. To the east the Scotchman Peaks raise their rugged heads to the sky, but the real treat is the panoramic vista of the pastoral setting of the Clark Fork River Delta and Lake Pend Oreille. Both sides of Bee Top and its ridgeline are exceedingly steep and rugged. At the summit are the rock walls and all that remain of the lookout that once perched on this stony pinnacle.

Trailhead: Bee Top Trail 63 veers off Bee Top-Round Top Trail No. 120 on the high ridges above the town of Clark Fork. The two best ways to get there is to follow Trail 120 from Wellington Saddle to the trail junction, or bushwhack up Porcupine Lake Trail No. 114, which is at the end of Porcupine Creek Road 642, which is being converted to a motorized trail open to off-road vehicles 50 inches wide or less. Trail users will have to ford Lightning Creek, which may be difficult during periods of high water. You get to Porcupine Creek Road 642 by taking Trestle Creek Road No. 275 off Highway 200 between Pack River and Hope to Lightning Creek Road No. 419, or by taking Lightning Creek Road No. 419 accessed from Highway 200 in Clark Fork.

Trail Length: 2 miles one-way, but the distance to the summit of Bee Top from the nearest roadside trailhead (if you can get there without a car) is approximately 10 miles

Trail Condition: fair

Elevation: start (junction with Trail 120) – 5,538 feet, end – 6,200 feet – 662 feet net gain

Estimated Duration of Hike: Once on Trail 63, it only takes an hour or so to get out to Bee Top.

Sweat Index: moderate

Mountain Bike Sweat Index: not suitable

Best Features: terrific views of Lightning Creek, Lake Pend Oreille and the Clark Fork River Delta; excellent ridgeline hiking in grassy meadows and rocky openings

Availability of Water Along the Trail: none

Stream Crossings: none

Campsites: There is a primitive site at the junction of trails 63 and 120.

Alternate Hikes: This trail branches off Trail 120 eight miles from Wellington Saddle and about 4.5 miles from Porcupine Lake Trail 114.

Area 6: Johnson Creek to Green Monarchs
Trails in this area:

Green Monarch Divide Trail No. 69

Schafer Peak Trail No. 68 and Teepee Gulch Trail No. 105

Most of the land on the east side of Lake Pend Oreille is public land managed by the U.S. Forest Service. It also is its most rugged shoreline. The mountainsides of the Green Monarchs plunge steeply into the depths of the lake, and evidence of a large forest fire is still obvious on its flanks. There is visible evidence of the large wildfire from 1991 on the flanks of Green Monarch Mountain and Shafer Peak, accessed via fabulous trails with equally fabulous views of the lake.

Green Monarch Divide Trail No. 69

This is a Family Fun Hike

Destination: Green Monarch Mountain, 5,076 feet

Best Suited For: hiking, horseback riding, mountain bikes, motorbikes

How Much Use: A Little * A LITTLE MORE * A Lot * A Lot More * Excessive

USGS Map: Packsaddle Mountain, Hope, Clark Fork **GPS:** N48 05 55.3 W116 17 30.9

The 1991 forest fire opened up dramatic views on Green Monarch Divide Trail (Jim Mellen)

What's it like?

This trail begins in Johnson Saddle in an old overgrown clear-cut. It follows a skid road for nearly half a mile, then enters a forest of lodgepole pine. The grade is a gentle but steady climb over one knob, then the trail undulates toward a deep notch in the ridge before ascending Green Monarch Mountain. The family fun hike is apropos at least as far as the summit of Green Monarch Mountain. The forest obscures views of the lake until you come to where a forest fire burned from near the lakeshore to the top of the ridge in 1991. The fire opened up dramatic views of the lake and the Cabinet Mountains to the north. Once over Green Monarch, the trail descends through brushy openings into another notch where it joins Trails 105 and 68. Much of Trail 69 makes for a terrific mountain bike ride, but the section leading up to Green Monarch Mountain is quite steep. Although the net elevation gain is quite small, the total elevation gain is much larger due to the undulating nature of this trail.

Trailhead: In downtown Clark Fork turn southwest off Idaho State Highway 200 onto Stephen Street next to the gas station. The road crosses railroad tracks and bears left to the bridge over the Clark Fork River. At the south end of the bridge, turn right. Continue about 2.5 miles to Johnson Creek Road No. 278. Cross the cattle guard and creek and follow this road seven miles to Johnson Saddle. Stay on Road 278 to the right, but go only 100 feet or less to a spur road that goes a short ways to the trailhead. There is parking here for four to six vehicles.

Trail Length: 4.3 miles one-way to the junction of trails 68 and 105, about 3 miles to the top of Green Monarch Mountain (approximately 5.5 miles to Schafer Peak from this trailhead via Trails 69 and 68.)

Trail Condition: good

Elevation: start (Road 278 at Johnson Saddle) – 4,700 feet, Green Monarch Mountain 5,076 feet, junction with Trails 68 and 105 – 4,600 feet – 476 feet net gain (total gain is much higher)

Estimated Duration of Hike: 2 to 3 hours to Green Monarch Mountain, 3 to 4 hours if continuing to Schafer Peak

Sweat Index: moderate

Mountain Bike Sweat Index: difficult

Best Features: mountaintop, views of the lake, forest fire remains

Availability of Water Along the Trail: none

Stream Crossings: none

Campsites: at the trailhead but none along the trail

Alternate Hikes: This trail connects to Schafer Peak Trail No. 68 and Teepee Gulch Trail No. 105.

— — — — — — — — — — — — — — — — — —

Schafer Peak Trail No. 68 and Teepee Gulch Trail No. 105

Destination: Schafer Peak, 5,210 feet
Best Suited For: hiking, horseback riding
How Much Use: A Little * A Little More * A LOT * A Lot More * Excessive
USGS Map: Packsaddle Mountain, Hope **GPS:** N48 06 22.3 W116 20 58.2

What's it like?

The most common way to attain the summit of Schafer Peak is to continue from Trail 69 to where it joins Trail 68 in a saddle between Green Monarch Mountain and Schafer Peak. But you can shave off half the distance by taking Trail 105 to that same saddle, though the elevation gain is much greater. Trail 105 climbs through a dense forest with brush pressing in closely on both sides. But once in the saddle, the hike to the top is relatively easy. Trail 68 joins an old logging road for several hundred yards, then climbs onto the ridge – climbing steadily to the top. A little evidence of a lookout that once stood here still remains. The views of the lake are excellent.

Trailhead: Trail 68 can only be reached by following Trail 69 (see directions to trailhead on page 307) or by taking Trail 105, which is accessed most easily by taking Road 278 from Johnson Saddle about four miles to the junction of Road 1063, then take that road half a mile to the trail. The trail actually crosses this road, descending half a mile to Road 2706 or climbing about a mile and maybe 1,200 feet to its junction with trails 68 and 69.

Trail Length: Trail 105 from Road 1063 is about 1 mile in length, and Trail 68 also is about a mile long.
Trail Condition: Trail 105 is fair; Trail 68 is good.
Elevation: start (Trail 105 at Road 1063) – 3,700 feet, junction with Trails 68 and 69 – 4,600 feet, Schafer Peak (via Trail 69) – 5,210 feet – 1,510 feet net gain
Estimated Duration of Hike: 1.5 to 2 hours up, 1 to 2 hours down
Sweat Index: moderate
Mountain Bike Sweat Index: not suitable
Best Features: mountaintop hike, views of the lake
Availability of Water Along the Trail: There may be a trickle where Trail 105 crosses Road 1063.
Stream Crossings: none
Campsites: none
Alternate Hikes: These two trails connect with Green Monarch Trail No. 69.

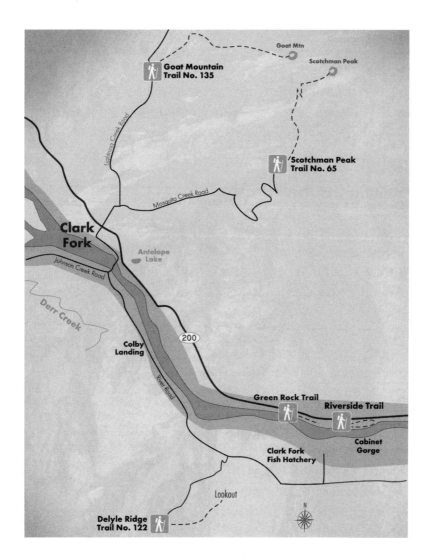

Area 7: Clark Fork River to Cabinet Gorge
Trails in this area:

Goat Mountain Trail No. 135

Scotchman Peak Trail No. 65

Delyle Ridge Trail No. 122

Riverside Trail and Green Rock Trail

The Cabinet Mountains north of Clark Fork hold two trails, one of which is a classic renowned for its beautiful vistas of Lake Pend Oreille and the presence of mountain goats. Nearby

Goat Mountain surely got its name from the prevalence of that same mammal. The trails that lie to the south of this part of the river are on U.S. Forest Service land. A lookout worth hiking to is perched on Delyle Ridge and looks north over the entire Clark Fork Valley. Finally, a new hiking-and-biking trail system along the Clark Fork River was developed at a 40-acre access site. Riverside and Green Rock trails provide access to the water and surrounding forest.

- - - - - - - - - - - - - - - - - - -

Goat Mountain Trail No. 135

Destination: Goat Mountain, 6,380 feet
Best Suited For: hiking
How Much Use: A LITTLE * A Little More * A Lot * A Lot More * Excessive
USGS Map: Clark Fork **GPS:** N48 11 27.3 W116 09 29.7

What's it like?

It used to take a 30-foot scramble to get up off the road, and in that short distance it was easy to miss the trail, which bears right into some thick brush and young trees. But a new sign marks the start of the trail and some maintenance has cleared the path. For more than half a mile the trail might be densely overgrown but still discernible. This trail did receive some maintenance in 2007. A volunteer crew did some brush clearing. It switchbacks up a steep mountainside dotted with lots of open, rocky meadows. As you climb higher the views to the southwest become increasingly spectacular. In just over a mile the trail reaches a small level bench overlooking Lightning Creek and an awesome vista of Bee Top. A short ways farther the trail gains a small grassy opening on

Jim Mellen, right, and friends on Goat Mountain with Scotchman Peak in the background

top of a knob with a grand view of Scotchman No. 2. All along the way the trail is steep and full of loose rock until it enters heavy timber. The trail is particularly brushy here and difficult to follow for several hundred vertical feet. But finally it gains a level ridgeline and some easy walking to a point that affords an incredible, panoramic view of Goat Mountain, Scotchman Peak and Scotchman No. 2, not to mention the mushroom-shaped dome on Black Top Mountain. At the summit, the view is even more dramatic, both of the lake and the Scotchmans. This trail affords some of the finest views on the north side of Lake Pend Oreille, especially for such a difficult climb on a poorly maintained path.

Trailhead: In downtown Clark Fork turn north on Main Street next to the Chevron station. Go one-half mile to Lightning Creek Road and turn left. Travel three miles to the trailhead. What looks like a steeply ascending game trail on the uphill side of the road is the start of Trail 135.

Trail Length: 3.5 miles one-way
Trail Condition: poor
Elevation: start – 2,330 feet, end – 6,380 feet – 4,050 feet net gain
Estimated Duration of Hike: 3 to 4 hours up, 2 to 3 hours down
Sweat Index: strenuous
Mountain Bike Sweat Index: not suitable
Best Features: fantastic views of the lake, Lightning Creek and Scotchman Peak
Availability of Water Along the Trail: none
Stream Crossings: none
Campsites: several primitive fire rings located along the trail
Alternate Hikes: From Goat Mountain it is only a mile of bushwhacking to the shoulder of Scotchman Peak. A fine, open loop hike can be had with this trail and Trail 65.
Wild Notes: Bears frequent this mountain because Sandberg's biscuitroot is plentiful. This diminutive plant, which is in the carrot family, is a favorite of bears in early spring. They dig up the fleshy roots and consume them by the dozens. When a hungry bear finds a good patch of this species of biscuitroot, it is not unusual to find whole meadows torn up as though a farmer plowed them with his tractor. One of the largest black bears I have ever seen was from this trail.

Scotchman Peak Trail No. 65

Destination: Scotchman Peak, 7,009 feet
Best Suited For: hiking, horseback riding
How Much Use: A Little * A Little More * A LOT * A Lot More * Excessive
USGS Map: Clark Fork, Scotchman Peak **GPS:** N48 09 52.1 W116 05 54.8

What's it like?

This steep trail passes through a variety of forest types and a wonderful subalpine meadow on its way to the highest peak in Bonner County, Idaho. At midslope there are some fine specimens of old Douglas fir trees. The lower section is rutted by erosion and crowded with brush. The jagged summit of Scotchman Peak is a jumble of rocks and dizzying cliffs at 7,009 feet. A lookout tower once sat upon this peak. It has been removed, but some evidence remains. A large wildfire burned to the ridgetop in 1994, and the effects of that are seen up close within a mile of the summit. The views from along this trail are magnificent, especially as the hiker gains elevation and the expanse of Lake Pend Oreille dominates the vista to the southwest. From the peak, the rugged nature of the proposed Scotchman Peaks Wilderness to the north is obvious, and the panorama of the high

Mountain goat atop Scotchman Peak (Jolanda Van Ooyen)

country of the Cabinet Mountains Wilderness to the east is awesome. Mountain goats can often be seen or heard at the summit. You don't want to miss the most fascinating feature of this hike, if they are still there – the hundreds of pieces of rock art that hikers have built near the summit over the years. It is an incredible gallery of unique art. The harsh climate tends to knock these impromptu sculptures down over time, but some of them are often rebuilt.

Trailhead: In downtown Clark Fork, turn north by the Chevron station onto Main and go 2.3 miles, passing the school and the former site of Clark Fork Field Campus. At the junction of Road No. 2295, take a right and go 1.1 miles to Road 2294, then left for another 0.4 miles, then left again on 2294A for 2.3 miles to the trailhead. The trailhead parking is limited to along the road due to flood damage in 2006.

Trail Length: 4.2 miles one-way
Trail Condition: good
Elevation: start – 3,300 feet, end – 7,009 feet – 3,709 feet net gain.

Estimated Duration of Hike: 3 to 4 hours up, 2 to 3 hours down

Sweat Index: strenuous

Mountain Bike Sweat Index: not suitable

Best Features: spectacular views of Lake Pend Oreille and the west Cabinets

Availability of Water Along the Trail: The trailhead is located near Mosquito Creek, but there is no water along the trail.

Stream Crossings: none

Camping: A primitive campsite is at the trailhead.

Alternate Hikes: With a short bushwhack, an open loop hike can be done with this trail and Goat Mountain Trail No. 135. Several other primitive trails access the west side of the Scotchmans from Lightning Creek. Look for these trailheads along Lightning Creek Road No. 419 for Goat Mountain Trail No. 135, Regal Mine Trail No. 556 and Morris Creek Trail No. 132.

Delyle Ridge Trail No. 122

This is a Family Fun Hike

Destination: Delyle Ridge Lookout, 4,498 feet

Best Suited For: hiking, mountain biking, horseback riding

How Much Use: A Little * A Little More * A Lot * A LOT MORE * Excessive

USGS Map: Clark Fork **GPS:** N48 2 53.88 W 116 8 55.95

What's it like?

Overall, this trail goes downhill to its destination at the old lookout. It drops rather steeply for a short ways then undulates along a beautiful forested ridge with occasional views of Dry Creek. The trail skirts the edge of an area selectively logged several years ago. The final 300 yards climbs stiffly to the rocky pinnacle where the ramshackle lookout has rested for decades. The views are magnificent all the way around, but the best is out over the town of Clark Fork and the vast river delta feeding Lake Pend Oreille. Much of this trail makes for a grand ride on a mountain bike.

Trailhead: In downtown Clark Fork turn southwest off Highway 200 onto Stephen Street next to the gas station. The road crosses railroad tracks and bears left to the bridge over the Clark Fork River. Continue on this road nearly six miles to Dry Creek Road No. 203 and turn south. Go seven miles to Delyle Forks and take Road No. 203E for 1.25 miles to the end of the road and the trailhead. The parking area is a gravel pit with room for lots of vehicles.

Trail Length: 1.5 miles one-way

Trail Condition: good

Elevation: start – 4,480 feet, end – 4,440 feet undulating – 40 feet net loss

Estimated Duration of Hike: 1 hour each way

Sweat Index: moderate

Mountain Bike Sweat Index: easy

Best Features: historic lookout structure, views of the Clark Fork Valley

Availability of Water Along the Trail: none

Stream Crossings: none

Campsites: An established campsite with a fire ring is located about a mile from the trailhead along the access road, and the trailhead parking area is plenty big enough for camping.

Precautions: The lookout is deteriorating and is unsafe for any kind of occupancy; it also sits on the edge of a sheer cliff, so be careful of loose rock.

Alternate Hikes: The trailhead for Twin Creek Trail No. 77 can be found at Delyle Forks. Also in this area are Delyle Creek Trail No. 75 and Derr Point Trail No. 66.

Wild Notes: For several years the lofty perch upon which Delyle Ridge Lookout is situated was used in releasing peregrine falcons into the wild, a place called a hack site. A rare bird that until 1999 was on the Endangered Species List, the peregrine is making a comeback in parts of the American West.

— — — — — — — — — — — — — — — — —

Riverside Trail and Green Rock Trail

portions wheelchair accessible

This is a Family Fun Hike

Destination: Clark Fork River

Best Suited For: hiking, mountain biking

How Much Use: A Little * A LITTLE MORE * A Lot * A Lot More * Excessive

USGS Map: Cabinet **GPS:** N48 05 33.8 W116 05 46.6

What's it like?

On the north bank of the river, the 40-acre Clark Fork Access Site is a recently redeveloped recreational opportunity on the river and borders Bureau of Land Management land on the east end. There are two hiking trails on-site that also are open to mountain bikers. The Riverside Trail goes upstream for almost two miles. From the west end, the first one-half to two-thirds of a mile is an old roadbed, but then the trail parallels the river through a beautiful forest of big fir, ponderosa pine, larch and cedar trees. Along the way are five side trails down to the water as access for anglers and swimmers. The Green Rock Trail branches off the shoreline trail about one mile in and becomes a singletrack uphill loop for another three-quarters of a mile. A portion of the Riverside Trail is wheelchair accessible from the west entrance with a developed vista point two-thirds of a mile from the parking area. The east entrance offers limited wheelchair accessibility.

Trailhead: From downtown Clark Fork, follow Idaho State Highway 200 for another five miles. The site is just past the River Delta Resort. The west entrance is directly off a newly constructed section of Highway 200 between mileposts 60 and 61, two miles west of the state line. The east entrances are accessed via the old highway. The entire site is located across the highway from a privately owned rock quarry with steep cliffs, a visible landmark. From Highway 200, two parking areas can accommodate eight to 10 vehicles at both the west and east ends. Another paved entrance at midpoint can hold up to three vehicles. A small gravel launch ramp at the west entrance is accessible only to kayaks, canoes, rafts and other small car-top boats.

Trail Length: just over 2 miles combined
Trail Condition: good
Elevation: approximately 2,200 feet
Estimated Duration of Hike: 45 minutes each way
Sweat Index: easy
Mountain Bike Sweat Index: easy
Best Features: water access, sites for anglers and swimmers, mature forest
Availability of Water Along the Trail: Most of the Riverside Trail runs along the river.
Stream Crossings: none
Campsites: none

CHAPTER TWELVE

FISH AND FISHING

Many Waters, Many Fish
By Kevin Davis

*F*ishing in northern Idaho has been a way of life for hundreds of years. American Indians of this area, specifically the Kootenai and Kalispel tribes, relied on fish from Lake Pend Oreille to supplement their diet. Even in the past century, locals fished to help feed their families as well as make a living.

"My father would catch enough fish to feed our whole family right over there at the mouth of Lightning Creek," said one angler, a lifelong Clark Fork resident. He pointed across the river, just upstream of Lake Pend Oreille, as he explained how they used to feast on kokanee and trout caught from these waters.

To this day we still rely on the bountiful harvest local waters provide, but the focus is more on maintaining and renewing the fishery for sportsmen to enjoy. The most unique part of our fishery may well be Lake Pend Oreille, a veritable "inland sea" that is home to numerous native and introduced fish.

Many anglers wait patiently to feel the sudden tug of the elusive Kamloops, also known as Gerrard rainbow – a fish that can reach epic proportions. Kamloops were introduced here in 1941 and are endemic to Kootenay Lake in British Columbia, a lake of similar natural qualities. Because

317

of their beautiful coloring, tasty flesh and tenacious fighting, the Kamloops quickly became the prized fish of Pend Oreille. In 1947 Wes Hamlet caught the world record, a 37-pounder.

Another introduced species that has fared well, the lake trout (also called mackinaw), was brought here in 1925. They like deep, cold waters and adapted well to Pend Oreille's abyssal depths. The lake record, a whopping 43-pounder caught by Jim Eversole in 1994, is the largest fish ever caught in Lake Pend Oreille.

The lake also harbors the strongest population of bull trout in the Pacific Northwest. Adfluvial fishes, they reside as adults in the lake but return to the tributaries to spawn. The state and world record bull trout was caught in Pend Oreille by Nelson Higgins in 1949, weighing 32 pounds. Bull trout harvest is closed since it was listed as a threatened species in 1995 under the Endangered Species Act.

What makes Lake Pend Oreille grow such big fish? The answer is kokanee – a land-locked subspecies of sockeye salmon native to the Pacific Northwest but not to Lake Pend Oreille. They arrived in 1933 when a spring flood swept them out of Flathead Lake in Montana and down the Flathead and Clark Fork rivers. Kokanee thrived on the abundant food source in Lake Pend Oreille, and few natural predators existed to control their numbers. By the 1950s a commercial kokanee fishery evolved with 1 million fish harvested annually. Ultimately, this species became a plentiful food base for prized game fish that were introduced later.

Kokanee populations are now at an all-time low in the lake. The decline started in 1966 when the U.S. Army Corps of Engineers changed the regulation of Albeni Falls Dam from primarily flood control to production of hydroelectric power. Fluctuating lake levels come at a critical time when kokanee are spawning naturally in the lake. In response to their plight, Idaho Fish and Game closed harvest of kokanee in Lake Pend Oreille in 2001. Catch and release rules apply. Additional measures such as gill netting have been tried as well as increasing harvest limits and setting bounties on Kamloops and mackinaws in an attempt to reduce their numbers since they are the kokanee's main predator.

Other fish species that fishermen may

Ward Tollbom and Boots Reynolds (shown) caught these 23 lake trout, or mackinaw, in three and a half hours on June 24, 2008 (Ward Tollbom)

Legendary Lake Pend Oreille

be rewarded with in the Pend Oreille watershed include a feisty Idaho native, the westslope cutthroat trout. This fish prefers the cold, well-oxygenated waters that flow crystal clear from the mountains. Catch and release is recommended. A pretty little transplant to be found in tributary streams and in the lake as well is the brook trout.

Fisheries resources still thrive in the Panhandle and excellent opportunities abound both in Lake Pend Oreille and the many streams that feed it, but the integrity of these resources remains at a critical stage.

Anecdota: The Days of Commercial Fishing on Pend Oreille
By Marianne Love

During the winters of the early 1900s when it was hard to keep mill ponds from freezing, mill workers had to seek other employment. Many found their prosperity swimming in the lake under the ice. A bulletin of the U.S. Fish Commission reported that 1.3 million Lake Superior whitefish fry (maturity stage following egg stage) were planted in Lake Pend Oreille in 1889, adding to an already healthy stock of native whitefish. Without much competition for food, the fish thrived. By the turn of the century, a healthy commercial fishing industry was born, and who better to tell its story than Finlander Rauno (Ron) Raiha. The owner of the former Pend Oreille Sport Shop for 23 years, Raiha came to Sandpoint as an 18-year-old in 1962 while touring the West in search of a place to settle.

"I fell in love with the lake when I crossed the bridge, saw water on both sides, and mountains on both sides," he recalls. "It was spring. The snow came halfway down the mountains. I said to myself, 'There must be fish there.' Of course, I'd already cheated," he adds. "I had a book given to me in 1959 with a picture of a man standing by the Long Bridge, holding a 25-pound Kamloops in one hand and a fishing pole in the other." The man in the photograph turned out to be Jim Parsons Sr., whose fishing rods and reels Raiha eventually repaired in his shop.

Ron Raiha with a whitefish caught in the lake in winter

Parsons, a journalist, had spent years chronicling and promoting both Kamloops trout and kokanee salmon fishing in Lake Pend Oreille, which eventually grew into the biannual events that are known today as the spring and fall K&K (shorthand for Kamloops and kokanee) fishing derbies on the lake. Raiha worked for many years on K&K projects and was the lucky person to weigh in a 32-pound Kamloops caught by Van Sawyer in 1969. "When I see the postcard, I have a special feeling for that fish," Raiha says of the Ross Hall photograph of the amazing catch.

Ron Raiha also has played a major role helping Idaho Fish and Game harvest kokanee eggs at the Granite Creek fish trap (see related story on page 67) for growing the fish at the Cabinet Gorge Fish Hatchery on the Clark Fork River.

While working behind the counter of his sports shop, Raiha listened to plenty of the local lore about the whitefish commercial fishing of the past. "It was employment for out-of-work loggers, especially in little villages like Cabinet, Sourdough Point and Hailey's Bay (between present day Contest Point and Sourdough Point)," he explains. In those years the lake had colder temperatures and more ice, and a different water level (no dams). Oden Bay and Bottle Bay would freeze over.

"There'd be little tar paper houses all over, sometimes as many as 150 at a time," he says. "Anglers would drop their hand lines and No. 10 hooks – half-wrapped with red wool yarn, the other half covered with a maggot."

Where there wasn't ice, the fishermen would take to their five-plank boats (three boards on the bottom, one on either side), with a wood stove and little chimney between their legs. The boats

For $2 a day, including lunch and all equipment, people could angle for whitefish from inside *SS Fish House*, shown in 1931, during the heyday of commercial whitefishing (Ross Hall)

were built low to the water for efficiency in hand lining. "With your hand a few inches from the water, you could flip the fish off the hook quickly and not waste any time," he explains. "If you could catch 10 a day, that was good. You earned five cents a fish."

Whitefish that measured 12 to 14 inches were smokers. Anglers would sell them to fish buyers, mainly the Evans family, who accepted fish at various spots on the lake including Evans Landing, Idlewilde Bay, Bottle Bay, Sheepherder Point and Sunnyside's Fisherman Island. The Evans family and Bill Zinter owned processing houses where they smoked and packaged the fish into 20-pound boxes, ready for rail transport to Spokane and other cities.

"Sometimes that was the only freight picked up by the train (on its daily stop)," Raiha said. "Pallet after pallet went out all over the country."

Commercial fishing for whitefish continued until the late 1930s when a number of factors caused the population to quickly dwindle. Among these was competition from kokanee. The land-locked salmon found their way to the lake after a 1933 Flathead Lake flood took them to waters emptying into Pend Oreille. Suddenly, whitefish were competing for the same food as the newly arrived kokanee. Then a disease ran through the whitefish population; they became wormy, skinny and their fat content diminished. "The oil disappeared from the fish. They wouldn't smoke up any more, so people lost interest," Raiha says. Dead fish washed up on shore in droves, creating a tremendous smell.

Raiha said the whitefish demise led to the rise of interest in kokanee. Also called bluebacks or silvers, the fish had established themselves in the lake and had grown in size Fishing for kokanee is similar to whitefish, but not as subtle, says Raiha. They aren't as crafty, making them easier to catch. "At first nobody knew if you could eat them, but then they started smoking them and 'Hurrah!' " he adds. Those who held whitefish licenses became commercial kokanee fishermen.

With commercial limits and sport fishing limits at 250 and 50 per day, respectively, the kokanee industry thrived until the early 1960s when, again, several factors eventually led to the end of commercial kokanee fishing on Lake Pend Oreille in 1969. Cabinet Gorge Dam (1952) and Albeni Falls Dam (1955), designed to provide power for the post-war economy and to curb lake flooding, played havoc with the fish population by cutting off spawning streams and disrupting shoreline spawning because of fluctuating lake levels. Moreover, the introduction of mysis shrimp into the lake with hopes of enhancing the kokanee population backfired because instead of becoming prey, the shrimp competed for the same food as young kokanee. Abuse of commercial fishing limits also contributed to the kokanee demise. Predator species of fish washing down the river to the lake and Kamloops, or Gerrard rainbow trout, brought in from Canada only exacerbated the problem as the kokanee became their primary diet. Predation, along with continual degradation

Dave Ivy with his award-winning 31-inch rainbow trout caught during the 2008 Thanksgiving K&K Derby (Clint Nicholson)

of the food chain and increasing streambed siltation caused by hydroelectric dam operations, have left the kokanee at critically low populations and will continue to do so. Fishing for the species ended in 2001.

Although various efforts continue to enhance the lake's kokanee population, Ron Raiha doubts if the kokanee fishery will ever rise again to its former prominence; and nor will the whitefish fishery, even though it has regained some of its numbers. Nonetheless, Lake Superior whitefish can still be caught at Whiskey Rock, Garfield Bay and Sheepherder Point near the Hope Peninsula and for native whitefish, anglers should concentrate on waters from the Sandpoint City Beach west to Priest River.

"People today are different folk than those of the '20s and '30s," Raiha says. "The majority of people just want to catch a few fish that taste good, and they're happy to take home six."

Fish Tales: Kamloops and Sport Fishing
By Marianne Love

Lake Pend Oreille and its contributing streams continue to satisfy an angler's hunger to catch a big one or a good mess of pan fryers. Besides whitefish and kokanee, the lake supports other game fish, including perch, several trout species, crappie and bass.

Like the commercial fishing industry, the introduction of Kamloops to Lake Pend Oreille satisfied a need. Local sportsmen of the 1940s had heard stories about a species of giant trout in Canada in the Kootenay and Trout lakes and the Lardeau River near Gerrard, British Columbia. Many of these men were community leaders seeking a fun but profitable way for the local economy to bounce back from Depression-era stagnation. Though World War II activities hampered their efforts a bit, these visionaries persevered and forged ahead with their plan to introduce Kamloops, or Gerrard rainbows, in the lake.

Laurin Pietsch co-owned and operated the weekly *Sandpoint News Bulletin*. He also played a key role in stocking Lake Pend Oreille with Kamloops rainbows. Photographer Ross Hall reported in a 1978 "Leisure Time" supplement to the *Sandpoint News Bulletin* that some key men led a large team of locals in introducing Kamloops to the lake and later to the world. He listed sportsmen's association president Pietsch, fisherman Jim Weaver, hatchery superintendent Ross Brown and public-relations specialist Jim Parsons Sr., aka the Pied Piper of the Kamloops.

"Jim Weaver was such a fishing enthusiast that he induced reverential quiet in the boat when Kamloops were in the waters," Hall wrote. "Laurin and Jim on their first fishing trip together in 1938 in Kootenay Lake ... caught 5- to 12-pound Kamloops. Out of that fishing experience was born the conviction that Kamloops rainbows would be the answer to the need to have trophy-size fish in Pend Oreille."

Under Pietsch's leadership, the group spent the next four years introducing thousands of Kamloops fry, from eggs obtained in Kaslo, B.C, to the lake. Unfortunately, they experienced a setback when the first batch of fry in 1941 caught a virus and most of them died. With Brown's guidance, the group obtained more eggs the next year and let half of them mature to fingerlings in the warmer climate of Hagerman, Idaho, and the other half in Sandpoint. This time, they saw success.

"They released 20,000 from 6 to 9 inches into the lake in the fall of 1942," Pietsch wrote in the *News Bulletin*. With an additional 60,000 released in 1943, Lake Pend Oreille Kamloops were left to grow, and in 1946, on opening day, large numbers of fish from 10 to 20 pounds were hauled in around the lake.

To promote the new fishery, a fishing derby was organized called K&K – Kamloops and Kokanee Days – by the Bonner County Sportsmen's Association, an event that offered a total of $1,500 in prizes. Big fish in the 20-pound range were caught, but the most famous fish brought in was a 15-pounder caught by Bing Crosby. The news media nationwide devoured the story.

Opening day in 1947, May 1, was not a disappointment for Pend Oreille anglers. C.C. Shepherd of Opportunity, Washington, successfully landed a 36-pound Kamloops in Garfield Bay.

Ironically, as he posed for newsmen and photographers the next day, he hefted the fish for a picture, only to lose his grip, and the new world record slipped back into 14 feet of water. Shepherd was heard to say, "I always heard they threw 'em back if they weren't 40 pounds." Remarkably, Claude Simon, chief of the Sandpoint Fire Department, was able to retrieve the enormous fish by welding several large hooks to a 4-foot length of pipe and then dragging the area where the fish had disappeared.

Later that year, Wes Hamlet of Coeur d'Alene caught a 37-pound Kamloops. This world record still stands. The legend is that General Dwight D. Eisenhower ate the fish for his Thanksgiving dinner, and sportsmen around the lake gave thanks for a new form of angling recreation.

Kamloops fishing involves savvy, a good boat and sophisticated fishing tackle. In many cases, a good guide can enhance "lunker luck." Consequently, marinas, charter services and sporting goods shops began appearing in key places around the lake — Bottle Bay, Garfield Bay, Hope, Bayview, Glengary and Sandpoint. Restaurants and sporting lodges popped up to feed and house all those anglers. The K&K event lured another wave of outdoors lovers to

Wes Hamlet and his world-record, 37-pound Kamloops
(Ross Hall)

the area, and continues to do so more than 60 years later. The Lake Pend Oreille Idaho Club now sponsors the Spring K&K Fishing Derby in April and another derby around Thanksgiving. These biannual events continue to draw anglers to Lake Pend Oreille for Kamloops rainbow and lake trout, although catching kokanee is no longer permitted. Thousands in cash and prizes are still given out in the spring derby, but today's trophy fish are much smaller than in the early years. The winning rainbow in a recent derby was only 16 pounds, while the winning mackinaw was 19 pounds. Proceeds from the K&K derbies go toward education programs and field projects to enhance the lake's fishery and water quality.

The Kamloops sports fishery definitely boosted the local economy, but the thrill of Kamloops fishing still lingers deep within the souls of countless residents and visitors to Lake Pend Oreille.

"Pair of Kokanee," 1988 (Eileen Klatt illustration)

LAKE PEND OREILLE FISH GUIDE

Two dozen species of fish live in Lake Pend Oreille; 17 species are considered game fish – that is, the fish that sportsmen most enjoy catching. Many of these fish are also delicious to eat. However, before venturing onto the lake with a fishing pole in hand, be sure to check the state rules and regulations and have the proper license. Whereas catch and release was once the preferred method of fishing for the trophy fish, in recent years Idaho Fish and Game has not only encouraged keeping the big predators – Kamloops rainbow trout and mackinaw, or lake trout – in order to help recover the kokanee, their primary prey, the agency now also pays money to anglers for catching big fish. Commercial netting of rainbows and lake trout also is helping to reduce the predator fish populations. Nonetheless, the kokanee fishery is still on the verge of disappearing.

Regardless of your intent – whether you want to fish for sport or put a few nice fillets in the frying pan – the fishing on Lake Pend Oreille historically has been some of the finest in the world. With cooperative management efforts, it can be that way again.

All of these fish can be caught in Lake Pend Oreille, but it takes a wide variety of angling techniques and equipment to be successful, from lightweight fly fishing to heavy-duty 40-pound test line trolled up to 500 feet behind and 160 feet below a charter boat. Almost any kind of angler can find a challenge on this enormous lake. You can stand on the shore, wade shallow bays and

Fish and Fishing   325 sloughs, or glide across the waters in vessels of any size. Fishermen find a paradise of angling opportunities here, from perch the size of your hand, to Kamloops as long as your leg. And at least one day a year, usually in early June, Idaho has a Free Fishing Day. No license is required on that day, but all other fishing rules and bag limits apply. Enjoy!

Game Fish

Bull Trout (*Salvelinus confluentus*) – native species

Green to blue-gray back, with silvery sides; no spots on dorsal fin; yellow, orange or red spots dot its sides. Pelvic pectoral and anal fins have white leading edge. Illegal to harvest. Listed as threatened under the Endangered Species Act. Secretive and almost impossible to see in streams unless spawning. Grow up to 32 pounds. Commonly seen in open water and high in the water column. Bull trout have been observed in deep water (to 1,000 feet), but are more regularly at depths to 100 feet or more. During spring and fall, often found along shorelines, with some staging at the mouths of spawning tributaries in late summer-early fall.

Cutthroat Trout (*Oncorhynchus clarki*) Idaho State Fish – native species

Bright red-orange streak in the fold under the jaw. Native to mountain streams, lakes and rivers throughout Idaho. One of the most popular sport fishes in the state. Primarily found in proximity to shorelines. They enter tributaries to spawn in early spring and may be found off of the mouths of tributaries during that time.

Rainbow Trout, and Kamloops or Gerrard rainbow (*Oncorhynchus mykiss*) – introduced species

Silver colored with black spots over its body, dorsal and caudal fins. Adults have a distinctive "rainbow" band. Popular with Idaho anglers and widely distributed in accessible waters. May grow to more than 30 pounds. Virtually all rainbow trout found in Pend Oreille are derived from Gerrard-strain Kamloops trout. They occupy the open water portions of the lake almost exclusively, feeding on kokanee. Depth varies with water temperature at the surface; they are deeper in the summer, when the surface water is warm, and near the surface much of the remainder of the year. They are springtime tributary spawners, and can be found off the mouths of the Pack and Clark Fork rivers in late winter and early spring.

Lake trout, or Mackinaw (*Salvelinus namaycush*) – introduced species

Dark gray with numerous light gray spots on sides; tail deeply forked. May grow to more than 30 pounds. Typically found at lake bottom at depths to 200 feet; most habitat is in the north end of the lake around the islands and interface of the Monarchs with Clark Fork Delta, but also near Whiskey Rock, off Cape Horn, and at the southern end of the lake. Commonly taken in open water by fishermen trolling for rainbow trout. Spawning congregations develop in September-October on the east shoreline near Windy Point and just south of Lakeview.

Brook Trout (*Salvelinus fontinalis*) – introduced species
Back dark green with pale wavy lines, or worm-like markings; sides a purple sheen with blue-haloed red spots. No black spots. Originally native to the eastern United States and Canada. Introduced into Idaho waters in the early 1900s. Uncommon in Pend Oreille; may be found in shoreline areas near the mouths of tributary streams.

Brown Trout (*Salmo trutta*) – introduced species
Golden brown with large black spots and red spots with pale halos. Native to Europe. Introduced into Idaho waters in 1892. Wary and hard to catch. Uncommon in Pend Oreille, but large specimens are occasionally taken from the north end and off the mouth of the Clark Fork River; typically caught by anglers trolling for rainbow trout.

Kokanee Salmon (*Oncorhynchus nerka*) – introduced species
Greenish-blue back with faint speckling; silver sides and belly. Introduced in 1933. Kokanee fishing is closed in Lake Pend Oreille; catch and release rules apply. Usually to one pound, but can grow larger. Except during spawning, these small salmon use the open water areas of the lake. Shoreline spawning occurs during the late fall-early winter, with the highest concentrations in Scenic Bay, but numerous historic shoreline spawning sites exist around the lake where gravel conditions are suitable. Garfield Bay and Ellisport Bay are important sites when kokanee numbers are high. Early spawners (September) use tributaries such as Trestle and Gold creeks. Granite Creek hosts a large number of late spawners, as the Idaho Fish and Game egg-taking facility is there; some kokanee also ascend the Clark Fork River during the fall.

Mountain Whitefish (*Prosopium williamsoni*) – native species
Large scales, no spots and small mouths without teeth. Body a bronze-white or greenish-white color. Native to many waters of Idaho. Most anglers seek whitefish during winter. Relatively uncommon in the lake, but a healthy population in the lower Clark Fork River contributes some fish to the north end of the lake.

Lake Whitefish (*Coregonus clupeaformis*) – introduced species
Large scales, no spots, and small mouths without teeth. Body an olive green to light brown, not silvery. Not native to Idaho. Summer the preferred angling season. Very common at depths to 200 feet, associated with the lake bottom. Most habitat exists at the north end of the lake, the extreme south end of the lake, and areas such as Whiskey Rock and Cape Horn. Can be found in shallower water in late fall and winter.

Pygmy Whitefish (*Prosopium coulterii*) – native species
Silvery except for olive brown back, with its mouth overhung by snout; they seldom exceed 6-8 inches in

length. Not much is known of their distribution in Pend Oreille, but reportedly spawn in shallower, gravelly shorelines, and spend the remainder of their time in deeper water.

Largemouth and Smallmouth Bass (*Micropterus salmoides, M. dolomieu*) – both introduced species

Dark green on the back and sides with a white belly. Reddish eyes, a dark olive to brown back, bronze sides and a white belly. Introduced to Idaho in the late 1800s. Smallmouth bass, or bronzeback, acclaimed by many sportsmen to be America's most fighting game fish. Largemouth are primarily associated with shallower and weedy areas of the lake, mostly on the north end and down the Pend Oreille River. Smallmouth are found primarily in association with rocky shorelines and generally high in the water column. Smallmouth have expanded to much of the lake's shoreline.

Northern Pike (*Esox lucius*) – introduced species

Long, slender body with light spots on dark greenish background. Upper part dark green, becoming lighter, almost milk-white, along the belly. Large mouth with many teeth; dorsal fin far to the back of the body. Washed downstream from waters in Montana. Found in shallow weedy bays on the north end of the lake and down the Pend Oreille River.

Black Crappie (*Pomoxis nigromaculatus*) – introduced species

Olive to silvery-green with lighter sides. Black or olive flecks on sides randomly arranged. Possibly the most popular table fish caught in Idaho today. Generally found in bays on the north end, such as Denton Slough and off the mouth of Fry Creek.

Yellow Perch (*Perca flavescens*) – introduced species

Greenish-yellow down the back, with dark colored bands on sides; orange fins. Readiness to bite makes them popular with anglers, especially in winter. Found in bays on the north end and down the Pend Oreille River, often associated with the bottom in water to 30 feet deep. Popular ice fishing spots are located near the Long Bridge and along the north shore near Sunnyside.

Bluegill (*Lepomis macrochirus*) – introduced species

Yellowish-olive to olive-green above with bluish luster; blue sides and yellow belly. Body compressed, short and deep. Great fun for light tackle techniques and teaching kids. Uncommon, may be found in shallow and weedy areas of the lake and Pend Oreille River.

Bullhead (*Ictaluras melas, I. nebulosus*) – introduced species

Back yellowish brown to almost black with an undersurface of yellow to white. Nocturnal feeders, so fishing best at night. Shallow water with muddy/silty bottom, mostly at the north end of the lake.

Walleye (*Stizostedion vitreum*) – introduced species

Greenish-yellow on the back, brassy-silver on the sides and whitish on the belly; the fairly large mouth has numerous teeth. It has a double dorsal fin, the first spiny, the second having soft rays. The gill cover has a razor-sharp edge. Generally, average two pounds or less, but will grow up to 11-plus pounds. Walleye are thus far not widely distributed in the lake but are of interest due to potential impacts on kokanee and native fish. They have entered the lake via the Clark Fork River and the reservoirs in Montana above the Cabinet Gorge Dam where they were illegally introduced. Though not abundant, they are occasionally caught near the mouths of the Clark Fork and Pack rivers, or around rocky points and shoals in the Pend Oreille River.

Non-game Fish

Northern pikeminnow (Ptychocheilus oregonensis) – native species

Yellowish body with dark olive-green back, grayish-silver sides and a yellow-white belly. Tail fin distinctly forked; large mouth. No spots on fins. Native fish caught and eaten since aboriginal times – hence, its older name of squawfish. Found lake-wide, primarily along shorelines; occasionally in open water. Typically in the upper part of the water column.

Other non-game species include tench, longnose sucker, largescale sucker, redside shiner, longnose dace, sculpin and peamouth.

For complete information on the identification, life cycle, diet and fishing tips for fishes found in Lake Pend Oreille, see Idaho Fish and Game's Web site, http://fishandgame.idaho.gov.

- - - - - - - - - - - - - - - - - - - -

The Future of Lake Pend Oreille's Fishery

Understanding the complexities of managing the fish in Lake Pend Oreille in the first decade of the 21st century is no easy task. The lake and its inhabitants have undergone considerable changes over the past 100 years and what exists now barely resembles what the early settlers found here.

Beginning in 1916, the first dam in the region was built on the Clark Fork River at Thompson Falls, Montana. This was the beginning of a drastically altered system inhibiting the natural spawning runs of fish like bull trout and mountain whitefish. By the mid-1950s, three new dams had been constructed in the basin: Cabinet Gorge and Noxon Rapids upstream on the Clark Fork River and Albeni Falls downstream on the Pend Oreille River. Spawning habitat was suddenly and significantly altered for bull trout and for kokanee, its prey.

Kokanee and bull trout have both been identified as "keystone species" in Lake Pend Oreille: bull trout because of its status as a native and kokanee because of its value as the most important food source for the Kamloops trophy fish and for their own value as a sport fish. Lake trout, or mackinaw, is also an aggressive predator to kokanee, and is now considered more of a threat than an asset to Lake Pend Oreille.

Fisheries managers have spent the past several years trying to fully understand the dynamics of these fish in Lake Pend Oreille. What is known for certain is that for successful spawning, the kokanee need a higher winter lake level than the 2,051-foot elevation of the typical drawdown. Even a difference of just 4 feet can have a huge positive influence. But predation is the single most important factor. Those giant rainbows and lake trout are voracious, and too many kokanee are being consumed before each generation can replace itself in its life cycle. The adult kokanee have been at record low numbers despite an abundance of fry.

Kate Wilson of the Pend Oreille Basin Commission, left, and Captain Kurt Artner of Pend Oreille Charters fishing on Lake Pend Oreille (Tina Friedman)

Legendary Lake Pend Oreille

According to Chip Corsi, regional supervisor for Idaho Fish and Game, no lake has ever been able to sustain simultaneous populations of lake trout, rainbow trout, bull trout and kokanee for long. Priest Lake and Flathead Lake have both experienced the collapse of its kokanee population due to lake trout with additional losses of rainbows, bull trout and cutthroat trout. Predator reduction has to occur if the kokanee are to survive. Current efforts include a combination of angling incentives — paying cash for every lake and rainbow trout caught longer than 12 inches, as well as gill netting and live trapping. Many anglers are unhappy over the use of nets, believing fishermen can better control the predator fish by catching them. Fish and Game's goal is to cut the rainbow trout and lake trout population in half.

The solution to the problems facing the Lake Pend Oreille fishery will not be easy. The demands on the lake's water downstream must be balanced with the needs of its fish, but which fish species to manage for is a complex matter in itself. Regaining the predator/prey balance is essential. In deciding how to manage Lake Pend Oreille in the future, Ned Horner, the Idaho Fish and Game biologist who has been at the forefront of these issues for years, believes: "Clear choices will have to be made with a full understanding of the consequences. Not everyone will be happy."

These consequences are a matter of what fish has the brightest future. Bull trout continue to dictate much of the management direction because of their threatened status and because Pend Oreille is a stronghold for this species. The trophy rainbow will not thrive without the kokanee. Lake trout are known to dominate a system if left unchecked. And recently, walleye have been finding their way into the Pend Oreille drainage in the Clark Fork and Pend Oreille rivers. It's a tangled web of life. As Horner explains: "When you combine ... social and political issues with a very complex and dynamic biological system, you can begin to understand there are no simple solutions to fishery recovery efforts."

Editor's note: Thanks to Ned Horner, Melo Maiolie, Hobe Jenkins, Kevin Davis, Kate Wilson and Bill Schaudt for helpful information from their published news or feature articles. Thanks also to Chip Corsi and Jim Fredericks of Idaho Fish and Game for information on the different species. They are all concerned with or involved in the efforts to restore and preserve the Lake Pend Oreille fishery.

Kalispels Lucy Bluff and Paul Tom, circa 1934 (Northwest Museum of Arts & Culture/Eastern Washington State Historical Society, Spokane Washington, William Ryan, S.J. Collection. Digitally restored, for authorized publication, per financial support of the Kalispel Tribe of Indians L97-26.17)

CHAPTER THIRTEEN

LAND OF THE KALISPEL

A version of this story first appeared in Sandpoint Magazine *in the Summer 1997 issue.*

By Jane Fritz

I have a fertile imagination. There have been times while out paddling my canoe in the watery reaches of the Clark Fork River Delta after the fishermen have called it a day, or past rocky outcroppings where petroglyphs of grizzly and black bear tracks are etched into stone, that I am captured by an ancient time; pulled backwards into the primordial landscape that existed before machines and metals transformed life here in Idaho's panhandle.

During these solitary sojourns, I gain insights into a balanced, more generous way of life. If I stay open to my surroundings, I might hear indigenous voices chanting from the forest, or see old Indian faces in the rocks sculpted by the long shadows of near-evening light. Sometimes, if I squint my eyes while passing a stretch of undeveloped shoreline wet with an autumn rain, the willows will appear as tule mat lodges encircling campfires thin with woodsmoke. It is here on water that my imagination swells and bursts into some story of the past ...

An old woman watches from shore as her granddaughters paddle their canoe toward open water. She sings a song of protection for all the women, knowing that it will take several days to paddle down river and across the lake until they come to the large river valley where the bulrushes grow. The old woman remembers her own youth and the many hours she passed gathering tules for the woven mat coverings of her band's summer lodges and winter longhouse. Singing the special gathering songs made the work go easier.

So did the canoes. Tapered at both ends like the snout of a sturgeon and covered with white pine bark, the canoes allowed the rush gatherers to easily slice through waves on open water and slip through the delta's marshy wetlands without getting stuck. But she liked to work the shallows, standing calf deep in the cool water and using her best stone knife to cut the spongy, insulating plants. She and the others would gather them until nearly dark. With morning light, the canoes filled, they would make the long journey home, camping always in new places, telling stories under a starry sky, howling back to Wolf and Coyote, falling asleep to the lullabies of Loon ...

Maybe the spirits enjoy teasing my imagination, but this fantasy is also based in fact. These waters are part of the ancestral homeland of the Upper and Lower Kalispel bands of Indians, also known as Pend d'Oreilles, the name given them by French fur traders in the early 1800s. The tribe's aboriginal territory once comprised more than 4 million acres and followed the great river and lake system from the Mission Mountains of Montana down the Clark Fork River, west across Lake Pend Oreille and downstream along the Pend Oreille River almost to Chewelah, Washington, and north to Canada's Salmo River. Their territory also included the Priest River drainage and Priest Lake. It is estimated that at the time they first encountered explorer David Thompson in 1809, the tribe numbered close to 2,000 people living in a number of different bands along the upper and lower reaches of the Pend Oreille system.

The Kalispel were canoe people. In this great watery terrain it was the most practical way to

A Kalispel canoe and tule mat lodge is situated on the shores of the Pend Oreille River at Seneacquoteen across from an American camp in this Boundary Commission photo taken in 1860 (Bonner County Historical Society)

get around. They would venture out into the mountains for spiritual reasons and to pick huckleberries and to hunt deer, bear and caribou, but their villages and encampments were near water.

Although summer would find the people camped anywhere they chose along the shores – there were literally hundreds of camping sites – there were also summer and winter village sites. Village sites were more stable and better protected, especially against the long winters. Winters were spent along the Pend Oreille River near the present-day towns of Laclede and Priest River, Idaho, and Newport, Usk and Cusick, Washington, for the Lower Kalispel bands; and Bayview and Clark Fork, Idaho, and Thompson Falls in Montana for the Upper Kalispel bands. The snows were usually too deep in other places to live comfortably.

Former Washington State University professor, Dr. Allan Smith, was a Yale doctoral student in the early 1930s when he began his ethnographic study of the Kalispel. He had planned to write a book about the tribe but never did. After his death, some 1,800 pages of extensive research notes were donated to the tribe's cultural resource department with a copy given to the Lewis-Clark State

Alec Revais and Catherine Pierre Manwolf Frye, Francis Cullooyah's grandmother, standing on Frog Island in 1936. "The Village," on the banks of the Pend Oreille River, is in the background (Northwest Museum of Arts & Culture/Eastern Washington State Historical Society, Spokane, Washington. Digitally restored, for authorized publication, per financial support of the Kalispel Tribe of Indians, L84-327.746)

College library archives. From these materials, we learn that the Kalispel were an easy-going and peaceful people. They weren't a warrior society, nor were they prone to formulating a lot of rules and rituals to live by, as were the Plains tribes farther east. The Kalispel lived more spontaneously. They shared almost all property in common – discovered eagle nests and creeks claimed by the placement of a fishing weir being perhaps the only exceptions – and there existed a specialization of work.

The tasks of daily living created cohesion among the different bands and extended families. The responsibilities of hunting and gathering were informally assigned to certain groups. One group might be caribou hunters; the woodland caribou (now an endangered species) once outnumbered the deer in the surrounding mountains, and its hide and meat were favored over deer. Another group hunted bear. There were groups of fishers, root diggers, berry pickers and canoe builders.

The tules or bulrushes used for building their lodges were abundant in the Clark Fork River delta, so those designated as tule gatherers would travel there by canoe and collect them. They would weave the tules into mats and layer them around a conical structure of poles resembling a teepee. Women normally did this work. The Kalispels moved frequently throughout their territory as they gathered these gifts of nature. The people shared freely; interdependence resulted. Generosity abounded. The people also ventured beyond the waterways, frequently traveling the established trails overland to visit and trade with the Spokanes to the west (crossing the Pend Oreille River at Seneacquoteen near present-day Laclede) and their relatives, the Upper Pend d'Oreilles, in the Mission Valley to the east. These tribes spoke the same Salish language with variations in dialect. In Montana, the Kalispel would hunt buffalo, a task made easier after the horse was introduced. They had good relations with the Blackfeet, a warrior tribe who lived in the Great Plains of north-central Montana. The Kalispel also would trade a great deal with the various tribes of the Colville region of Washington to the west. Relations with the Kootenai to the north, and Coeur d'Alene and Nez Perce to the south occurred, but were sometimes strained.

The Kalispel wandered this vast territory utilizing all of nature's resources and trading with the many other tribes. It wasn't always an easy life, but it was a good life.

But its days were numbered. Their life in harmony with nature was dramatically changed after white contact. First came the diseases they had no immunity against, like measles and

smallpox. Hundreds died. As waves of white settlers began to move into their territory, beginning in the later 1800s, they increasingly found themselves barred from traveling through traditional lands to hunt, fish, and gather roots and berries. The burgeoning settlement by the whites created conflicts, but unlike tribes who warred

The Kalispel Indian village where many Kalispels remained until new homes were built for them with judgment-fund monies in 1966 (Northwest Museum of Arts & Culture/ Eastern Washington State Historical Society, Spokane, Washington. Digitally restored, for authorized publication, per financial support of the Kalispel Tribe of Indians, L87-410.42) with the settlers, the Kalispel tribe as a whole never carried out hostilities against the whites.

Eventually some of the Kalispel – those who became known as Upper Pend d'Oreilles – followed Jesuit missionaries up the Clark Fork River to the Flathead Reservation in St. Ignatius, Montana. Those who stayed behind – the Lower Pend d'Oreilles – settled at one of their winter village sites near Usk and Cusick in Washington. In 1914 formal recognition as a sovereign people was granted by the executive order of President Woodrow Wilson. A small strip of land, consisting of only 4,600 acres along the Pend Oreille River near Usk, was given to the tribe for a reservation.

From the 4 million acres they knew as their homeland, the people had been uprooted, displaced and forced from northern Idaho and western Montana. Their way of life was devastated. Within 100 years of that first contact with David Thompson, only about 150 Kalispels remained.

"The spirit of the people probably died at that time," say Francis Cullooyah, the Kalispel's cultural and spiritual leader. He wonders how his ancestors survived such dramatic losses. "I would not be able to live very well. I wouldn't be able to go through it."

Cullooyah says it was especially difficult being displaced from northern Idaho. "How things would be so good if I was able to walk on the shores of Lake Pend Oreille today and say this is mine. I still say this is mine, but I'm only kidding myself. We have places we just can't go anymore." He respects the no trespassing signs that bar him from important traditional

Masseslow, chief of the Kalispels, circa 1910 (Northwest Museum of Arts & Culture/Eastern Washington State Historical Society, Spokane, Washington. Edward S. Curtis photo digitally restored, for authorized publication, per financial support of the Kalispel Tribe of Indians, L87-410.13)

places on the lake and rivers, like the islands in Lake Pend Oreille, but it bothers him. He says his spirit suffers, and he believes most non-natives don't understand what this separation means to the Kalispel.

"It's always in the back of our minds to reestablish our presence around Lake Pend Oreille," says Cullooyah, which is why reacquisition of lands that once belonged to the Kalispel is now a primary goal of the tribe's leadership. Already, more than 3,000 acres have been purchased in eastern Washington and in Bonner County, Idaho. Several hundred acres of land in East Hope was close to being deeded to the tribe by longtime local resident Claudia Stearns before her death

One unidentified woman, left, and five men, likely a mixture of Upper and Lower Pend d'Oreilles (Kalispels), in a store in Hope (Bonner County Historical Society)

at 101 years, but the trustees of her estate instead created a nonprofit foundation and the transfer didn't happen. It was a tremendous disappointment for the tribe, Cullooyah says.

"In the non-Indian society there are changes being made constantly," Cullooyah says, "but as Indian people, it's the things that we need and the things that we utilize that come from our Creator that are important to us. There are a lot of differences, and that's where we run into conflict." The cultural conflicts that arose in those first 100 years after David Thompson's arrival often were rooted in misunderstanding or ignorance. The Kalispel did their best to survive the changes while maintaining traditions, but many of the old ways began to slip away. Each new generation of Kalispels adapted to European lifestyles, including destructive ones like alcohol. But even with new trials and ongoing losses, their spirituality and connectedness with nature remained strong.

Catherine Pierre Manwolf Frye and Annie Nick fishing on Pend Oreille River, sometime in the 1940s (Northwest Museum of Arts & Culture/Eastern Washington State Historical Society, Spokane, Washington. Digitally restored, for authorized publication, per financial support of the Kalispel Tribe of Indians, L92-86.49)

After white settlement, up until the mid-1900s, the Kalispel would still travel around their former territory to hunt, fish and gather traditional foods. The marshy country of the Lower Kalispel along the Pend Oreille River was camas country. Each spring the camas plants' blue flowers would color the landscape so abundantly that grassy meadows appeared as water.

The camas plant was a food source so important to the Kalispel that they were known as "Camas People." The camas bulb, about the size of a woman's thumb, provided a staple food whose nutritional value exceeds brown rice. Indian women would dig for the bulbs in early to midsummer, then roast the peeled bulbs underground with heated stones and between layers of black lichen. They would make them into loaves and cakes and store them for winter use. Hiking the interpretative historic trail at Pioneer Park along the Pend Oreille River in Newport, Washington, offers a glimpse of the Kalispel's ancient food preservation system including the excavated remains of camas ovens.

Today tribal members still roast and preserve camas bulbs in the traditional way. However, the invader plants introduced since white settlement have out-competed the camas and sharply reduced their numbers.

Shirley Sandoval is granddaughter of the last formal chief of the tribe, Chief John Big Smoke. She still digs what camas can be found and roasts the bulbs underground in the way her mother, Alice Ignace, taught her. Sandoval has shared this knowledge with her children and other tribal members. She believes as a member of a traditional hunter-gatherer society, it's important to maintain the preparation of not only traditional foods but medicinal plants as well. "Some of these things are falling out of our basket along the way," she says, referring to the traditional ways. "Some are left behind. Some lost completely. But some remain."

Unidentified Kalispel women on horseback, circa 1890 (Bonner County Historical Society)

Kalispel ties with the vast waters and lands of northern Idaho remained, at least until the early 1950s. Lake Pend Oreille's shoreline continued to be a gathering place for the Kalispels in summer. There are a few old-timers left who remember the Indian encampments that took place near the hay farms at the mouth of the Clark Fork River. Families from a number of tribes around the area, including the Spokane, Bitterroot Salish, Kootenai, Coeur d'Alene, Nez Perce and others, would join the Kalispel near the present-day Clark Fork Drift Yard, a traditional gathering site, which the whites called "Indian Meadows." The Indians fished and dried their catch on sticks at warming fires near their lodges. They would also hike or ride horses up into the surrounding Cabinet Mountains to hunt and pick baskets and baskets of huckleberries.

Charlie Seymour and children at Indian Meadows during an encampment, circa 1930
(Bonner County Historical Society)

My late friend, Henry SiJohn, would speak of these times. Each year as a boy until he was 15 years old, he traveled with his family to join all the grandmothers and grandfathers at Indian Meadows until 1932 (see "Tribal Gatherings at Indian Meadows," page 205). Although he has been gone for several years now, I can still picture him standing at the shore of Lake Pend Oreille, his eyes welling up with tears and his voice quivering, telling me that those years spent at Indian Meadows were as close to a utopian lifestyle that a person could live.

Henry was in his 80s when he died, and it was a gift to know such a wise man. Those tears in his eyes would be there again when he spoke of the destruction to the meadows caused by the building of the Cabinet Gorge and Albeni Falls hydroelectric dams. The dams flooded the meadows, killing the native bulrushes, cottonwoods and old-growth cedar. Important religious sites and ancient rock petroglyphs were submerged. Subsequent shoreline development added to the impacts. "Nothing can ever replace what we had," Henry said.

Another important gathering place for the Kalispel and neighboring tribes was the annual powwow grounds just east of what is now City Beach in Sandpoint. Supported by the City of Sandpoint, the annual powwows usually lasted three days with the first day spent conducting memorials, giveaways and other tribal ceremonials. Non-natives didn't attend the powwow until the second day. Then there would be dancing and lots of gambling games like the traditional stick game.

But the powwows were discontinued in the early 1950s. Tribal members stayed to their small reservation far downstream near Usk, and the Kalispel presence in northern Idaho diminished to virtually nothing until recent years. Their reservation hugs the Pend Oreille River, but at nine miles long and only a mile wide, it is located on a clay floodplain with poor soils for agriculture. Unemployment within the tribe was high. Alcohol became the salve for their collective grief. For the next 30 years or so, the Kalispel, like many other tribes, had a very difficult time walking the line between assimilation into mainstream culture and retaining their traditions.

But that has changed dramatically. Beginning in the mid-1980s, the tribe began to renew ties to its ancient heritage and to make a collective commitment to sobriety.

In 1999, a renaissance of sorts took place that would have made their ancestors proud. For the first time in 50 years, a tribal gathering at the Clark Fork Delta Drift Yard led by Francis Cullooyah took place, bringing together tribal elders from several tribes, native drummers, singers and dancers, and a couple hundred non-natives from the area to celebrate what this special place still means to tribal people today. The gathering was blessed by the animals, too: a bald eagle circled overhead as well as a pair of ospreys and, to punctuate a brilliant red sunset, came the cry of the common loon.

Then in September 2000 a few months before Sandpoint's centennial was to be celebrated, a powwow and feast of traditional foods was held for the public at Lakeview Park in Sandpoint, nearly 50 years after the

Kalispel students Elisha Edmiston and Kevin Bowman act out one of the tribe's traditional stories in the Salish language, in 2008

last powwow was held at City Beach.

The tribe also is active in natural resource management. As part of mitigation settlements with the Bonneville Power Authority over Albeni Falls Dam, the tribe has developed 400 acres along the Pend Oreille River – the Flying Goose Ranch – into a wildlife and waterfowl refuge, and a bass fish hatchery, to make up for some of the lost native fish species in the river. It is hoped that bass fishing will benefit the tribe commercially.

The Kalispel have two other projects that have raised their standard of living – the Northern Quest Casino and the Camas Institute, both situated off the reservation in Airway Heights, Washington, near Spokane.

"The gaming enterprise has enriched most aspects of our lives," says Cullooyah. He says it has not only provided jobs for tribal members, but has provided the financial means to improve tribal community buildings, government offices and the powwow grounds in Usk. One of these tangible improvements opened in December 2007 – the Camas Center for Community Wellness. It provides an array of services to meet the social and health needs of tribal members and those in the surrounding rural communities. Casino revenues also have generated the resources to reacquire lands once belonging to the tribe. Cullooyah is particularly proud of the Camas Institute. It offers a holistic segue to higher education for young adults in the tribe, integrating college

Kalispel Tribe members Wilma Cullooyah, center, and Jamie Samuels, left, peel camas bulbs with Kalispel Encampment participants in June 2009 for the David Thompson Bicentennial. Wilma and Francis Cullooyah's grandson, Louis Cullooyah, is at Wilma's side (Billie Jean Plaster)

preparatory coursework and technology with the Kalispel culture. He sees the institute as one of the tribe's keys to the future. At home on the reservation, Cullooyah and his assistant J.R. Bluff also are working hard to keep the *qlispe* ("kully-speh") language alive – the key to keeping their culture thriving. With few elders still living that speak it fluently, a significant effort is under way to both record and teach the Kalispel dialect of Salish to young adults in the tribal language center and to elementary students across the Pend Oreille River in Cusick.

Reconnecting language and culture to place, Shirley Sandoval hopes that eventually her small tribe – now around 390 members strong – will reclaim some of its traditional territory around Lake Pend Oreille, something her people once thought impossible.

"I think of having land – even partial pieces of our aboriginal boundaries where the Kalispel used to be free to come and go – I think that would be totally amazing," she says. "It would be overwhelming for some of my people to be able to drive by Clark Fork and to say we got some of this back. I think it would be a miracle almost."

Cullooyah shares her dream and with every passing year its realization becomes more possible. In June 2009, as part of the David Thompson Bicentennial celebration, the Kalispel Tribe hosted a firsthand experience of their cultural traditions tied to its aboriginal lands and waters in Bonner County. A three-day tribal encampment at a guest ranch only a few miles east of their traditional gathering site at Indian Meadows in the Clark Fork Delta introduced the public to the setting up and taking down of teepees, the uses of native plants, traditional camas baking and venison jerky making, and fish weir and basket construction. At the end of the weekend, Cullooyah thought seriously about the idea of owning the very property they were using to help restore this ancient connection to place.

The Kalispel creation legend says when Creator brought the first animals to Earth in his great canoe and they touched land and Bear left his tracks on the still hardening rock, the bond between the Kalispel and the Earth was forged. For the Kalispel people, it remains a sacred trust.

"Map of North America from 84° West," David Thompson's 1820 map prospectus, shows Lake Pend Oreille, center, as Kullyspel (Public Record Office, Kew, Engl

CHAPTER FOURTEEN

DAVID THOMPSON

In 1809, fur trader and surveyor David Thompson came from present-day Canada, and he and his party of voyageurs became the first recorded white men to lay eyes on Lake Pend Oreille. He also established the first documented business operation between tribes and traders in Idaho, the Kullyspel House on the Hope Peninsula. Thanks to his detailed journals, today we can reconstruct much of Thompson's early explorations here.

By Dennis Nicholls

Across the Divide, 1807

On the night of June 18, 1807, on the North Saskatchewan River west of present-day Edmonton, Alberta, a black bear visited the tent in which slept David Thompson. A shot fired in the dark scared the bear off, but it returned the next morning. This time, "the Hunter" who shared the tent with Thompson killed the curious bruin.

"At dawn of Day the Hunter killed a black Bear at our Tent Door – we had fired at him last Night at our Door, but it was too dark to aim with precision." Thus was how Thompson recorded the event in his journal.

This was three days before Thompson gained the "Height of Land" later called Howse Pass and had his first look into the vast country to the west that lured him across the Continental Divide. In this gap between rugged peaks of the Canadian Rockies, Thompson found a passage to the much longed-for Columbia River and a route to the Pacific Ocean.

It would be four more years before David Thompson arrived at the mouth of the Columbia, but during those intervening years the man who mapped and surveyed more of northwestern North America than anyone else set about untangling the confusing geography of the Kootenai, Pend Oreille, Clark Fork and Columbia rivers and established a fur trading empire in the name of the North West Company of Montreal. Included in those days of exploration were three periods of time he spent along the "Saleesh" River (now Clark Fork and Pend Oreille Rivers) and Lake Pend Oreille. In all, between September 1809 and March 1812, Thompson spent approximately 365 days in the Clark Fork-Pend Oreille Valley, all the way from Cusick, Washington, to Dixon, Montana.

"Looking for a Portage, McGillivray's River," watercolor painting by British Army officer Henry James Warre, 1845. The river was later renamed Kootenai River

McGillivray's River, 1808

Within a month of crossing the Divide, Thompson's men began work on the first of four fur trading posts and several other temporary encampments within the North West Company's Columbia Department. Kootanae House was erected a short distance north of the outlet of Windermere Lake on what Thompson originally referred to as the Kootenay River, after the native people that inhabited the area. Little did he know then that he had already discovered the headwaters of the Columbia River.

Once the post was established, Thompson decided to explore the country to the south at the invitation of a Flat Bow Indian named Chief Ugly Head, a man with uncharacteristically curly hair. They left Kootanae House on October 2, 1807, and shortly after 5 p.m. Thompson rode his horse over the imperceptible divide now known as Canal Flats to "McGillivray's River, a bold clear rapid stream of about 150 yards wide … " This was his first look at what would become one of the most traveled routes in all his journeys through the western mountains -- the Kootenai River (spelled "Kootenay" in Canada). His first name for it, McGillivray, was after a man who was David Thompson's boss within the North West Company.

Unable to spare much time for this initial foray to the south, Thompson returned to Kootanae House within a week. Autumn passed into winter and Thompson remained at the post. But by the fourth week in April 1808, Thompson was ready to explore the region once again. The morning of April 20, 1808, dawned stormy with rain, but nonetheless, Thompson began arranging the gear he and his men would need to travel the unknown course of McGillivray's River.

The next day, frost covered the new grass as the party set off at 6 a.m. They crossed McGillivray's Portage (Canal Flats) and for the second time Thompson began downstream along what would later become the Kootenay River. It took 17 days to follow the river to present day Bonners Ferry, Idaho. The first week of May was characterized by cold mornings, illustrated by this journal entry: "May 3rd (1808) Tuesday, a sharp frost, Ice 1/4 inch thick." On May 8, Thompson's party spied a camp of Kootenai and Lake Indians comprised of 10 lodges. They pulled ashore and spent five days with this band of natives. This camp was likely a little east of the confluence of Deep Creek with the Kootenai River.

Thompson continued down McGillivray's River toward a lake he knew to exist farther downstream, Kootenay Lake. He turned around and retraced his route up McGillivray's River to Bonners Ferry. The country was so severely flooded there was nothing else to do but return to Kootanae House.

Third time's a charm, 1809

More than a year would pass before Thompson's next opportunity to push south from Kootanae House. In the summer of 1808, he went all the way back to Rainy Lake House, just west of Lake Superior, with a load of furs. Thompson stayed all of two days before once more setting his sights on the Rocky Mountains. He was back at Kootanae House on November 10. In five months he had traveled over 3,000 miles.

His second winter at Kootanae House passed, and in the spring Thompson and Finan McDonald transported more packs of furs over the Divide, two and a half tons worth, exceeding even Thompson's expectations. But by late June 1809 – four years after the Corps of Discovery had passed through Idaho on the Clearwater and Snake rivers farther south – Thompson was on the Kootenay River again and may have had an inkling that the north-flowing river on which he had established his first post west of the divide may well have been the Columbia. He boldly decided to temporarily abandon Kootanae House and turn his full attention to finding out exactly what lay to the south. On a cloudy August morning that was, according to Thompson's journal, "as usual very smoky," indicating forest fires in the region, Thompson's party set off at 4:45 a.m. It was August 20, 1809. For the third time, he was heading down McGillivray's River.

Five days of clouds, with rain on at least one day, and several very cold mornings with northeast gales ushered in a spell of classic summer weather in the Northern Rockies. Friday, August 25, 1809, was the first of 17 consecutive "fine" or "very fine" days as Thompson descended McGillivray's River. On the fifth day of that stretch of good weather, the party, wrote Thompson, "arrived at the Great Road of the Flat Heads and camped as it is here we must procure Horses to take us to the Flat Head River where we hope, please Heaven, to pass a good quiet Winter."

Thompson referred to the stream he had yet to see as the Flat Head River, but he later named it the Saleesh River, both above and below Lake Pend Oreille, after the Salish-speaking peoples who lived along it.

This site at the head of the Great Road of the Flat Heads was near where he had camped in May 1808 near present-day Bonners Ferry. His goal this time was to go south. Knowing this was new country with new contacts, Thompson and his men spent several days "arranging our Goods for the Horses etc., and examine and dry every thing so as to have the whole in good order for Trade and Preservation." He obviously wanted to make a good first impression.

Lake Pend Oreille, 1809

Thompson departed the Kootenai River on September 6, 1809, following a course of south 15 degrees east for three miles. This brought them "to the foot of the high banks. At 11:30 a.m. we had much Trouble to get up it, the Horses often rolling down with their Loads." This may well have been in the vicinity of the Mirror Lake Golf Course south of Bonners Ferry and it took nearly four hours to get everything to the top of this steeply rising slope.

They covered eight miles the first day, five of them after gaining the top of the high banks, and camped "near a small brook." T.C. Elliot, in a footnote to *David Thompson's Narrative of His Explorations in Western America, 1784-1912*, identified this brook as Brown's Creek barely two miles north of Naples, Idaho. From here the route becomes confusing. Exactly how Thompson got from Brown's Creek to Pack River is a mystery and probably always will be.

Nearly 17 miles of travel on September 7, beginning from the camp at Brown's Creek, took the party around Elmira Peak and into the Pend Oreille Valley for the first time. Here the trail could easily have struck off southeasterly, as Thompson recorded, across the valley northeast of Pack River. But it is likely that he arrived on the shore of Lake Pend Oreille at Boyer Slough. To get there, he would have had to go virtually due south once he crossed the Pack. By the end of that day, they were probably at Grouse Creek not far from Pack River, where they "put up" in "much fine Woods … of several Kinds of Fir and Pine and plenty of Cedar."

On September 8, the fifteenth straight "very fine day," morning came with frost. The party set off at 7:15 a.m. and within one-half mile they came "to a Brook which we followed South 40 East 1/2 mile then crossed it – it is 15 yards wide, deep and very easy Current." They had just waded Pack River. This put them on the south side of the river and on a course, he recorded, of south 20 degrees east for six miles. After those six miles, they came to a "rill of water," which they followed, Thompson wrote again, south 40 degrees east for a mile and a half "to the lake." Those southeast readings are suspect because Boyer Slough slides due south to the lake a little over six miles in a straight line south of the confluence of Grouse Creek with Pack River.

Thompson's distances indicated they went seven and a half miles after crossing Pack River, and 33 and a quarter miles from the Kootenai River near Bonners Ferry to the shoreline of Lake Pend Oreille. It was probably late morning, perhaps nearing 11 a.m. when they arrived at the north shore of the lake. Wherever they were, the party continued another mile along the shoreline then met a fleet of canoes manned by local Indians. When you read his journal for September 27, 1809, and again for October 6, it becomes clearer that, in all likelihood, David Thompson indeed did first arrive at the lake near Boyer Slough.

Kullyspel House and the Pend Oreille River, 1809

Of all the things one might notice about Lake Pend Oreille, upon seeing it for the first time, Thompson's first record in his journal, after plying its waters along its northeast shore, was this: "We held on southeast 4 or 5 miles and put up at 2:30 p.m., the Wind blowing too hard for the Canoes to hold on." This was September 8, 1809.

If indeed Thompson met the canoes near Kootenai Point southeast of Boyer Slough, and took the time to load a great deal of gear into them, as he describes in his journal, then set out into a stiff wind, it is no wonder they only got four or five miles. The wind forced them to shore after probably about two hours of toiling, and they pitched camp, apparently just off Hawkins Point at the mouth of Pack River.

Thompson did not note the time they set off the morning of September 9, still heading southeast on the lake toward the mouth of the Clark Fork River, but the wind came up again and gathered such strength that they soon put ashore. "The Canoes were obliged to lighten and reload part of the horses," Thompson recorded. Not long after, at 2 p.m., they rounded Sheepherder Point, the southernmost tip of Hope Peninsula, and, as Thompson remarked in his journal, "We all at length arrived in safety, thank God, at the mouth of the River where we camped for the night." It was Thompson's second night on the shores of Lake Pend Oreille. He originally called it "Kullyspel

Lake" after the Kalispels who lived here.

Thompson's expedition came upon a large encampment in the delta east of present-day Denton Slough reportedly "of about 80 men" and their families from four different tribes. The camp could have numbered in the hundreds. These friendly people, who almost certainly had heard of the coming of these white men, greeted Thompson and his men with, as Thompson relates in his Narrative, "an acceptable present of dried Salmon and other Fish, with Berries and the meat of an antelope." In his journal, Thompson called the gift "a handsome present."

The next day, Sunday, September 10, was the final "very fine day" of that two and a half week stretch. Thompson set out with two Kalispel Indians in search of a suitable place to build a trading post. They found a place somewhere in the vicinity, though it was less than ideal (the currently accepted site, after much debate by historians and archaeologists, is on the Hope Peninsula facing Memaloose Island). "At length found a place somewhat eligible but labours under the want of good Earth," Thompson wrote. The crew moved to this spot later in the day.

Monday dawned cloudy with rain showers, but work began on Kullyspel House, which was completed about two weeks later. On September 21, Thompson spent four hours exploring the peninsula on which he had built Kullyspel House. That evening, Jaco Finlay arrived with his family.

Jim Parsons Sr. inspects an inscribed tree on Hope Peninsula, circa 1948. It reads "Kullyspell House Duncan McDonald" and was presumably carved in 1923 by the son of fur trader Angus McDonald, who enlisted the help of aged Kalispel Alex Kai Too in order to locate the former trading post site (Ross Hall)

Various Indian groups came to make presents to and trade with the white men. September 13, a Wednesday, was a very busy day. Even though construction of the trading post had barely begun, Thompson "Spent much of the Day in trading with the Indians who brought about 120 or 130 Skins ... "

Exactly two weeks later, at noon, Thompson had set off with his man Joseph Beaulieu and an "Indian Lad ... to examine the Country below us." Work was still in progress on the post and Indians were steadily coming in to trade, but Thompson was anxious to explore the country to the west. They crossed the "isthmus," or Hope Peninsula, in 45 minutes, rounded Hope Point and got

Legendary Lake Pend Oreille

as far as Pack River where they put up for the night. It had been a "rainy," "cold," "blowy" and "cloudy" day. Thursday, September 28, was no better. "A cold cloudy Morning, wind northerly," wrote Thompson. This is when he discovered the glass face and the needle had fallen off his compass, making the instrument useless. Thompson was rather chagrined. Nonetheless, the three-man exploratory expedition continued along the lakeshore, traveling about 12 miles to the Pend Oreille River.

This day would have been Thompson's first time past the site of modern Sandpoint. A couple of miles west of the "Pointe of Sand" coming down into the lake from Sand Creek, Thompson noted that the Pend Oreille River was 350 to 400 yards wide with an easy current. Two days later, beneath skies that had remained cloudy, foggy and rainy for five days, having passed by Priest River and Albeni Falls, Thompson came to an area of enormous trees. He noted in his journal "Red Fir, Fir Pine," and "much gummy white Fir" that were often three fathoms, or 18 feet, in circumference, "and a chance one a little larger." This grove of trees, which were probably Douglas fir, western white pine and western hemlock, would have been six feet or more in diameter and probably many hundreds of years old.

"Indian Fishing Station on the Kalispel Lake and River": In 1845, British Army officer Henry James Warre painted this watercolor sketch of a Kalispel village near Cusick, Washington, very close to a place where David Thompson met Kalispel people in the fall of 1809

By noon they arrived at an Indian village in the vicinity of Cusick, Washington. From there Thompson and Beaulieu, with an Indian guide, explored the river another 30 miles downstream almost to Box Canyon in a borrowed, but very leaky, canoe. When it became clear their guide had never been on that part of the river, and the current had increased dramatically, Thompson took to heart some information that the lower Saleesh River (from Box Canyon to its confluence with the Columbia) was not navigable. He turned around and started back for Kullyspel House.

Four more days of rain and clouds, making nine in a row, marked Thompson's return trip up the Pend Oreille River. When he arrived back at Sandpoint, on October 6, where he had a good view out across the lake to the east, he noted the course to "a large Point, the one this side of the Rivulet (Pack River), is about East 5 miles." He was looking across open water to the southwest tip of Sunnyside at Fisherman Island. Later that day, Thompson, Beaulieu and the Indian lad arrived back at Kullyspel House where, "thank God," Thompson wrote, "we found all well." He must have been especially pleased that Finan McDonald had carried on with much successful trading: "Mr. McDonald had traded ab^t 2 Packs of good Furrs in my Absence, mostly from the Pointed Hearts (Coeur d'Alenes) ... " Two packs of furs would have weighed approximately 180 pounds and would have contained about 100 beaver skins.

The Clark Fork River and Saleesh House, 1809

Five days after Thompson returned from his excursion down the Pend Oreille River, he turned his attention upstream along the Clark Fork River. In 1809, it was all the "Kullyspel Lake" or Saleesh River to him. He was due to meet James McMillan of the North West Company, who was coming with supplies all the way from Rainy Lake House, somewhere on the Kootenai River. Curiously, however, Thompson decided to travel through unexplored territory that turned out to be nearly twice as far to the confluence of the Fisher and Kootenai rivers in Montana as following the Great Road of the Flat Heads back to Bonners Ferry and then up the Kootenai from there.

On his second journey down the Kootenai in the spring of 1808, Thompson had been aware of a trail called the Kootanae Road southeast of Libby, Montana, that went south to the Flathead River, but he was not sure of the exact location of this road. This time, leaving Kullyspel House on October 11, 1809, he intended, with the help of his man, Beaulieu, a young Indian hunter and his father the guide, to find that trail.

The route from the Clark Fork Delta to Camas Prairie in Montana, up the Little Bitterroot River to Wolf Creek, then down the Fisher River to the Kootenai encompassed 160 miles, which took Thompson and his men 10 days to traverse. But it worked. They found a party of Indians on the opposite bank from the mouth of the Fisher along with two French Canadians who informed him that McMillan was just downstream. By the final day of the month, they arrived at Kullyspel House by way of the Pack River.

Two days later Thompson was on the move again, heading back up the Clark Fork with a crew of seven men. He headed for an area he noted for fine meadows with lots of grass where he had seen a herd of about 40 unattended horses only a couple of weeks earlier. He planned to build another trading post – Saleesh House – where, today, the town of Thompson Falls, Montana, is located not far from the mouth of Thompson River. The second journey up the Clark Fork was even more difficult than the first. By the time they reached Thompson Falls, the men were starving and the horses were in such bad shape, they were too poor to eat. Though they had been on site for a week, Thompson's men were too weak with hunger to work, until, on November 14, Jaco Finlay showed up with all kinds of food. Work commenced on the post, where Thompson remained until late February 1810.

Thompson's Final Days West of the Divide, 1810-1812

Beginning February 22, 1810, Thompson spent almost a month and a half of incredible travel up and down the Saleesh River, including another adventure down the Pend Oreille River to Cusick. He traveled from Thompson Falls to Dixon three times, where a large group of Salish Indians were wintering near the confluence of the Jocko and Flathead rivers, and later descended the river to Lake Pend Oreille and back to Kullyspel House. On May 9, 1810, Thompson left the trading post on Lake Pend Oreille with the intention of returning to eastern Canada. For all but nine of the previous 212 days, Thompson had been somewhere along the Saleesh River and the lake. Those nine days found him on the Kootenai River meeting James McMillan and escorting him back to Kullyspel House. Before leaving, he assigned Finan McDonald responsibility for Saleesh House, James McMillan for Kullyspel and Jaco Finlay was dispatched to the Spokane River to build a new trading post there.

Almost exactly one year later, Thompson arrived at Saleesh House by way of the Kootanae Road from Fisher River, only to find it empty. By June 6, 1811, he was at a deserted Kullyspel House and so paddled down the lake and the Pend Oreille River to Cusick, where he learned McDonald had moved all the way to the new Spokane House built by Jaco Finlay. Thompson made his first visit there, arriving eight days later. During this quick run through the Clark Fork-Pend Oreille Valley, Thompson spent a mere 30 to 35 days in his old stomping grounds.

He was to return, however, after finally surveying the Columbia River all the way to the ocean and then all the way from Kettle Falls to its big bend at the northern tip of the Selkirk Mountains. By mid-November, he was rebuilding Saleesh House, where he spent another winter. Come spring, David Thompson left Saleesh House and the Clark Fork-Pend Oreille Valley for the last time. He traveled to the far northern reaches of the Columbia and on May 6, 1812, he set off from Boat Encampment on foot over Athabasca Pass.

There is no indication that he returned to Lake Pend Oreille for a fond farewell. Within five months, he had settled down with his wife and growing family (eventually 13 children) on the outskirts of Montreal. Though he never ventured out West again, by 1814 he had drawn the most accurate map of the northwestern lands yet created – so accurate, in fact, that 100 years later it remained the basis for many maps issued by the Canadian government. Despite his achievements, Thompson encountered financial misfortune and died a pauper in 1857. His legacy was resurrected by historians in the 1920s.

Altogether, David Thompson spent a total of some 365 days, or the equivalent of one full year, along the Clark Fork River, Lake Pend Oreille and the Pend Oreille River between September 1809 and April 1812. This greatest of North American geographers left an indelible mark on this region, and during the 2007-2011 bicentennial of his travels here and beyond, we would do well to remember his pioneering efforts.

Mr. and Mrs. Don Eagen, early pioneers at Trestle Creek, display a fine potato harvest (Bonner County Historical Soci

CHAPTER FIFTEEN 15

THE LAST 200 YEARS

By Marianne Love

Ripples in Time: A Glimpse at White Settlement on Lake Pend Oreille

Over the past 200 years, white settlement around Lake Pend Oreille has come in trickles, ripples and waves since fur trader David Thompson built Kullyspel House in 1809. The story is a colorful saga of development, disappointment and drama as the white world gradually descended upon the lake's shores and used its natural resources, hoping for individual bonanzas — from simple homesteads to once-notable logging empires to thriving recreational attractions.

On a calm day at Sam Owen campground a person can stand among the rocks facing the lake's vast expanse and skip a piece of shale at least five or six times across the glass-like, serene surface. Within a split second, stillness returns, leaving no indication of any recent disturbance. Likewise, Lake Pend Oreille's documented historical timeline provides few clues to outside influences for decades immediately after Thompson left the area where Kalispel Indians had lived off the land and the lake for thousands of years. By all accounts, with the exception of other fur traders and Jesuit missionaries, their tranquil existence continued for decades thereafter.

Then, gold fever struck in nearby areas during the 1860s, bringing throngs of miners to the lake en route to Montana or British Columbia, Canada. From that point on, the indigenous

355

Steamboat *Northern* at City Dock in Sandpoint; note cordwood on dock (Bonner County Historical Society)

inhabitants around Lake Pend Oreille began to feel the pinch of an outside world slowly discovering and surely changing their homeland forever. A sad example of this intrusion is evident in the Sandpoint Treaty of 1887 that was never ratified, when the Kalispel inhabitants around the lake were ordered to vacate their lands to make way for the Northern Pacific Railway's transcontinental line. The route was destined to go through areas the Kalispel had inhabited for centuries, and the U.S. government supported the railway. The displaced Kalispel either followed missionaries to Montana's Flathead Reservation to live or stayed at traditional village sites along the Pend Oreille River near present-day Usk, Washington, until in 1914 a reservation was created for them by executive order.

As the outside world gradually discovered northern Idaho's geological jewel, a cast of fascinating personalities and ordinary folks from all walks of life arrived here from all corners of the globe and for a myriad of reasons. Pend Oreille's cast has included fur trappers, missionaries, steamboat pilots, railroad executives and laborers, lumbermen, homesteaders, farmers, sailors, entrepreneurs, resort owners, anglers and a lot of transplants with a simple romantic yearning to lead a quiet life far away from it all.

Steamers and miners

Lake Pend Oreille's major waves of settlement were punctuated by modes of travel and the

356   Legendary Lake Pend Oreille

ease with which people or goods could get from one place to another. During the fur-trading era in the first half of the 1800s, horses, canoes and foot travel enabled frontier-savvy adventurers to find areas where wildlife roamed abundantly around the lake. Trappers reportedly hunted for furs down the eastern shore and around Bayview, but they moved on, seldom leaving much evidence of their presence.

City Dock in Sandpoint (Bonner County Historical Society)

Then came the era of the steamboat and a relatively convenient and comfortable method for transporting people, supplies and livestock. Steamboat travel provided a handy passageway during the Montana and Canadian gold-mining rushes. The boats also aided later mining projects in Clark Fork and Hope, several sites along the eastern shore south to Lakeview and up the western shore to Bayview, Blacktail and Talache. Steamboats also supported railroad construction in the late 1800s and helped usher in a thriving lumber industry of the early 20th century. From the 1860s until an organized road network developed in early 1930s, the big boats, mostly stern-wheelers, powered by steam from wood fires, dominated lake transportation, keeping commerce on the move.

Discovery of gold in the mid-1860s at Wild Horse Creek in British Columbia and Last Chance Gulch near Helena, Montana, served as a catalyst for the lake to provide a pathway to the gold fields. Prospectors heading north over land from the Spokane River crossing along Pend Oreille's western and northern shorelines faced days of slow, difficult travel through mucky areas, especially with their mule-drawn wagons heavily loaded with supplies.

Steamer *Mary Moody* waits for pack strings, on their way to mines, to be loaded at Pen d'Oreille City in 1869
(Bonner County Historical Society)

Enter what would become the first lady of steamboats – the *Mary Moody*. Lake Pend Oreille's first steamboat was sanctioned by the Oregon Steam Navigation Co. (OSN), recognizing the great business potential of extending its service beyond the Columbia River during the gold rush of the 1860s. Zenas Moody, as the OSN representative, built the vessel in four months during 1866 at Seneacquoteen, one of the area's first towns with its trading post and ferry crossing on the Pend Oreille River near present-day Laclede. Constructed from rough-cut local lumber, the boat sported a 20-horsepower engine originally from Wilmington, Delaware.

Moody's 85-ton, 108-foot long vessel carried 85 pack animals, 10,000 pounds of freight (at 13 cents per pound) and 50 passengers on her maiden voyage, which embarked from Pen d'Oreille City at the south end of the lake. Some passengers stepped off the boat at Mud Slough (later Boyer Slough near the town of Kootenai) and set off on the arduous journey up the Lake Indian Trail to the Kootenai River, which they would cross on their way to the mines near Canada's Kootenay Lake.

From Mud Slough, the *Mary Moody* (named for pilot Zenas Moody's wife) moved on to Cabinet Landing, east of present-day Clark Fork, where customers went ashore and portaged for seven miles before boarding another steamer along the Clark Fork River to the Montana mining areas. It also saved approximately six days from what had been an eight-day trip around the lake over trails with little grass for the animals to eat but with more than enough mud to mire them down.

Before boarding the *Mary Moody*, miners or riders carrying "the express," meaning mail, money transfers, etc., bound from Walla Walla for Missoula, Montana, could enjoy the few conveniences available at Pen d'Oreille City. Moody founded the village of five houses, one hotel, a bar and pool hall, and a grocery store. The site, one of several ghost towns associated with the lake, is now known as Steamboat Landing on Idlewilde Bay near Farragut State Park.

During the nearly 70-year steamboat run, 60-plus vessels that crisscrossed the lake fulfilled numerous needs, including delivering mail to small communities located near the 11 landings along the shoreline. *The Western*, built by Charles Spealman and the Northern Navigation Co., after making its last mail run in 1938 along the south part of the lake, was dismantled and burned. With its ashes, went a lifestyle known for decades by residents in remote areas, depending on the steamers for basic needs, social lives, connection to the outside world and a sense of regularity, as penned by Dorothy Nelson in *Beautiful Bonner*.

Nelson wrote of typical days spent on the roadless peninsula (east of Sagle Hill, bordered by Bottle Bay, Glengary Bay and Garfield Bay).

Boats brought in fresh bread from Sandpoint on Monday, Wednesday and Friday, which were the "early boat days," Nelson explained. On Tuesdays, Thursdays and Saturdays "late boat days," the boat came from Bayview. The arrival of the boat with its "jingling bells and tooting whistles" was the event of the day.

"Both captain and engineer appeared on the deck, tossed the mail sacks to the dock and lowered the gangplank down which to assist passengers and slide the freight and empty cream cans," Nelson added. "During an exchange of pleasantries, joshing, and gossip, outgoing mail was tossed on deck, full cream cans were hoisted up and the passengers were helped aboard. The bells and whistles chimed their signals and the Western was on its way again."

If the *Mary Moody* was the matriarch of the Pend Oreille steamboat era, Canadian transplant Ed Elliott might reign as undisputed king of the boatmen. After moving to Sandpoint and working as a cobbler, he founded the Northern Navigation Co. (1906) and built his 102-foot-long majestic boat *The Northern*, a 250-passenger and freighter double-decker steamer. Some writers called her "the queen of the lake." Elliott's fleet grew to five boats. For several years, he held the mail/freight contract, which meant cruising the lake's 110-mile perimeter every day. His route from Sandpoint took him first to Hope and on to Bayview before moving up the west channel to homeport. Along his route, Elliott stopped at 11 landings – Hope, Granite Creek, Whiskey Rock, Cedar Creek and Lakeview to the east and Bayview, Blacktail (Talache), Garfield Bay, Glengary and Bottle Bay. For a time, Sunnyside on the lake's north shore also served as a steamboat-repair landing. Later, Elliott diversified his navigational services by loading his magnificent boat with passengers for picnic and moonlight dancing cruises on the lake. In 1912, President Theodore

Roosevelt joined other passengers for a *Northern* cruise. By 1919, Elliott decided he had had enough of the tours and began towing logs, claiming the work was much more rewarding because the logs "didn't talk back

like people did." In 1920, his crew reportedly broke a record by towing 5 million board feet of logs from the mouth of the Pack River to Priest River's Beardmore Mill. He died in 1965; Elliott Bay southwest of Hope honors his memory.

Ed Elliott shakes hands with Teddy Roosevelt in 1912 at the Northern Pacific depot in Sandpoint (Bonner County Historical Society)

Steamboats aid early local mining

During early northern Idaho mining eras, steamboats transported hopeful prospectors and tons of raw ore from one end of the lake to the other. For example, the towns of Panhandle (existing one year) and Ponderay sprang up in the early 1900s because of the Panhandle Smelting and Refining Co. The plant refined copper, gold, silver and lead, hauled by steamers from Lakeview, Blacktail, Granite Creek and Trestle Creek. In *Bayview and Lakeview: and Other Early Settlements on Southern Lake Pend Oreille*, Linda Hackbarth offers pictures and details about steamboats, including the *Dora Powell*, which "pushed barges holding railroad cars filled with crushed limestone from Lakeview to Bayview." Until D.C. Corbin's railroad line served Bayview, however, the *Bayview* hauled lime to the Northern Pacific railhead at Hope. The *C.H. Prescott* transported lime from Whiskey Rock, Lakeview and Bayview.

Pend Oreille's mining era began in 1881 when N.H. Porter and G.W. Ripley staked their claims south of Sandpoint on July 16. Many mining efforts along the lake's east side were a natural progression of activity occurring in the ore-rich Coeur d'Alene River area with gold discovery at Pritchard and silver at Bunker Hill.

During the 1880s, the Lakeview area attracted as many as 2,000 prospectors briefly after an article appeared in a San Francisco newspaper claiming that a rich vein of gold had been discovered. Names like Weber, O'Donnell and Donnelly dominated the Lakeview/Chloride gold and silver mining claims. In the 1900s, copper ore was discovered at the Green Monarch mine, while across the channel at Talache, the Armstead Mine set up a community for 125 workers and operated as one of Idaho's leading silver producers in the 1920s, grossing about $2 million when silver sold for less than a dollar per ounce. In the Hope and Clark Fork area, the Whitedelph, Lawrence and the Hope mines produced silver, lead and zinc from the 1920s to the 1950s. In Midas/Garfield Bay, shyster James McNicholas employed elaborate means to attract investors in his Midas operation. He set up a hotel to attract tourists and miners to the area that netted only a large dose of fool's gold.

Steamboats *Daisy* and *Northern* on either side of barge with a group of people gathered around
(Bonner County Historical Society)

Disputes closed some mines, while falling silver prices closed others. "In fact, our road in town is paved with about 3 ounces to the ton of silver," long time Lakeview resident Harry Heavner said. "They got more money for it as gravel as road building than they did for ore."

Railroads and their construction bring settlers aplenty

First launched August 17, 1881, at Steamboat Landing, the 150-foot *Henry Villard* helped open the way for a new mode of transportation that would change the face of Pend Oreille's north shoreline forever. Rail transport also would expose the area to thousands of potential residents and usher in a logging industry that dominated northern Idaho for decades. The vessel's namesake, Henry Villard, a Bavarian immigrant and journalist, served as president of Northern Pacific (NP) Railway which pushed its transcontinental route along the north shore of Lake Pend Oreille from 1881 through 1883. Numerous land features associated with the lake were named for NP employees, and some are still in use today, including Picard Point, Strong Creek and Johnson Peak.

Time-consuming and difficult construction of the line required up to 6,000 workers (more than half were Chinese). Especially challenging was building the 6,500-foot-long wooden trestle, completed in 1882, across the mouth of Pack River from Hawkins Point to Trestle Creek. After the NP (now Montana Rail Link) line was completed, a number of Chinese remained in Hope, raising beautiful gardens, selling imported goods from China and running a local laundry.

Looking southwest above the Northern Pacific tracks, view of Pack River with remnants of the old trestle visible in the lake in the background (Bonner County Historical Society)

With railroad construction workers constantly on the move, boomtowns, also known as "front towns" or railroad camps, like Ventnor, Hangtown (near the south end of Sandpoint's railroad bridge) and Cabinet (east of Clark Fork) would spring up but disappear quickly. Others like Hope and Clark Fork, Kootenai and Sandpoint would remain permanent communities. When the Great Northern (now Burlington Northern-Santa Fe Railway) constructed its line through northern Idaho in 1892, Dover, Laclede and Priest River were born. Sandpoint's importance as a railroad center grew. Eventually, in 1906, a third railroad called the Spokane International (now Union Pacific), running from Spokane to Canada passed through Sandpoint.

In the early 1880s, the *Henry Villard* steamer transported supplies up the Clark Fork River to Cabinet, then a front town along the NP construction line. Cabinet saw population spurts several times. The population really exploded during its front town existence. Cabinet fit the typical wild and woolly mold of these temporary communities. An article about Cabinet by T.J. Sanders in the *Northwest Tribune* in 1882 characterized "a free fight in the streets" as "the order of the day since payday." After all, 2,600 Chinese and 1,400 Euro-American railroad workers built shacks and pitched tents in Cabinet for three months. With 33 temporary saloons, things were likely to get rough. It comes as no surprise that executives recognized recreational potential as they oversaw construction and took in the breathtaking views of the lake and its islands from the north shoreline

362   Legendary Lake Pend Oreille

of Pend Oreille. Hope, named for the railroad construction crew's veterinarian, served as site of the Inland Empire's first resort when the NP built the Highland House in 1885. The company hoped to lure wealthy Easterners as summer tourists to its three-story "luxury" resort surrounded by beautifully landscaped grounds and offering 17 guestrooms.

The railroad operated the Highland House for two years before its caretaker Charles Smith, a Swedish immigrant, and his family assumed ownership and rented out rooms for the next five years. During this time, Civil War General William Tecumseh Sherman spent the summer of 1888 there. Word was he couldn't catch a fish in the lake or even in Hope's Strong Creek, which teemed with trout at the time.

Hope enjoyed a heyday when the NP moved its round house from Heron in 1889. The town grew quickly with six transcontinental trains stopping each day and with a revival of steamboat traffic bringing ore or limestone from mines around the lake. The increased traffic brought in a rough element and a Wild West atmosphere with the main street being lined with saloons. Railroad importance for the community changed drastically, however, in 1894 when a devastating flood washed out dozens of homes and considerable railway track bed. Hope's demise later turned Kootenai into a temporary boomtown when the round house was eventually moved there.

Meanwhile, at the south end of the lake, the name D.C. Corbin conjures up more railroad talk. Corbin constructed a spur line off from his Spokane International into what's now Bayview on Scenic Bay. The line was called the Coeur d'Alene and Pend Oreille. Limestone brought by steamboat from quarries at Whiskey Rock, Lakeview and Bayview was deposited on its cars and then hauled to Spokane for use in construction sites like the Davenport Hotel and Long Lake Dam, saving considerable time over past years when lake transport involved a trip north to Hope.

"If you build it, they will come," certainly fit the development story of Bayview. Corbin and other Spokane businessmen envisioned using the railroad spur line as a way to transport tourists to their new resort town designed around 1910. After designing a plat, the business partners built a street network, created a water system, constructed a hotel and set up an office in Spokane to sell Bayview real estate. On its official opening day, April 30, 1911, the partners hosted 500 Spokane citizens to view the new community. Bayview would attract new residents and recreationists through several decades, especially thanks to the eventual prominence of next-door Farragut Naval Training Station, which later turned into a state park.

From gandydancers to river pigs

Small local railroad lines extending to the logging camps in drainages like Pack River, Gold Creek and Grouse Creek to the east and Carr Creek to the west contributed significantly toward transporting logs to one giant mill pond called Lake Pend Oreille. The timber industry became a

"River Pig Rescue," 1949: An unidentifed man gets help after losing his footing on a log jam and falling into the river. Fellow loggers steady the log with a peavey and pike pole (Ross Hall)

dominant force in the 1890s and especially during the Humbird Lumber Co. era from the early 1900s until 1931. By 1900, upper Midwest forests were nearly exhausted, so when word of plentiful western white pine spread to lumber barons with names like Humbird, Deary (eventually Potlatch Corp.) and Weyerhaeuser, they wasted no time coming west to establish their presence in pre-designated areas.

Humbird purchased the Sand Point Lumber Co. mill in 1899 and Kootenai's Ellersick Mill in 1903. The owners operated a state-of-the-art facility for the times. The need to harvest trees for lumber and matches brought on a new breed of rough-and-tough workers, ranging from sawyers and teamsters, to "river pigs" who worked the log drives along fast-moving, dangerous rivers. Crosscut saws, peaveys, caulk boots with high-water pants held up by suspenders, millponds, chutes and flumes became a part of the local vernacular. Virtually all aspects of logging were dangerous; many men died or were crippled from woods-related accidents. Logging camps complete with laundry facilities and well-supplied cookshacks served as homes to hundreds of lumberjacks for five days a week. Trees were cut, limbed and later decked with the power of horse teams. Some trees were branded to identify the logging company, dumped in rivers and herded downstream by river pigs. In other cases, narrow gauge railroads, consisting of geared-down Shay Locomotives, lugging loaded flat cars down steep grades, hauled logs from the mountains to the lake where they would be stored in brails (basically a log and cable fence line surrounding

364   Legendary Lake Pend Oreille

other loose logs) and later towed by steamers to the larger mills in Kootenai, Sandpoint, Dover, Laclede or Priest River. Ed Elliott and his Northern Navigation Co. crew began towing log booms for lumber companies in 1919. Along the shoreline at Hope, Kootenai and Sandpoint where sailboats and motorized crafts now rest in marina slips, expansive reddish-brown seas of logs floated in protective lake water. The water kept the logs from drying out and becoming checked; and it was the only way to move the logs into the mill in that era. Eventually, the logs were processed and shipped by rail to other parts of the country. "Humbird built a 'railroad dock,' extending hundreds of feet out over the lake," Doug Thurlow explained in *History of Bonner County*, "in order for trains to be able to drive out and unload logs into the water."

The huge presence of Humbird Lumber Co. in Sandpoint and Kootenai signaled assurance that the timber industry was here to stay. With 20,000 acres of timberland purchased from the Northern Pacific, jobs were plentiful. The mill employed more than 350 men. Housing was in demand. Sandpoint became a Humbird Company town as its economy thrived and it received distinction as the lumbering capital of Idaho.

Whether it was the 1929 Wall Street Crash, the gradual depletion of white pine in the area or a general loss of profits, the Humbirds left Sandpoint and moved on to Canada. The logging industry slowed considerably during the next decade, as did most everything during the Great Depression years. The Dust Bowl brought droves of new settlers from the Midwest to northern Idaho by rail. Many of these transplants with strong rural roots transformed stump ranches into working farms, establishing an agricultural industry in the area. Road building also began around the lake, especially with help from the Civilian Conservation Corps. This ushered in yet another new era. Motorized logging trucks could reach areas once served by the small railroads and horse teams. Steamboat travel turned virtually obsolete.

World War II and the need for supplies and the subsequent post-war baby boom housing demand breathed renewed energy into the timber industry. A couple of Spokane brothers, Jim

"Idaho Jammer": Loading logs with a jammer, circa 1950 (Ross Hall)

and Larry Brown, capitalized on these demands and built a logging empire throughout eastern Washington, Canada and Montana, lasting nearly 50 years. Jim Brown Jr. moved to Sandpoint and started his successful lumbering career with "sinkers." In 1940, he established Deadhead Logging Co. along Sand Creek by retrieving logs that absorbed too much water and sank to the bottom. From there, Brown's empire took off, eventually expanding to 15 mills. One of those mills at Dover operated at the same site as the A.C. White mill where today's Dover Bay waterfront community continues to unfold. Besides producing lumber, the Dover Mill served as a research facility for Jim Brown, who was always looking for production efficiency with logs. In the 1950s, the term "tenex" eventually became a fixture locally as an addition to the mill began producing the particleboard product by compressing wood shavings with steam-operated pressure and applying a resin coating. Brown's daughter, Bobbie Huguenin, said the process was the first of its kind in the wood industry. The mill employed hundreds of people for four decades before closing in the early 1990s. Pack River Lumber Co. continually diversified its interests, and Jim Brown would influence a rapidly growing recreational and tourist industry through his ownership of Schweitzer Mountain Resort.

Recent influences: recreation and real estate development

A number of influences have granted Lake Pend Oreille dramatic nationwide and worldwide exposure since the early 1960s. The opening of Schweitzer Ski Basin (now known as Schweitzer Mountain Resort) and its continued marketing strategy of tying the ski area to the lake below ("Ski the big bowl; see the big Hole") have attracted continuing migrations of transplants to the area. Exposure also came through several Scout gatherings in the 1960s and 1970s at Farragut State Park, numbering up to 30,000 visitors at a time. Even a controversial "church picnic," sponsored by the Universal Life Church brought in at least 20,000 rock-music revelers for a weekend in 1971.

Once the place had been discovered, and as hopping on a commercial airplane or Learjet became more the rule than the exception for travelers, the area around the lake saw an influx of new residents representing diverse careers and cultures. In addition, more leisure time meant more time for recreation. An economy based more on tourism has slowly pushed aside the farming, logging or railroad lifestyles that so dominated the lives of hard-working citizens in earlier decades. The demand for this recreational playground opened a thriving real estate market and the way for development of farmland into subdivisions generally ranging from half-acre to 5-acre plots.

More and more resorts and private communities catering to golfers, skiers and recreationists have dotted the shoreline during the past 30 years. Sandpoint's small but vibrant arts and culture, with the Panida Theater and events like the Festival at Sandpoint, have served as another lure to the so-called "amenity migrants." The quality of life has also been an asset to attract talented employees for a variety of younger companies, such as Coldwater Creek,

Litehouse Foods and Quest Aircraft. Other modern trends, such as the Internet, have enabled many micro-companies to locate here yet pursue national markets. Coupled with a high rate of new arrivals – county population increased 54 percent in just 18 years, from 26,622 in 1990 to 41,168 as of 2008, according to the U.S. Census Bureau – the change in the employment base away from the traditional resource industries has created dramatic changes in the demographics of the population. Lake Pend Oreille and environs have become a magnet for a wealthier, leisure class as well as for those whose families have lived in and loved the area for generations.

Nonetheless, Lake Pend Oreille remains a valuable jewel continually casting its magic spell on most anyone who lays eyes on its glistening waters. Though tarnished a bit, the jewel remains vibrant and alive. Fortunately, many who use the lake recognize its fragility. Though development on the lake seems overwhelming, miles and miles of quiet, unspoiled public land exists along the shoreline and can still thrust visitors into a tranquil time warp. If the lake is to remain a precious gem to be cherished 200 years from now, developers, residents and visitors must work together to actively exercise one simple guideline for its future: Leave it in better shape than you found it.

A newly built home on Moose Mountain at The Idaho Club's gated community (Jerry Luther)

TIMELINE FOR RECORDED WHITE SETTLEMENTS ALONG LAKE PEND OREILLE

September 1809: North West Company surveyor and fur agent David Thompson, his clerk, Finan McDonald, and their men establish the Kullyspel House on Hope Peninsula.

1811: Thompson abandons Kullyspel House. McDonald concentrates his efforts on Spokane House.

1820s-1860s: Occasional fur trading takes place around the lake; but no permanent settlements.

1830s-40s: Catholic missionaries visit the "Bay Indians" at Blackwell Point at southernmost end of Lake Pend Oreille, a winter village of Upper Kalispel people. The Kalispel lands were eventually claimed by the U.S. military, which built Farragut Naval Training Station on this site.

Mid-1860s: Gold strikes in British Columbia's Kootenay Lake area and Montana bring thousands of miners through the area via the Wild Horse Trail.

Ferry crossing at Seneacquoteen (Bonner County Historical Society)

1860: Thomas Forde establishes the first commercial ferry at Seneacquoteen, a traditional Kalispel crossing called *Sin yaq' tn*, on the Pend Oreille River near present-day Laclede.

1866: *Mary Moody* steamboat is constructed at Seneacquoteen on Pend Oreille River. Owned by

Oregon Steam Navigation Co.

1867: *Mary Moody* begins transporting miners and their supplies bound for Montana gold mines; the route is from Pen d'Oreille City on south end of Lake Pend Oreille to Cabinet Landing on the Clark Fork River.

1867: *Harper's New Monthly Magazine* features descriptive story in October edition by Colonel Cornelius O'Keefe (pen name for Thomas Francis Meagher, a Civil War brigadier general of the Irish brigade) about a steamboat journey he supposedly had taken on Lake Pend Oreille in 1866.

1869: W. Milnor Roberts, U.S. Civil Engineer pens *Special Report of A Reconnoissance [sic] of the Route for the Northern Pacific Railroad between Lake Superior and Puget Sound via the Columbia River.* Roberts describes trip taken around the lake on the *Mary Moody.* He finds the northern and western shores suitable for railway construction.

1882: Northern Pacific construction of the railway through Hope.

1882: For three months, Cabinet, on the Clark Fork River serves as a "front town" for railway construction. More than 4,000 workers, including 2,600 Chinese laborers, pitch their tents near the landing where the *Mary Moody* and *Henry Villard* steamboats dock.

1885: Dr. Wilbur Hendryx, formerly of Grand Rapids, Michigan, establishes Kootenay Mining and Smelting Co. (KMS Co.) headquarters, a boarding house, general store and a sawmill at the NP's Kootenai Station.

1886: Northern Pacific Railway constructs the Highland House in Hope – the first major resort in the Inland Northwest. The 22-bedroom lodge is built for $3,949.64.

1886-87: Mineral discoveries around the southeast end of Lake Pend Oreille lead to a "rush," as more than 2,000 prospectors move into that district.

1887: The unratified Sandpoint Treaty sets the stage for the forced removal of all American Indian residents from the Lake Pend Oreille drainage by the beginning of the 20th century.

1887: Albeni Poirier, a French Canadian farmer from Blanchard, builds log cabin near waterfalls on Pend Oreille River.

1888: Northern Pacific Idaho/Rocky Mountain division point is moved from Heron, Montana, to Hope, Idaho.

1888: R.J. Perry surveys and plats Hope town site and names three streets: Main, Highland Avenue and Ridgewood.

1891: Kootenai enjoys population boom during construction of the Great Northern Railway when it serves as the supply point for a 100-mile section of track.

1892: Albeni Poirier adds barn, combined saloon, dance hall and blacksmith shop to his hotel and café after Great Northern Railway completes its link to Troy, Montana. A ferry eventually operates from his location, which attracts travelers from Spokane.

1894: The "High-Water" year. Heavy snowpack melts rapidly during a sudden hot spell causing flooding and the loss of Northern Pacific track near Hope.

1899: Otto Smith buys the Highland House at Hope for one dollar. The structure eventually becomes a school.

1898: Great Northern Railway agent L.D. Farmin plats Sandpoint town site.

1899: Approximately 1,300,000 Lake Superior whitefish fry are transplanted in Lake Pend Oreille.

1900: Lakeview Landing becomes a prosperous village because of earlier mining boom.

1901: Herman Ellersick and sons establish Kootenai Bay Lumber Co., a single-band sawmill, two miles north of Sandpoint on Greenough's Spur. The complex includes the sawmill, planer, homes and company store.

1901: Kootenai County Board of Commissioners incorporates the town of Sandpoint. Judge Whitaker is appointed first chairman of the five village trustees.

1903: Ellersick family sells Kootenai Bay Lumber Co. to Humbird Lumber Co., a subsidiary of Weyerhaeuser Co. At sale time, 123 employees are working six 10-hour days. Laborers earn 20 cents for an hour's labor while sawyers, filers and foremen earn 60 cents an hour.

1903: Ground is broken for the Panhandle Mining and Smelting Co. at Ponderay, Idaho.

1903: Panhandle, Idaho, is established at present-day Ponderay by I.H.M. Williams of Spokane.

1904: Panhandle, Idaho, is vacated and replaced by Village of Ponderay.

1904: The present-day railroad bridge across Lake Pend Oreille from Sandpoint is built replacing earlier wooden trestle.

1905: First road on Sagle peninsula is constructed from one mile north of Glengary to Sagle, built by volunteers paying off taxes.

1906: Ed Elliott, a shoe repairman on First Avenue, begins his Northern Steam Navigation Co. His longtime boat business begins with the steamboat *Nancy*.

1906: Present-day town of Dover is known as "Welty."

1907: Ed Elliott builds the steamer *Northern*, a 250-passenger and freight steamboat. He secures the mail-freight contract for delivering mail from Hope to Bayview to Sandpoint. Makes 120-mile per day circuit around the lake.

1907: Bonner County is formed after being cut off from Kootenai County by act of the Idaho Legislature on February 2.

1907: Village of Sandpoint becomes City of Sandpoint. Mayor and council form of government is formed. Dr. O.F. Page is elected first mayor; serves one term from 1907-1909.

1908: Ye Old Midas Inn opens for both tourists and miners at what's now the Forest Service picnic ground at Garfield Bay. Owner James McNicholas promises a bright future for the area that he names Midas, due to his Midas-Galena mining interests.

1908: Realignment of Great Northern Railway cuts off Albeni Poirier's enterprise from the Pend Oreille River.

1908: First fish hatchery is established in Bonner County, and the third one in Idaho after Idaho's Ninth Legislature passes legislation for fish and game funding. Located at Murphy Bay and built on 20 acres, the Sandpoint Hatchery supports native cutthroat trout and eastern brook trout.

1908-09: First Long Wagon Bridge is built across Lake Pend Oreille, dramatically enhancing commerce for Sandpoint.

1910: Approximately 500 people from Spokane spend day viewing the newly planned resort town of Bayview. Business leaders foresee the spot on Beauty Bay as a resort playground for Spokane residents.

1910: Massive forest fires ravage Idaho Panhandle and some lakeside communities.

1910: Commercial whitefish industry on lake becomes regular source of winter income for many men and their families affected by seasonal logging and mining employment.

1911: Ad in *Pend Oreille Review* newspaper lists 10 landings along the lake for the *Northern* steamboat. They include Bayview, Lakeview, Cedar Creek, Whiskey Rock, Granite Creek, Blacktail (later Talache), Garfield Bay, Glengary, Hope and Sandpoint.

1912: The town of Clark Fork is incorporated.

Talache Mine (Bonner County Historical Society)

1917: Talache Mines of Boise incorporates Armstead Silver Mine at Blacktail (later known as Talache).

1919: The Northern Navigation Co. starts towing logs on the lake.

1920: Northern Navigation Co. breaks a record by towing 5 million board feet of logs from Pack River to the Beardmore Mill in Priest River.

1922-23: More than 50 homes, warehouses and even the present Dover Community Church are moved by barge from Laclede to Dover. Fire at A.C. White Mill precipitates decision to relocate to Dover.

1922-26: Talache District ranks as one of Idaho's leading silver producers, grossing about $2 million with silver selling for less than a dollar per ounce.

1927: Ed Elliott's $15,000 steamer, the Northern, is gutted by fire just after last trip of the season.

1930s-'50s: Civilian Conservation Corps and U.S. Forest Service build a network of roads around the lake, diminishing importance of steamboat commerce.

1931: Humbird Mill liquidates, shutting down all logging and sawmills in Sandpoint and Newport. Its mill in Kootenai closed the previous year.

1933: Completion of the second wooden driving bridge across Lake Pend Oreille.

Tugboats pulling a boom of logs on Lake Pend Oreille (Ross Hall)

1942: First successful stocking of Kamloops rainbow trout in Lake Pend Oreille.

1942-45: Farragut Naval Training Station is built. The inland base serves as training ground for nearly 300,000 sailors preparing to serve in World War II.

May 1, 1946: Beginning of Kamloops and Kokanee (K&K Days) Fishing Derby on Lake Pend Oreille.

1946: Decommissioning of Farragut Naval Training Station leads to Farragut College and Technical Institute, a two-year vocational school. The college lasts only two years and is closed in 1949.

1947: Barge operator Fred Kennedy opens Sandpoint Marina at the Old Power House.

1947: Herschel Weaver builds his Litehouse Restaurant at Hope.

1947: Harlan and Margaret Walker, along with Wayne and Ruth Anderson, establish Talache Lodge in Talache mining district on west side of Lake Pend Oreille. The fishing resort attracts Hollywood stars like Bing Crosby.

View of the 1948 flood looking east toward the breakwater at Sandpoint City Beach (Ross Hall)

1948: Pend Oreille's waters rise above the shoreline to flood level, cause havoc, and leave debris throughout Sandpoint residential areas and its streets.

1951-53: Construction of Cabinet Gorge Dam on the Clark Fork River.

1955: Albeni Falls Dam west of Priest River is completed. Structure is named for Albeni Poirier of Blanchard. Dam construction allows regulation of waterline height around the lake, thus dramatically reducing the possibility of flooding.

1956: The third Long Bridge is constructed and opened. A new fill is created southeast of

Sandpoint for this structure.

1957: Last ferry closes down in Bonner County at Seneacquoteen.

1963: Schweitzer Mountain Resort opens. Its influence throughout the Northwest and Canada propels Sandpoint into a resort community.

1965: Farragut State Park hosts the National Girl Scout Round-up.

1967: World Boy Scout Jamboree is held at Farragut State Park, attracting 12,000 participants.

1967: Kamloops, a U.S. Navy large-scale submarine model arrives at Acoustic Research Detachment (ARD) at Bayview. The Bayview ARD site begins to play an increasingly important role in submarine silencing. Another model named Kokanee later joins the operation.

1968: Village of Ponderay, which had existed since 1904, is renamed and incorporated as the City of Ponderay. Attorney Jim Hunt serves as first mayor.

1969: Farragut State Park hosts the National Boy Scout Jamboree.

1971: Controversial Universal Life Church Picnic, a rock festival compared to Woodstock, over Fourth of July weekend at Farragut State Park attracts 15,000 to 30,000 participants during the two-day event.

1973: Farragut State Park hosts another National Boy Scout Jamboree. Comedian Bob Hope entertains at the event.

1981: The present-day Long Bridge at 6,080 feet is completed. Third Long Bridge is converted into a walking/jogging/biking structure.

1986: Cabinet Gorge Fish Hatchery opens as part of Avista Utilities (formerly Washington Water Power) mitigation effort from loss of spawning streams for kokanee after construction of Cabinet Gorge Dam in the early 1950s.

1988: Dover is incorporated as Idaho's 111th city. First mayor is Bill O'Donnell.

1996: Disc golf course is established at Farragut State Park.

2000: Entering abandoned mines in northern Idaho's five counties without a permit becomes illegal, according to closure order from the Bureau of Land Management. Violators face a possible maximum penalty of one year in jail and a $1,000 fine.

2000: U.S. Navy christens *Cutthroat* (LSV2), the world's largest unmanned autonomous submarine for conducting research experiments in Lake Pend Oreille.

2002: U.S. Navy opens a new $7.7 million Acoustic Test and Analysis Center (ATAC) in Bayview. The center consolidates offices, computer laboratories and industrial research facilities into a single, modern facility.

2003: Work begins to transform Sandpoint Fish Hatchery on Lakeshore Drive into "WaterLife Discovery Center," with fish viewing windows, living stream and interpretive trail.

2004: *Sunset Magazine* names Sandpoint "West's Best Small Town." Other prominent

Ross Hall snowshoeing above Lake Pend d'Oreille, circa 1937

THE ROSS HALL COLLECTION

Arriving in Sandpoint in 1931, photographer Ross Hall spent half a century capturing richly detailed images of the community, people and landscapes here. He gained national recognition with photos in the *New York Times*, *National Geographic*, *Life* and others, prompting Eastman Kodak in the 1940s to name him one of the top 10 scenic photographers in the country. With wife Hazel, he operated the Ross Hall Studio. Ross died in 1990 and Hazel in 2009, but their stunning photographic record remains in The Ross Hall Collection, managed by son Dann at the Hallans Gallery in Sandpoint.

The Ross Hall Collection

Moonlight Tête-à-Tête 1939   Overlooking Memaloose Island near Hope

Legendary Lake Pend Oreille

Early Stiles 1964 Austrian racing instructor Werner Beck on Stiles Run at Schweitzer

The Ross Hall Collection

The Snyedrens, circa 1906. Pictured clowning between expeditions of Lake Pend Oreille are two sisters, of the ski club.

Legendary Lake Pend Oreille

Lake Pend d'Oreille in Winter 1939 Looking toward the Clark Fork drainage from Talache

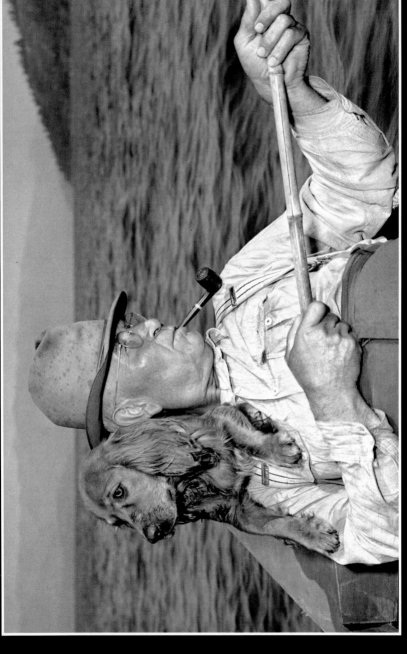

Bo and Teddy, 1946. Pend d'Oreille fisherman laureate Bo Johnson and his dog, Teddy.

Legendary Lake Pend Oreille

Cottage and Pearl 1935 The islands of Cottage and Pearl photographed from Hope

Showboatin' on the Fourth 1933 A Fourth of July crowd gathers at the Cedar Street Bridge in Sandpoint

Legendary Lake Pend Oreille

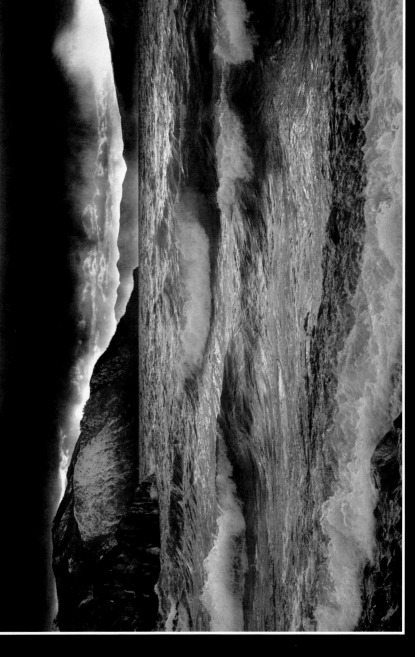

The Silver Storm 1939 Lake Pend d'Oreille looking south toward the Green Monarchs

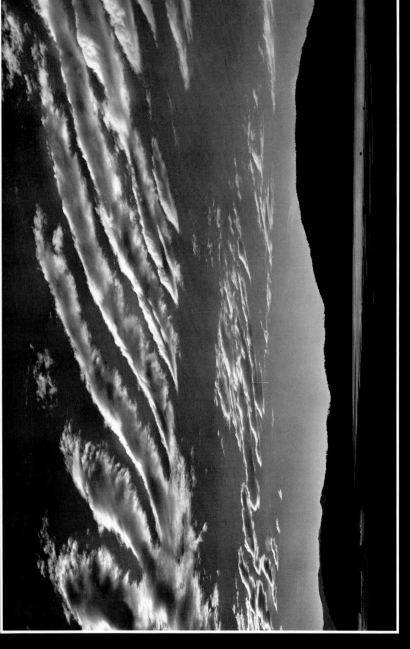

Sunset Quills 1940 The western sky from the Long Bridge

Legendary Lake Pend Oreille

Sisters in Silhouette circa 1940   Three bathers at Sam Owen beach on the Hope Peninsula

The Ross Hall Collection

The Indian Stick Game 1931 The last stick game at Sandpoint at the final powwow held at present-day City Beach

Farragut 1944 Overlooking Idlewilde Bay toward Farragut Naval Training Station

The Ross Hall Collection

Gypsy Rose Lee, circa 1943. Legendary entertainer Gypsy Rose Lee recreating at Lake Pend d'Oreille

The Waterdoggers 1933 The first "wake boarders" take to Lake Pend d'Oreille

The Ross Hall Collection

Kamloops and Cheesecake circa 1948

Legendary Lake Pend Oreille

publications echo town's praises. Real estate sales go off the charts and million-dollar resort developments spring up in Dover, Sandpoint, Hope, Trestle Creek and along the Pend Oreille River.

2005: U.S. Navy christens *Sea Jet*, a 133-foot model representing a destroyer-size surface ship, on August 24 and puts her "to sea" November 28 in Lake Pend Oreille at Bayview. Rear Admiral Jay Cohen attended the christening ceremony.

2008: The U.S. Highway 95 Sandpoint Bypass construction along Sand Creek commences, a 2.1-mile alignment that runs from the north end of the Long Bridge to the Highway 95-Highway 200 interchange. Entailing five bridgeways and 65 retaining walls, the bypass construction is expected to last until 2012.

2009: The Bonner County Historical Society in conjunction with the North American David Thompson Bicentennials Partnership commemorates the fur trader's arrival here in 1809 with a Kalispel Encampment and other events on and around Lake Pend Oreille.

Bud Moon as a child at Garfield Bay (courtesy Pat Moon)

Barracks inspection at Farragut Naval Training Station (Ross H...

CHAPTER SIXTEEN

FARRAGUT NAVAL TRAINING STATION

This article first appeared in Sandpoint Magazine *in the Summer 1996 issue.*

By Marianne Love

Sailors Ahoy: Farragut Naval Training Station's era on Lake Pend Oreille

*I*t served as a small slice of life's big picture and ignited like a field of tinder dry weeds. It faded so quickly, like a wisp of smoke.

Yet in spite of its momentary flutter, the sights, sounds and memories of Farragut Naval Training Station at the southern tip of Lake Pend Oreille flame within the hearts and minds of thousands of World War II veterans as if they happened yesterday. Its embers floated far from Farragut's boundaries, sparking nearby communities into an era of excitement and new blood. These days, cracked cement foundations, the brig, a few pump houses and two giant water towers have survived as the few visible vestiges of an era when the urgency of the war effort thrust northern Idaho into a vital role.

Farragut Naval Base rose almost overnight on wide-open fields and rolling hills that had once served as a seasonal stop for early Indian and pioneer migrations. In late 1941, the U.S. government snapped up the land from private owners, Kootenai County and a railway company to establish an inland naval base more than 300 miles away from the Western coastline, where the

377

Aerial view of Farragut Naval Training Station after World War II and before the World Boy Scout Jamboree in 1967. The base was situated on the southern end of Lake Pend Oreille between Scenic and Idlewilde bays (Ross Hall)

nation feared a Japanese invasion. For the next nine months more than 22,000 men worked 10-hour shifts for 13 of every 14 days for Walter Butler Construction Co. to build mess halls, libraries, movie theaters, living quarters, chapels and other buildings. In the great hurry and with a supply crunch, many of the 776 buildings were constructed with green wood. The flurry of construction activity provided a giant, economic shot-in-the-arm for surrounding communities like Sandpoint, still mired in a slow revival from the Great Depression of the 1930s.

"They paid $1.60 an hour," recalls Hope resident Fred Kennedy, who later operated a tugboat/barge service on Lake Pend Oreille. "No one had ever heard of such wages." Carpenters, laborers and tradespeople from throughout the Sandpoint area worked at Farragut.

The summer of 1996 marked the 50th anniversary of the decommissioning of Farragut. Between its opening in September 1942, and its decommissioning in June 1946, this stunning expanse of 4,000 acres served as temporary home to almost 300,000 naval recruits. Located about 30 miles from Sandpoint at the far end of the lake, the Farragut Naval Training Station – briefly to become Idaho's largest city – served as boot camp for "Blue Jackets." During basic training, recruits left home for the first time, came to Farragut and learned to how march, row, swim and use firearms before heading off to the Mediterranean Sea or the South Pacific. Others received additional training as signalman's gunner's mates, the hospital corps or radiomen. WAVES (women naval officers) served as nurses at the base hospital.

378   Legendary Lake Pend Oreille

Other soldiers, some as young as 16 or 17, arrived at Farragut from Europe. Wearing shirts inscribed with "PW," 750 German prisoners of war, many from Austria, worked side by side with American soldiers. They ran loose in camp and trimmed shrubbery or mowed lawns at the facility named in honor of the Navy's first admiral, David Farragut.

Base personnel also played a major role in Sandpoint daily life during those years. They brought their spending cash with them while on furloughs here. Retired business woman Edith Jennestad, whose family owned a clothing store on First Avenue, remembers Farragut's impact on the community. "We were amazed when we opened the paper and learned that they were going to have this base," she recalled. "That was a real plum for Idaho." Her father, Ole, had opened Jennestad's at 317 N. First in 1908. "Farragut really boosted business," she recalled. "Father sometimes wouldn't get home until 1 a.m." The Jennestads outfitted the prisoners of war with boots and socks, and once Ole was asked to go to Farragut and measure base commander Commodore Frank Harrison Kelley for uniforms. "He heard my father fit people well," Edith said.

Farragut's presence also meant new friends, Jennestad recalled. Her next door neighbors, the Racicots, kept sailors. In fact, Sandpoint families often invited the lonely men over for holiday dinners. And many young women from Sandpoint were torn between these men and their sweethearts already involved in military action abroad. Zelma Carter was barely 19 when she went to work in the dry cleaners at Farragut in 1943. "There really wasn't anything special you wanted to do but go to work," she recalled. "At the time you were interested in boys, they were all gone." In her leisure time, Carter enjoyed weekend social activities when, according to a newspaper report, "the streets downtown on a Saturday afternoon would be literally navy blue ... masses of sailors walking down streets arm-in-arm, whistling at every girl. The invasion meant fun Saturday nights to Carter and her friends. "My mother never knew how many to cook for because we always brought home sailors," she remembered. "We would go off dancing and Daddy would come with us."

Following the Naval base's decommissioning after the war, a vocational/technical college opened in 1946, but it quickly folded from lack of funding. Later, the land comprising the training station was turned over to the State of Idaho. During the '60s and '70s, Farragut hosted worldwide Boy and Girl Scout jamborees. Even a controversial Universal Life Church picnic, referred to by some as "Idaho's Woodstock," brought nationwide attention to the area in 1971.

The spot now serves as one of Idaho's premier state parks. During summer months, bikers and horseback riders play on its fields where scores of sailors once practiced marching. Swimmers, boaters and campers enjoy spectacular scenery around Buttonhook Bay where young recruits learned basic seamanship. Across the bay on their high perches, mountain goats seemingly stand watch over the rolling hills where six camps of 5,000 men each resided. In a large open field just inside the park, remote controlled model airplanes often buzz the skies above the parade grounds.

In the 1990s the park's museum drew hundreds of silver-haired memory seekers. Typically, the 70- to 80-year-old visitors started at their camp sign-in sheet, thumbed through 1,100 laminated group photographs and eventually spotted themselves among the neatly organized rows of youthful sailors. Then, the stories would flow. "When they find their picture, that seals the memory," Farragut State Park assistant manager and historian Al Leiser says. "The experience (at Farragut) was a very powerful period in these men's lives."

Anyone within listening distance could eavesdrop and learn vivid details about half a century ago when the "cattle wagons" brought young men from the Athol train station seven miles away and dropped them off for shots, uniforms and general processing. They were eventually assigned to one of Farragut's six camps, which remained their world for more than two months before they left for faraway places to do their part in the war effort. Some recruits had dismal memories of northern Idaho, while others were charmed enough by the area to find their way back.

Montana native Paul Mikelson returned to Farragut for a visit in 1995. He completed boot camp and radio school before heading to the South Pacific. Besides the cold and general misery, he recalled many recruits contracting rheumatic fever. In fact, his hometown buddy had to go home after being stricken.

In 1943, a 28-year-old mortician from Clarinda, Iowa, arrived at Farragut after receiving his draft notice. After completing boot camp, Harlan Walker stayed another 16 weeks and attended the hospital corps service school before spending the rest of the war at the Seattle Naval Hospital, treating casualties straight from Iwo Jima.

"About the time I was discharged, I began to read about those great big Kamloops trout in Pend Oreille," he recalled. "I had an excellent job with a good (mortuary) firm in Des Moines, but I'd seen enough death in that hospital. It made this country look that much better. I also knew the resort facilities on the lake were not too great ... I couldn't get Sandpoint out of my mind." Walker, his wife, Margaret, and

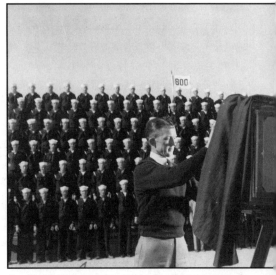

Recording World War II era: Ross Hall was the official photographer for Farragut Naval Training Station

their partners bought 800 acres of mining property southeast of Sagle and opened Talache Lodge. The premier fishing resort attracted the likes of Bing Crosby, Lon Chaney, Phil Harris and even two-time presidential candidate Adlai Stevenson.

About the same time, Don Samuelson, another Iowa transplant who had served as Farragut's weapons instructor and gunsmith throughout the war, came to Sandpoint and opened the Pend Oreille Sport Shop with his friend Jim Breinich. The two maintained their partnership until the mid-'60s when Samuelson became involved in politics, first as a state senator and then for one term as Idaho's governor. In August 1966, he upset incumbent Governor Robert Smylie in the Republican primary and defeated Democratic opponent and fellow state senator, Cecil Andrus.

Hazel Hall, upper right, along with a group of Farragut officers and their wives on a boat ride (Ross Hall)

The Farragut experience helped fulfill Samuelson's childhood dream. "When I was in the fifth grade, I read a book on Idaho history," the former governor explained. "It had pictures of the statehouse and Bunker Hill. From that time on, I wanted to come to Idaho." His first deer hunt in the mountains above Bayview and hikes up Bernard Peak, which overlooks Farragut, helped set the stage for the move back to Sandpoint.

At 83 in 1996, he still enjoyed trips to the park and was looking forward to September's 50th anniversary of Farragut's decommissioning. Samuelson, Carter and Walker would be among a few hundred returning personnel who hope to swap stories and rekindle a few of the flames of youth that once burned so brightly in the place "where fightin' Blue Jackets were made."

Epilogue: At the time of this publication, many of the people interviewed in 1996 for this story have since passed away. The last formal Farragut reunion for World War II Naval recruits was held at the park in 2006.

CHAPTER SEVENTEEN

PEND OREILLE PADDLER

Traditionally, the Kalispel Indians told stories of large sturgeon in Lake Pend Oreille and there were rituals practiced to avoid encounters with them. With the arrival of non-Indians, fish stories were replaced with monstrous, prehistoric-looking creature stories. In 1984 James R. McLeod led a group of North Idaho College students in a study of Lake Pend Oreille and the mystery surrounding a "monster" alleged to be swimming its waters. The following is an edited version of the report prepared by McLeod and the North Idaho College Cryptozoology Club, originally published by Wordcraft Publishing, 1987.

Mysterious Lake Pend Oreille and Its "Monster": Fact and Folklore

*T*he basis for the claim of a "monster" in the lake is directly traceable to a single event occurring in the summer of 1944. Although much national attention had been focused on another reputed monster, "Slimy Slim" (or "Sharlie"), in Payette Lake in central Idaho in the early and mid-1940s, the 1944 event at Lake Pend Oreille received little note. It might have been lost to modern memory had not monster lore documentarian Loren Coleman, in his interesting book *Mysterious America*, listed Pend Oreille as one of many lakes having monsters.

An article appearing in the *Utah Humanities Review* in 1948 made passing reference to the sighting in Pend Oreille: "As late as the summer of 1944, the mysterious appearance of such a monster was reported from the Farragut Naval Training Station on Lake Pend Oreille in Idaho."

A tongue-in-cheek allusion to this event appeared on the front page of the October 19, 1944, issue of *Farragut News*. The article satirized the lake monster rumor, publishing a hoaxed photograph showing a gigantic horny toad against a backdrop of Bayview. There was a strong implication that the sightings in the lake were alcohol-related.

References, both published and unpublished, of something large in the lake began to appear again until the early 1970s. In a January 1970 article, Mrs. Lillian E. Hall, a resident of 59 years at Kilroy Bay, observed: "Talk of some kind of 'monster' in the lake," which she hears from time to time, "mostly comes from a bottle. " This attitude certainly was consistent with the *Farragut News* treatment in 1944. However, in another North Idaho College Cryptozoology Club (NICCC) interview, an Athol resident said that when she moved to the area prior to 1972, there were many stories coming out of Bayview regarding a "big animate" object in the lake – of particular interest to NICCC because people interviewed all around the lake repeated them. These included reports that the animate object had been picked up on sonar; a huge sturgeon 50 to 60 feet long living in the "trench" in the lake; boats being pulled "all over the lake" and "lines being snapped"; large shadows just under the surface; logs rolling over and diving; and fins.

What was certainly the most sensational surface sighting of the late 1970s occurred in early September 1977 when a young girl was reportedly attacked by the monster near Sandpoint City Beach. The tabloid *What's Happening* published a photo of the creature that journalists dubbed the "Pend Oreille Paddler" and stated that the creature was a "cousin" of the Loch Ness Monster. This sensational report apparently left many grade school students afraid to venture into the lake. Years later, the stories that it spawned were a primary impetus for NICCC's investigation.

For several years in the early 1980s, the club sought information on the report's source. In late 1984 the mystery was finally solved. The photo of the Paddler turned out to be a 12-foot papier-mâché catfish used in a play that had appeared in Sandpoint in October 1974. The story behind this hoax is too lengthy to recount here, but it is interesting to note that the individuals involved very much believed in the oft-repeated lore that there really was a large "prehistoric creature" in the lake, and they maintained that the article was merely trying to draw attention to its existence. At least two of these individuals claim to have actually had unusual sightings themselves, one before 1977 and one after. The one prior to 1977 occurred between Dover and Sandpoint in the summer and involved an observation of "humps" for some minutes. The second happened about 1979 during the summer about 6 p.m. While the informant was fishing off the dock near Lakeshore Drive in Sandpoint, he noticed a seagull "attack" the water just 30 yards offshore. Then a "giant head" appeared with eyes as "big as basketballs." The informant threw a line over it, but it quickly submerged. Though this account certainly strains credulity, the observer gave every indication of seriousness and is a respected member of the community. In any case, the 1977 story is of particular note in that it coined a new name for the creature, for the "Paddler" has been the most frequent label since that time.

Another monster account comes from a Sandpoint resident and his cousin who were fishing near Warren Island in June 1981. They had started fishing and were on their "first beer" when the informant's cousin's mouth "dropped open." The informant turned to see a "grayish-silver, serpentine" back emerge out of the water, "kinda like a sturgeon, but not rigid," "undulating" a quarter mile away. The cousin turned to the informant and said, "What the hell can that be?" The creature, at least "15 to 20 feet long," was between Hope and the boat, and the two men could clearly see the shore. The sighting occurred on a sunny, flat, calm day between 1 p.m. and 2 p.m.

With the exception of the foregoing report, the monster hypothesis was not attracting much attention during the early 1980s until an article entitled "Where is the Monster?" appeared in a fishing newsletter, *The Red Herring,* in January 1983. The tongue-in-cheek editorial called for the creation of a monster legend and went so far as to rechristen the monster "Orville" rather than the Paddler. The article also included a sketch of a dragon-like creature in the lake. The following two years were to see a virtual explosion in interest in the Paddler, beginning with the summer 1984 Cryptoquest expedition by NICCC; for example, an appearance of an article in *USA Today* in July 1984 and an order from The British Museum Department of Natural History.

NICCC is not entirely ready to shut the door on the possibility that a large, possibly prehistoric animal does exist in the lake. After all, the lake is extremely large. Moreover, it remains one of the least explored areas in Idaho and, for that matter, in the United States as a whole.

Perhaps the most compelling argument that unknown species may dwell undiscovered in Lake Pend Oreille is that it has already been known to happen, though certainly not on so dramatic a scale as alleged Paddler sightings. The head project engineer for the U.S. Naval Acoustic Research Detachment at Bayview confirmed in 1984 the discovery of a small, white, lizard-like creature, which appeared to be blind. He reported that it was observed in 1965 during a deep submersible dive. Another, though unconfirmed, report of this small animal contends that a specimen was actually brought to the surface and kept in a fruit jar by a Navy wife as a curiosity. (Just for the record, NICCC does not believe this new, lizard-like creature is the larva of the Paddler! A.L. Wilson, a Washington State University zoologist, thought it could be an unknown species of a salamander.)

In summary, Lake Pend Oreille may have many mysteries yet to be revealed. Where the monster is concerned, the history of hoaxes and publicity stunts, the absence of photographs, the reticence of many area residents, and the silence of the Navy at Bayview on this subject do not make NICCC optimistic that, after its three years of research, a flood of further information is likely to be forthcoming. The lake is without a doubt an area rich in history and folklore, and it rests in a spectacular setting that will give any explorer much satisfaction, monster or no monster.

CHAPTER EIGHTEEN

CROSSING OPEN WATER

This story first appeared in Sandpoint Magazine *in the Summer 1993 issue.*

By Jane Fritz

t is a rare occasion that I take to open water. Where I usually hug the shoreline while canoeing alone, tonight I am drawn by a desire for adventure, a lust for spring's wildness. Guided by honking geese skimming the lake's surface, I stretch a line with my cedar canoe from Glengary Bay to the island, arriving at dark. Pitching a tent quietly and without a flashlight is as much a ritual for me as watching the moon ripen. As geese couples make their raucous night music, calling to each other and those nesting on other islands, I lie awake listening, a respectful voyeur. The geese seem to accept my interloping and recognize that it is, after all, their ecstasy I came to experience.

For many years now, flat water canoeing on the lakes and rivers of the Panhandle has been my preferred form of travel. These solitary sojourns garner remarkable encounters with nature: I've been chased by beaver and visited by mink, and in between the paddling I have swum with the loons and talked with the stars.

Perhaps it is this love of watery wilderness that has endeared me to another so bold to canoe it alone. He is Russell Keene, who lives in the mountains high above Talache at a place called Castle Rock. Russ is the proverbial king of the mountain, approaching 84 years, and

Russell Keene at Talache (Jane Fritz)

as much like an old grizzly bear as any human I know. His first love is the forest his family homesteaded in 1914 – a 200-acre tree farm overlooking Lake Pend Oreille that he now shares with his son's family, two young couples, and friends and relatives when they come to visit. Russ was the only one of the nine children in his family that didn't trade mountain living for a home in the city. For him, Castle Rock has become the living memorial to his mother, Sarah, the woman who taught him to seek the spiritual gifts of nature as well as its more pragmatic offerings.

The view of the lake from Castle Rock's cliffs is spectacular. At 450 feet above the water, the vista spans from Sunnyside to the Clark Fork River to the Green Monarchs to Bayview. Sandpoint is hidden behind Grouse Mountain. With such abundant visual beauty, it seems strange that it would be something Russ heard that brought him to explore the lake by canoe.

He recalls that when he was 7 years old he begged his brother, who was 17 years older, to take him down to the water to fish. There, far out on the lake, he heard a loon wailing. He figured his brother was pulling his leg when he told him it was a bird. "Philip being a great storyteller and all ... I couldn't feature it being a bird," Russ muses. "Its cry was like a wild animal, calling for help." He fell in love with the shadowy song and vowed someday to get to know the bird's mysterious domain — "the loon being more of a mystic creature and all."

Despite that experience, Russ didn't actually canoe the shores of Pend Oreille until many years later. In 1967 he moved back to the area after living and working in California for 30 years, first for the Forest Service and then as a hydro-surveyor in the Sierra Nevada Mountains for a utility company. That first summer home he and his son, Rob, canoed whenever they could, but with all the work to be done on the tree farm, they weren't often on the water. The next summer they tried a small motor on the canoe, thinking it would help them explore more of the lake, but it was noisy and they actually traveled less. After that they resumed paddling their canoe.

A favorite and frequent jaunt began at the southern end of the lake at Bayview. Five hours later, Russ' wife, Lily, would pick them up at Talache Landing and there would be a catch of new stories to feast on around the supper table.

It wasn't until his son went away to college that Russ began to venture out alone. Lily never joined her husband on the water, he says, because she was terrified of the lake. But he enjoyed it so much that he canoed in solitude at every opportunity. Rarely, though, was he really alone. Russ recalls one quiet autumn paddle toward Maiden Rock that was disrupted by a pack of coyotes chasing a panicked deer out of the forest and into the lake. He tried to head the deer off, knowing she couldn't swim far with her winter coat. He succeeded in stopping the deer, talking to her all the while. "Her eyes just blazed, you know," Russ says. "I told her she had to go back. Meantime, I let out a tremendous holler and scared the coyotes back up the hill, them running from bush to bush. The doe turned back, crawled behind a big log and laid down, she was so tired. So I told her, 'You stay here, those coyotes will be back in about an hour.' She must have listened: When Russ canoed back from Maiden Rock, she was still there, browsing leaves along the bank.

Many times in dry weather and late in the evening when a downdraft from the mountains would prevent the wildlife from smelling what's out on the lake, Russ would paddle slowly and silently past animals who had come down to the shore for a drink: opossum, raccoon, deer, a mama bear and her cubs, lynx and an occasional cougar.

Sometimes the encounters Russ has with wild creatures are less enviable, like those times bald eagles have "dive-bombed" him after following his canoe awhile. He says they make "the weirdest sound, a funny grunting roar" as they pull out of the dive, coming quite close. (The lake's ubiquitous ospreys have never done that to him.) His experiences on the lake have given him a special knowledge of these creatures. He says eagles usually fish the shallows with the sun at their back in order to blind the fish, dragging their talons in the water as they hunt in their own shadow. Unlike osprey, they cannot fly if they get their feathers wet. "A wet eagle has to get to shore pretty quick, or he's in trouble," Russ says.

During those many years of adventuring, the Keenes lost a canoe to thieves and one to the weather. Then Russ bought an Old Town "Katahdin" that was shorter and wider than a standard canoe and would accommodate a rowing machine. It was the summer of 1988 when Russ Keene "started canoeing alone in earnest."

You'll hear him say that with a bit of a chuckle at the understatement. In the past five years, Russ has rowed his canoe nearly 4,000 miles on the big lake. He started out slow, he says, rowing only 600 miles the first year. Then each year commencing with the celebration of his 80th birthday, he covered much more of the aquatic territory: 700 miles in 1989, 800 miles in 1990 and peaking at 1,000 miles in 1991. In 1992, he didn't quite reach his goal of another 1,000 miles.

You might imagine that by now, Russ had taken to crossing open water – miles of it. Some days he rows to Hope and back, or Clark Fork, maybe even Sandpoint. Often he'll spend the night camping under the stars before returning to Talache. Crossing over to Kilroy Bay has become a favorite route, following a familiar path he says elk can swim in an hour and a half. He's seen them do it.

Despite his zest for water travel, Russ Keene doesn't fish, unless it's for trouble. Pend Oreille is known for its unpredictable weather and being out in the middle of the lake, miles from any shore, is not where you want to be when a 20 mph wind suddenly comes raging. Russ always reads the clouds before he crosses open water: "Horsetails, they're dangerous. Trade winds. And I never trust the weatherman." But if he gets caught, he will ride the waves at a 45-degree angle to safety, although more than once fishermen have come to his rescue.

With all those miles, though, he's never once swamped his boat. "I have great respect for this lake. I know it can kill me," says Russ. "But you got to roll with it. You got to live with the wilderness of water, not just be there. You have to be part of it. This lake gets in your blood, I guess. You're living on your own strength. It's a lot more fun than motorboating and it doesn't cost you anything. And there's a certain thrill in pitting yourself against a wild thing like this lake, and believe me, when it gets rough, it's wild – terrifying!"

Russ also has seen dramatic changes in the lake. He worries about Pend Oreille's water quality and that of the Clark Fork River, which he says "has always been muddy." And although there have been plenty of times when he's been on the lake and never seen another soul, his canoe trips are becoming more and more populated with people in motorboats. But he doesn't hold it against them; he believes these folks are just out there to enjoy the same splendid wildness that he does. And if it gets a little too crowded, he says, he just takes his glasses off and the boats disappear into the fuzzy horizon.

Russ tells me he gets lonely in cities, even those the size of Sandpoint. But he's never lonely on the lake. Those times when nobody is out there but him, Russ says it's peaceful and a lot like praying. "It's a feeling that you're alone with the Creator, and you listen to the deep calm of it," he muses. "The wilderness of water has a spiritual vastness that's almost greater than any wilderness of land." I know exactly what he means.

There's one other passion Russell Keene and I share. His favorite spot to canoe skirts the Green Monarch Mountains. "It's beautiful there, where the cliffs come right down to the water and there are little bays and you just barely get through without getting stuck." It's here that he also gets close to the singing loons of his childhood dreams. If he's very, very quiet, they'll come around. Sometimes a loon even will call to him early in the morning off Indian Point. It's a kindred spirit, to be sure.

Epilogue: Russell Keene died in 1997 at the age of 88. He spent the final year of his life bedridden, a challenge for him given his frequent traveling and exploration of his beloved water – and mountain – wilderness home. His last words were an enthusiastic greeting to the morning sun rising over the Monarchs.

APPENDIX 1:
BOATING & FISHING
--

Boating Services

Following are marinas, boat rentals, charters and services, organized by communities around the lake.

Bayview
Bitter End Marina
Bayview, Idaho • 208-683-2534
Sailboat marina with moorage for transients by reservation.

MacDonald's Hudson Bay Resort
Bayview, Idaho • 208-683-2211
www.macdonaldsresort.com
Full marina services, boat service and repair, year-round boat launch, store on-site. Rental of paddle, sail and power boats.

Scenic Bay Marina and JD Resort
Bayview, Idaho • 208-683-2243
www.scenicbaymarina.com
Moorage for boats, adjacent RV sites and camping, near grocery store and restaurants.

Bottle Bay
A Day on the Lake Boat & Sea Doo Rentals
115 Resort Way, Sandpoint, ID 83864
208-687-1450 or 877-890-2444
www.adayonthelake.com
Located at Bottle Bay Resort, with rentals of ski boats, fishing boats, pontoons, and Sea-Doos.

Bottle Bay Resort Marina
115 Resort Road, Sagle, ID 83860
208-263-5916
Fine dining beneath tall cedars at this lakefront restaurant and cocktail lounge and cabins for vacation rentals.

Dover
Dover Bay Marina
651 Lakeshore Avenue, Dover, ID 83825
208-263-5493 • www.doverbayidaho.com
A full-service marina in Dover with boat launch and deep water, café and market on-site.

Garfield Bay
Garfield Shores Resort and Marina Club
1835 Garfield Bay Road, Sagle, ID 83860
208-263-9595 • www.garfieldshores.com
Marina with 24-hour fuel, boat slips for powerboats and sailboats, convenience store, adjacent restaurant located in Garfield Bay.

Hope
Holiday Shores/East Hope Marina
Hope, Idaho • 208-264-5515
www.sandpointwaterfront.com
Located off Highway 200 in Hope with 24-hour fuel, marine supplies, dockside power and water and on-site café and convenience store.

Hope Marine Services
47392 Highway 200, Hope, ID 83836
208-264-5105 • www.hopemarine.com
Full-service, year-round marina. Boat sales, full-service shop, accessories, boat rentals; the Floating Restaurant located on-site.

Kramer's Marina
46820 Highway 200, Hope, ID 83836
208-264-3021
Powerboat and sailboat long-term moorage.

BC&M Houseboat Vacations
Hope, Idaho • 208-755-0970 or 208-755-0073
www.sandpointhouseboats.com
Three houseboats available for rent, out of Hope.

Sandpoint
Alpine Shop
213 Church Street, Sandpoint, ID 83864
208-263-5157
Repair, storage and equipment for boaters and water-skiers, along with a wide selection of sporting goods.

Full Spectrum Tours
321 N. Second Avenue, Sandpoint, ID 83864
208-263-5975 • www.kayaking.net
Kayak tours on Lake Pend Oreille and Priest Lake.

Also classes, rentals and equipment sales.

Lake Pend Oreille Cruises
427 Fry Creek Road, Sagle, ID 83860
208-255-5253 or 1-888-726-3764
www.lakependoreillecruises.com
Private charters and public cruises on the
Shawnodese, a unique customized passenger ferry
boat. Jet boat tours and rentals also.

Outdoor Experience
314 N. First Avenue, Sandpoint, ID 83864
208-263-6028 • www.outdoorexperience.us
Kayak rentals and sales, plus paddle and outdoor
goods.

Pend Oreille Houseboat Rentals
Hope, Idaho
208-263-2675 or 208-290-5756
Houseboat rental out of Hope.

Sandpoint Marina
120 E. Lake Street, Sandpoint, Idaho 83864
208-263-3083 • www.sandpointwaterfront.com
Full-service marina with all amenities and 24-hour
gas, in downtown Sandpoint. Rentals of power and
ski boats, pontoon craft, kayaks and canoes.

Sandpoint Marine & Motor Sports
195 N. Triangle Drive, Ponderay, ID 83852
208-263-1535
www.sandpointmarineandmotorsports.com
Marine dealership with factory-certified mechanics.
Powerboat and pontoon boat rentals. Located behind
Wal-Mart.

Windbag and City Beach marinas
City Beach, Sandpoint • 208-263-3317
www.cityofsandpoint.com/Parks_Rec/
Marinas operated by the City of Sandpoint with long-
term moorage for sailboats and powerboats.

Fishing Charters & Services

Eagle Charters
Hope, Idaho • 208-264-5274
www.eaglecharters.net
Captain Dave is the fishing guide for fishermen after
trophy size trout or Lake Pend Oreille bass.

Sandpoint Outfitters
400 Schweitzer Plaza Drive, Ponderay, ID 83852
208-263-9119 • www.sandpointoutfitters.com
Fishing equipment, classes and local source of
advice for fishermen.

Diamond Charters Fishing Excursions
P.O. Box 153, Hope, Idaho 83836 • 208-265-2565
www.diamondcharters.com
Captain Ed Dickson guides fishing for the lake's big
rainbows and lake trout, or he takes people out on
the lake for sightseeing.

Pend Oreille Charters
Hope, Idaho • 208-265-6781
www.pocharters.com
Captain Kurt Artner guides fishing for trophy
rainbows and lake trout for parties up to six on his
28-foot cabin cruiser. Year-round, all gear supplied.

Seagull Charters
P.O. Box 217, Clark Fork, ID 83811 • 208-266-1861
www.seagullcharters.net
Captain Ken Hayes guides for giant rainbow and
mackinaw, or just for sightseeing, on his large 34-
foot cruiser that can accommodate two to 12 for
fishing, up to 30 for cruising.

APPENDIX 2:
WHO TO CONTACT

- -

Environmental & Advocacy Organizations

Clark Fork-Pend Oreille Conservancy
P.O. Box 2123, Sandpoint, ID 83864
208-263-9471 • www.cfpoconservancy.org
Land trust that works with landowners and organizations in the Clark Fork River and Lake Pend Oreille watersheds to protect, maintain and enhance natural resources and recreational values.

Friends of Pend d'Oreille Bay Trail
P.O. Box 1607, Sandpoint, ID 83864
208-265-9565 • www.pobtrail.org
Nonprofit group promoting creation of a walking and biking trail on the Lake Pend Oreille shoreline from Sandpoint to Black Rock in Ponderay.

Friends of Scotchman Peaks Wilderness
P.O. Box 2061, Sandpoint, ID 83864
www.scotchmanpeaks.org
Promoting wilderness designation for the magnificent 88,000-acre Scotchman Peaks roadless area just a stone's throw from Sandpoint. Also providing frequent group hikes and events for all to enjoy.

Idaho Conservation League – Sandpoint
208-265-9565 • www.wildidaho.org
Sandpoint office of statewide group advocating clean water, clean air and wilderness for Idaho.

Idaho Mythweaver
P.O. Box 2418, Sandpoint, ID 83864
208-264-5724 • www.mythweaver.org
A nonprofit educational arts and humanities organization with a mission to support the authentic presentation and preservation of cultural traditions, oral histories and storytelling.

Lake*A*Syst
1224 Washington Ave., Ste. 101, Sandpoint, ID 83864
208-263-5310 • www.plrcd.org/lakeasyst
A voluntary educational program to assist shoreline property owners in making well-informed decisions in the management of their lakefront property through free land use consultation and water quality guidebook. Also performs on-the-ground activities that prevent pollutants from entering the lake.

Lake Pend Oreille Idaho Club
P.O. Box 1589, Sandpoint, ID 83864
208-448-1365 • www.lpoic.org
Mission to protect and enhance Lake Pend Oreille, striving for clean water and ways to restore lake fisheries to their productive past.

Lake Pend Oreille Waterkeeper
P.O. Box 732, Sandpoint, ID 83864
208-597-7188
www.lakependoreillewaterkeeper.org
Striving through education, partnership and advocacy to protect the water quality of Lake Pend Oreille and improve the health and viability of its people and ecosystem.

Panhandle Chapter Trout Unlimited
P.O. Box 1853
Priest River, ID 83856
208-448-0520
Working to conserve, protect and restore Idaho's trout and salmon fisheries and their watersheds.

Pend Oreille Basin Commission
120 E. Lake Street, Suite 301, Sandpoint, ID 83864
208-263-4984 • www.lakescommission.com
Created by the Idaho Legislature in 2003, and also known as the Lakes Commission, this group works on water quality and quantity issues in Lake Pend Oreille, Pend Oreille River, Priest Lake and Priest River.

Rock Creek Alliance
P.O. Box 2636• Sandpoint, ID 83864
208-265-8272 • www.rockcreekalliance.org
Working to protect water quality in Lake Pend Oreille's watershed from the proposed Rock Creek Mine.

Selkirk Conservation Alliance
P.O. Box 1809, Priest River, ID 83856
208-448-1110 • www.scawild.org
SCA works for the conservation and protection of the crucial and sensitive natural resources of the Selkirk Mountains, their watershed, forests, lakes, streams and rivers, in an area that encompasses the northernmost counties of Idaho.

Tri-State Water Quality Council
101 N. Fourth Avenue, Suite 105
Sandpoint, ID 83864
208-265-9092 • www.tristatecouncil.org
A partnership of diverse community interests working together to improve and protect water quality throughout the 26,000-square mile Clark Fork-Pend Oreille watershed.

-- --

Recreation & Visitor Information

Bayview Chamber of Commerce
P.O. Box 121, Bayview, ID 83803
208-683-8040 • www.bayviewidaho.org

Greater Sandpoint Chamber of Commerce
P.O. Box 928, Sandpoint, ID 83864
800-800-2106 • www.sandpointchamber.com

**Hope-Clark Fork
Chamber of Commerce**
310 East Fourth Avenue, Clark Fork, ID 83811
208-266-1101

Idaho Fish and Game
P.O. Box 25, Boise, ID 83707
208-334-3700 • www.fishandgame.idaho.gov

Idaho Panhandle National Forest
Sandpoint Ranger District
1602 Ontario Street, Sandpoint, ID 83864
208-263-5111 • www.fs.fed.us/ipnf/sandpoint/

Idaho Parks and Recreation
P.O. Box 83720, Boise, ID 83720-0065
208-334-4199 • www.idahoparks.org

Lake Pend Oreille Yacht Club
P.O. Box 13, Bayview, Idaho 83803
http://web.lpoyc.org

North Idaho Bikeways
www.northidahobikeways.com
123donate@northidahobikeways.com

Pend Oreille Pedalers
P.O. Box 2451, Sandpoint, ID 83864
www.pendoreillepedalers.com
info@pendoreillepedalers.com

SandpointOnline.com
405 Church St., Sandpoint ID 83864
208-263-3573 • www.sandpointonline.com

Sandpoint Parks and Recreation
1123 Lake Street, Sandpoint, ID 83864
208-263-3613 • www.cityofsandpoint.com

Sandpoint Sailing Association
Sandpoint, Idaho 83864
www.sandpointsailing.com

APPENDIX 3:
TRAIL INDEX BY NAME

APPENDIX 4:
TRAIL INDEX BY NUMBER

Clark Fork, 239–240
Clark Fork Access Site, 246–248
Colby Landing, 243
Derr Creek Property, 241–242
map, 234m

R
radio channels, weather, 15
Raiha, Ron, 67-68, 93, 319, 320, 321, 322
railroads
    Area 3 (Greater Sandpoint), 152
    Area 4 (Pack River to Hope), 170, 180, 184
    basics, 5, 361-363, 369-370, 371-372, 373
    bridges, 97, 114, 171, 240, 362, 381
    Cabinet and, 245, 369
    Kalispel and, 356
    logging and, 364
    museum, 123
    scuba diving and, 22-23, 171
    steamboats and, 357, 362
rainbows, 9cp
rainbow trout, 16cp, 67, 85, 321, 325, 326, 330-331
regulations, 13, 15, 16-17, 168
rentals, boats, 18. see also charters
resorts
    Area 1 (Bayview), 47, 49, 69, 77
    Area 3 (Greater Sandpoint), 98, 99, 103, 104, 114-115, 129, 136, 290, 293-294
    Area 4 (Pack River to Hope), 159, 180-181, 183
    Area 5 (Hope Peninsula to Clark Fork Delta), 189, 195, 363
    Area 7 (Clark Fork to Cabinet Gorge), 248
    history, 374, 380-381
Revais, Alec, 335
Reynolds, Boots, 318
rivers, 3. see also specific rivers
roads, 6, 30, 69, 365, 371, 373. see also driving tours; specific roads
rock climbing, 4cp, 232, 233
Rocky Point, 290
Roosevelt, Theodore, 180, 359-360
rope swing, 112p
Round Lake, 94-95
RVs, 94, 189, 195, 237

S
sailing, 3cp, 17, 18-19, 49, 101-102, 104, 107-108. see also marinas; Points of Sail (Huisman)
Saleesh River, 348, 352, 353
Salish language, 109, 117, 198, 208, 223, 253, 340, 353
salmon, 67-68, 81, 253. see also kokanee
Sam Owen Campground, 195-197
Samuels, Jamie, 342
Sand Creek, 108, 112p
Sand Creek Bridge, 103
Sandoval, Shirley, 339, 343
sandpipers, 147
Sandpoint, city of, 5, 341, 351, 356, 359, 370, 371
Sandpoint Bike Week, 88

Sandpoint City Beach, 11cp, 12rh, 100, 103-106
Sandpoint Sailing Association, 101, 102, 107
Sandpoint Wooden Boat Festival, 109
Scenic Bay, 44, 47, 48, 50-51
scenic byways, 15cp, 99, 158, 169, 189
Schweitzer Mountain, 7, 101, 139-140, 286, 366, 374
Scotchman Peak, 3, 29, 211, 235, 239, 312
scuba diving, 16, 22-23, 47, 52-53, 158, 171
Selkirk Mountains, 3
Selle, Dale, 148-149, 150p
Seneacquoteen, 23, 117, 334, 336, 358, 368
serviceberry, 176
Seymour, Chief, 340
Shawnodese (boat), 24, 183-185
Shepherd Lake, 94
shrimp, 321
SiJohn, Henry, 34, 207, 340
silver, 360, 361
silvers. see kokanee
skiing, 2rh, 3rh, 4rh, 294
smoke house, 107
smugglers, 66
snakes, 26-27
snorkelers, 16
snow, 6, 7, 61. see also winter
sockeye salmon, 68
sounds, 182p, 190, 224, 227, 275, 387
special events
    Area 1 (Bayview), 48, 53
    Area 3 (Greater Sandpoint), 31, 104, 109
    basics, 30-31
    biking, 88, 293-294
    fishing, 23, 229, 320, 322, 323, 324, 373
    horseback riding, 185-186
    scouting, 53, 94, 366, 374, 375, 379
Spokane Tribe, 206, 340
Springy Point, 133-134
SS Fish House (commercial houseboat), 320
Steamboat Rock, 51, 57
steamboats. see also specific steamboats
    Area 1 (Bayview), 57, 65
    Area 2 (Garfield Bay), 91, 93
    Area 3 (Greater Sandpoint), 140, 356
    Area 4 (Pack River to Hope), 184
    Area 7 (Clark Fork to Cabinet Gorge) and, 245
    basics, 5, 356-361, 369, 371
    gold rushes and, 358
    landings, 152, 372
    museums and, 123
storms, 14cp, 161-162, 229-230
Studebaker, William, 126p
Sullivan Springs, 66, 67-68
sunbathing, 17
Sunnyside, 100, 145, 148-149, 150p, 151-155, 286, 352, 359
swans, 8, 191
sweat indexes, 259
swimming, 4cp, 11rh, 15rh, 21-23, 61, 111, 117, 169. see also beaches
swinging bridge, 246

ABOUT THE AUTHOR

Jane Fritz is an award-winning environmental journalist and oral historian whose articles, documentaries and independent radio productions have been showcased in many media, including National Public Radio and the BBC. She is the director of The Idaho Mythweaver, an educational arts and humanities organization. An area resident for more than 30 years, she lives in Hope with her five cats.

CONTRIBUTING WRITERS

Kevin Davis is a hydrologist for the U.S. Forest Service, where he works in many of the tributaries to Lake Pend Oreille to improve water quality and fish habitat; he's also a frequent writer on outdoor topics for *Sandpoint Magazine*.

Gary Hassler was a writer for the *Sandpoint Reader* when he had his first brush with moonlight kayaking; he's also contributed to *The River Journal* and the 2008 coffee-table book *Sandpoint: A Small Town with a Big Heart*.

Cate Huisman is a Sandpoint freelance writer for *Sandpoint Magazine* and other Northwest publications; she enjoys exploring the lake in her family's 20-foot Ranger shoal-draft sloop, as well as hiking, biking and skiing hereabouts.

Marianne Love, a Sandpoint native of 60-plus years, taught English and journalism at Sandpoint High for 33 years and, aside from hundreds of stories for regional publications, has authored three humorous books on her escapades in town and classroom. She mutters daily about life in Sandpoint and her Selle Valley farm on her blog, SlightDetour.com.

Heather McElwain is a native of Wisconsin's lake country who transitioned naturally to life along Lake Pend Oreille in 2000. She's founder of Turtle Bay Editorial & Design and, aside from her own writings, has helped many others bring their work to print.

Patrick McManus was born in his family's old farmhouse just north of Sandpoint in 1933; growing up here somehow produced enough adventures to fuel an illustrious career as one of the nation's top humor writers, with hundreds of magazine and newspaper pieces, 21 books and five stage plays under his belt.

Dennis Nicholls was a forester by training who became founding publisher of *The River Journal* and authored two definitive hiking guidebooks for the area, *Trails of the Wild Cabinets* and *Trails of the Wild Selkirks*. Nicholls wrote an initial draft for *Legendary Lake Pend Oreille* in 2005, including chapters 11 and 14; he died in May 2009.

Jim Mellen is an avid hiker, skier, mountain biker, snowboarder, gardener and photographer; he also spends a little time working at Encoder Products Co., designing and building assembly and test fixtures. He edited and provided revisions to the second edition of *Trails of the Wild Cabinets* by Dennis Nicholls and chapter 11, "Hiking, Mountain Biking and Horse Riding Trails," in *Legendary Lake Pend Oreille*.